THE ROUTLEDGE INTRODUCTION TO ENGLISH CANADIAN LITERATURE AND DIGITAL HUMANITIES

The Routledge Introduction to English Canadian Literature and Digital Humanities is a guide to the concepts and theories at the intersection of Canadian literary studies and digital humanities (DH). Equal parts theoretical and practical, it focuses on debates that overlap the two domains. This book historicizes the connections between the two by surveying the history of DH in Canada, the tradition of Canadian writers engaging with technology, and DH analyses of Canadian literature. It also situates both CanLit and DH with respect to contemporary concerns about alterity and it demonstrates how digital technologies allow writers and scholars to intervene in them.

This book complements its theoretical discussions with a practical introduction to DH methods. Using Canadian literary texts and examples from projects at the intersection of CanLit and DH, it introduces key DH approaches to novice readers. Topics covered include data collection, data management, and textual analysis, as well as essential DH tools and the Python programming language. A concluding case study guides readers interested in applying the ideas presented throughout.

Paul Barrett is an Associate Professor in the School of Theatre, English, and Creative Writing and the Culture and Technology Studies program at the University of Guelph.

Sarah Roger is the project manager for the Linked Infrastructure for Networked Cultural Scholarship and an Adjunct Assistant Professor in the School of Theatre, English, and Creative Writing at the University of Guelph.

Routledge Introductions to Canadian Literature
Series Editors:
Robert Lecker, *McGill University*
Lorraine York, *McMaster University*

Routledge Introductions to Canadian Literature is a series that provides critical introductions to important trends, issues, authors, historical, cultural and intellectual contexts in Canadian Literature. The series draws on the work of experts in the field to provide a detailed but accessible commentary on those works or conceptual issues which are taught with undergraduate students in mind but also graduate students and instructors.

The Routledge Introduction to Gender and Sexuality in Literature in Canada
Linda Morra

The Routledge Introduction to the Canadian Short Story
Maria Löschnigg

The Routledge Introduction to Twentieth- and Twenty-First-Century Canadian Poetry
Erin Wunker

The Routledge Introduction to English Canadian Literature and Digital Humanities
Paul Barrett and Sarah Roger

For more information about this series, please visit: https://www.routledge.com/Routledge-Introductions-to-Canadian-Literature/book-series/RICL

THE ROUTLEDGE INTRODUCTION TO ENGLISH CANADIAN LITERATURE AND DIGITAL HUMANITIES

Paul Barrett and Sarah Roger

NEW YORK AND LONDON

Designed cover image: Todd Kowalski

First published 2025
by Routledge
605 Third Avenue, New York, NY 10158

and by Routledge
4 Park Square, Milton Park, Abingdon, Oxon, OX14 4RN

Routledge is an imprint of the Taylor & Francis Group, an informa business

© 2025 Paul Barrett and Sarah Roger

The right of Paul Barrett and Sarah Roger to be identified as authors of this work has been asserted in accordance with sections 77 and 78 of the Copyright, Designs and Patents Act 1988.

All rights reserved. No part of this book may be reprinted or reproduced or utilised in any form or by any electronic, mechanical, or other means, now known or hereafter invented, including photocopying and recording, or in any information storage or retrieval system, without permission in writing from the publishers.

Trademark notice: Product or corporate names may be trademarks or registered trademarks, and are used only for identification and explanation without intent to infringe.

ISBN: 9781032331287 (hbk)
ISBN: 9781032331256 (pbk)
ISBN: 9781003318323 (ebk)

DOI: 10.4324/9781003318323

Typeset in Sabon
by codeMantra

*To the members of our online Canadian literature
short story book club (2020–2024) for showing us
a new way to read—and connect—digitally.*

CONTENTS

List of Figures   xiv
Acknowledgements   xv

   Introduction: Beyond the boundaries: digital
   humanities and Canadian literature   1
   Boundaries and borderlines 3
   Canada in DH, DH in Canada 5
   Quickstart and contexts 7
   Works cited 11

PART I   **13**

1 What is English Canadian literature?   15
   Histories of digital humanities and Canadian
      literature 19
   The shape of Canadian literary criticism 21
   New critical formations 23
   Further reading 27
   Works cited 28

2 What are digital humanities?   30
   What of the humanities? 32
   A provisional, historical, collaborative definition 34

Methodological 36
Theoretical 36
Methodological + theoretical 37
Further reading 38
Works cited 39

PART II   **41**

3 Early interventions: the history of humanities computing and Canadian literature   43
Early Canadian humanities computing 44
Emerging organization 48
Burgeoning humanities computing community 50
Towards a digital humanities 56
   Artmob 58
   The Orlando Project 59
   Implementing New Knowledge Environments 61
   A proliferation of projects 62
Further reading 65
Works cited 66

4 National literatures, infrastructural developments: emerging concepts of Canadian literature and digital humanities   70
Humanism and the nation 71
Other histories 73
Institutional support for digital humanities 75
New institutional initiatives 80
Further reading 84
Works cited 84

5 Digital humanities spaces: archives, collaboratories, laboratories, and centres   87
Digital archives 88
CanLit and the digital archive 90
Collaboratories 92
   Collaboratory for Writing and Research on Culture 93
   Editing Modernism in Canada 94

SpokenWeb 95
DH laboratories and centres 96
Further reading 99
Works cited 100

PART III   103

6   Canadian literary criticism and the digital sphere   105
   Sea change of the digital 106
   Canadian critical interventions 108
   Early Canadian literary-digital scholarship 110
     The Hypertext Pratt 111
     The Digital Page 113
   Contemporary Canadian literary-digital
     projects 114
     AMM Bibliography 114
     Distant Reading Mennonite Writing 115
     Fred Wah Digital Archive 115
     The People and the Text 116
   Digital poetics, creative praxis 116
   Further reading 122
   Works cited 122

7   Canadian literature as data   125
   Methodological opportunities 127
   Project goals, methodological challenges 131
   Expanding DH's rubric 133
   Further reading 135
   Works cited 135

PART IV   139

8   Intersectional digital humanities   141
   A call to (intersectional) action 143
   Subjects and subjectivity 147
   Projects 149
     The Orlando Project 149
     LGBTQ+ and feminist archives 150
     Yellow Nineties 2.0 151

Lesbian and Gay Liberation in Canada 151
Principles and practices 152
Further reading 155
Works cited 156

9 Race, power, and digital culture 160
Digital humanities and (the absence of) race 162
A call to action 166
Race, literature, and culture 169
Challenging the human *in digital humanities* 173
Further reading 175
Works cited 175

10 Indigenous digital humanities 179
Data sovereignty and data management 182
Projects 188
  Voices of the Land 189
  FourDirectionsTeachings.com 189
  Kiinawin Kawindomowin / Story Nations 191
  Native Land Digital and Whose Land 191
  Terrastories 192
  The People and the Text 192
  Great Lakes Research Alliance for the Study of Aboriginal Arts & Cultures 193
  Wikipetcia Atikamekw Nehiromowin 193
  #HonouringIndigenousWriters 194
Literary interventions 194
Further reading 202
Works cited 202

PART V **207**

11 Data acquisition 209
Finding data 211
Large-scale text repositories 212
Aggregators and specialized archives 213
Supplementary materials 214
Born-digital and emerging resources 215
From corpus to curation 215

Further reading 218
Works cited 219

12 Data management — 221
    RDM planning basics 222
    Best practices through FAIR data 224
        Findable data 225
        Accessible data 227
        Interoperable data 229
        Reusable data 230
    Linked open data as a model for best practice 231
    The costs of data management 232
    Further reading 234
    Works cited 234

13 Steps towards analyzing text — 237
    Minding the gap 237
    Analyzing the corpus using GUI-based tools 240
    Analyzing the corpus programmatically 242
        Text encoding 243
        Text analysis using Python 245
        Sentiment analysis 246
        Network analysis 246
        Topic modeling 247
    Further reading 250
    Works cited 250

14 Programming — 253
    Building blocks 256
    Data types 259
    Control structures 261
    Application Programming Interfaces 263
    Libraries 263
    Data cleaning 267
    Bringing it all together 268
    Further reading 271
    Works cited 271

15 Mary Prince and Susanna Moodie, a case study 272
Starting points 272
Mary Prince and Susanna Moodie 273
Data acquisition 276
Analyzing the texts using Voyant 278
Analyzing the texts using Python 281
Further reading 288
Works cited 288

PART VI **291**

16 Future thinking: developments and predictions for
the twenty-first century 293
Works cited 304

*Appendix I: Digital humanities laboratories and centres
at Canadian universities* 307
Carleton University—Hyperlab 307
Carleton University—Cultural Heritage Informatics
Collaboratory 308
McGill University—Digital Scholarship Hub 308
McMaster University—Lewis & Ruth Sherman
Centre for Digital Scholarship 308
Simon Fraser University—Digital Humanities
Innovation Lab 309
Toronto Metropolitan University—Centre for Digital
Humanities 309
Université de Montréal—Centre de recherche
interuniversitaire sur les humanités
numériques 309
University of Alberta—Digital Scholarship
Centre 310
University of British Columbia Okanagan—AMP
Lab 310
University of Guelph—The Humanities
Interdisciplinary Collaboration Lab 311
University of Ottawa—Labo de données en sciences
humaines / The Humanities Data Lab 311

University of Toronto—Critical Digital Humanities
  Initiative 312
University of Victoria—Electronic Textual Cultures
  Lab / Digital Scholarship Commons 312
York University—Digital Scholarship Centre 313

Appendix II: Digital humanities projects, tools and
platforms, resources, and organizations   314
  Projects 314
  Tools and platforms 316
  Resources 317
  Organizations 318

Index   319

FIGURES

3.1	Infographic of humanities computing needs (Lancashire 1983)	53
13.1	*Voyant* analysis of eleven issues of the journal *Canadian Literature*	241
13.2	Search for multiculturalism in *Google Ngram Viewer* and *HathiTrust Bookworm*	243
14.1	*Jupyter* notebook combining Markdown and code sections	259
15.1	Plain text of *The History of Mary Prince*	277
15.2	*Voyant* analysis of *The History of Mary Prince*	279
15.3	*Voyant* trends analysis of the word *free* in *The History of Mary Prince*	280
15.4	*Voyant* analysis of Susanna Moodie texts available on gutenberg.org	281
15.5	A selection of *Voyant*'s keywords-in-context for the word *slave* in the Moodie corpus	287

ACKNOWLEDGEMENTS

The strength of digital humanities in Canada is thanks to the generosity of its community. We drew on the knowledge of friends, colleagues, collaborators, and members of the broader digital humanities community in writing this book, including Jason Boyd, Constance Crompton, Sandra Djwa, Rebecca Dowson, Shawn Graham, Neta Gordon, Marcela Isuster, Graham Jensen, Ian Lancashire, Aaron Mauro, Willard McCarty, Kris Joseph, Harvey Quamen, Geoffrey Rockwell, Karis Shearer, Ray Siemens, Danielle Taschereau Mamers, Bri Watson, Darren Wershler, and Andrea Zeffiro—and especially our colleagues at the University of Guelph, Susan Brown and Kim Martin. Thank you to all of them for answering our questions, chatting with us about the field, and for all their contributions to the community of practice that is Canadian DH. Thanks also to Todd Kowalski for the cover art, to Dani Spinosa for comments on an early draft, to series editors Robert Lecker and Lorraine York for inviting us to write this volume and for providing feedback on the manuscript, and to Bryony Reece and the team at Routledge for all their hard work in creating this book.

INTRODUCTION

Beyond the boundaries: digital humanities and Canadian literature

* * *

It was 3 a.m. in Vancouver and I was half-asleep, scrolling through the usual algorithmic sludge, when my AI—affectionately named Zed—started texting me existential questions about the meaning of art, and honestly, I wasn't sure if it was a glitch or if Zed had finally outgrown me. *Zed.exe*, a novel generated by ChatGPT in response to the prompt, "Write me the opening sentence of a Canadian novel about generative AI in the style of Douglas Coupland."

A July 22, 2023, article in the *Globe and Mail* describes the Writers' Union of Canada's efforts to "protect Canadian authors from the damage" (O'Kane 2023) of *ChatGPT* and related technologies. Canadian author Mona Awad, meanwhile, has sued OpenAI, the company behind *ChatGPT*, for using her copyrighted works to train their artificial intelligence (AI) models. She argues that her books were used illegally as part of *ChatGPT*'s training data, which, as a result, can produce "very accurate summaries" of her writing (Creamer 2023). The rise of large language models and generative AI is the cause of great concern among Canadian writers; Canadian novelist Danny Ramadan is not alone in his sentiment that technology companies' use of writers' works "feels like imperialism" (O'Kane 2023). Even Margaret Atwood, who has embraced technology in her use of the LongPen device[1] and has championed the fanfiction site *Wattpad*, responded to generative AI with an essay entitled "Murdered by My Replica?" (Atwood 2023). For Awad, Ramadan, Atwood, and others, digital

DOI: 10.4324/9781003318323-1

systems that transform our concepts of creation and ownership represent a profound threat to writers and the works they produce.

When Awad asked the court to determine whether digital technology can "read" literary works and, if so, how this is distinct from ingesting works into a digital system, she was, in effect, asking the government to weigh in on behalf of authors. Ramadan's metaphor of technology as imperialism might seem hyperbolic, and Atwood's article wry and humorous, but like Awad's court case, both highlight the relationship between technology and systems of power—a resonant connection for a country grappling with the ongoing effects of colonialism. The pushback against *ChatGPT* raises questions about who should be responsible for protecting Canadian writers (and indeed all cultural workers) from market forces and emerging technologies. One could argue that this is a job for government, for publishers, or for authors themselves. One could even assume that tech companies would recognize that it is in their—and collectively our—best interests to safeguard artistic production. This is, undoubtedly, wishful thinking.

Authors' concerns about generative AI are exemplary of the questions that we address throughout this book. What is the relationship between emerging digital technologies, literary culture, and literary studies? How has Canadian literature been responsive to, and transformed by, technology? How have the digital humanities (DH) contributed to—and, subsequently, affected—understandings of Canadian literature? What is the history of digital experiments with literature and literary experiments with computers in Canada, and how can these histories help us understand present and future paradigms of reading and writing? What ethical questions should DH practitioners ask before treating literature as data?

At the time of our writing in 2024, *ChatGPT* is a hot topic. By the time you read this, *ChatGPT* may be old news and something else may have taken its place. The tenor of the discussion about large language models follows the same pattern as that of the technologies that have preceded it, including smart phones, the Internet, personal computers, pocket calculators, and more; undoubtedly, future conversations about yet-to-be imagined technologies will elicit a similar dual sense of panic and promise. Some will worry that the new technology signals the end of all things good, while others will be convinced that the technology brings improvement for everyone, everywhere. Theorists will reflect on the broader social implications, while advocates will conceive of ways to harness power while minimizing drawbacks. Indeed, as Lynne Coady reminds us in *Who Needs Books? Reading in the Digital Age* (2016), the original technological object of alarm was writing itself. Yet, as time progresses and new technologies become integrated into everyday life, they become virtually invisible to the people who rely on them. As we write this book and as you read it, the technologies that make it possible—the screens, computers, Internet connections, data centres, networked infrastructure, servers, and other forms of data transmission—all fade into the background. Technology appears to be a kind of translucent mediator that cleanly conveys information.

Yet one of the lessons of the digital humanities is that technology is never unobtrusive. We design it and adapt it to our needs, but we also adapt our needs to its design. DH therefore calls upon us to subject technology to scrutiny. When N. Katherine Hayles asks in *Writing Machines*, "Why have we not heard more about materiality?" (2002, 19), she is appealing for a critical interrogation of that which we no longer see. Behind the smooth, impressive functionality of large language models, for instance, are the authors whose texts have been ingested to power the models, the programmers who have coded the models that perpetuate worldviews, and even the server farms where tens of thousands of computers engage in intense computation with terrible environmental effect. Researchers estimate that training *ChatGPT-3* required 700,000 litres of fresh water to cool the computers used just during the training process. If their present estimates are accurate, the "operational water withdrawal of global AI may reach 4.2—6.6 billion cubic metres in 2027, which is more than the total annual water withdrawal of 4–6 Denmarks or half of the United Kingdom" (Li et al. 2023, 2).[2] DH critically interrogates the social, cultural, material, and infrastructural supports that make our technological engagements possible by asking questions such as: How is our act of reading changed by reading on a screen? How do hyperlinks, embedded images, and videos shape our engagement with and understanding of a text? How is literary culture altered by cutting, pasting, remixing, and reposting? What happens to a field of knowledge when scholars predominantly cite research that is accessible online? How are conceptions of the digital transformed by ideas of the nation?

Boundaries and borderlines

The two terms that animate this collection—Canadian literature and DH—do not appear to be a natural pair. Canadian literature (CanLit) is a region-specific identification of literature and literary production that may or may not be concerned with varying conceptions of Canada and nationhood. The digital humanities, meanwhile, are a loosely connected set of methods that use digital technology to study topics in the humanities. DH is not spatially bound like CanLit, nor is it singularly tied to literary study. It may have its origins in literary studies (see Chapter 2), but it equally attracts scholars of history, philosophy, gender studies, game studies, computer science, and mathematics, among others. For Julie Thompson Klein, DH is not a field but rather a paradigm: "an overarching framework that remakes all disciplinary research and education" (2015, 21). It is "*boundary work* ... a composite label for the claims, activities, and structures by which individuals create, maintain, break down, and reformulate boundaries between knowledge units" (2015, 5; emphasis added). Analogously (and to our minds not coincidentally) Marshall McLuhan describes Canada as a "borderline case," arguing that Canada exists at the borderlines of numerous geographic, linguistic, cultural, and historical forces (1977, 241). Throughout this volume, we consider how CanLit and DH exist at the edges of other disciplines and intellectual histories, each of which plays a role in their definitions. The boundaries of both DH and Canadian literature provide insight into the composition of the two fields and allow us to understand their constitution and limits. In Chapter 1, we survey Canadian literature's history, a significant portion of which has been spent defining, arguing about the definition of, and subsequently redefining the term. In Chapter 2, we examine DH as the site of definitions that overlap, nuance, and contradict one another. Once we have (failed to singularly) define the terms of the book's title, we spend the remaining chapters considering what happens to our understanding of the digital and the literary as each crosses the boundaries of, and is refashioned by its interactions with, the other.

The goal of this book is not to bring together the digital humanities and Canadian literature under some broad argument that the two have always been (or even currently are) inextricably interrelated. Rather we examine the borderlines to uncover, for example, the histories of digital scholarship in Canada, digital scholarship concerned with Canadian literature, and Canadian literary engagements with the digital. We also reflect on the changing idea of nation—and of national literature—within the new digital world. In doing so, we join Susan Brown and Cecily Devereux in asking,

> How ... have the particulars of Canadian culture, infrastructure, and academic structures affected digital literary and cultural studies? Which local, regional, organizational, institutional, or national factors have inflected the relationship between culture and technology in Canada? Are our diverse identities, histories, politics, and infrastructures reflected in how we read, write, and research digitally? What have digital approaches contributed to our understanding of Canadian literature, culture, and identity categories?
>
> *(2017)*

To these questions, we add some more of our own: What are the points of connection between Canadian literature and the digital humanities? How has Canadian literature, a particularly regional concern, been transformed by digital forms of literary production and scholarship? What is the relationship between regional, provincial, and national identities and digital culture? How has the long history of Canadian concern with emerging technologies affected our understanding of the digital? What opportunities does the digital offer for intersectional and decolonial approaches to understanding Canadian literature?

Canada in DH, DH in Canada

Canada has always been well represented within the field of DH. Chris Alen Sula and Heather V. Hill's (2019) analysis of two key journals in DH—*Computers and the Humanities* (1966–2004) and *Literary and Linguistic Computing* (1986–2004)—found that Canada was the third-most-represented country among those of the authors in the journals' history. Their findings affirmed the impressions of Willard McCarty, an early advocate for DH in Canada, who insists that there are "Per capita more digital humanists in Canada than anywhere else in the world," and that "The Canadians have done marvels in convincing the government and setting up structures of funding" for digital scholarship (McCarty et al. 2012). Mary Vipond reminds us that, given the oversized presence of Canada in theories of media (via figures such as Harold Innis, George Grant, and McLuhan), "It has long since become a cliché to suggest that the key to Canada lies in communications" (2003, 1). Canada is the birthplace of the *Humanist* listserv, the Digital Humanities Summer Institute, and foundational digital projects including *The Orlando Project*, the *Collaboratory for Writing and Research on Culture* (formerly the *Canadian Writing Research Collaboratory*, CWRC), and the home of *Voyant Tools*, "one of the most widely used DH tools globally" (Brown 2023, 407). In Chapters 3 and 4, we explore the many reasons for the success of DH in Canada, among them the energy of individual researchers, early Canadian experiments with computation, and government support for digital research and teaching.

One of the aims of this book, therefore, is to view the significance of Canada (as both place and idea) to DH through the substantial history of its applications to Canadian literature. In Chapter 3, for instance, we discuss Sandra Djwa's experiments in the 1960s with mainframe computers to build a concordance of contemporary Canadian poetry—work that led her, some forty years later, to collaborate with Zailig Pollock on *The Digital Page: The Collected Works of P. K. Page*, a CWRC-hosted DH project on the work of Canadian poet P. K. Page. Similarly, Frank Davey and Fred Wah's digital poetry magazine, *SwiftCurrent* (1983–1986), was hosted on a VAX mainframe computer at York University; fredwah.ca would be developed as part of the *Artmob* project in the late 1990s and would be transformed into the *Fred Wah Digital Archive* by Deanna Fong and Ryan Fitzpatrick in the 2010s. One of the lessons of DH in Canada is that historical precedents play a role in shaping future developments. These are just a few of the many examples of Canadian literature and DH overlapping and informing one another.

Unfortunately, the ephemerality of digital scholarship means that a sizeable portion of this history has been lost. This ephemerality is, therefore, a significant part of this history. Research support funds dry up and institutional priorities change, leaving digital projects to struggle and eventually disappear. For example, the *Canadian Poetry Collection* at the University of New Brunswick, a vast digitized collection of Canadian poetry, does not survive in either digital or print form. *L'infocentre littéraire des écrivains québécois*, an early digital project on Québécois literature, is only sporadically updated and therefore increasingly outdated. The aforementioned *SwiftCurrent* now exists only as a print collection; the files and servers that were once at the heart of the project are no longer available. Jennifer Wemigwans (Anishnaabekwe, Ojibwe/Potawatomi) confronts this problem with her ongoing project:

> FourDirectionsTeachings.com, uploaded to the World Wide Web in 2006, has been maintained by my company, Invert Media. Access to the site is free. I pay the annual hosting costs for the website since currently there is no funding body specifically committed to online Indigenous Knowledge projects. That said, I have been fundraising to upgrade the site from its original flash HTML to HTML 5, a mobile responsive technology. In its current state, the website is accessible to less than 50 percent of potential Internet users.
>
> *(2018, 18)*

As the number of digital projects grows, so too will out-of-date content, broken links, and obsolete interfaces. As Melissa Terras explains, "The sustainability of digitized content is … concerning. It is highly expensive to maintain a digitized resource, and, without careful maintenance, online resources quickly become outmoded and unusable" (2012, 58). This problem has been exacerbated by the war against so-called "Diversity, Equity, and Inclusion" (DEI) in the United States, which has resulted in digital projects focused on antiracism, feminism, LGBTQ+ topics, and subaltern histories being hastily defunded and taken offline. In the course of reviewing the proofs for this book in March 2025, several previously available sites—all archives and DH projects that fall under the umbrella of DEI—are no longer online. We have included URLs for these sites in our lists of works cited and in our appendix of DH resources, both as a record of the DH landscape at our time of writing and in hopes that they will come back online. There are lessons to be learned here: the ease with which materials can disappear heightens the importance of thinking about preservation strategies and the location of the servers that host digital projects; we are also reminded of the responsibility DH researchers have in taking a stand against authoritarian efforts to silence marginalized and dissenting voices. We address some of these concerns in Chapter 3, where we highlight the difficulty of recovering the history of digital projects, and in Chapter 12, we discuss recent efforts to develop Canadian preservation resources such as *The Endings Project* and the Canadian *Federated Research Data Repository*.

Alongside digital engagements with Canadian literature, we explore the lengthy history of Canadian literary engagements with the digital, both in content and form. For example, on the content side, William Gibson invented the term *cyberspace* while writing *Neuromancer* (1984) in Vancouver. Hugh MacLennan's little-known final novel, *Voices in Time* (1980), describes a dystopian society managed by complex computational systems. Bridging content and form are works such as Douglas Coupland's *Microserfs* (1995), a Microsoft-themed epistolary novel, and *JPod* (2006), written partly in emails, about lives of employees at a BC-based video game company. Sean Michaels's *Do You Remember Being Born?* (2023), about a poet commissioned to write a collaborative piece with an AI chatbot, was itself written in collaboration with a specially trained AI chatbot. Examples of form-led engagements include Earle Birney's computer-assisted poem, "Space Conquest: Computer Poems" (1968), bpNichol's *First Screening* (1983) and his early experiments with computational poetry, Caitlin Fisher's interactive hypertext narratives, such as *These Waves of Girls* (2001), and Jordan Abel's digital transformations in *Injun* (2013) and *Un/inhabited* (2014). Toronto-based Coach House Press, meanwhile, was one of the first presses to use computers for book production. To understand the conditions that have resulted in so many successful Canadian DH projects and fostered so much literary engagement with technology, we also consider the role played by institutions and organizations—from small networks of likeminded scholars to cross-Canada, government-funded projects. In Chapters 3–5, we map the terrain of material supports that make DH in Canada possible.

Quickstart and contexts

This book has been written for readers who have some familiarity with— but do not consider themselves experts in—either or both of DH and

Canadian literature. As such, we introduce both fields, focusing on the overlaps between them. There are many excellent guides to DH and to Canadian literature, which provide more detail than we can offer; the end of each chapter has a short list of recommended resources. To borrow from the language and format of technology, we offer readers this quickstart guide:

- Part I introduces this book's two key concepts, Canadian literature (Chapter 1) and digital humanities (Chapter 2).
- Part II traces the course of digital humanities in Canada, starting with a historical overview of humanities computing in Canada (Chapter 3), followed by a look at the forces—such as government policies and academic trends—that have shaped both Canadian literature and digital humanities (Chapter 4), and an exploration of how digital humanities has carved out space on university campuses via archives and labs (Chapter 5).
- Part III turns to the intersection of digital humanities and Canadian literature, looking at how Canadian literary criticism makes use of digital humanities (Chapter 6), and then at how digital humanities creates data out of Canadian literature (Chapter 7).
- Part IV turns to minoritized literatures, where the application of digital methods can be most fraught, but also where there may be the most to gain: first intersectional digital humanities, with a focus on feminist and LGBTQ+ projects (Chapter 8), followed by racialized literatures and the connections between race and computing (Chapter 9), and finally digitally inflected Indigenous literatures and digital humanities projects that engage with Indigenous communities and information (Chapter 10).
- Part V provides practical information for getting started with digital projects, covering data creation and acquisition (Chapter 11), data management (Chapter 12), text analysis (Chapter 13), and programming (Chapter 14). A case study at the end of this section pulls together ideas from this section—and across the book—to show how they could be used in a digital humanities project (Chapter 15).
- Part VI offers a forward-looking conclusion by bringing together emerging technologies with current and ongoing concerns in digital humanities (Chapter 16).

Since this book is both technologically and critically oriented, we situate our writing within several contexts. To start, we note that because we are tracing the intersections of two fields, we move between theoretical discussions, project histories, and case studies with attempted deftness but, sometimes, necessary clumsiness. The topics overlap at many points, and we know that many readers will not tackle the chapters in sequential order (or even read them all). To this end, we have provided ample cross-references—think of them like the old-fashioned version of hypertext—to help readers navigate the book in whatever order they choose. Where we move from describing the field to providing practical steps for getting started with DH (Chapters 11–14), we switch to a more informal style, addressing *you* (the second-person reader) directly.

Additionally, we note that the limits of this book will become apparent as the reader progresses. We focus almost exclusively on Anglo-Canadian literature. This is an effect of the limits of the scope of the book and the ongoing "two solitudes" separating English- and French-Canadian literatures. In DH, the divide is not as acute, but it remains all the same. Although we mention French projects in the history of humanities computing, our discussion of Canadian literary DH has a notable Anglo bias. Likewise, our discussion of the technical dimensions of DH works—for example, stylistics, mapping, and statistical approaches—is limited by space and the scope of the project.

We have also sought to balance our practical, applied discussion of DH methods with reflections on methodology. From Tanya Clement's notion of differential reading to Alan Liu's meaning problem, theorizing about and interrogating methodology is central to DH. At best, DH approaches invite questions about the methods of analysis; at worst, DH research must be defended against critics who challenge the very tenets on which it is based (see Chapter 2). In DH research, the *how* is often as important as the *why*. As such, we consider *how* digital approaches to literature challenge or nuance more traditional literary scholarship to reflect on, and express, a clear methodology.

As part of this approach, we extend the discussion of methodology to offer readers a vocabulary for a more broadly informed critical DH praxis. Chapters 8–10 place DH into dialogue with critical race theory, Indigenous studies, feminist studies, and queer studies: how do these theories transform DH methodology? DH too often either treats considerations of power and difference as an afterthought, or it justifies its own presence in the humanities mechanically or by drawing on a rarefied, Arcadian vision of scholarship that is inadequately attuned to the concerns of race, class, power, and gender (Barrett and Roger 2023). Indeed, the debates over the meaning of the digital humanities have tended to focus solely on the digital, treating the humanities as either settled or unworthy of examination. Recent debates over Canadian literature remind us that the humanities, as concept and practice, are never settled and, indeed, are at their most vibrant when their very tenets are examined. Canadian literary studies has been productively affected by a practice of unsettling, examining the nation-state to which it lays claim, its colonial origins, and its participation in present-day forms of oppression. We raise the same questions concerning DH and we subject the humanities to scrutiny, arguing that the humanities draw on a legacy of humanism concerned with deciding who does—and does not—count as a person. Our inquiries are guided by Edward Said, who argues that "It is possible to be critical of humanism in the name of humanism" (2005, 11) and who calls for a humanism that is worldly and cosmopolitan.[3] We draw on the lessons of Sylvia Wynter and others to read the legacies of oppression within the humanities and humanist discourse, digital and otherwise. Indeed, the humanities can be perceived as a kind of social technology aimed at producing readers and citizens. We therefore analyze it like the other technologies discussed in the book to ask what vision of the humanities, and the human, a critical DH endorses. Of course, these are not exhaustive discussions (not just beyond the scope of this book but also impossible), but rather pathways for readers to develop their own understanding.

Canadian literature has been complicit with the colonial project, constructing a vision of the nation that disavows its colonial origins. We join in the work of challenging the notion of Canadian literature throughout this book, and we start by identifying our own position in relation to Canada. Paul Barrett is a settler in Canada, born in the United Kingdom, who migrated here at a young age. Sarah Roger is a fourth-generation settler whose displaced ancestors displaced others in turn. We both work and live in Guelph and Toronto, which means we are guests on lands with longstanding and ongoing historical relationships with the Anishinaabeg, Haudenosaunee, Attawandaron, Chippewa, and Mississaugas of the Credit. Both Guelph and Toronto are included in the territory of the Dish With One Spoon treaty—the Haudenosaunee and Anishinaabeg formal commitment to peaceably sharing the land.[4]

Notes

1 The LongPen is a device that enables an author to sign books at a distance using a tablet and robotic hand. Conrad Black used the technology to remotely sign books while unable to leave his Florida home after being forced to surrender his passport to a US court (CBC News 2007).
2 For a digital humanities response to the environmental impacts of computing, see "The Digital Humanities and the Climate Crisis: A Manifesto" (Baillot et al. 2021).
3 Said defines humanism as

> the exertion of one's faculties in language in order to understand, reinterpret, and grapple with the products of our language in history, other

languages and other histories. ... [H]umanism is not a way of consolidating and affirming what "we" have always known and felt, but rather a means of questioning, upsetting, and reformulating so much of what is presented to us
(2005, 28)

4 Any land acknowledgement, while helpful, cannot account for the complexity of the ties and historical and present-day responsibilities to the land. Guelph, for example, is near the Grand River. The Mohawks of the Six Nations at Caledonia were promised the land 6 miles on either side of the Grand River, encompassing present-day Kitchener, Waterloo, Cambridge, and areas near Guelph—a complex history that cannot easily be conveyed in the short space of a land acknowledgment. We also recognize that land acknowledgments can become rote exercises meant to assuage feelings of guilt or acts of institutional box-checking. We are aware of how academic institutions embed terms like decolonization and diversity in their mission statements while neglecting the actual work of decolonization and antiracism. We provide our background and a land acknowledgment as a first step in our commitment to substantive anticolonial and antiracist work.

Works cited

Abel, Jordan. 2013. *Injun*. Vancouver: Talonbooks.

Abel, Jordan. 2014. *Un/inhabited*. Vancouver: Talonbooks.

Atwood, Margaret. 2023. "Murdered by My Replica?" *The Atlantic*, August 26, 2023. https://www.theatlantic.com/books/archive/2023/08/ai-chatbot-training-books-margaret-atwood/675151/.

Baillot, Anne, James Baker, Madiha Zahrah Choski, Alex Gil, Kaiama L. Glover, Ana Lam, Alicia Peaker, Walter Schloger, Torsten Roeder, and Jo Lindsay Walton. 2021. "Digital Humanities and the Climate Crisis: A Manifesto." https://dhc-barnard.github.io/dhclimate/about/.

Barrett, Paul, and Sarah Roger. 2023. *Canadians Read*. Accessed October 10, 2024. https://canadiansread.ca/.

Birney, Earlie. 1968. "Space Conquest: Computer Poem." *Gronk2*. Toronto: Ganglia Press.

Brown, Susan. 2023. "Afterword: The Landscape and the Horizon." In *Future Horizons: Canadian Digital Humanities*, edited by Paul Barrett and Sarah Roger, 407–23. Ottawa: University of Ottawa Press.

Brown, Susan, and Cecily Devereux. 2017. "Introduction: Digital Textualities/Canadian Contexts." *Studies in Canadian Literature / Études en littérature canadienne* 42, no. 2: 145–53. https://id.erudit.org/iderudit/scl42_2art07.

CBC News. 2007. "Long Pen of Conrad Black to Touch Down in Toronto." *CBC News*. https://www.cbc.ca/news/entertainment/long-pen-of-conrad-black-to-touch-down-in-toronto-1.661365.

Coady, Lynn. 2016. *Who Needs Books? Reading in the Digital Age*. Edmonton: University of Alberta Press. https://doi.org/10.1515/9781772121438.

Creamer, Ella. 2023. "Authors File a Lawsuit against OpenAI for Unlawfully 'Ingesting' Their Books." *The Guardian*, July 5, 2023. https://www.theguardian.com/books/2023/jul/05/authors-file-a-lawsuit-against-openai-for-unlawfully-ingesting-their-books.

CWRC. n.d. *Collaboratory for Writing and Research on Culture.* Accessed July 12, 2024. https://cwrc.ca/.

Davey, Frank, and Fred Wah. 1986. *The SwiftCurrent Anthology.* Toronto: Coach House Press.

Djwa, Sandra, and Zailig Pollock. n.d. *The Digital Page: The Collected Works of P. K. Page.* Collaboratory for Writing and Research on Culture. Accessed October 10, 2024. https://cwrc.ca/project/digitalpage.

The Endings Project. 2024. *The Endings Project,* July 7, 2024. https://endings.uvic.ca/.

Fong, Deanna, and Ryan Fitzpatrick. 2024. *Fred Wah Digital Archive.* https://fredwah.ca/.

Hayles, N. Katherine. 2002. *Writing Machines.* Cambridge: The MIT Press. https://doi.org/10.7551/mitpress/7328.001.0001.

Invert Media. 2012. *FourDirectionsTeachings.com.* https://www.fourdirectionsteachings.com/.

Klein, Julie Thompson. 2015. *Interdisciplining Digital Humanities: Boundary Work in an Emerging Field.* Ann Arbor: University of Michigan Press. https://doi.org/10.3998/dh.12869322.0001.001.

Li, Pengfei, Jianyi Yiang, Mohammad A. Islam, and Shaolei Ren. 2023. "Making AI Less 'Thirsty': Uncovering and Addressing the Secret Water Footprint of AI Models." *ArXiv* 2304. https://doi.org/10.48550/arXiv.2304.03271.

McCarty, Willard, Julianne Nyhan, Anne Welsh, and Jessica Salmon. 2012. "Questioning, Asking and Enduring Curiosity: An Oral History Conversation between Julianne Nyhan and Willard McCarty." *Digital Humanities Quarterly* 6, no. 3. https://www.digitalhumanities.org/dhqdev/vol/6/3/000134/000134.html.

McLuhan, Marshall. 1977. "Canada: The Borderline Case." In *The Canadian Imagination,* edited by David Staines, 226–48. Cambridge: Harvard University Press.

O'Kane, Josh. 2023. "Generative AI Copyright Lawsuits Likely Won't Yield Results for Creative Workers Any Time Soon: Margaret Atwood, Mona Awad among Canadians Demanding AI Services Ask Permission to Use Writers' Work and Provide Compensation." *The Globe and Mail,* July 22, 2023. https://www.theglobeandmail.com/arts/books/article-generative-ai-copyright-lawsuits-likely-wont-yield-results-for/.

Orlando. 2023. *The Orlando Project.* https://orlando.cambridge.org/.

Said, Edward. 2005. *Humanism and Democratic Criticism.* New York: Palgrave.

Sula, Chris Alen, and Heather V. Hill. 2019. "The Early History of Digital Humanities: An Analysis of *Computers and the Humanities* (1966–2004) and *Literary and Linguistic Computing* (1986–2004)." *Digital Scholarship in the Humanities* 34, no. 1: i190–i206. https://doi.org/10.1093/llc/fqz072.

Terras, Melissa. 2012. *Digital Humanities in Practice,* edited by Claire Warwick, Melissa Terras, and Julianne Nyhan. Cambridge: Cambridge University Press.

Vipond, Mary. 2003. "The 2003 Presidential Address of the CHA: The Mass Media in Canadian History: The Empire Day Broadcast of 1939." *Journal of Canadian Historical Association / Revue de la Société historique du Canada* 14, no. 1: 1–21. https://doi.org/10.7202/010317ar.

Wemigwans, Jennifer. 2018. *A Digital Bundle: Protecting and Promoting Indigenous Knowledge Online.* Regina: University of Regina Press. https://doi.org/10.1515/9780889775527.

PART I

1
WHAT IS ENGLISH CANADIAN LITERATURE?

* * *

English Canadian literature has been as broadly defined as anything written by a Canadian in English, anything written in English by a person while they were in Canada, and anything written in English by someone who was *once* in Canada.[1] Because the relationship between national identity, geography, and literature is tenuous and shifting, readers and critics alike have puzzled over whose work should define the field. Modern Canadian readers will likely be familiar with names such as Margaret Atwood, Michael Ondaatje, and Lawrence Hill, while readers of an earlier generation would have recognized the names of Farley Mowat, Hugh MacLennan, and E. J. Pratt. Some, such as Lucy Maud Montgomery, have remained popular over time while others, such as Mazo de la Roche, have moved from the centre to the margins. Indeed, it is striking how many once-major figures in Canadian Literature—for example, Mavis Gallant, Clark Blaise, and Gabrielle Roy—are largely forgotten by contemporary readers and critics.

The changing face of Canadian literature has led critics to ponder what the term means today. Laura Moss and Cynthia Sugars organize their *Canadian Literature in English: Texts and Contexts* (2008) anthology around three central questions: "What, if anything, is distinctive about Canadian literature? … What is the connection between literature and nation? How does Canadian literature fit within an international literary context" (xv)? Although these questions have driven discussions since CanLit's earliest days, they have evolved in recent years as we move from understanding literature as a reflection of nation to trying to understand

DOI: 10.4324/9781003318323-3

how literature can transform and challenge ideas of nation. A program such as CBC's longstanding *Canada Reads*, a Canadian literature battle of the books, organizes its seasons around themes such as "The Book Canadians Need Now," "One Book to Move You," and "A Novel to Change Our Nation," all of which suggest the pedagogical and nation-building dimensions of Canadian literature; featured texts range from the canonical to the lesser-known, for example, Hubert Aquin's *Prochain episode* (1965), Miriam Toews's *A Complicated Kindness* (2004), and Heather O'Neill's *Lullabies for Little Criminals* (2006). As Leon Surette argues, "Canadian literary criticism has always been an enterprise in which the central purpose was the discovery of the Canadian-ness of the literature written in this country" (1991, 17).

Canadian literature predates the existence of Canada insofar as there has been writing and storytelling in this place prior to the establishment of Canada as a nation. Yet the emergence of the institution of Canadian literature, the formalization of the field, and the establishment of CanLit as a genre and object of study are all more recent phenomena, which can be traced, for some, to the public recognition of a range of Canadian writers, to the establishing of Canadian literature courses on university campuses, or to the publication of the *Literary History of Canada* (1965). Compiled by a team of leading Canadian literary scholars, including Carl Klinck and Northrop Frye, the *Literary History* is often considered the starting point for modern Canadian literature, particularly as it surveys a range of historical texts and includes Frye's infamous conclusion, where he proposes the notion of a garrison mentality in Canadian literature: the idea that Canadian culture perceives itself within the walls of a garrison and must defend itself against all that lurks beyond those walls. The *Literary History* is probably best known for Frye's oracular observation,

> Canadian sensibility has been profoundly disturbed, not so much by our famous problem of identity, important as that is, as by a series of paradoxes in what confronts that identity. It is less perplexed by the question, "Who am I?" than by some such riddle as "Where is here?"
>
> *(1965, 826)*

Frye's invocation of the "series of paradoxes" and his phrase "some such riddle" suggests that "Where is here?" is but one of the vexing puzzles that confront Canadian identity. For Frye, literature—and other forms of artistic expression—are where the problems of cultural identity are worked out.

The *Literary History* is a productive starting point for contemporary articulations of Canadian literary discourse because it establishes much of the critical vocabulary that has defined Canadian literature (even in opposition) in subsequent decades. It offers the basis for notions of thematicism, regionalism, and spatial concerns that position Canada between America and Britain, places Canadian literature in the context of its environment, and establishes the identifying literary divisions between English and French Canadas. Furthermore, the *Literary History* is one of the first major efforts to establish Canadian literature as a distinct object of scholarly study and to theorize it as such.

Unsurprisingly, however, critics remain divided on the import of the *Literary History*. While Robert Lecker argues that "in Canada the canonical departure point is marked by the publication of the first *Literary History of Canada* in 1965" (1990, 661), Nick Mount eschews it in favour of the cultural and economic forces in the Canada that led to the "CanLit boom" of the 1960s (2017, 31).[2] Dermot McCarthy, meanwhile, insists that "The *Literary History of Canada* does not represent an act of literary autogeny" but rather finds its origins in "the nineteenth-century anthologies" (1991, 32) as well as in A. J. M. Smith's *Book of Canadian Poetry* (1943). Furthermore, D. M. R. Bentley, and others have argued that, despite its continued influence, the *Literary History* represents a narrow and regional (notably, Toronto and Montréal-centric) vision of the national literature. The *Literary History* arrived at a time of great national patriotism in Canada and aimed to establish the very literary tradition it purported to describe. The collection was published just prior to the 1967 centenary and other nation-building events of the 1960s. Yet, to bring this literary culture into being as an identifiable field of study, the editors excluded a great number of works that might have complicated, or even undermined, the collection's organizing logic.

Debates concerning the origins of Canadian literature, the relationships between scholarly and public interest in books, and the regional and linguistic differences that shape the Canadian literary field are some of the salient features of Canadian literary scholarship. Indeed, the field has been marked by sometimes-complementary expressions of both the need for a national literary tradition and of the inadequacy of that tradition. Thomas D'Arcy McGee's position is representative of the view of literature as nation-building enterprise: "Every country, every nationality, every people, must create and foster a National Literature, if it is their wish to preserve a distinct individuality from other nations" (1985, 43). Nationalist critics, dominant throughout the nineteenth and early-twentieth centuries, insisted that for Canada to be recognized as a nation, it must possess a distinct national literature—an insistence that led critics throughout the twentieth century to struggle to differentiate Canadian literature from British, French, and American traditions.[3]

Margery Fee (1981) refers to the critics seeking a nationalist—and not just national—literature as the *romantic nationalists*, because they transposed onto Canada the German Romantic philosophers' ideas of the bond between folk, land, and literature. For example, William Arthur Deacon writes in "The National Character,"

> if we see the Canadian Race emerging a distinct, a unique people; and if we believe that the world's salvation depends ... upon the development of that type—then we are justified in erecting about ourselves walls of words, like constitutions, or walls of stone, like the Great Wall of China.
> *(1923, 63)*

Deacon's highly problematic metaphor evokes the image of the walled garrison while also envisioning literature as a great cultural monument. In this context, the establishment of literature seems integral to defining the nation and identifying Canadians as a distinct people. This is but one example of Canadian literature's origins in an explicitly humanist discourse that employs culture to articulate a particular mode of communal and national belonging. Fee thus argues that, in the mid-nineteenth century,

> The ideas of German Romanticism spread rapidly throughout the West, and, as part of the ideology of nationalism, still flourish, especially in regions struggling for cultural or political self-determination. Romantic nationalist critics, then, were not necessarily sentimental patriots (although they may have been), but critics who, using a set of assumptions first developed during the Romantic period, saw the nation as the primary literary category. These critics could not, ultimately, conceive of literature outside the national context.
> *(1981, 1)*

Perceiving the "nation as the primary literary category" means reading literature as a reflection on, or response to, the idea of Canada. While explicit articulations of Romantic nationalist criticism in Canada peaked during the late nineteenth and early twentieth century, the ongoing effects of this critical trend continue today in the form of the competing roles of French and English literary traditions, the differences in regional articulations of Canadian literature, the role of environment in shaping national literature, and—since the early 1970s—the importance of marginalized voices to challenge and transform Canadian writing. The debates over Canadian literature have largely eclipsed, in scholarly contexts at least, the literature itself, leading Robert Fulford to observe that Canadian cultural production often "looks like a giant tomato cannery: dozens of canning machines, hundreds of workmen trained to run them, scores of trucks waiting to transport the finished product—but no tomatoes" (quoted in Fee 1981, 21).

Histories of digital humanities and Canadian literature

The contours of the debates over the meaning of Canadian literature and the state of the field are too complex to trace in their entirety here. However, the pattern of thesis and antithesis, with little sign of synthesis, is general across this history. Part of what this book aims to show is the role that humanities computing and digital humanities have played both in terms of challenging any emerging consensus concerning national literature and querying what it means to "read" more generally. Digital humanities offers the tantalizing possibility of allowing critics to read broadly, to observe a whole field, rather than a small subset of texts. As a result, it can both shore up and challenge the idea of the nation as the primary literary category. It can also complement or challenge traditional forms of literary scholarship by providing data-rooted perspectives on the books Canadians read, the broad themes in those books, what books critics write about, how those books are related to other fields, and more.

An early example of the complementary relationship between traditional forms of reading and digital scholarship comes from the mid-1960s. While Klinck, Frye, and their co-editors were completing the first edition of the *Literary History of Canada*, in Vancouver, BC, a graduate student named Sandra Djwa was engaged in an entirely different form of Canadian literary history. Djwa, who would go on to be one of the most important Canadian literary critics of her generation, found the assessments of the *Literary History* to be inadequate; she was particularly annoyed by Frye's argument that the environment—the cruel north—shaped both the Canadian psyche and Canadian writing. Djwa was a Newfoundlander and her dissatisfaction with Frye's assessment may have been informed, in part, by her experience growing up in a place where the sea was far more significant than ideas of the north or the wilderness. For Djwa, Frye's oversimplification handpicked a few examples as metonyms for what was a vast, complex, diverse tradition.

Serendipitously, Djwa's home institution at the time, the University of British Columbia, had recently opened a Campus Computing Centre and was eager for researchers to start taking advantage of the new computing power. The centre housed an IBM 7044 mainframe computer and Djwa had the idea of using the computer to challenge the emerging Canadian literary orthodoxy by developing a digital concordance of Canadian poetry. In general terms, a concordance is a kind of index that lists the occurrences of a word, theme, or image across a collection of texts. As we show in subsequent chapters, concordances were some of the first projects that humanities computing scholars would develop. Djwa describes her project thus:

> Between 1966 and 1968, the published books of seven poets, Isabella Valancy Crawford, Sir Charles G. D. Roberts, Archibald Lampman, Duncan Campbell Scott, E. J. Pratt, Earle Birney and Margaret Avison were key-punched. Between 1968 and 1970, seven other poets—Charles Mair, Charles Sangster, Bliss Carman, A. J. M. Smith, A. M. Klein, Irving Layton and P. K. Page—were added.
>
> The procedure followed was the same in all cases. Each poet's published books in chronological order were key-punched on computer cards at the rate of one typographical line per computer card. The [300,000] computer cards containing the poet's canon were then fed into an IBM 7044 computer for printout. Following proofreading and necessary corrections, the computer drew up a word frequency count. This is an alphabetical index listing every word that a poet uses and indicating its frequency of appearance.
>
> *(1970, 44)*

Djwa's work at the UBC Computing Centre is one of the first digital humanities projects in Canada, and it is certainly the first effort to use nascent digital humanities methods to intervene in the debate over the historical origins and contemporary makeup of Canadian literature.[4] While the goals and results of her project merit their own attention (Roger et al. 2023), her work predicts the ways Canadian authors and critics have gone on to use digital methods to challenge critical orthodoxies. Alongside her computationally powered critique of Frye and the *Literary History*, Djwa asserts a canon of Canadian poetry and identifies a novel method of reading its patterns, a few years ahead of Atwood, whose own CanLit-defining work, *Survival*, "outlines a number of key patterns" (1972, 13) in Canadian literature. Djwa's work is also the first in another pattern: as CanLit has continued to be a site of contestation, it is often emerging scholars, dissident voices, minoritized writers, and those at the margins of the critical field who have employed digital and computational methods to challenge Canadian literature's orthodoxies.

There is a longstanding history of Canadian critics and poets using digital and computational methods to intervene in Canadian literary debate and to produce Canadian literature. Frank Davey and Fred Wah ran *SwiftCurrent* (1983–1986), the world's first online literary magazine, on a VAX mainframe hosted at York University and made accessible via the Datapac network (a precursor to the Internet). Sheila and Wilfrid Watson engaged in a decade-long correspondence with Marshall McLuhan such that McLuhan's ideas about media were informed by Sheila Watson's ideas about modernism and vice versa. Robert Cluett's *Canadian Literary Prose: A Preliminary Stylistic Analysis* (1990) details more than a decade of work using computational methods to identify Canadian literary style. bpNichol was an early experimenter in electronic literature, creating *First Screening: Computer Poems* (1984) on his Commodore 64. Nicole Brossard's *Le désert mauve* (1987) was translated onto CD-ROM by artist Adriene Jenik. Erin Mouré's *Pillage Laud* (1999) was created, in part, out of the random sentences generated out of her copy of Mac Prose. The best-selling (by a wide margin) Canadian poet in 2020, Rupi Kaur, writes Instapoetry that blends the affordances of Instagram with her visual, aphoristic writing. As we demonstrate throughout this book, there are numerous points of connection and overlap between Canadian literature and the digital humanities.

Despite their differences, both Frye and Djwa were scholars and students of E. J. Pratt: Frye because Pratt mentored him early in his career, and Djwa because she was familiar with his poetry from her early life in Newfoundland and recognized the complexity in Pratt's combination of modern and classical poetic forms. While Frye saw in Pratt the evidence of a continuum of the great tradition, Djwa saw a syncretic combination of modernist themes and classical forms that evinced a unique poetic imagining of the place of the human in the modern world. Pratt's concern with the transformation of human life in relation to engineering projects, industrial systems, the power of the mechanical, and the alienation of the modern world offers the "man versus machine" sensibility that serves as a poetic analogue to the debates in the digital humanities. In many respects, Pratt's poetry anticipates the contemporary critical concern over what happens to the humanities and the human as they are changed by technological systems. These concerns live on in the works of writers as diverse as Hugh MacLennan, Liz Howard, Douglas Coupland, and Joshua Whitehead.

The shape of Canadian literary criticism

While Djwa's early computational work was largely ignored,[5] the *Literary History* and in particular Frye's conclusion, set the tone for Canadian literary criticism for years. The Frygian koan of "where is here?" became a vaguely understood mantra for Canadian critics of the 1960s, '70s, and '80s. These critics were interested in the relationship between place and identity and used Frye's statement as a guiding light in their thematic readings of Canadian literature. The title of Frye's collection of essays on

Canadian culture, *The Bush Garden: Essays on the Canadian Imagination* (1971), is revealing of this thematic-critical approach. Where today, Canadians might disagree with the notion of a single "Canadian imagination," Frye argued that the alchemy of place and identity shapes imagination such that a national culture, an expression of a collective experience, becomes coherent. Frye's view helped give rise to thematic criticism, the notion that a national literature can be identified by, and perhaps even reduced to, a particular theme. For Russell Brown, "The making of thematic statements is a reading act that follows from observing the existence of patterns that seem to have significance" (2001, 672). It is, as we shall see, a methodology well suited to some modes of digital reading, and which has parallels with Djwa's work on her thematic concordance. Crucially, where Djwa's approach to reading Canadian literary patterns works deductively, reading the texts computationally to find recurring themes, thematicism works in the opposite direction, employing Frye's "inductive basis" (1965, 821) to assert a thematic pattern and then find the supporting evidence in the texts.

Atwood's *Survival: A Thematic Guide to Canadian Literature* (1972) is the best known of the thematic arguments, beginning with the "sweeping generalization ... that every country or culture has a single unifying and informing symbol at its core" (31). This is the thematic statement *par excellence,* and Atwood argues that "The central symbol for Canada ... is undoubtedly Survival, *la Survivance*" (32). Atwood deftly splits *survival* along linguistic lines and thus sets out to identify "a series of characteristics and leitmotifs, and a comparison of the varying treatments of them in different national and cultural environments" (xx). Notably, she wrote *Survival* to support Coach House Press after a fire threatened financial ruin. Coach House had published a book about venereal disease that had sold well, and Atwood hoped that *Survival* would serve as a "VD of Canadian Literature" (Brown 2017, 173); as Susan Brown archly notes, "Appropriately, it went viral" (2017, 173). Atwood's book is deeply influenced by Frye (she was his student at the University of Toronto), and *Survival* can be seen as a popular gloss of his work on Canadian literature. Despite the many objections to the book's premises, arguments, and conclusions by reviewers, critics, and casual readers, *Survival* was a best-seller and became a key text on Canadian literature syllabi; its thematic view of Canadian literature set the tone for public discussion of books in Canada for years.

Thematicism was (perceived as) a dominant trend in Canadian literary criticism until the publication of Frank Davey's "Surviving the Paraphrase" (1976), a title that blends Cleanth Brooks's "The Heresy of Paraphrase" with Atwood's *Survival*. Davey argues that "It is a testimony to the limits of Canadian literary criticism that thematic criticism should have become the dominant approach to English-Canadian literature," and he excoriates

Canadian criticism for ignoring "the literary work," particularly "matters of form, language, style, structure, and consciousness as these arise from the work as a unique construct" (1976, 5). For Davey, theme is a lazy kind of critical shorthand that ignores the complexities of a literary work. Alas, Davey's critique of thematicism retains all the weaknesses of the tradition of New Criticism upon which it draws.[6] Subsequent reassessments, meanwhile, argued that the dominance of Canadian thematic criticism has been overstated. As Smaro Kamboureli suggests, "it has not been so much thematicism that has governed Canadian criticism but the critics' obsession with the idea of it" (2012, 20).

New critical formations

In the years since Davey's broadside, Canadian critical discourse has substantially changed. The 1980s saw increased attention to difference and alterity and a related reassessment of the Canadian canon. Women writers, writers of colour, Black writers, Indigenous writers, and queer writers have all moved from the margins of Canadian literary discourse to being central to the composition of Canadian writing. Writers who were once staples on Canadian literary syllabuses—Timothy Findley, Mavis Gallant, Margaret Avison, Ethel Wilson, Al Purdy, and others—have now given way to writers such as Dionne Brand, Katherena Vermette, Souvankham Thammavongsa, Suzette Mayr, Esi Edugyan, and others. A representative moment in this transformation of the canon occurred with the publication of Marion Richmond and Linda Hutcheon's *Other Solitudes: Canadian Multicultural Fictions* (1990). Their title—with its reference to Hugh MacLennan's *Two Solitudes* (1945) and the English/French divide, as well as the tension it invokes between *fictions of multiculturalism* and *multiculturalism as fiction*—indicates a shift from *literature* as the assertion of signal national identity to *literatures* as reflecting the contradictions of the nation. *Other Solitudes* focused on the emerging group of "multicultural" writers including Austin Clarke, Rohinton Mistry, Michael Ondaatje, Tomson Highway, Himani Bannerji, and Rudy Wiebe. In doing so, *Other Solitudes* draws together writers who previously predominantly appeared in smaller anthologies that pushed at the margins of Canadian literature, such as Harold Head's *Canada in Us Now* (1977), a collection of Black writers in Canada with a title that suggests a complex relation to the politics of nation, and publications from M. G. Vassanji's TSAR Press. *Other Solitudes* follows in the footsteps of 1980s initiatives such as special issues of literary journals including *Descant* and *Tamarack Review* dedicated to minoritized and racialized writers. *Fireweed*, a significant source of women's and racialized women's writing in Canada, published a special issue on Asian Canadian women's writing that Larissa Lai has called "groundbreaking" (Markowicz 2019, 296) in its efforts to shift the map of Canadian writing. In channelling some of this energy, *Other Solitudes* has proven prescient of the changing landscape of Canadian literature.

More recently, definitions of Canadian literature have shifted to grapple with the field's colonial origins, literature's role in the process of nation-building, and the efforts to "recognize" or "make space for" Black, racialized, and Indigenous voices within Canada. For some critics and writers, this reckoning leads to a rejection of the very idea of national literatures, whereas for others this requires a reassessment of the relation between literature and nation. Kamboureli attempts to square these formulations by describing contemporary Canadian literature as

> a construct bounded by the nation, a cultural byproduct of the Cold War era, a nationalist discourse with its roots in colonial legacies, a literature that has assumed transnational and global currency, a tradition often marked by uncertainty about its value and relevance, a corpus of texts in which, albeit not without anxiety and resistance, spaces have been made for First Nations and diasporic voices. These are some of the critical assumptions scholars have brought to the study of CanLit, as we have come to call it for the sake of brevity, but also affectionately, and often ironically as we recognize the dissonances inscribed in the economy of this term.
>
> *(2011, vii)*

Kamboureli identifies the limits of the field, its uneven historical genealogy, and her own ironic, yet affectionate, distance from Canadian literature. As the complexity of their definition reveals, this history of Canadian literature is a broad sweep across a field of dispersed writers, discordant traditions, and moments of connection and disruption. Indeed, our own history misses many key moments and dimensions of Canadian literature, including the TISH poets, the Canadian modernists, regional concerns, and, of course, Québécois and other French-Canadian writing and the long history of Indigenous narrative, including that which predates the notion of Canada.

In recent years, the Canadian literary and critical landscape has faced an overdue reckoning with both the colonial origins of CanLit and the lengthy history of sexual assault, racism, and other abuses of power that have occurred in publishing houses, universities, and even authors' personal lives. After the revelations of sexual assault and predatory behaviour at the University of British Columbia and Concordia University, among others, Canadian literary criticism has turned its focus on the structural inequities that make this exploitation possible and that normalize white supremacy, sexism, and oppression. A number of these analyses were gathered in *Refuse: CanLit in Ruins* (2018), a collection of essays, poems, tweets, and polemics aimed at the institutions of Canadian literature.

Hannah McGregor, Julie Rak, and Erin Wunker, the editors of *Refuse* insist,

> At the heart of CanLit as a formation is colonial violence. That violence is what keeps CanLit supposedly open to Indigenous ways of knowing and making knowledge, but in fact closed to anything that would actively dismantle the innate moral authority assumed by its practitioners.
>
> *(21)*

The assessment of CanLit that Joshua Whitehead contributes to *Refuse* is revealing. He imagines it as "a collection of mirrors that have amalgamated into a reflective system spelling out nationalism—a whole thing rather than a web of fractures" (2018, 192). Whitehead's image is a reminder of the ways in which CanLit has been constructed to reflect a single vision of nation, one that denies its historical and present racism and colonial origins. Yet his critique overlooks the numerous histories of Canadian literature that have made the institutions, writers, readers, and voices far more fractious and diverse. M. NourbeSe Philip's work to expose structural racism and to insist on the importance of Black women's writing in Canadian literature, Lillian Allen's efforts to force the League of Canadian Poets to include dub poetry, or Lee Maracle's storming of the stage at the Vancouver Writer's Festival—these are all instances of how Black and Indigenous writers have refused their marginalization and, instead, transformed the terms by which literary recognition is offered. It is this history of struggle against marginalization that leads Karina Vernon to argue, "Not only is there a genealogy of struggle in CanLit, there is a genealogy of struggle *as* CanLit" (2019, 14, original emphasis).

It is telling that a work like *Refuse* sources some of the most stringent critiques of Canadian literature from the Internet. This is evidence of both the import of online spaces for marginalized writers to build community and speak back to institutional power, as well as of the increasing relationship between digital culture and Canadian literature. Like Djwa, whose early work predates social media by more than three decades, new critics and scholars have used digital forums and forms in order to challenge reigning Canadian literary orthodoxies. Canadian literature has moved online in a range of ways. *Canada Reads*, CBC's annual battle of the books, produces a lively online debate and discussion nominally about CanLit. Twitter was, for some years, a vital source of discussion of Canadian literature from the margins. More recently, Instagram and TikTok have become spaces to discuss books. Small magazines have moved online too, with digital incarnations of journals such as *The Puritan* (now *The Ex-Puritan*) and *Lemonhound* (no longer publishing) showcasing work from new writers. Digital spaces have played a significant role in shifting the grounds of Canadian literature in ways for which many of the contributors to *Refuse* called.

As we shall see, both Canadian literature and digital humanities are informed by their concern with the notion of the humanities. For Canadian literature, the investigation into the humanities involves understanding the relationship between literature and the nation in its numerous formations and manifestations. While the very category of Canadian literature has come under scrutiny—and is rejected by many authors writing in Canada today—the legacy of CanLit as a creative and critical practice continues to shape literary study in this country. For the digital humanities, the investigation into the humanities explores how the humanities is irrevocably transformed by emerging forms of technology, and how the lessons and principles of humanistic inquiry transform, in kind, our understanding of our technologically mediated world. In what follows we trace the development of Canadian literature and digital humanities and begin to discern the productive points of overlap between them.

Notes

1 Due to space and language constraints, we have almost entirely limited ourselves to a discussion of Canadian literature written in English. We make occasional references to literary works and digital humanities projects in French and Indigenous languages. While this decision does reify the traditional boundaries between English and French Canadian literatures, it is necessary as these traditions are so different that to try and bring them together in this volume, under some vague nationalist thesis, would do a disservice to both. Although we recognize the problems with using the terms *Canadian literature* and *CanLit* as stand-ins for *English Canadian literature* and *English CanLit*, the alternative (specifying that the works are in English) is clunky, and so we have opted to call out the language of the text only where relevant. We acknowledge that, in doing so, we are contributing to the problem of English Canadian literature unfairly and inaccurately serving as a metonym for all literature written by those from or located in or about the place referred to as Canada.

2 Mount's thesis combines cultural and economic histories to argue that the affluence of postwar Canada made possible the CanLit boom of the 1960s and early 1970s: "Affluence gave Canadians not just the means but also the time to consume and produce goods that are unnecessary to life" and this newfound "Affluence didn't just make the CanLit boom possible: it made it necessary" (2017, 31). Although Mount's work carefully traces the dramatic increase in the number of writers, publishing venues, magazines, and readers throughout the 1960s, it is anticipated, somewhat, by Desmond Pacey's 1954 question

concerning Canadian poetry output: "How are we to explain the surge of activity from 1944 to 1948, and the sudden slackening of 1949 and 1950? The last years of the war and the first years of peace were the high watermarks of the economic prosperity and of the sense of national well-being in Canada. The country was prosperous, prices were still controlled, and more people had money for relative luxuries such as books of verse" (1954, 256).

3 Edward Hartley Dewart is representative of the aspirational view of national literature:

> The literature of the world is the foot-prints of human progress; and unless all progress should cease, and mental paralysis arrest all human activity, these way-marks shall continue to be erected along the pathway of vanishing years ... A national literature is an essential element in the formation of national character. It is not merely the record of a country's mental progress: it is the expression of its intellectual life, the bond of national unity, and the guide of national energy. It may be fairly questioned, whether the whole range of history presents the spectacle of a people firmly united politically, without the subtle but powerful cement of a patriotic literature.
>
> *(1985, 50)*

4 In an example of two sets of scholars working independently on similar projects at the same time, as Djwa was working on her concordance, Robert Jay Glickman and Gerrit Joseph Staalman, both of the University of Toronto, published the *Manual for the Printing of Literary Texts and Concordances by Computer* (1966) as part of their *Integrated Series of Computer Programs for Literary Research* project (discussed further in Chapter 3).

5 Djwa recalls presenting her concordance at the 1970 *Learned Society* conference—the precursor to today's Congress of the Humanities and Social Sciences—and the audience being "stunned ... I don't remember any fuss or bother; it was just clapping. We were all very polite and very Canadian" (Roger et al. 2023, 148). After, Djwa was pleasantly surprised when P. K. Page reached out to inquire which metaphors Djwa had observed most regularly in her poetry.

6 Jonathan Culler challenges New Criticism's proposed ability to "just read" a text:

> New Criticism's dream of a self-contained encounter between innocent reader and autonomous text is a bizarre fiction. To read is always to read in relation to other texts, in relation to the codes that are the products of these texts and go to make up a culture.
>
> *(1981, 11)*

Further reading

Frye, Northrop. 1971. *The Bush Garden: Essays on the Canadian Imagination.* Toronto: Anansi.

Kamboureli, Smaro. 2000. *Scandalous Bodies: Diasporic Literature in English Canada.* Waterloo: Wilfrid Laurier University Press.

Moss, Laura, and Cynthia Sugars. 2008. *Canadian Literature in English: Texts and Contexts.* Toronto: Pearson Education.

Mount, Nick. 2017. *Arrival: The Story of CanLit*. Toronto: Anansi.
New, W. H. 1989. *A History of Canadian Literature*. London: Macmillan. https://doi.org/10.1007/978-1-349-19564-0.
Rak, Julie, Hannah McGregor, and Erin Wunker, eds. 2018. *Refuse: CanLit in Ruins*. Toronto: BookThug.
Walcott, Rinaldo. 1997. *Black Like Who? Writing Black Canada*. Toronto: Insomniac Press.

Works cited

Atwood, Margaret. 1972 (2012). *Survival: A Thematic Guide to Canadian Literature*. Toronto: Anansi.
Brown, Russell. 2001. "The Practice and Theory of Thematic Criticism: A Reconsideration." *University of Toronto Quarterly* 70, no. 2: 653–89. https://doi.org/10.3138/utq.70.2.653.
Brown, Susan. 2017. "Survival: Canadian Cultural Scholarship in a Digital Age." *Studies in Canadian Literature / Études en littérature canadienne* 42, no. 2: 171–200. https://id.erudit.org/iderudit/scl42_2art09.
Cluett, Robert. 1990. *Canadian Literary Prose: A Preliminary Stylistic Analysis*. Toronto: ECW Press.
Culler, Jonathan. 1981. *The Pursuit of Signs*. Ithaca: Cornell University Press.
Davey, Frank. 1976. "Surviving the Paraphrase." *Canadian Literature* 70, no. 5: 5–13. https://canlit.ca/article/surviving-the-paraphrase/.
Deacon, William Arthur. 1923. "The National Character." *Pens and Pirates*. Toronto: Ryerson.
Dewart, Edward Hartley. 1985. "Introductory Essay to Selections from Canadian Poets." In *Towards a Canadian Literature: Essays, Editorials, and Manifestos*, edited by Douglas D. Daymond and Leslie G. Monkman, 50. Ottawa: Tecumseh Press.
Djwa, Sandra. 1970. "Canadian Poetry and the Computer." *Canadian Literature* 46 (Autumn): 43–54. https://canlit.ca/article/canadian-poetry-and-the-computer/.
Fee, Margery. 1981. "English-Canadian Literary Criticism, 1890–1950: Defining and Establishing a National Literature." PhD diss., University of Toronto.
Frye, Northrop. 1965. "Conclusion." In *Literary History of Canada*, edited by Alfred Bailey, Claude Bissell, Roy Daniells, Northrop Frye, Carl Klinck, and Desmond Pacey, 330–61. Toronto: University of Toronto Press. https://doi.org/10.3138/9781487589363.
Frye, Northrop. 1971. *The Bush Garden: Essays on the Canadian Imagination*. Toronto: Anansi.
Glickman, Robert Jay, and Gerrit Joseph Staalman. 1966. *Manual for the Printing of Literary Texts and Concordances by Computer*. Toronto: University of Toronto Press.
Hutcheon, Linda, and Marion Richmond, eds. 1990. *Other Solitudes: Canadian Multicultural Fiction*. Oxford: Oxford University Press.
Kamboureli, Smaro. 2007. "Preface." In *Trans.Can.Lit: Resituating the Study of Canadian Literature*, edited by Smaro Kamboureli and Roy Miki, vii–xv. Waterloo: Wilfrid Laurier University Press. https://doi.org/10.51644/9781554581030-001.

Kamboureli, Smaro. 2012. "Introduction: Shifting the Ground of a Discipline: Emergence and Canadian Literary Studies in Canada." In *Shifting the Ground of Canadian Literary Studies*, edited by Smaro Kamboureli and Robert Zacharias, 1–22. Waterloo: Wilfrid Laurier University Press. https://doi.org/10.51644/9781554583966-003.

Lecker, Robert. 1990. "The Canonization of Canadian Literature: An Inquiry into Value." *Critical Inquiry* 16 (Spring): 656–79. https://doi.org/10.1086/448552.

Markowicz, Marcin. 2019. "'A Troublesome Weed Which Spreads Like Wildfire': *Fireweed: A Feminist Quarterly* and the Politics of Diversity." *Studies in Canadian Literature / Études en littérature canadienne*. 44, no. 2: 293–311.

McCarthy, Dermot. 1991. "The Canon and the Course." In *Canadian Canons: Essays in Literary Value*, edited by Robert Lecker, 17–29. Toronto: University of Toronto Press.

McGee, Thomas D'Arcy. 1985. "Protection for Canadian Literature." In *Towards a Canadian Literature: Essays, Editorials, and Manifestos*, edited by Douglas D. Daymond and Leslie G. Monkman, 20–30. Ottawa: Tecumseh Press.

McGregor, Hannah, Julie Rak, and Erin Wunker, eds. 2018. *Refuse: CanLit in Ruins*. Toronto: BookThug.

Moss, Laura, and Cynthia Sugars. 2008. *Canadian Literature in English: Texts and Contexts*, Vol. 1. Toronto: Pearson.

Mount, Nick. 2017. *Arrival: The Story of CanLit*. Toronto: Anansi.

Roger, Sarah, Paul Barrett, Kiera Obbard, and Sandra Djwa. 2023. "Canadian Poetry and the Computational Concordance: Sandra Djwa and the Early History of Canadian Humanities Computing." In *Future Horizons: Canadian Digital Humanities*, edited by Paul Barrett and Sarah Roger, 133–48. Ottawa: University of Ottawa Press. https://doi.org/10.2307/jj.17681834.13.

Smith, A. J. M., ed. 1943. *Book of Canadian Poetry*. Chicago: University of Chicago Press.

Surette, Leon. 1991. "Creating the Canadian Canon." In *Canadian Canons: Essays in Literary Value*, edited by Robert Lecker, 17–29. Toronto: University of Toronto Press.

Vernon, Karina. 2019. "CanLit as Critical Genealogy." *Canadian Literature* 239: 13–17. https://canlit.ca/wp-content/uploads/2021/04/CanLit_239_Final.pdf.

Whitehead, Joshua. 2018. "Writing as a Rupture: A Breakup Note to CanLit." In *Refuse: CanLit in Ruins*, edited by Hannah McGregor, Julie Rak, and Erin Wunker, 192–99. Toronto: BookThug.

2
WHAT ARE DIGITAL HUMANITIES?

* * *

Just as there is no agreed-upon definition of what constitutes CanLit, there is also no universal definition for digital humanities. The field encompasses everything from digital forms of reading to data visualizations, from social media analysis to augmented digital editions. Often referred to as a "big tent" (Pannapacker 2011), DH is a research methodology, a pedagogy, a stand-alone scholarly field, and also a toolkit used in more established domains. For some, it even stretches the bounds of what constitutes the humanities itself, pulling in contributions from social scientists, computer scientists, engineers, programmers, and user experience (UX) and user interface (UI) designers. Many members of the DH community hail from the galleries, libraries, archives, and museums (GLAM) sector, where they often, but not always, work with materials related to the humanities. The About page of the Alliance of Digital Humanities Organizations (ADHO), the umbrella organization for more than a dozen national and international DH societies including Canada's, nods to this expansiveness:

> Members in ADHO societies are those at the forefront of areas such as textual analysis, electronic publication, document encoding, textual studies and theory, new media studies and multimedia, digital libraries, applied augmented reality, interactive gaming, and beyond. We are researchers and lecturers in humanities computing and in academic departments such as English, History, French, Modern Languages, Linguistics, Philosophy, Theatre, Music, Computer Science, and the Visual Arts. We are resource specialists working in libraries and archival

centres, humanities computing groups, and other professional arenas. We are academic administrators, and members of the private and public sectors. We are independent scholars, students, graduate students, and research assistants. We are from countries in every hemisphere.

(ADHO, n.d.)

When DH's leading organization requires such a broad description to capture its membership, it is no surprise that DH is often viewed as a question of knowing DH when one sees it.

This wrestling over the definitions of digital humanities speaks to the novelty and diversity of the field. It isn't as clearly a demarcated object of study as, for instance, the other area of this book's focus, Canadian literature. This, in turn, raises the question of whether DH constitutes a field of study (with an assortment of defined objects and methods of inquiry) or whether it is more of a set of loosely related methods that bring digital technology to bear on preexisting domains, transforming them in the process. Our identification in the introduction of DH as a *boundary object* is one way to address this condition, by defining DH as something of a combination of both the field and the method. Another common way of addressing the question is deferral. Consider, for example, the editorial in the inaugural edition of *Digital Humanities Quarterly* (*DHQ*) in 2007:

> It is tempting, in the first issue of a journal by this name, to pose the question, "What is digital humanities?" and perhaps to attempt an answer. Instead, we defer this question to the future, with the expectation that it will be answered, or at least addressed, in the annals that are to be written and published here. Not the first issue, nor even the tenth, will give a sense of the emerging shape: it will take time for the range of submissions to represent the real contours of the field. And there will be a further dialectical process of reading and authorship, provocation and response, through which we can expect the field to evolve.
>
> *(Flanders, Piez, and Terras 2007)*

The editorial implies bounds will inevitably be drawn—just not yet. For Matthew Kirschenbaum, when they are, DH will "earn a place in histories of the profession alongside other major critical movements like the Birmingham School or Yale deconstruction" (2012). While it may be unclear what DH is, to some its value is still clear.

Yet the cycle between consensus on and division regarding what constitutes Canadian literature that we traced in Chapter 1 is matched by similar debates concerning the merits of the digital humanities. They perhaps begin with Stanley Fish's attacks on stylometrics in the 1970s—a line of criticism he has maintained for over forty years (Fish 2012)—and can be seen most recently in the *Critical Inquiry* forum responding to Nan Z. Da's 2019 critique of the field of computational literary studies (Da 2019) (see Chapter 7). It is telling that the field's major book series is entitled *Debates in the Digital Humanities*, with emphasis on the *debates*. It is perhaps only a slight exaggeration to say that community spirit has prevented internal debates from becoming into outright schisms. DH is routinely the subject of debate in part because the tools and technologies that constitute the *digital* are always changing. From Djwa's punch cards to the emergence of accessible, functional (although the latter is debatable) artificial intelligence in the mid-2020s, digital humanities has grown alongside the technologies that it employs and creates.

What of the humanities?

Just as digital humanities is generous in scoping its own domain, so too it allows for a broad understanding of what falls within the bounds of the humanities. A review of *Digital Studies / Le champ numérique*—the Canadian Society for Digital Humanities / Société canadienne des humanités numériques (CSDH/SCHN)'s peer-reviewed, online, open-access journal—shows that it includes everything from cultural studies and media studies to medicine and law to video games and digital maps. This breadth is in keeping with Kathleen Fitzpatrick's view that while "The field's background in humanities computing typically, but far from exclusively, results in projects that focus on computing methods applicable to textual materials … Digital humanities as it is currently practised *isn't just* located in literary studies departments" (2012, emphasis added). In other words, there is more to digital humanities than using computers to analyze texts. Yet there is a reason that this even needs to be said. At inception, DH was primarily a tool for literary-textual analysis, "more rooted in English than any other departmental home" (Kirschenbaum 2012). This early literary focus is a result of the relative ease of manipulating text with computers and strengthened by the continued growth of technologies for creating and accessing literary works.

An analysis of abstracts from ADHO conferences from 2004 to 2017 found that "The most-used keywords are unsurprising: 'Text Analysis' (tagged on 22 percent of submissions), 'Data Mining/Text Mining' (20 percent), 'Literary Studies' (20 percent)" meanwhile, other fields "have found a home in DH" but "their presence fluctuates, especially in comparison with the dominance of literary studies" (Eichmann-Kalwara, Jorgensen, and Weingart 2018; Weingart and Eichmann-Kalwara 2017). By contrast, in the analysis of the contents of humanities journals referred to in the introduction, Chris Alen Sula and Heather V. Hill show that across more than 1,300 scholarly articles, there is a strong representation of research involving sound, multimedia, and what they term "reflections on technology" (195).[1] With respect to the scholarly domain, they note that while English is indeed the most common departmental home for DH practitioners, "languages and literatures other than English are nearly as common, as are centres, labs, and non-academic affiliations" (2019, 197). Indeed, the strong representation of Francophone work in *Digital Studies / Le champ numérique* undercuts the notion that English departments (with emphasis on *English*) are the rightful home of DH. Unfortunately, the excellent work being done in French, both in digital humanities and Canadian literature, is beyond the scope of this book. In many cases, digital work in some humanities fields (music, art history, gender studies) may not get categorized as DH but fits any definition of the term. This indicates the continual need to revise definitions as the DH tent expands.

Broadening digital humanities to more than just textual analysis using computers is part of DH's tradition of extending and even challenging disciplinary boundaries. Traditionally, scholarship in fields such as art, history, literature, and philosophy has encouraged interpretations that are subjective and relative. Indeed, the humanities are largely concerned with aspects of human experience that are, to varying degrees, personal. By contrast, the digital implies something more positivist— not just the binary of computer code, but also the verifiability and repeatability of statistical analysis. Yet for most (or it is probably fair to say *all*) DH practitioners, computers are enlisted not to find the one correct, irrefutable interpretation, but rather to trouble dominant perspectives and the structures that enable them. In an often-quoted, now unavailable comment left on a Humanities, Arts, Science, and Technology Alliance and Collaboratory (HASTAC) blog post, Mark Sample says, "It's all about innovation and disruption. The digital humanities is really an insurgent humanities" (Svensson 2012), but he declines to specify: insurgent against *what*? In the *Digital Humanities Manifesto 2.0*, the unnamed authors call for the use of DH to (1) deconstruct "the very materiality, methods, and media of humanistic inquiry and practices," (2) affirm "the value of the open, the infinite, the expansive, the university/museum/archive/library without walls, the democratization of culture and scholarship," and (3) "collapse the boundaries between the humanities and the social and natural sciences" (2009, 8, 3). Patrik Svensson captures this aspirational, utopian thinking in his vision statement for the field, which reads (in part):

> The digital humanities clearly has the power to stimulate visionary and transformative thinking, and it can be a site for innovation, reconfiguration and exploration. This power, which should be acknowledged and

valued, comes from the broad and intersectional reach of the digital humanities, a sense of being situated at the periphery and fighting established structures, the non-disciplinary status of the field, and humanities-external interest and acknowledgement.

(2012)

Svensson's view is optimistic, even utopian, but contains echoes of the Silicon Valley disruptor discourse that often aims to reconfigure and transform all that it encounters, sometimes with little understanding of the implications of that transformation.

A provisional, historical, collaborative definition

While the variety of definitions makes it clear that digital humanities assembles around a shared vision more than a singular definition, we still need a working definition for this book. We start, therefore, from *A Companion to Digital Humanities* (2004):

> The real origin of that term was in conversation with Andrew McNeillie, the original acquiring editor for the Blackwell *Companion to Digital Humanities*. We started talking with him about that book project in 2001, in April, and by the end of November we'd lined up contributors and were discussing the title, for the contract. Ray [Siemens] wanted "A Companion to Humanities Computing" as that was the term commonly used at that point; the editorial and marketing folks at Blackwell wanted "Companion to Digitized Humanities." I [John Unsworth] suggested "Companion to Digital Humanities" to shift the emphasis away from simple digitization. ... I also appreciated the fact that it seemed to cast a wider net than "humanities computing" which seemed to imply a form of computing, whereas "digital humanities" implied a form of humanism. I also thought it would be an easier sell to the humanities community to have the emphasis on "humanities."
>
> *(Unsworth quoted in Kirschenbaum 2012)*[2]

While this origin story references the idea that DH was always meant to cast a wide net, it also highlights another aspect of digital humanities particularly relevant to this collection: collaboration (for example, see Chapter 5). Even DH's name has its genesis in an act of collaboration, since it appears in the title of a major edited collection that includes contributions from many of the discipline's best-known practitioners at the time; the title itself, as the quotation shows, is the result of dialogue between authors, editors, and even marketers. DH aspires to be inclusive and accessible, with its emphasis squarely on the human (or the humanist) rather than the digital. The choice of *digital humanities* rather than *digitized humanities* (with its implied limit to *digitized texts*) and rather than *humanities computing* (with its focus on the *computer*) feels prescient: at the moment of writing in 2024, DH practitioners are working with materials that are born digital (as well as those that have been digitized), while digital technologies have changed so dramatically that limiting DH to work done on a *computer* feels quaint.

This opening up to more than digitized or computer-based work is in line with the broader notion of DH as a community:

> The most important of those resources [required to do DH work] is human. We can't succeed as islands. We have to collaborate with one another and with the larger research centers if the field is going to succeed outside of major universities. More and more, we recognize that the old model of the individual scholar—if it was ever really viable, and not a romantic myth—has become completely dysfunctional.
> *(Pannapacker 2011)*

Pannapacker's foregrounding of the importance of the *human* as resource and Susan Schreibman, Ray Siemens, and John Unsworth's framing of DH as a "form of humanism" draw attention to the kinds of humanistic research DH enables and how that work reframes humanist discourse. Unsworth is right to identify the "implied forms of humanism" in the shift from humanities computing to digital humanities, yet that conception of humanism all too often remains unremarked upon. Indeed, as we discuss, historically, DH scholars have not always reflected on the humanistic values and practices that their projects reproduce or envision anew. In recent years, DH applications have increasingly foregrounded race, gender, sexuality, and other forms of difference and power. The notions of humanism that undergird humanities work have come under scrutiny and—in DH, as elsewhere—been revised by scholars using postcolonial, feminist, queer, Black, Indigenous, and intersectional frameworks.

Schreibman, Siemens, and Unsworth's collection is demonstrative of the collaborative nature of DH. It contains contributions from more than forty scholars, many of whom are still key players in the field; the follow-up volume published more than a decade later, *A New Companion to Digital Humanities* (2016), includes contributions from nearly sixty scholars. Co-authorship is the norm in digital humanities, which sets the field apart from disciplines that still venerate the solitary scholar, labouring away in isolation. As the five co-authors of *Digital_Humanities* (2012) state, "the Digital Humanities remains at its core a profoundly collaborative enterprise" (Burdick, Drucker, Lunenfeld, Pressner, and Schnapp 2012, ix).[3] This suggests the possibility that the best way to define DH is to do so collaboratively. The Day of DH (an international annual event, now organized by centerNet, but originating with Geoffrey Rockwell and the University of Alberta in 2009), invites digital humanists to contribute to a collective *day in the life* project, made up of photographs, social media posts, blog entries, and more, to capture a slice of what constitutes DH. Alongside these personal contributions, participants are asked to answer the question, "How do you define digital humanities?" More than 800 responses have been collated at whatisdigitalhumanities.com, which displays a single answer each time it is loaded (Heppler 2015). Definitions ranging from pithy to philosophical lend themselves to categorization[4] as either or both methodological (practical, application-oriented statements) and theoretical (conceptual, philosophical statements):

Methodological

I often say that humanities computing involves three distinct research areas. First, some researchers apply computing to research questions in the humanities. These might be questions they've always pursued but can now pursue faster or at a larger scale, or they may be questions that could not be addressed satisfactorily at all without computers. Second, some researchers take computing as an object of study using humanities methods. Examples include cyberculture and posthumanism. Third, some researchers take a generative approach, creating new online materials or tools for subsequent study and use. Most of my own work is in this third area.

(Stan Ruecker, University of Alberta)

A group of computer-related strategies and tactics that humanists use to accomplish their goals (from research and reading to writing and teaching, etc.).

(Harvey Quamen, University of Alberta)

Theoretical

I define Digital Humanities as the re-figuring of computing, a historically positivist field, in order to pose and answer the more speculative questions typical of the humanities.

(Constance Crompton, University of Ottawa)

The thoughtful use of computing in humanistic inquiry and the thinking through of computing from the perspective of the traditions of the humanities.

(Geoffrey Rockwell, University of Alberta)

Methodological + theoretical

Digital Humanities involves the use of computers, the Internet and related technologies to enable the creation and sharing of humanities scholarship in ways not possible in traditional humanities practice. Digital Humanities challenges traditional understandings of the Humanities by fostering interdisciplinary collaborations and providing new perspectives on the objects of humanistic inquiry.

(Jason Boyd, Toronto Metropolitan University)

Digital humanities is an interdisciplinary, often collaborative meeting place where computing addresses the interests and concerns founded in the humanities (and vice versa). At times, digital humanities is highly applied and, at other times, theoretical and reflective, but always diverse and complex.

(Milena Radzikowska, Mount Royal University)

Digital humanities involve situated and embodied engagement in humanities research and teaching through the development or application of digital technologies, in conjunction with the critical analysis using humanities frameworks and epistemologies of the implications of such activities. These inquiries bleed into considerations of mediation more generally, and of the transformative impacts of the digital turn, particularly of new modes of representation, publication, collaboration, dissemination, networking, and expression, on culture and society.

(Susan Brown, University of Guelph)

If gathered in a Venn diagram, those responses that combine method with concept would be located at the intersection—the shape of which is called a *lens*. This collocation is an apt metaphor for the digital humanities: a lens for focusing in on or refracting aspects of the humanities that researchers otherwise would not be able to see.

The final word on the matter goes to the late Stéfan Sinclair (McGill University), a highly respected and prolific scholar of DH, who—along with Rockwell—developed *Voyant Tools*.[5] His response takes us full circle, back to the idea of DH as a big tent, as undefinable, as a set of methodologies that can lead to all kinds of unexpected discoveries—fitting coming from someone whose contribution to DH was a resource for searching for patterns and meanings within vast quantities of seemingly undifferentiated materials. "How do you define digital humanities?" According to Sinclair, it is, quite simply, "The ineffably sublime."

Notes

1 Sound includes, for example, "programs for reproduction of sounds; correcting errors in musical databases; analysis of pronunciation," and multimedia, "digitizing *Beowulf* (manuscript images and text); recording live performance; video and speech generation," and technology, "artificial intelligence, computer-assisted language learning, mainframe and microcomputer file formats; MS word 3.0; PF474 string co-processor" (Sula and Hill 2019, 194). Media type alone does not dictate scholarly domain. *SpokenWeb* is a major, sound-based digital humanities initiative, and many of its recordings are readings of or materials related to CanLit (see Chapter 5).
2 Geoffrey Rockwell and Stéfan Sinclair's analysis of the *Humanist* listserv in *Hermeneutica* (2016) similarly locates the rise of the phrase "digital humanities" around 2004 when it gradually replaced the phrase "humanities computing." Rockwell and Sinclair identify several reasons for the transition from humanities computing to digital humanities including institutional formations, shifting research paradigms, and the rise of the web and networked computing.
3 Although citation conventions would abbreviate this list of authors to Burdick et al., it feels wrong to elide the names of four out of five authors when discussing the importance of collaboration.
4 Inspiration for this approach comes from "Day of DH: Defining the Digital Humanities" in *Debates in the Digital Humanities*; affiliations for individuals quoted are from 2024.
5 Canadian digital humanist Stéfan Sinclair (1972–2020) was one of the lead developers of *Voyant*, the tool we used to help us identify the methodological and theoretical patterns in the Day of DH responses. For more on Sinclair and his many contributions to the digital humanities community, see *Digital Humanities Quarterly* editorial team and ADHO's "Remembering Stéfan Sinclair" (2020).

Further reading

Burdick, Anne, Johanna Drucker, Peter Lunenfeld, Todd Presner, and Jeffrey Schnapp. 2012. *Digital_Humanities*. Baltimore: The MIT Press. https://doi.org/10.7551/mitpress/9248.001.0001.

Drucker, Johanna. 2021. *The Digital Humanities Coursebook: An Introduction to Digital Methods for Research and Scholarship*. Abingdon: Routledge. https://doi.org/10.4324/9781003106531.

Schreibman, Susan, Ray Siemens, and John Unsworth, eds. 2004. *A Companion to Digital Humanities*. Oxford: Blackwell. https://doi.org/10.1002/9780470999875.

Schreibman, Susan, Ray Siemens, and John Unsworth, eds. 2016. *A New Companion to Digital Humanities*. Chichester: John Wiley & Sons.

Siemens, Ray, Richard J. Lane, and Constance Crompton, eds. 2016. *Doing Digital Humanities: Practice, Training, Research*. London: Routledge. https://doi.org/10.4324/9781315707860.
Terras, Melissa, Julianne Nyhan, and Edward Vanhoutte, eds. 2013. *Defining Digital Humanities*. New York: Routledge.

Works cited

ADHO. n.d. "About." Alliance of Digital Humanities Organizations. Accessed July 12, 2024. https://adho.org/about/.
Burdick, Anne, Johanna Drucker, Peter Lunenfeld, Todd Pressner, and Jeffrey Schnapp. 2012. *Digital_Humanities*. Baltimore: The MIT Press. https://doi.org/10.7551/mitpress/9248.001.0001.
Da, Nan Z. 2019. "The Computational Case against Computational Literary Studies." *Critical Inquiry* 45, no. 3: 601–39. https://doi.org/10.1086/702594.
"Day of DH: Defining the Digital Humanities." 2012. In *Debates in the Digital Humanities*, edited by Matthew K. Gold, 67–72. Minneapolis: University of Minnesota Press. https://doi.org/10.5749/minnesota/9780816677948.003.0009.
The Digital Humanities Manifesto 2.0. 2009. https://www.humanitiesblast.com/manifesto/Manifesto_V2.pdf.
Digital Humanities Quarterly editorial team, and Association for Computers and the Humanities. 2020. "Remembering Stéfan Sinclair." *Digital Humanities Quarterly* 14, no. 2. https://www.digitalhumanities.org/dhq/vol/14/2/000493/000493.html.
Eichmann-Kalwara, Nickoal, Jeana Jorgensen, and Scott B. Weingart. 2018. "Representation at Digital Humanities Conferences (2000–2015)." In *Bodies of Information: Intersectional Feminism and Digital Humanities*, edited by Elizabeth Losh and Jacqueline Wernimont, 72–92. Minneapolis: University of Minnesota Press. https://doi.org/10.5749/j.ctv9hj9r9.9.
Fish, Stanley. 2012. "Mind Your P's and B's: The Digital Humanities and Interpretation." *Opinionator* (blog), *The New York Times*, January 23, 2012. https://archive.nytimes.com/opinionator.blogs.nytimes.com/2012/01/23/mind-your-ps-and-bs-the-digital-humanities-and-interpretation/.
Fitzpatrick, Kathleen. "The Humanities, Done Digitally." In *Debates in the Digital Humanities*, edited by Matthew K. Gold, 12–15. Minneapolis: University of Minnesota Press. https://doi.org/10.5749/minnesota/9780816677948.003.0002.
Flanders, Julia, Wendell Piez, and Melissa Terras. 2007. "Welcome to Digital Humanities Quarterly." *Digital Humanities Quarterly* 1, no. 1. https://www.digitalhumanities.org/dhq/vol/1/1/index.html.
Heppler, Jason. 2015. *What Is Digital Humanities?* Accessed July 12, 2024. https://whatisdigitalhumanities.com/.
Kirschenbaum, Matthew. 2012. "What Is Digital Humanities and What's It Doing in English Departments?" In *Debates in the Digital Humanities*, edited by Matthew K. Gold, 3–11. Minneapolis: University of Minnesota Press. https://doi.org/10.5749/minnesota/9780816677948.003.0001.

Pannapacker, William. 2011. "'Big Tent Digital Humanities,' a View from the Edge, Part 1." *The Chronicle of Higher Education*, July 31, 2011. https://www.chronicle.com/article/big-tent-digital-humanities-a-view-from-the-edge-part-1/.

Rockwell Geoffrey, and Stéfan Sinclair. 2016. *Hermeneutica: Computer-Assisted Interpretation in the Humanities*. Cambridge: The MIT Press. https://doi.org/10.7551/mitpress/9780262034357.001.0001.

Sula, Chris Alen, and Heather V. Hill. 2019. "The Early History of Digital Humanities: An Analysis of *Computers and the Humanities* (1966–2004) and *Literary and Linguistic Computing* (1986–2004)." *Digital Scholarship in the Humanities* 34, no. 1: i190–i206. https://doi.org/10.1093/llc/fqz072.

Svensson, Patrik. 2012. "Envisioning the Digital Humanities." *Digital Humanities Quarterly* 6, no. 1. https://www.digitalhumanities.org/dhq/vol/6/1/000112/000112.html.

Voyant. 2024. *Voyant Tools*. Version 2.6.14. https://voyant-tools.org/spyral.

Weingart, Scott B., and Nickoal Eichmann-Kalwara. 2017. "What's under the Big Tent?: A Study of ADHO Conference Abstracts." *Digital Studies / Le champ numérique* 7, no. 1: 1–17. https://doi.org/10.16995/dscn.284.

PART II

3
EARLY INTERVENTIONS

The history of humanities computing and Canadian literature

* * *

As the many definitions of digital humanities in the previous chapter demonstrate, there is a long history of humanities computing and digital humanities, which since the 1960s has been connected to the field of Canadian literary study in subtle ways. As humanities computing gained a foothold in Canadian universities throughout the 1980s and grew into the recognizable field of digital humanities in the early 2000s, the overlaps between DH and CanLit evolved into an explicitly theorized mutual engagement. While the general history of humanities computing is relatively well documented (see, for example, Hockey 2004), "The Canadian structural history is harder to gather" (Gouglas et al. 2012). This is, in part, because a history of Canadian-specific projects is unusual for the decidedly extra-national community of DH and, in part, because a great deal of the ephemera, notes, and logs about CanLit projects are scattered or have not been preserved. Yet the material that has survived reveals a history of experimentation and exploration that developed—unevenly and in disparate locations—into the humanities computing projects and programs of the 1980s. These projects laid the path for what eventually became the digital humanities in Canada.

Histories of humanities computing often adhere to an evolutionary or genealogical model that traces the relationship between major figures in the field.[1] Such a history often begins with Father Roberto Busa's searchable index of Thomas Aquinas's writing and his work on concordances. It then includes, for instance, the works of Sally Sedelow, a professor of

DOI: 10.4324/9781003318323-6

English *and* of Computer and Information Science at UNC-Chapel Hill, and one of the first scholars to examine methods for computational analysis of language.[2] Her "A LISP Program for Use in Stylistic Analysis" (1964) is one of the earliest efforts to use modern programming for literary analysis. Sedelow's graduate student, John B. Smith, extended her research, publishing statistical analyses of Joyce's work (among other writers) as well as the important "Computer Criticism" (1978). In turn, Smith's graduate student, Nancy M. Ide, participated in the Vassar workshops that helped connect humanities computing communities in the 1980s, wrote *Pascal for the Humanities* (1987), and launched the Text Encoding Initiative (TEI). Ide served as a mentor for Michael Sperberg-McQueen, who played a key role in developing TEI and was a member of the World Wide Web Consortium (W3C) technical team.

The implication of such histories is that the community of humanities computing is in a state of continuous evolution and that such evolution can be traced by identifying the key players and moments. Yet the history of humanities computing in Canada and elsewhere is far messier than this model allows, involving several false starts, dead ends, and people working in relative isolation rather than in a clear chain of influence. A history of Big Moments or Great People obscures the subtle connections and smaller, unheralded projects that shape the field. It also obscures the past by attempting to organize related, if discordant, events into a logical and causal narrative that appeals to a casual reader but neglects the complexity of the past. Furthermore, these evolutionary histories miss the ways in which the space of Canada, the institutional pressures and possibilities of Canadian research, and the concerns of Canadian scholars all affect how humanities computing has been envisioned here. We eschew this story of an ever-evolving vision of humanities computing and, instead, offer a survey of the field in which diverse critical interests, scholarly goals, and digital experiments cohere (or not) in uneven ways around the idea of digital humanities.

Early Canadian humanities computing

In the early days, humanities computing work in Canada often involved the use of computers to assist in the creation of concordances. The concordance that Sandra Djwa created as a graduate student at the University of British Columbia (see Chapter 1) identified themes in Canadian poetry (such as dream, vision, and mystery) and listed the poems and relevant lines where the theme occurred. At the University of Toronto, Robert Jay Glickman and Gerrit Joseph Staalman developed computational concordances and published, with the University of Toronto Press, their

Manual for the Printing of Literary Texts and Concordances by Computer (1966)—a guide for the use of punch cards and computers to create digital concordances. Their manual introduces their bespoke software, PRORA, the *Program for Research on Romance Authors* as a generic solution for developing concordances for diverse texts: "in addition to processing texts written in the Romance languages, PRORA can handle material written in other languages that use the Latin alphabet" (1966, 1). It is also an early attempt to think about the relation between the digital and the humanities:

> The philosophy behind all the programs is that intervention by the scholar should be limited to decision-making in the scholar's own field of competency (literature or linguistics, *not* computer science or technology); that complex pre-editing and coding of texts should be avoided; and that secretarial assistance should be rendered by a competent typist who has taken a short course in keypunching.
>
> *(1966, 1)*

It is unfortunate that Djwa did not have a copy of Glickman and Staalman's *Manual*, both for its methodological insights and to comment on both men's stated need for "secretarial assistance."

Djwa's and Glickman and Staalman's work represent early efforts to both practice and theorize how computation could enhance, transform, and challenge the tenets of literary criticism. Their projects demonstrate a pattern that emerges throughout the history of DH research in Canada: work tends to cohere around a few insider communities while others labour in relative isolation. Djwa's and Glickman and Staalman's areas of interest are also representative of two major foci in Canadian DH: on the one hand, efforts to use digital tools to better understand classical literature; on the other hand, efforts to use digital tools to read Canadian literature anew. While Djwa, along with her colleagues at the UBC Computing Centre, was largely inventing her methodology from intuited principles, Glickman and Staalman cite Busa's earlier work and had the support of the University of Toronto Press—a major cultural institution. It is not particularly surprising, given the elevation of male scholars over their female counterparts, that Busa, Glickman, and Staalman were all seen as pioneers of early DH scholarship whereas Djwa's work remains virtually unknown in DH and CanLit alike.[3] Yet within both concordance projects, one of the central problems of digital humanities research (a problem we return to throughout this volume) was emerging: namely, how to productively combine the humanities' engagement with ambiguity with the computer's requirement that ambiguity be reduced to discrete categories of data. This question would continue—and indeed continues—to animate debates and concerns about the nascent field of humanities computing in both project development and the establishment of the field.

Throughout the 1960s and '70s, Québec was a key site of early humanities computing projects. In 1964, Jean Baudot, a linguist and engineer, created *La Machine à écrire*, perhaps the first instance of computer-generated text in the world and possibly also "the first book-length publication of machine-generated poetry" (Eichhorn 2015, 514). Researchers at the Université de Montréal used mainframe computers and adapted "methodologies of the *Annales* School and historical demography to questions concerning the French population in New France" (Bonnett and Kee 2010). Jean-Guy Meunier was one of the earliest digital humanists involved in computer-aided text analysis. He launched the Centre d'application des médias technologiques à l'enseignement et à la recherche (CAMTER) in 1972 and went on to be a central figure in digital textual analysis. As Gouglas et al. note, in 1973, "researchers at the Université du Québec à Montréal implemented SATO (Systeme d'analyse des textes par ordinateur), a textual data processing system for literary and social sciences" (2012).

As computers became available to researchers at universities in the 1970s, humanities computing projects began appearing across the country. Outside Québec, Paul A. Fortier and J. Colin McConnel developed *THEME: A System for Computer-Aided Theme Searches of French Texts* at the University of Manitoba. Meanwhile, at the University of Toronto's Centre for Medieval Studies, Cameron Angus, Roberta Frank, and John Leyerle published *Computers and Old English Concordances* (1970), the proceedings of a 1969 conference on the same topic. These proceedings are a remarkable account of early humanities computing scholars working on digital concordances, and they include discussions of the limits of computing power, the state of the field, and prognostication on future work, all phrased in a Wodehousian gentleman scholarly tone. The participants speculate, for instance, that a "linkage of computers, can do more than ten ordinary unlinked machines, and not ten times more but thousands of times more, if interchangeable programs are developed so that all workers in Old English are using compatible and converging programs" (Angus, Frank, and Leyerle 1970, 8). While each of these projects developed in relative isolation, these individual nodes marked the beginning of the emerging network of digital scholarship in Canada.

The 1970s and '80s were a period of establishing computational centres, hosting conferences, and building "the linkages of computers" and networks between research projects. Many of the major topics of the day were discussed at the Third International Conference on Computing in the Humanities. Held at the University of Waterloo in August 1977, it featured more than one hundred papers, including work from "colleagues in music, ballet and the graphic arts," which challenged the notion that humanities computing was largely the domain of literary scholars. Papers ranged from T. K. Bender's "Authorial Privilege in Joseph Conrad" to D. Srinivasan's "Style in Syntax: A Computer Aided Quantitative Study" to discussions of "Literary Data Management," "Computer Interpretation of Dance Notation," and "A Computer-Aided Analysis of Canadian Folksongs." These titles only hint at the diverse topics and interests of individual scholars who dabbled with their computers, only to find their research profoundly transformed by their experiments.

It is telling that so much of what survives of early humanities computing records and archives are traditional forms of scholarship: monographs, articles, and conference proceedings. The concordances themselves, the code, the software, and the machines are largely lost to time and there are lessons here for the digital humanities projects of the 1990s and 2000s concerning archiving and preservation: without a data and project preservation strategy, digital forms of research are in danger of disappearing. The implications of the ephemeral nature of DH scholarship have been taken up by many, including *The Endings Project* at the University of Victoria (see Chapter 12).

A book that does survive is Barron Brainerd's *Weighing Evidence in Language and Literature: A Statistical Approach* (1974).[4] Brainerd, a professor of Mathematics and Linguistics at the University of Toronto, taught a "Statistics for Linguists" undergraduate class. His goals are laudable:

> In recent years, there has been a tremendous development in the area of quantitative and statistical analysis of linguistic and literary data ... However, except for a few rather specialized examples, there has been no truly introductory text in statistics and quantitative analysis dedicated to the needs of language scholars. This work was written especially to fill the gap.
>
> *(1974, i)*

Brainerd's book remains useful today for offering the kind of statistical background necessary for quantitative literary study, although his text opens with the sort of deluge of mathematical maxims that tend to scare off humanities scholars. His identification of the "tremendous development in the area of quantitative and statistical analysis of linguistic and literary data," meanwhile, is indicative of the computational work being done in stylistics, and other forms of computational literary analysis, at the time. Meanwhile, Susan Hockey's *A Guide to Computer Applications in the Humanities* (1980) serves as a record of humanities computing projects developed throughout the 1960s and '70s, including R. A. Wisbey's computational work on German texts at Cambridge and King's College, London, Alvar Ellegård's statistical analysis of *The Junius Letters*, and others. Hockey's book is designed as an introductory text for interested readers and includes clear definitions of terms such as input, output, compilation, tape readers, delimiters, keywords in context, and so forth. Her analysis of collocations and vocabulary studies predicts many of the tools that digital humanities scholars have developed in the subsequent forty years. Together, Brainerd's and Hockey's books provide useful introductions to humanities computing and attendant computational methods.

Emerging organization

While Brainerd's and Hockey's books are notable markers in the development of the field, they are not representative of the kinds of humanities computing activities that tended to occur in the 1970s and early 1980s; these projects tended to be smaller and experimental. Yet as humanities computing found a foothold in institutions, there were also many efforts to establish humanities computing centres, programs, and partnerships across Canada. In 1982, McGill philosophy professor Alistair McKinnon sought Social Sciences and Humanities Research Council of Canada (SSHRC) funding for a humanities computing centre. At McMaster University, Elaine Nardocchio was a tireless advocate for humanities computing; she went on to serve as founding president for both the Ontario Consortium for Computing in the Humanities and the Consortium for Computers in the Humanities in Canada / Consortium pour ordinateurs en sciences humaines (COCH/COSH). Grace Logan was regularly involved in humanities computing in Ontario via her position at the University of Waterloo's Arts Computing Office. Glyn Holmes at the University of Western Ontario was the editor of *Computers and the Humanities*, and Ann Gilmour-Bryson at York University, Glendon, published *Computer Applications to Medieval Studies* in 1984. At York University, Robert Cluett organized the York Computer Inventory of Prose Style, a humanities computing project that attempted to map the stylistic features of literature using Fortran IV and mainframe computers. Cluett's *Canadian Literary Prose: A Stylistic Analysis* (1990) is a chart-heavy attempt to use computational stylistics to map the stylistic features of Canadian literature. Likewise, Ian Lancashire worked diligently at the University of Toronto to establish a computing centre, to collaborate with partners at IBM in nearby Markham, Ontario, and to envision the ways in which computing technology could not merely aid but transform the work of humanities researchers. Alan Heyworth of the University of Toronto Computing Services was supportive of these efforts but worried, presciently, that "the Humanities will require a lot of handholding" (1982).

The papers collected for the Sixth International Conference on Computers and the Humanities include contributions from a number of Canadians and provide a sense of the concerns of the day. Antonette diPaolo Healey offered a paper describing "The Dictionary of Old English and the Design of its Computer System" (248) and C. Stuart Hunter of the University of Guelph presented "A Novice's Guide" to a system for "computer-assisted preparation of an annotated bibliography ... produced on the University of Guelph's Amdahl 470 V5 mainframe" (299). University of Alberta librarian Brian Champion gave a paper entitled "A Cat Among the Pigeons: An Opinion on the Effects of the Computer in the Humanities Library," which concludes, "High technology is incompatible with the humanities library because high tech is an extension of technique, that combination of machines and attitudes that reduces the significance of man" (87). Virginia M. Doland of Biola University is less pessimistic, wondering, "Can a TRS-80, Model II Find Happiness in Working with an 18th-century Novel?" (Burton and Short 1983, 121). She concludes, probably yes.

Gilmour-Bryson's contribution to the published essays from the conference, "From Medieval MSS to Homicide Investigation" (Burton and Short 1983, 206) is an example of the kinds of unique projects made possible by computing. She used a computer to transcribe, and subsequently collect data relevant to, "the edition of a medieval manuscript" detailing "the trial of the Templars in the Patrimony of Saint Peter and parts of the Abruzzi" (206). From this, she developed code to annotate and interpret the trial documents relevant to all of the Templar trials, including the testimonies of over 925 people and 117,745 unique answers. Her project is compelling in its own right, yet while working on her distant reading of the Templar trials, Gilmour-Bryson read about a case in the *Toronto Star* in which a person who had murdered four patients at a local hospital was also accused of killing other patients using the heart drug digoxin. The newspaper detailed the difficulty of the police investigation given the large number of patients that might have been affected. Gilmour-Bryson "wrote the Attorney General of Ontario describing the kind of work I had been doing" (207) and was subsequently invited to participate in the investigation by adapting her data analysis of the Templar trials to the criminal investigation. She then spent months revising her code to suit the hospital's needs and produced a clear dataset for officers to assess as a basis for identifying additional victims. Sadly, the results of Gilmour-Bryson's interventions in policing appear to be lost to time.

It is striking how many of the earliest digital projects focused on classical texts and areas of research. This is, in part, because scholars in

Medieval Studies, Classics, and Ancient Languages had a lengthy history of working with concordances, and computational methods provided a convenient way of modernizing these existing research paradigms. Michael Sperberg-McQueen recalls stumbling across the proceedings of the humanities computing Medievalist conference at the University of Toronto and being amazed at the possibilities that computers offered. He explains,

> As a Medievalist I had spent a lot of time, as everyone I knew in Medieval Studies or Classics did, transcribing glossary entries on to index cards and transcribing locations of occurrences of words onto index cards so I could sort them and re-sort them and analyse them ... so the idea that you could generate a concordance automatically seemed like magic.
> *(Sperberg-McQueen and Nyhan 2016, 179)*

Many classical works had already been digitized in a variety of forms and were readily available for use. In contrast, Canadian literary studies in the early 1980s were defined by intense interest in literary nationalism and understanding where Canadian identity was expressed in Canadian literature; digital methods did not provide a clear way to address those questions.

Burgeoning humanities computing community

A shift began, however, in 1985 with the publication of the two-part "Special Canadian Issue" of *Computers and the Humanities*, edited by Paul Bratley at the Université de Montréal. The issue is representative of an emerging diversity of digital research, including H. M. Logan's efforts to use computers to measure sound and metre in poetry, Barry Truax's overview of "The Computer Music Facility at Simon Fraser University," Nick Cercone and Carole Murchison's early theorizing of "Integrating Artificial Intelligence into Literary Research," and Ian Lancashire's "Letter from Toronto." Nardocchio's "Structural Analysis of Drama: Practical and Theoretical Implications" describes

> the process of transforming into a computer analysis a hand procedure used to study three plays produced in Québec in the 1970s ... The elements of the plays, *Les Belles-Soeurs* by Michel Tremblay, have been encoded and a retrieval system, written in Fortran for the VAX 11/780 at McMaster University, has been developed.
> *(1985, 221)*

Her article grappled with the complexity of language in Tremblay's work (blending French, joual, and English) as well as the relationship between the structural and textual dimensions of the play. The Canadian contexts of Nardocchio's research required specific software design, and her initial forays into digital theatre analysis would lead to Nardocchio and her team developing, two years later, *Theatre: Software for the Analysis of Dramatic Dialogue*—a program that allowed "the user to record his or her analysis of a dramatic dialogue and its stage elements in a database and then to manipulate and selectively retrieve the data" (McCarty 1987, 3).

At the University of Waterloo, humanities and computing faculty were involved in developing the *New Oxford English Dictionary* project, an early effort to digitize the OED. Throughout the 1980s and early '90s, faculty at the University of Waterloo, in collaboration with Oxford University Press, designed databases and tools for text editing, searching, and display. The project was a major undertaking, with Harry Logan suggesting that the prospect of "publishing an integrated OED by 1989 … seemed like science fiction, more computer futuristics" (1989, 385), yet it was a resounding success. It was so successful, in fact, that the OED project led to the creation of a spin-off company, OpenText, which, in 2024, had revenue of over $5 billion.

Conferences during this time also helped develop international networks of humanities computing scholars. In 1986, Teaching Computers and the Humanities courses were held at Vassar College and served as something of a prototype for later DH workshops and summer schools such as the Digital Humanities Summer Institute (DHSI). The Vassar workshop featured presentations from Hockey, Lancashire, Ide, Robert Tannenbaum, and others. Likewise, the Computers and Teaching in the Humanities '88 conference, held in Southampton, UK, with the subtitled theme, "Redefining the Humanities," brought together international humanities computing scholars.

These early groups of scholars were instrumental in beginning to define the field of humanities computing and in setting up the institutional supports that would make humanities computing possible. Lancashire was tireless in this regard, and in 1983 he began teaching a "computer applications" novice humanities computing course to English doctoral students at the University of Toronto. In the same year, he also organized a collaboration between IBM and Toronto, outlining the "Needs of Researchers in the Humanities," including "data collection and communication with Oxford and U.S. universities that have databases of text, … database packages … printing of high quality documents … various software packages," and, perhaps most importantly, "improvement of the interface between the researcher and the microcomputer." Lancashire also presented "An Overview of Activities of Researchers in the Humanities that Could Benefit from Computerized Support," where he argued that computational humanities activities could include "authorship simulation, database applications, statistical applications, concordances, collocational studies, editing / formatting, typesetting, [and] word processing." His early back-of-the-envelope speculation on what digital humanities scholarship might entail is surprisingly accurate—particularly from the perspective of literary studies. He then attempted to map these applications to traditional categories of humanities inquiry such as "history of ideas, literary criticism, explication of text, ... stylistics" and "literary theory" (1983).

Lancashire included, as an appendix to the June 2, 1983, "Minutes of the Meeting of the Advisory Committee for the IBM/U of T Cooperative Agreement", a figure where he attempts to convey researchers' humanities computing needs (see Figure 3.1). The graphic is impressively prescient and still represents a significant amount of the work that computational literary studies scholars engage in. Indeed, Lancashire's speculation predicts (and likely informs) Willard McCarty's 2003 conception of the humanities computing as a "methodological commons," a field united more by practices of "database design, text analysis, numerical analysis, imaging, music information retrieval, communications" (2003, 1224) than shared objects of study.

A great deal of Lancashire's efforts were aimed at supporting the burgeoning humanities computing community at the University of Toronto, efforts that went hand in hand with attempts to acquire the necessary computing tools and develop the partnerships that would enable that community to engage in research. His work resulted in the establishment of the Centre for Computing in the Humanities (CCH) at the University of Toronto in 1985. The 1986 *Centre for Computing in the Humanities Newsletter* outlines Lancashire's success and details a range of events and activities, including a humanities computing software fair, instructions for accessing extended ASCII characters, a "programmer's corner" column, reports from departments, and a list of forthcoming conferences.

Lancashire worked diligently to organize connections across institutions, including a trip to San Jose, Palo Alto, Stanford, and Berkeley, California, for "Toronto computing humanists" to visit IBM's labs and learn about new developments in computing technology. The researchers stayed at the IBM ranch and heard presentations on topics such as "Storage Technology Trends," "Trends in Printer and Display Technology," "Text Processing Research and Development," and "EZ Draw using the IBM PC" (Lancashire 1983). McCarty recalls the collaboration with IBM being very fruitful for Toronto researchers:

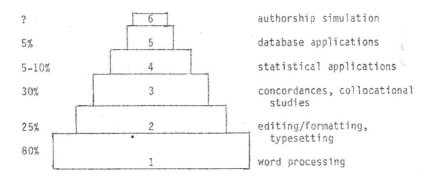

FIGURE 3.1 Infographic of humanities computing needs (Lancashire 1983).

IBM was very forward thinking, very forward-looking in developing a field that was manifestly not going to do very much of commercial interest but they ... poured lots of money into the Humanities. So, the University of Toronto was awash with money, in the 1980s, 300,000 Canadian dollars a year[5] budget for this little centre, which was quite a bit of money then.

(2013)

Subsequent efforts to establish an accredited graduate program in humanities computing did not come to fruition, yet Toronto remained a major centre for DH work throughout the '80s until the sudden shuttering of CCH in the early '90s. Lancashire's 1985 "Letter from Toronto" describes the University of Toronto's "Department and College facilities have now grown up" and he details the equipment and labs available to scholars and students as well as the *Computer Applications in Literary Studies: A User Book for Students at Toronto*, published by the CCH. Scholars and programmers working in Toronto would produce the *Text Analysis Computing Tools* (TACT), a "text-analysis and retrieval system for MS-DOS that permits inquiries on text databases in European languages" (DiRT, 2012). A precursor to *Voyant Tools*, TACT was free software, available via the web and FTP; a corresponding manual was published by the MLA in 1996. Lancashire used TACT in his "Computer-Assisted Critical Analysis: A Case Study of Margaret Atwood's *Handmaid's Tale*" (1993). Throughout the 1990s, Lancashire also built and maintained *Representative Poetry Online*, a free, online version of the poetry anthology used to teach University of Toronto undergraduates for decades. Toronto was thus a hub of early humanities computing research, and many scholars who would become central figures in Canadian digital humanities, including McCarty, Ray Siemens, and Geoffrey Rockwell, all worked at Toronto in various capacities. As Patricia Clements writes, "Ian Lancashire's early and continuing work at the University of Toronto launched a succession of Canadian graduate students on new approaches to literary study" (2006, xxxvi).[6]

In 1987, also at the University of Toronto, McCarty established *Humanist*, a digital humanities listserv, operating on Netnorth/Bitnet (precursors to the Internet), which he still moderates to this day. The wonderfully preserved *Humanist* listserv is a rich resource for understanding the development of the digital humanities in Canada and beyond. *Humanist* is an early example of the networked nature of humanities computing and demonstrates how Canadian researchers were always in dialogue with international colleagues. Early discussions include "proposals toward a set of principles for making, sharing, and using machine-readable texts" (Sperberg-McQueen, August 25, 1987) as well as McCarty's own insightful predictions about DH methods:

> If, as it seems to me, computational scholarship in the humanities tends to reveal the theoretical bases of interpretation, then we have a natural affinity for the study of criticism, historiography, and, in general, semiotics. ... Computational methods allow the semiotician to construct and improve upon models of interpretation. Others of us (like me) are content to computerize the observable aspects of our favourite methods because our interests really lie elsewhere, with the texts themselves & the

hermeneutical act rather than theories of how texts are read. ... Computing in the humanities seems to be where many things meet ... (this is a very Canadian statement), it is essentially a field populated by people from somewhere else, with the off "native" specialist in theory.

(August 25, 1987)

McCarty's observations evoke the metaphor of the boundary discussed in the introduction to this book, and they are representative of the kind of vibrant analysis and debate on *Humanist*.[7] His hope that humanities computing would "reveal the theoretical bases of interpretation" intuits some of the core debates in subsequent digital humanities scholarship. Furthermore, his conception of DH as a place "where many things meet," a "very Canadian statement," suggests the subtle ways in which his location in Canada informs his position in the broader debates about how computational systems and interpretive acts come together.

Humanist also features "Humanist Biografys," descriptions of scholars involved in humanities computing. These biographies include Canadians whose names otherwise rarely appear in surveys of Canadian DH history and demonstrate both the desire to build community and to receive recognition for that community building. Early posts on the listserv include discussions of the Oxford Text Archive, questions of academic credit for "computer activity," a code of practice for digital text archives, an advertisement for all *eight volumes* of the University of Toronto's *Academic's Guide to Microcomputer Systems: Second Edition*, and, of course, someone accidentally spamming the list with their out-of-office message.

Like *Humanist*, the *Ontario Humanities Computing Newsletter*, published by the Ontario Consortium for Computing in the Humanities (OCCH) is indicative of the kinds of projects happening in the 1980s. The 1987 newsletter includes a discussion of the "ENGLISH" listserv run out of the University of Guelph, which served as a "means to exchange ideas about using computers in teaching and research" (McCarty 1987, 2). There is also a report describing efforts by four humanities departments at the University of Alberta to establish a joint computer lab to serve humanities research. Nardocchio advertised the release of *Theatre: Software for the Analysis of Dramatic Dialogue*. Researchers at the University of Waterloo announced the development of *The Analytic Criticism Module*, a software package designed to aid teachers in creating language lessons for the ICON computer. This newsletter is a record of the large number of projects, of varying scale and levels of complexity, at Canadian universities. Nardocchio's 1987 collection of OCCH members estimates 280 faculty interested in humanities computing work, thus indicating the size of the community. Canadian poet and critic Frank Davey is listed as the York University contact for the OCCH for his work with "electronic typesetting through the

Coach House Press" and the establishment of *SwiftCurrent* (Ontario Consortium 1987, 97) (for more on Davey and *SwiftCurrent*, see Chapter 6).

The 1980s ended, fittingly, with The Dynamic Text conference held in Toronto, a collaborative event that combined the Third International Conference on Computing in the Humanities with a meeting of the International Association for Literary and Linguistic Computing. Lancashire writes in his foreword to the conference guide, "The conference theme and title ties together incompatibles in an oxymoron" (1989, v) while stressing that

> The "text" with which this joint conference deals includes not only conventional language and literature, a web of writing or speech, but also the non-literate textures of the distribution graph ... spatial models ... speech waves ... and even images.
>
> *(v)*

Perhaps to force these "incompatibles" into some kind of troubled dialogue, Northrop Frye was recruited to give one of the keynotes. The conference program lists a series of panels and workshops that blend the pedagogical concerns of teaching language and literature using computers with philological concerns over the meaning of *text, reading, heuristics,* and similar terms. Participants considered the function of computers in author attribution studies, discourse analysis, language pedagogy, and whether humanities computing formed a discipline in its own right. Even at this early point, scholars were already using their experiences with computing as the basis to reflect upon the broader meanings of humanities research.

Towards a digital humanities

Where the key objective in the 1980s was "Simply getting the technology into the hands of students and faculty" (Gouglas et al. 2012), by the early 1990s personal computers were more accessible and the need shifted from equipment and centralized projects to building links between researchers, developing a firmer methodology for the emergent field, and supporting larger research infrastructure projects. Humanities computing found a foothold within Canadian universities throughout the 1990s with the development of professional organizations, the establishment of labs, and the necessary infrastructural support from universities, government funding agencies, and external partners. During this time the OCCH became the Consortium for Computers in the Humanities / Consortium pour ordinateurs en sciences humaines (COCH/COSH). This, in turn, became the Society for Digital Humanities / Société pour l'étude des medias interactifs (SDH/SEMI) and then the Canadian Society for Digital Humanities /

Société canadienne des humanités numériques (CSDH/SCHN), the current acronym. As Gouglas et al. note, "the shift from a 'consortium' to a 'society' in 2005–2006 is important" because it marks a move away from the import of DH centres and towards a network of scholars distributed across a range of sites.

As the field became more formalized, the methodological questions that would define digital humanities research became more important. At the University of Alberta, David S. Miall published "Beyond the Word: Reading and the Computer" (1993) in which he advocated for the efficacy of digital forms of reading (particularly using TACT) which enable

> students ... to define their own questions and work singly or collaboratively on projects that make effective use of the computer as an investigative tool. In the process, however, students become more aware of their own reading process and more aware of the dialogic nature of literary texts.
>
> *(323)*

Miall also edited *Humanities and the Computer: New Directions* (1990), a collection that investigated "the principles raised by the use of computers in Humanities disciplines: how the Humanities are conceptualized, what models of thought and communication they embody, and questions about the nature of learning" (1). In the same volume, David A. Bantz's "The Values of Humanities Computing and the Values of Computing" poses a question that remains at the core of digital humanities work (and this book): "Are the tacit values of humanities scholarship and humanistic learning at odds with the widespread and intensive use of computing and computing techniques?" (1990, 27).

Yet, even as the methodological and theoretical foundations of digital humanities began to be more formally and explicitly articulated, researchers continued to encounter skepticism and resistance when attempting to establish DH research programs and centres. As Rockwell observes, "Computing, in the humanities, has been plagued by resistance" (Meunier 2009); researchers throughout the decades have wrestled with the confusion and reluctance among institutions and colleagues to recognize the merits of humanities computing. The burgeoning humanities computing community at the University of Toronto was scattered with the closing of CCH in the early 1990s, leading McCarty, Lancashire, Rockwell, and others to move elsewhere. At McMaster University, Rockwell and Stéfan Sinclair developed a multimedia program that included many facets of digital humanities research. Rockwell taught courses with titles such as "Introduction to Computers in the Humanities," "Quantitative Methods in the Humanities," and a graduate-level "Computer Research Methods" while also organizing the *Text Analysis Portal for Research* (TAPoR) project. The multimedia program was a major success and helped entrench a form of computer-aided humanities at McMaster.

The transition from *humanities computing* to *digital humanities* in the early 2000s broadened the scope of the research, teaching, and creative practices that defined the field; by taking the emphasis off of computers, computing, and the language of programming and opening the field to other interventions (e.g., those done using web-based tools), space was made for the diverse, field-defining projects that would comprise DH work throughout the 1990s and early 2000s. These projects were larger and far more interdisciplinary than their forebears, as they focused on a range of cultural and historical material and involved diverse methods as part of their approach to DH. Both the rise of networked computing and the increasing accessibility of personal computers resulted in several new digital projects. Large Canadian projects with connection to literature that emerged during this time include *Artmob* at York University, *The Orlando Project* and the *Canadian Writing Research Collaboratory* (now the *Collaboratory for Writing and Research on Culture*; CWRC) at the University of Alberta, Implementing New Knowledge Environments Partnership (INKE) based out of the University of Victoria, the Digital Humanities Summer Institute (DHSI) at the University of Victoria (now at Université de Montréal), the *Editing Modernism in Canada* (EMiC) project at Dalhousie University, and others.

Artmob

Artmob, organized by Darren Wershler, Rosemary J. Coombe, and Christopher Innes, was an early CFI-funded DH project that led to the production of a number of online poetry sites still in existence today, including *bpnichol.ca*, the *Fred Wah Digital Archive*, *UbuWeb*, and others. An open-source content management system designed for arts archives, *Artmob* was driven by the twin goals of supporting the creation of digital archives and developing cultural policy recommendations rooted in the experiences of creating these sites. It was largely driven by Wershler's experiences working at Coach House Press and as a web designer (and writer of *Starcraft* strategy guides!) in the 1990s, alongside Coombe's interest in the transforming cultural policy considerations emerging in response to new digital technology. While *Artmob* effectively dissolved after their Canada Foundation for Innovation (CFI) grants ended, many of the projects they supported are still active on the web.

That *Artmob* was started by Wershler as a result of his work with Coach House is unsurprising, given that Coach House has long been a hub of literary computing activity, beginning with their purchase of a mini-computer in 1974 for $40,000. In the mid-1970s, Coach House had an in-house programmer, David Slocombe, who developed bespoke software that would allow editors to typeset manuscripts using the computer. Coach House benefited from proximity to the University of Toronto (their office is directly north of the central library on bpNichol Lane) and its accumulated computing expertise. By the mid-1980s, Coach House ran a network connection, via the university, to the burgeoning Internet and was "the first Unix-based, networked connected publisher" in Canada, "possibly in the world" (Maxwell 2015). Around the same time, Slocombe, along with Yuri Rubinski and others, developed SoftQuad, a spinoff company that published SGML and other digital publishing software. SoftQuad would eventually be purchased by Corel. While the history of Coach House's engagement with digital technology is well beyond the scope of this book, it is a notable spoke emerging from the digital humanities hub in place in Toronto from the 1970s onwards.

The Orlando Project

On the other side of the country, *The Orlando Project*, an "experiment in literary history" (Brown 2017, 187) is exemplary of the kinds of multi-institutional projects that became possible with the "linkages of computers." *Orlando* was initiated at the University of Alberta in 1995 by Clements, Hockey, Isobel Grundy, and Susan Brown. Having worked on *The Feminist Companion to Literature* (1990), the *Orlando* team realized, "The index to the Companion—which offered readers a few basic pathways into the several inches of densely packed information in the book—was a hundred A4 pages in typescript. Printing it would have broken the bindings. Literally" (Brown et al. 1997). In this respect, "The Orlando Project begins in a book too big for its bindings," driving the team to computational methods to manage their textual data:

> For the Orlando Project, technology has become much more than a simple tool. It is altering the way we are conducting our research and changing the ways in which we approach the problems of literary history. We think the technology will allow us to do a different, and in some ways a better, kind of history. We want computers to help us to bring together and into focus the complex relationships that inform literary history. The hype of hypertext's ability to create multiple pathways for users through electronic material has become a bit stale, but the possibility of offering multiple rather than single trajectories, of fracturing the single, monological narrative, retains its freshness for us. The possibility

of offering parallel and intersecting narratives, interlinked with non-narrative material, allows us to make the user of our electronic history an active partner—another collaborator—in the history.

(Brown et al. 1997)

The electronic medium did not merely offer a practical solution to the problem of an expansive literary history but also a new paradigm for creating "multiple pathways" for interpretation. The *Orlando* team's reflections comprise some of the earliest shifts away from the hacker ethos of humanities computing, where the computer is often conceived as a tool to aid in research. Instead, it marks a turn towards broadly conceived, carefully theorized interdisciplinary work that develops new forms of research and teaching in dialogue with computation.

The development of *Orlando* mirrors that of many DH projects where humanistic inquiry is reshaped by (and reshapes) software's capability. The *Orlando* leads learned that the creation of "categories demanded careful thought" particularly as "Lines had to be drawn where history offers a continuum rather than a sharp divide" (Brown et al. 2007, 136). Clements explains that for the *Orlando* research team, "it has been an entirely new way of working ... Our research methodologies, familiar now to scholars in humanities computing, were foreign to our experience at the outset" (2006, xxxviii). In their acts of discovery, the *Orlando* team posed incisive questions to humanities computing that cut to the core of the practice. For instance, as a team comprised mostly of women, they drew attention to the gendered dimensions of humanities computing and the use of technology more generally. They explain,

> We feel, as a team, that we are involved in the domestication of computing for the humanities. For us, this gendered metaphor highlights the obvious and important fact that we are a team predominantly composed of women, working to reshape, in the interests of feminist inquiry, the tools of a field very markedly dominated by men. ... We understand gender as cutting across every element of our project, from the time past we are constructing together to the time present in which we are working together to construct it. So while this domesticating labour is also productively underway in many other arenas in the humanities, we think we have a particular angle on the potential servitudes and freedoms of writing with computers, on the politics of knowledge this work produces, and on the ways that we may seek to possess the means of electronic production rather than being dispossessed by them.

(Brown et al. 1997)

Orlando had many important successes, including hosting the international "Women and Literary History" conference held at the University of Alberta in 1997, creating a significant textual database of women's writing, starting the careers of innumerable researchers, and tackling major methodological questions concerning digital literary study. Despite these successes, however, *Orlando* did not receive a second Major Collaborative Research Initiative (MCRI) Grant from SSHRC, in part because "no books had been written and [SSHRC] deemed that the project had been insufficiently productive" (Brown et al. 2007, 141). *Orlando* faced a challenge that would become familiar to DH scholars: namely, the difficulty of engaging in innovative forms of scholarship while trying to ensure that scholarship was legible to Canadian funding agencies. Clements describes the project as a "case study in the shift of a research paradigm" (2006, xxxviii), particularly as the researchers' understandings of humanities work was reshaped by computational possibilities and as granting agencies found it difficult to assess the merits of emerging digital paradigms. *Orlando*'s shifting of research paradigms went on to inform subsequent DH projects including CWRC, EMiC, *SpokenWeb*, and other large digital projects that emerged in the 2000s (see Chapter 5). Clements went on to be a board member of the CFI (see Chapter 4) as well as the president of the Canadian Federation for the Humanities and Social Sciences, playing an integral role in shaping humanities at the beginning of the present century—one undoubtedly informed by her DH work.

Implementing New Knowledge Environments

The second issue of *Digital Studies / Le champ numérique* includes an article from Ray Siemens, Claire Warwick, Richard Cunningham, Teresa Dobson, Alan Galey, Stan Ruecker, and Susan Schreibman, "Codex Ultor: Toward a Conceptual and Theoretical Foundation for New Research on Books and Knowledge Environments," which outlines the goals of the Implementing New Knowledge Environments Partnership (INKE). The partnership, developed with $13 million in funding from SSHRC's MCRI project, began as a "large international, interdisciplinary research team, including over thirty-five researchers from more than twenty institutions," and with the aim of studying how textuality, reading, and interpretation are transformed by the migration of text to new digital environments (Siemens et al., 2009). Its ambitious goals included

> [1] the evolution of reading and writing technologies from antiquity to the present; [2] the mechanics and pragmatics associated with written forms of knowledge; [3] strategies of reading and organization within

those forms; and [4] the computational possibilities latent in written forms and manifest in emerging technology.

(Siemens et al., 2009)

Its membership, meanwhile, is a veritable *who's who* of the digital humanities community of the 2010s; in this respect, INKE's numerous "birds of a feather" gatherings were highly successful in the collaborations they fostered and the connections that they formed.

Initially, INKE was divided into a series of research groups, including Textual Studies, User Experience, Interface Design, and Information Management, each of which applied a particular lens to the transformation of textuality, reading, and interpretation. As Christian Vandendorpe explains, INKE aimed

> not only to import the affordances of the book on a computer, but to create the best possible space for working on information and producing knowledge, devising tools for manipulating text and implementing interfaces suited to a variety of tasks.
>
> *(2012, 5)*

Its groups developed prototypes such as "The Paper Drill," "Just in Time Research," "Wrkflux," and "New Radial"—each of which provided proof of concept but did not see widespread use and are now unavailable. Other projects live on, such as the *Architectures of the Book* site, a series of "open-access, peer-reviewed … richly illustrated essays about specific design features in the history of the book." In recent years, INKE has continued its work via a SSHRC Partnership Grant with a move away from textual studies and towards Open Social Scholarship; its *Canadian HSS Commons* (HSS standing for *humanities and social sciences*) is a "resource for research, education, and collaboration [where] members can share, access, develop, re-purpose, and preserve scholarly data and resources" (Canadian HSS Commons 2024). INKE also sponsors the Open Scholarship Policy Observatory and the Canadian-Australian Partnership for Open Scholarship.

A proliferation of projects

The issue of *Digital Studies* that sets out the goals of INKE is dedicated to "The Computer and Canadian Scholarship: Recent Trends in the Humanities and Social Sciences—Volume 1." Although INKE has been longstanding, many of the other projects it describes are now defunct. For example, Shawn Graham's discussion of his *PatronWorld* model of patronage network interactions in Roman history appears to have been absorbed into his subsequent work, while B. G. Robertson's *Fawcett Toolkit* for the Semantic Web is no longer available. Yet, as Graham convincingly argues in *Failing Gloriously and Other Essays* (2019), the failure of digital projects is to be celebrated, as it often lays the groundwork for future projects, further collaboration, and renewed opportunities to think about the goals of digital humanities work. Not all the projects achieve their goals or persist indefinitely; many more inform subsequent research, support students, build collaborations, and develop key infrastructure.

As we discuss in the subsequent chapters, much of this infrastructure was the result of two things: on one hand, the communities that formed through projects such as *Artmob*, *Orlando*, and INKE; on the other hand, the establishment of formal government programs in the late 1990s and early 2000s, which subsidized DH research in new ways. Burgeoning communities and stable funding led to an increase in the number of DH programs and projects across Canada. Projects such as EMiC offered models for bringing students into the DH orbit. Similarly, the founding of DHSI, and its explosive growth in the 2000s, made Victoria a hub for DH scholars. What began as isolated projects now had professional organizations, networks of communication, formal methods of mentorship, training workshops, and government funding.

Alongside large projects such as those discussed above and in Chapter 5, the 2000s also saw the emergence of many of the smaller projects discussed in subsequent chapters, among them Zailig Pollock and Sandra Djwa's *The Digital Page: The Collected Works of P. K. Page*, and Deanna Fong and Ryan Fitzpatrick's *Fred Wah Digital Archive* (Chapter 7). There is a clear genealogical connection between EMiC and Graham Jensen's subsequent *Canadian Modernist Magazines Project* (Chapter 7). Likewise, *The People and the Text,* an Indigenous literary archive organized by Deanna Reder (Cree-Métis), Madeleine Reddon (Métis), Alix Shield, Margery Fee, and Susan Glover brings attention to largely unknown or forgotten works while offering necessary cultural contexts for interpreting Indigenous literatures (Chapter 10). Sinclair and Rockwell's important *Hermeneutica: Computer-Assisted Interpretation in the Humanities* (2016) can be seen as a descendant of Brainerd's aforementioned *Weighing Evidence in Language and Literature*. Sinclair's doctoral work on OuLiPo poetry at Queen's University led to him creating *Hypertexte Potentiel* (*HyperPo*), an online textual analysis tool. Sinclair and Rockwell, whose work with *Hypercard* and TAPoR had convinced them of the need for an easy-to-use textual analysis tool, collaborated to create *Voyant Tools* (Chapter 13).

Since the 2000s, there has been a proliferation of DH projects, courses, and publications, spurred, in part, by the recognition of DH within some academic institutions and formal (financial) support for digital forms of research. In the next chapter, we discuss this most recent evolution. Many of the earliest concerns of humanities computing scholars, as seen in this chapter, remain at the heart of digital humanities today. Writing in 1981, Richard W. Bailey's "Computing in the Humanities" claims that "Even a brief and incomplete survey of this volume suggests that the motives inspiring humanists to use a computer are by no means new" and that "The extension of humanistic inquiry through data processing is merely scholarship carried out by other means" (1). This would remain a contentious point and both critics and practitioners of humanities computing would insist that the use of computing to address humanities concerns represents a significant modification of the humanities. These debates continue. One of the biggest methodological challenges for DH research is that of theorizing the relationship between computation and interpretation in their varying forms, for example, as done by Rosanne Potter in her "Literary Criticism and Literary Computing: A Difficult Synthesis" (1989) and echoed by Alan Liu in his "The Meaning of the Digital Humanities" (2013) and, more recently, in Katherine Bode's "What's the Matter with Computational Literary Studies?" (2023).

Other, ongoing challenges are best captured by unanswered questions, such as: How can computation aid in, or further complicate, the kinds of interdisciplinary work that DH makes possible? How can DH forms of infrastructure and community building be recognized within academia, and how can labour on DH projects be fairly distributed? This history has demonstrated how DH researchers have initially addressed these challenges, in part, through their participation in communities of practice and research, and with the aid of institutions willing to support their explorations. It has also demonstrated how precarious that institutional support can be such that the whim of a dean or administrator can shutter a burgeoning DH program and break up a community. In the next chapter we focus more squarely on the institutions that have supported DH research and survey how DH and CanLit scholars alike have adeptly aligned their research aims with institutional goals.

Notes

1 Sula and Hill are critical of the canonical histories of humanities computing and digital humanities. They argue that this history "privileges certain disciplines, projects, and tools," and that "most accounts of DH fail to chart an actual historical course from humanities computing … to present DH work in all its variety" (191). They also argue that the "standard history precludes

historicizing and contextualizing DH work that falls outside text analysis" and, as a result, "it obscures connections to other fields" (2019, 192). Other scholars have challenged the standard early DH history. Manfred Thaller, for instance, writing on the *Humanist* listserv, argues that John. W. Ellison created a computational concordance prior to Busa (2021). Likewise, Arun Jacob's "Punching Holes in the International Busa Machine Narrative" (2020) offers a compelling counternarrative to the Busa origin story.
2 Sedelow's work on the *Automated Analysis Language* project aimed to "use the computer to characterize a non pre-edited natural language text" including "identification of individual authors or speeches as well as permit the description of the content of their remarks." Her work was supported, in part, by the Information Systems Branch, Office of Naval Research, and she thus takes efforts to indicate that the work would aid in the "verbal structuring of diplomatic documents or upon the interpretation for intelligence purposes of verbal materials" (1970, 7).
3 Melissa Terras has demonstrated that Busa employed a team of women who, as programmers, developed the punch cards for his research, but who have subsequently been erased from history. She writes, "it shouldn't be that surprising to us that women were so important in Father Busa's pioneering computing project: in the early 1960s computer programmers were commonly women" (2013).
4 Brainerd's text can be included alongside Karl Kroeber's *Styles in Fictional Structure: Studies in the Art of Jane Austen, Charlotte Brontë, George Eliot* (1971) and Louis Tonko Milic's *A Quantitative Approach to the Style of Jonanthan Swift* (1967) as early instances of computational literary studies.
5 $300,000 in 1983 is equivalent to $820,000 in 2024.
6 Sadly, a great deal of Lancashire's and McCarty's efforts were undone with the shuttering of the Centre for Computing in the Humanities in the early 1990s. In what appeared to be an administrative whim, years of work to establish humanities computing at Toronto were erased, the centre was closed, and the relevant files were placed in the hallway for anyone to take. Toronto would not have a significant DH presence again until the creation of the Digital Humanities Network in 2016.
7 In a moment of notable, rare lack of prescience, McCarty reflects, "Experience with HUMANIST suggests that the new medium," email, "carefully managed, may be just what is needed to foster widespread humanistic discussion and collaboration in a world largely indifferent to its goals." He continues, "Because e-mail is restricted to verbal expression, it tends to favor those with highly developed rhetorical skills" (McCarty 1992, 206). As readers will know, McCarty's predictions about highly articulate, rhetorically savvy, widespread humanistic discussion and collaboration via email would not prove true.

Further reading

Gaffield, Chad. 2015. "The Surprising Ascendance of Digital Humanities: And Some Suggestions for an Uncertain Future." *Digital Studies / Le champ numérique* 6, no. 1. https://doi.org/10.16995/dscn.2.

Gouglas, Sean, Geoffrey Rockwell, Victoria Smith, Sophia Hoosein, and Harvey Quamen. 2012. "Before the Beginning: The Formation of Humanities Computing as a Discipline in Canada." *Digital Studies / Le champ numérique* 3, no. 1. https://doi.org/10.16995/dscn.244.

Hockey, Susan. 2004. "The History of Humanities Computing." In *A Companion to Digital Humanities*, edited by Susan Schreibman, Ray Siemens, and John Unsworth, 3–19. Oxford: Blackwell. https://doi.org/10.1002/9780470999875.

Ide, Nancy, and C. M. Sperberg-McQueen. 1995. "The TEI: History, Goals, and Future." *Computers and the Humanities* 29: 5–15. https://doi.org/10.1007/BF01830313.

McCarty, Willard. 2004. "As It Almost Was: Historiography of Recent Things." *Literary and Linguistic Computing* 19, no. 2: 161–80. https://doi.org/10.1093/llc/19.2.161.

Works cited

Angus, Cameron, Roberta Frank, and John Leyerle. 1970. *Computers and Old English Concordances*. Toronto: University of Toronto Press.

Bailey, Richard W. 1981. "Computing in the Humanities." In *Computing in the Humanities*, edited by Richard W. Bailey, 1–6. Oxford: North Holland Publishing Company.

Bantz, David A. 1990. "The Values of the Humanities and the Values of Computing." In *Humanities and the Computer: New Directions*, edited by David S. Miall, 27–38. Oxford: Clarendon.

Bode, Katherine. 2023. "What's the Matter with Computational Literary Studies?" *Critical Inquiry* 49, no. 4: 507–29. https://doi.org/10.1086/724943.

Bonnett, John, and Kevin Kee. 2010. "Transitions: A Prologue and Preview of Digital Humanities Research in Canada." *Digital Studies / Le champ numérique* 1, no. 2. https://doi.org/10.16995/dscn.106.

Brainerd, Barron. 1974. *Weighing Evidence in Language and Literature: A Statistical Approach*. Toronto: University of Toronto Press.

Brown, Susan. 2017. "Survival: Canadian Cultural Scholarship in a Digital Age." *Studies in Canadian Literature / Études en littérature canadienne* 42, no. 2: 171–200. https://id.erudit.org/iderudit/scl42_2art09.

Brown, Susan, Patricia Clements, Isobel Grundy, Sharon Balazs, and Jeffrey Antoniuk. 2007. "The Story of the Orlando Project: Personal Reflections." *Tulsa Studies in Women's Literature* 26, no. 1: 135–43. https://doi.org/10.1353/tsw.2007.a220810.

Brown, Susan, Patricia Clements, Isobel Grundy, Terry Butler, Susan Hockey, Sue Fisher, Kathryn Carter, Kathryn Harvey, and Jeanne Wood. 1997. "Tag Team: Computing, Collaborators, and the History of Women's Writing in the British Isles." Plenary at the Association of Canadian College and University Teachers of English, June 1997. https://sites.ualberta.ca/ORLANDO/publications/o-ACUT97.htm.

Burton, Sarah K., and Douglas D. Short, eds. 1983. *Sixth International Conference on Computers and the Humanities*. Rockville: Computer Science Press.

Canadian HSS Commons. Implementing New Knowledge Environments Partnership. 2024. https://hsscommons.ca/en/.

Clements, Patricia. 2006. "Introduction: Ink and Air: Computing and the Research Culture of the Humanities." In *Mind Technologies*, edited by Ray Siemens and

David Moorman, xxxiiii–xlii. Calgary: University of Calgary Press. https://doi.org/10.1515/9781552384039.
Cluett, Robert. 1990. *Canadian Literary Prose: A Preliminary Stylistic Analysis*. Toronto: ECW Press.
CWRC. n.d. *Collaboratory for Writing and Research on Culture*. Accessed July 12, 2024. https://cwrc.ca/.
DiRT. 2012. *Digital Research Tools Wiki*. Accessed August 20, 2024. https://digitalresearchtools.pbworks.com/.
Eichhorn, Kate. 2015. "The Digital Turn in Canadian and Québécois Literature." In *The Oxford Handbook of Canadian Literature*, edited by Cynthia Sugars, 512–23. Oxford: Oxford University Press. https://doi.org/10.1093/oxfordhb/9780199941865.001.0001.
EMiC. n.d. *Editing Modernism in Canada*. Accessed July 12, 2024. https://editingmodernism.ca/.
Fong, Deanna, and Ryan Fitzpatrick. 2024. *Fred Wah Digital Archive*. https://fredwah.ca/.
Gilmour-Bryson, Ann. 1984. *Computer Applications to Medieval Studies*. Kalamazoo: Medieval Institute Publications, Western Michigan University.
Glickman, Robert Jay, and Gerrit Joseph Staalman. 1966. *Manual for the Printing of Literary Texts and Concordances by Computer*. Toronto: University of Toronto Press.
Gouglas, Sean, Geoffrey Rockwell, Victoria Smith, Sophia Hoosein, and Harvey Quamen. 2012. "Before the Beginning: The Formation of Humanities Computing as a Discipline in Canada." *Digital Studies / Le champ numérique* 3, no. 1. https://doi.org/10.16995/dscn.244.
Graham, Shawn. 2019. *Failing Gloriously and Other Essays*. Grand Forks: The Digital Press at the University of North Dakota.
Heyworth, Allan. 1982. Allan Heyworth to D. Nowlan, November 5, 1982.
Hockey, Susan. 1980. *A Guide to Computer Applications in the Humanities*. Baltimore: Johns Hopkins University Press.
Hockey, Susan. 2004. "The History of Humanities Computing." In *A Companion to Digital Humanities*, edited by Susan Schreibman, Ray Siemens, and John Unsworth, 3–19. Oxford: Blackwell. https://doi.org/10.1002/9780470999875.
Ide, Nancy M. 1987. *Pascal for the Humanities*. Philadelphia: University of Pennsylvania Press.
INKE. n.d. *Implementing New Knowledge Environments*. Accessed November 2, 2024, https://inke.ca/.
Jacob, Arun. 2020. "Punching Holes in the International Busa Machine Narrative." *IDEAH: Interdisciplinary Digital Engagement in Arts & Humanities* 1, no. 1. https://doi.org/10.21428/f1f23564.d7d097c2.
Jensen, Graham, Deseray Manuel, et al. 2022. *Canadian Modernist Magazines Project*. University of Victoria. https://modernistmags.ca.
Kroeber, Karl. 1971. *Styles in Fictional Structure: Studies in the Art of Jane Austen, Charlotte Brontë, George Eliot*. Princeton: Princeton University Press.
Lancashire, Ian. 1983. "Minutes of the Meeting of the Advisory Committee for the IBM / U of T Cooperative Agreement." Unpublished document, June 2, 1983.
Lancashire, Ian. 1985. "Letter from Toronto." *Computers and the Humanities* 19: 251–53.

Lancashire, Ian. 1989. "Foreword." In *The Dynamic Text: Conference Guide*, edited by Ian Lancashire, v–vii. Toronto: Centre for Computing in the Humanities.

Lancashire, Ian. 1993. "Computer-Assisted Critical Analysis: A Case Study of Margaret Atwood's *Handmaid's Tale*." In *The Digital Word: Text-Based Computing in the Humanities*, edited by George P. Landow and Paul Delany, 293–318. Cambridge: MIT Press.

Liu, Alan. 2013. "The Meaning of the Digital Humanities." *PMLA* 128, no. 2: 409–23. https://doi.org/10.1632/pmla.2013.128.2.409.

Logan, Harry. 1989. "Report on a New OED Project: A Study of the History of the New Words in the New OED." *Computers and the Humanities* 23: 385–95. https://doi.org/10.1007/BF02176644.

Maxwell, John W. 2015. "Coach House Press in the 'Early Digital' Period: A Celebration." *Devil's Artisan: A Journal of the Printing Arts* 77: 9–20.

McCarty, Willard, ed. 1987. *Ontario Humanities Computing Newsletter*. Centre for Computing in the Humanities, University of Toronto.

McCarty, Willard. 1992. "HUMANIST: Lessons from a Global Electronic Seminar." *Computers and the Humanities* 26: 205–22. https://doi.org/10.1007/BF00058618.

McCarty, Willard. 2003. "Humanities Computing." In *Encyclopedia of Library and Information Science*, edited by Miriam Drake, 1224–35. New York: Marcel Dekker.

McCarty, Willard. 2013. "The Future of Digital Humanities is a Matter of Words." In *A Companion to New Media Dynamics*, edited by John Hartley, Jean Burgess, and Axel Bruns, 33–52. Hoboken: Blackwell. https://doi.org/10.1002/9781118321607.ch2.

Meunier, J. G. 2009. "CARAT—Computer-Assisted Reading and Analysis of Texts: The Appropriation of a Technology." *Digital Studies / Le champ numérique* 1, no. 3. https://doi.org/10.16995/dscn.263.

Miall, David S. 1990. "Introduction." In *Humanities and the Computer: New Directions*, edited by David S. Miall, 1–12. Oxford: Clarendon.

Miall, David S. 1993. "Beyond the Word: Reading and the Computer." In *The Digital Word: Text-Based Computing in the Humanities*, edited by George P. Landow and Paul Delany, 319–42. Cambridge: The MIT Press.

Milic, Louis Tonko. 1967. *A Quantitative Approach to the Style of Jonathan Swift*. Berlin: De Gruyter. https://doi.org/10.1515/9783111400358.

Nardocchio, Elaine. 1985. "Structural Analysis of Drama: Practical and Theoretical Implications" Special issue, Activities in Canada. *Computers and the Humanities* 19, no. 4: 221–23. https://doi.org/10.1007/BF02259575.

Nyhan, Julianne, and Andrew Flinn. 2016. *Computation and the Humanities: Towards an Oral History of the Digital Humanities*. New York: Springer. https://link.springer.com/book/10.1007/978-3-319-20170-2.

Ontario Consortium for Computing in the Humanities. 1987. *Directory of Membership*.

Orlando. 2023. *The Orlando Project*. https://orlando.cambridge.org/about/introduction.

Potter, Rosanne G. 1989. "Literary Criticism and Literary Computing: A Difficult Synthesis." In *Literary Computing and Literary Criticism: Theoretical and Practical Essays on Theme and Rhetoric*, edited by Rosanne G. Potter, 93–106. Philadelphia: University of Pennsylvania Press.

Reder, Deanna, Madeleine Reddon, Alix Shield, Margery Fee, and Susan Glover. n.d. *The People and the Text: Indigenous Writing in Lands Claimed by Canada*. Accessed September 8, 2024. https://thepeopleandthetext.ca/.

Representative Poetry Online. n.d. Accessed July 12, 2024. https://rpo.library.utoronto.ca/.

Robertson, Bruce G. 2009. "'Fawcett': A Toolkit to Begin an Historical Semantic Web." *Digital Studies / Le champ numérique* 1, no. 2. https://doi.org/10.16995/dscn.112.

Rockwell, Geoffrey, and Stéfan Sinclair. 2016. *Hermeneutica: Computer-Assisted Interpretation in the Humanities*. Cambridge: The MIT Press. https://doi.org/10.7551/mitpress/9780262034357.001.0001.

Sedelow, Sally. 1964. "A LISP Program for Use in Stylistic Analysis." SDC Document TM-1753.

Sedelow, Sally, Martin Dillon, Gerald Fisher, Walter Sedelow, and Walter Smith. 1970. *Automated Analysis of Language Style and Structure: 1969–1970*. Chapel Hill: University of North Carolina at Chapel Hill.

Siemens, Ray, Claire Warwick, Richard Cunningham, Teresa Dobson, Alan Galey, Stan Ruecker, Susan Schreibman, and the INKE Team. 2009. "Codex Ultor: Toward a Conceptual and Theoretical Foundation for New Research on Books and Knowledge Environments." *Digital Studies / Le champ numérique* 1, no. 2. https://doi.org/10.16995/dscn.270.

Smith, John B. 1978. "Computer Criticism." *Style* 12, no. 4: 326–56.

Sperberg-McQueen, Michael to *Humanist* mailing list. August 25, 1987. https://dhhumanist.org/archives/Converted_Text/humanist.1987-1988.txt.

Sperberg-McQueen, Michael, and Julianne Nyhan. 2016. "I Mourned the University for a Long Time: Michael Sperberg-McQueen and Julianne Nyhan." In *Computation and the Humanities: Towards an Oral History of Digital Humanities*, edited by Julianne Nyhan and Andrew Flynn, Springer Series on Cultural Computing, 177–94. Cham: Springer. https://doi.org/10.1007/978-3-319-20170-2_12.

SpokenWeb. 2024. *SpokenWeb*. https://spokenweb.ca/.

Sula, Chris Alen, and Heather V. Hill. 2019. "The Early History of Digital Humanities: An Analysis of *Computers and the Humanities* (1966–2004) and *Literary and Linguistic Computing* (1986–2004)." *Digital Scholarship in the Humanities* 34, no. 1: i190–i206. https://doi.org/10.1093/llc/fqz072.

TAPoR. n.d. *Text Analysis Portal for Research 3*. Version 3.0. Accessed July 10, 2024. https://tapor.ca/home.

Terras, Melissa. 2013. "For Ada Lovelace Day—Father Busa's Female Punch Card Operatives." *Melissa Terras, Adventures in Digital Cultural Heritage* (blog), October 15, 2023. https://melissaterras.org/2013/10/15/for-ada-lovelace-day-father-busas-female-punch-card-operatives/.

TEI. 2023. *Text Encoding Initiative*. https://tei-c.org.

Thaller, Manfred. 2021. "The First Computer-Generated Concordance." *Humanist*, March 9, 2021. https://dhhumanist.org/volume/34/264/.

Vandendorpe, Christian. 2012. "Foreword: The Work of Implementing New Knowledge Environments Community." *Scholarly and Research Communication* 3, no. 1: 21 pp. https://doi.org/10.22230/src.2012v3n1a88.

Voyant. 2024. *Voyant Tools*. Version 2.6.14. https://voyant-tools.org/.

4

NATIONAL LITERATURES, INFRASTRUCTURAL DEVELOPMENTS

Emerging concepts of Canadian literature and digital humanities

* * *

The histories of humanities computing and digital humanities (outlined in the previous chapter) and Canadian literary criticism have all been shaped by the support—or lack thereof—from funding institutions. Indeed, both Canadian literature and digital humanities have relied on government (and non-government) funding bodies for their development and support. Willard McCarty's comment that there are "Per capita more digital humanists in Canada than anywhere else in the world" (McCarty et al. 2012) is the result of the energy of motivated individuals, but it is also the product of the financial support that DH has received in Canada. McCarty notes that "The Canadians have done marvels in convincing the government and setting up structures of funding" (McCarty et al. 2012) for digital humanities research. Likewise, the establishment of Canadian literature as a discipline is partially attributable to a similar combination of individual energy and vision with support from government programs and other institutions.

Yet government support often comes at a cost. Scholars must make their research legible to funding agencies, and funding agencies must justify their spending to a wider public in turn. In this sense, there is a dialogical relationship between researcher and funding agency, expressed, in part, through a shared language of humanism, wherein scholars and funding bodies argue that research activity constitutes some notion of public good. Predictably, researchers have adapted the rhetoric and goals of their activities to this institutional humanist discourse (yesterday's "public good" is today's "knowledge mobilization") to secure the necessary funding.

DOI: 10.4324/9781003318323-7

Writing in 1944, for instance, the University of Manitoba English professor Arthur Phelps described a sense of

> national interest in the Arts, stimulated not only by widespread national awakening which is political and economic, but also by the modern conditions of easier communication suited to draw together an erstwhile too much dispersed country. ... [There is] a conviction already matured in the consciousness of the Canadian people: the conviction that the artistic interests of Canadian life need recognition and encouragement now, and that recognition and encouragement can be practical on a large scale now.
> *(Phelps quoted in Litt 1992, 18–19)*

For Phelps, a national program supporting the arts is necessary for the expansion of cultural life and relies on both the "national awakening" in Canadian politics and the emergence of communication technology that can bring together an otherwise "dispersed country." Throughout the history of Canada's institutional supports for both literature and digital humanities, national culture has relied on networks of communication technologies. Beginning with the Massey Commission and the subsequent establishment of the Canada Council for the Arts, this chapter outlines the history of the institutional developments of this discourse of public good and nation-building.

Humanism and the nation

It is telling that the *Royal Commission on National Development in the Arts, Letters, and Sciences* (1951), informally known as the "Massey Commission," includes an epigraph from St. Augustine's *The City of God*: "A nation is an association of reasonable beings united in a peaceful sharing of the things they cherish; therefore, to determine the quality of a nation, you must consider what those things are" (Government of Canada 1951, xxiii). This passage locates the goals of the commission squarely within a Christian humanist construction of national culture. As George Henri Lévesque explains, "au départ, la philosophie humaniste qui inspirait fortement notre commission" (from the start, humanist philosophy strongly inspired our commission) (Litt 1992, 91); Paul Litt describes the Commission, tellingly, as "a crusade for Canadian cultural nationalism" and as helping to usher in "the dawn of a new era in Canadian cultural affairs" (1992, 3). The Massey Commission would thus establish a vision of social development through support for the arts inspired, in part, by the humanist ideas of the early twentieth century—a vision of the arts as a source of social improvement that remains evident today in Social Sciences and Humanities Research Council of Canada (SSHRC) and Canada Council funding programs and in programs like *Canada Reads*.[1]

The Massey Commission determined that Canadian "literature has taken a second place ... far behind painting" in national culture, and it asked whether "we are a people without a literature"? The Commission's answer, drawing on the expert reports of authorities, was decidedly yes: "neither in French nor in English have we yet a truly national literature" (Government of Canada 1951, 223). Included among the commission's conclusions is the recognition that

> the Canadian writer suffers from the fact that he is not sufficiently recognized in our national life, that his work is not considered necessary to the life of his country; and it is this isolation which prevents his making his full contribution. It seems therefore to be necessary to find some way of helping our Canadian writers to become an integral part of their environment and, at the same time, to give them a sense of their importance in this environment.
>
> *(227)*

According to the Commission, the isolation that affects Canadian writers is due to the size of the country, the lack of a substantial reading public, and the absence of infrastructure supporting a literary industry. The Commission aimed to overcome these particularly Canadian problems by recommending supports for Canadian authors and the Canadian publishing industry.

The Commission paid little attention to the burgeoning Canadian literature of the late nineteenth and early twentieth century and completely ignored early Indigenous writing and narratives. Yet in its support of the creation of the Canada Council for the Arts, and its call for broader support for Canadian writers, presses, and institutions, the Commission was instrumental in establishing Canadian literature as a field. Canadian literature, as it is recognized today, would not exist were it not for the Massey Commission. As E. D. Blodgett argues, the report "led to the formation of such institutions as the National Library and the Canada Council," and without it, "such histories as Carl F. Klinck's, not to mention countless other texts, would very probably never have appeared" (2003, 94).[2] Nick Mount is less sure about the Council's early significance, noting that in the Canada Council's first fiscal year, the "only grant for a writer was $1,000 for E. J. Pratt ... for recognition on his 75th birthday," although subsequently

> Council money let Al Purdy find *North of Summer* on Baffin Island. It helped Graeme Gibson finish *Five Legs*, and it helped Anansi publish it.

It helped Mordecai Richler write *Duddy Kravitz* in France and Dennis Lee write *Civil Elegies* in Nathan Philips Square.

(2017, 43–44)

Inadvertently, Mount demonstrates, too, how in the early days, the Canada Council mostly benefitted established (white, male) writers creating literature in a specific mold; resources for emerging writers and those writing in other styles were not as readily available.

Other histories

While this history of large-scale funding institutions has been thoroughly mapped by traditional Canadian critics, Canadian digital humanists have made valuable contributions by uncovering the lesser-known histories of Canadian literature, including the types of creative and critical work that eschewed the humanist ethos espoused by funding bodies. Dean Irvine and Graham Jensen's digital projects on Canada's "marginal modernisms" (Kronfeld 1992) have employed archival and distant reading practices to highlight Canada's extensive modernist literary production that has heretofore gone unrecognized. Likewise, Deanna Reder (Cree-Métis), Madeleine Reddon (Métis), Alix Shield, Margery Fee, and Susan Glover's *The People and the Text* overturns dominant literary history in Canada by identifying a genealogy of Indigenous writing and storytelling as resistance and survivance (Vizenor 2008) in contrast to Atwood's notion of Canadian literature as survival (see Chapter 1). These digital projects offer a richer, more complex understanding of the shape of Canadian literature, thus demonstrating how Canadian literary digital humanities projects provide a necessary correction to the Canadian literary canon by highlighting marginalized or minoritized writing. Irvine's *Editing Modernism in Canada* (see Chapter 5) was funded through a Strategic Knowledge Cluster Grant and the *Canadian Modernist Magazines Project* was supported by a SSHRC Postdoctoral Fellowship; *The People and the Text* was funded through a SSHRC Insight Grant.

These DH projects and the works they foreground remind us that the relationships between institutional support and cultural and scholarly works are very uneven. Canadian literature is replete with authors who have shaped the field without substantial support from major funding institutions, including Austin Clarke, Mavis Gallant, and Rohinton Mistry. Relatedly, there are numerous moments of institutional hubris where organizations are overconfident in their ability to predict—and even shape—Canadian scholarship and culture. The national Conference on the Canadian Novel, held in Calgary in 1978, for instance, concluded with an "Official Ballot for the Selection of Canadian Novels," ranking them as

"Major," "Significant," or "Of Secondary Importance" (Steele 1982). The list is, in retrospect, hilariously lacking, and the entire process affirms the cliché that a camel is a horse designed by committee.[3]

In a more recent and more apt manner, Diana Brydon questions the institutional reframing of Canadian literature into a kind of "TransCanada." She argues,

> Those who care about literature … and about informed reading practices as taught through literary study need to ask how that reframing fits within larger institutional changes, when most disciplines are asking about their methods and mandates, when universities are shifting their financing and their functions, when science and all forms of knowledge production are being brought into question, and when states are reorganizing their priorities.
>
> *(2007, 2)*

Brydon's vision calls on Canadian literary scholars to grapple with the ways in which institutional and social changes, the transformation of the nation within global contexts, and the once-assumed notion of the public good have affected disciplinary expectations and critical practices. Brydon's concerns, meanwhile, are inspired, in part, by the kinds of research and institutional developments brought about by DH. Factor in evolving ideas of nation, national literature, and the value of the humanities in a globalized world, and Brydon argues that it is no longer enough for Canadian literary critics to focus on the world of the text or even literature; they must adapt their work to understand the broader social circumstances that inform it. Scholars must change their practices to reflect on the relationship between literary study, public life, and new modes of expression and communication.

Some of the changes Brydon calls for have been reflected in the research paradigms supported by funding bodies that have had significant effects on Canadian literary and digital humanities research. The 2001 report from SSHRC's Working Group on the Future of the Humanities (a group that included prominent Canadian literary scholar, Linda Hutcheon) attempted to understand the shifting grounds of humanities research, including increasing the role of new digital technology in humanities work. In an opening comment that remains eerily true today, the working group identifies their first goal being "to address what it regards as one of the most important challenges for humanists in today's university environment—the profound malaise infecting their disciplines" (SSHRC 2001, 10). The report cites the Massey Commission's call for new supports for Canada's cultural existence and "recognizes the need for increased funding for humanities education and research" (8). Furthermore, it identifies that "New information technologies represent one of the major impacts on humanities teaching and research. They also present an exciting opportunity for scholars, teachers and students" (21). The report represents, on one hand, a sobering appraisal of the challenges for humanities scholars at the beginning of the century, and on the other hand, an optimistic assessment of the opportunities for humanists. The authors call on humanists to use their training to meet the emerging challenges of the new century, writing,

> The position here is that we can apply the traditional humanistic virtues of broad cultural literacy and analysis and interpretation of complex intellectual and social issues to new contexts; the confidence here is that these intellectual skills will always be highly relevant, whatever the technological or social landscape—that the old wine remains an incomparable vintage, whatever the shape or hue of the new bottles.
>
> *(20)*

This report led, in part, to the creation of SSHRC's Image, Text, Sound, and Technology program in 2003, a fund designed to support research investigating "new digital media, multimedia, and text-based computing technologies" as well as to "facilitate the creation of national and international networks" of researchers working in this field (SSHRC 2009). As Lynne Siemens notes, a significant amount of SSHRC's digital humanities funding flowed through the "Image, Text, Sound and Technology (ITST) fund with additional funding through discipline-specific committees and some strategic grants, such as the Digging into Data Challenge" (2013).

Institutional support for digital humanities

Although the SSHRC report from the 2000s heralded money to come, DH struggled in the early days to find institutional support. While Ian Lancashire generated funds in the 1980s from IBM for humanities computing at the University of Toronto (see Chapter 3), this kind of private backing was atypical. Because funding bodies are legislated to support particular kinds of activities, research that is novel or interdisciplinary—such as DH work, especially in the early days—often seems unrecognizable and is therefore rendered ineligible. Even humanities computing and digital humanities research and teaching in universities often depended (and still depends) on limited funding requiring renewal or is tied to a support from a computer centre. It is telling that a project as successful as *Orlando* was unable to renew its SSHRC funding because it did not produce the revered object of scholarly work: a monograph. Despite producing a network of engaged scholars, systems and methodologies for ingesting, tagging, and structuring data, a growing database of writing, a series of conferences, and more, SSHRC could not see the value in a project that did not produce a scholarly book. Were it not for the timely arrival of funds from the Canada Foundation for Innovation (CFI), *Orlando* very well may not have continued.

The CFI has played a significant role in the development of DH research in Canada. It was established, in part, thanks to an unexpected $500 million federal government surplus in 1997. In the mid-1990s, the Liberal Chrétien government implemented a tough program of fiscal austerity meant to combat the perception that Canada's growing deficit would turn Canada into, in the *Wall Street Journal*'s phrasing, a "Banana republic of the north" (CFI 2016). After discovering a surprise surplus, the federal government established the CFI—an independent funding body to support projects under the wide (vague) rubric of innovation. While CFI funds were primarily funnelled towards modernizing scientific equipment and laboratories, digital humanities was one of the few humanities areas of study that could justifiably request funds for labs and equipment. CFI funds also contributed to the establishment of the Canada Research Chairs program, which counts among its funded positions several DH chairs, including those held by Constance Crompton (University of Ottawa), Laura Estill (St. Francis Xavier University), Susan Brown (University of Guelph), Ray Siemens (University of Victoria), and Lai-Tze Fan (University of Waterloo). CFI funds also support DH projects including the *Linked Infrastructure for Networked Cultural Scholarship* and the *Collaboratory for Writing and Research on Culture*, and many of the DH labs and centres described in Chapter 5.

Like other funding bodies, the CFI supports particular kinds of research, with the result that digital humanities scholars have had to adapt their projects to CFI requirements in order to secure funding. A quick assessment of the funded projects reveals the qualities of humanities research that the CFI deems worthy of funding—ones with an emphasis on deliverables typical of science and engineering research. The CFI's mandate is to support equipment, labs, and systems; a great deal of humanities research requires none of these. Furthermore, CFI funding privileges team-based research, organized around humanities lab spaces. In 2024, of the CFI's thirteen members and thirteen directors, Sophie Bouffard is the lone humanities scholar. The remaining twenty-five are from science, engineering, and the private sector. It is little surprise, then, that humanities scholars in search of the often-substantial CFI funds have had to frame their research to be legible to this group of adjudicators.

One of the CFI's—and DH's—great successes is the Canadian Research Knowledge Network (CRKN). Beginning as a librarian-organized initiative in 1999, the *Canadian National Site Licensing Project* (CNSLP), as it was originally called, was supported with over $20 million in CFI funds to make its scholarly content widely available. In the early 2000s, the CNSLP became the CRKN, and it substantially expanded its humanities holdings to include a sizable collection of open-access journals and merged with *Canadiana*, an archive of Canadian cultural heritage. CRKN's work preserving and providing access to Canadian cultural heritage and academic resources is a major achievement in Canadian humanities digital infrastructure.

Following CFI's lead, other funding bodies have also begun to value—and therefore support—digital humanities. The Council of Canadian Academies' 2006 report, "The State of Science and Technology in Canada," recognized humanities computing as one of the areas in which Canadian researchers were gaining ground. For some, this acceptance or even ascendancy of the digital is not simply an indication of due support finally being received, but rather as the salvation of the humanities more generally. As Chad Gaffield explains,

> declining enrolment and research funding are consistent with a larger devaluing of the humanities often by unwarranted claims about "return on investment" from the perspective of a corporatized campus. The extent to which and how DH can successfully and appropriately contribute to the re-enchantment of the humanities in this challenging context deserve robust discussion as well as specific initiatives to demonstrate promising approaches.
>
> *(2015)*

Where once DH research was once largely illegible to funding models, SSHRC has adapted their criteria in a range of ways. In place of privileging a monograph, for instance, SSHRC now requires researchers to participate in the more general activity of "knowledge mobilization," defined as the "reciprocal and complementary flow and uptake of research knowledge between researchers, knowledge brokers, and knowledge users—both within and beyond academia" (2021). SSHRC's "Guidelines for Effective Knowledge Mobilization" rely heavily on the self-evidently digital, such as "data sharing through online repositories, social media, … websites," and many more that lend themselves to digital formats and use of DH methodologies (e.g., oral histories, videos) (2023). Plans for data management and open access provisions are de facto in grant applications; Canada's "Tri-Agency Research Data Management Policy," to which adherence is required for securing most federal funding, includes an expectation that publications are open access and that research projects have plans for long-term, public domain data storage (2021). In the same way that the federal government shifted the needle towards CanLit through policy decisions in the 1950s, current requirements for receiving federal research funding are nudging scholars and students to include digital components and develop technological competencies.

The shift in funding has been accompanied by a shift in teaching, with the intertwining of emerging technologies and the traditional domains of a liberal arts education offering a way for universities to tout DH as a route to marketable skills. Consider, for example, the promotional text on the webpage for the University of Alberta master's in digital humanities:

> Digital Humanities integrates computational methods and theories with research and teaching in the Arts and Humanities. *It addresses the demand for Arts graduates to be able to work* either in the realm of arts and humanities research and teaching or *in the emerging job markets of information management and content delivery over the Internet.* We have a great record of *placing our students in* library positions, *computer lab positions*, research projects, PhD programs *and industry jobs.*
> (2024, emphasis added)

These changes to funding and teaching have taken place alongside a shift in what we collectively consider worthy of investigation. Whereas a study of social media would have been impossible thirty years ago and unheard of even fifteen years ago, research that engages with social platforms and public discourse is now standard fare. Even SSHRC's priority research areas, as described in the *Imagining Canada's Future* initiative, have significant digital components. Areas include "working in the digital economy," "the emerging asocial society," "humanity+," "the arts transformed," and "evolving narratives of culture"; sub-topics, meanwhile, range from "art and big data" to "social media and participatory culture" to "enhanced humanity."

The evolution of SSHRC's funding metrics and adjudication policies has contributed to the flourishing of DH projects and centres (see Chapter 5). Yet many humanities scholars are concerned about funding models prioritizing a limited vision of the humanities at the expense of more traditional research. Daniel Coleman and Smaro Kamboureli, for instance, describe this as the "development of research capitalism" which is having a "significant impact on the structure of internal and external university relations" (2011, xvii). They cite Claire Polster's argument that "The new importance of research grants" constitutes a "reallocation of university resources based on grant generating ability" that "has the potential to restructure the university's core and its periphery" (Polster 2007, 605). While programs like the Centres for Excellence, CFI, and CRC provide necessary funds to the humanities, they tend to prioritize projects that achieve some broad notion of impact (perhaps today's expression of *public good*). With their emphasis on deliverables and knowledge mobilization, these funding models undervalue some forms of humanities research that are less self-evidently impactful. Critics also question the value of DH-specific funding—suggesting, for example, that the money spent to build humanities labs and purchase computers would be better allocated to individual researchers based on their research goals rather than infrastructural needs. Others argue that the funds required to support large-scale digital humanities projects come at the expense of smaller, more traditional humanities projects. The worry is that SSHRC is fostering a culture of *research capitalism*—a particular form of humanities work that eschews traditional scholarship in favour of work coded in the scientific terms of labs, research teams, datasets, and deliverables.

Adding to the complexity of this dynamic is the increasing number of digital humanities researchers who are precariously employed by universities and (grant-funded) research projects. Part of the move towards research capitalism has been to shift labour away from tenured, academic positions towards contractually limited positions, sessional work, alt-ac, and other forms of *so-called* part-time work (*so-called* because the employees typically work as much as their full-time colleagues but receive less compensation and have little job security). The increase in precarious labour at universities has changed researchers' relationship both to their institutions and their own scholarship, and funding organizations have done little to support those engaged in this type of work. The aforementioned Canada Research Chairs program, for instance, contributes to an academic star system that exacerbates the inequity of research. Additionally, the obligations associated with precarious work—be it teaching, administration, or technical labour—make it more difficult for those employed in these positions (especially at the start of their careers) to develop their own research. As Graeme Jensen (2023), Dani Spinosa (2021), and Deanna Fong and Ryan Fitzpatrick (2023) have noted, the increased precarity of researchers also curtails research freedoms: precariously employed scholars depend on approval from team leads and administrators for their contracts to be renewed. Projects are often directed by senior, tenured colleagues, while the bulk of the labour is contributed by employees on short contracts, by postdoctoral fellows, and by graduate and undergraduate students. DH projects that provide a lifeline (in the form of a salary) to precarious scholars may also curtail their career prospects, as a condition of funding from SSHRC, among others, is that grant funds cannot be used to pay grant applicants and collaborators, thus forcing those who make a living from grant-funded work to choose between receiving a paycheque or receiving intellectual credit for their contributions.

New institutional initiatives

Over the years, funding models have changed in response to researchers who have worked to identify cracks through which digital scholarship has fallen. For example, the Sustaining Digital Scholarship for Sustainable Culture group was assembled to propose "strategies for maintaining the vitality of humanities scholarship and the cultural sector by means of electronic scholarly activity, including archiving, editing, and dissemination" (2010). Members included notable DH scholars such as Brown, Irvine, and Siemens, as well as Canadian literature and theatre scholars including Ashok Mathur, Susan Rudy, Ann Wilson, and Darren Wershler. The group collaborated on "Lasting Change: Sustaining Digital Scholarship and Culture in Canada," a report that "reviews the current state of knowledge about the sustainability of digital scholarship and related cultural activity in Canada and identifies research opportunities that emerge from consideration of the literature" (Bretz, Brown, and McGregor 2010, 1). Although the authors do not address DH's dependence on precarious labour discussed above, they identify a number of other problems, including "the difficulty of tracking and acknowledging the often invisible labour of both student researchers and technical assistants," "the issue of tracking and rewarding labour for innovative or non-traditional work," and the need for a "national digital preservation strategy, the fostering of strategic partnerships and greater support for innovative research and development" (18, 1). While some of these requests have been met, their calls for a "national metadata strategy, a national tool repository and ... a set of national sustainability standards and practices" (1) remain unheeded. It is notable that while the Massey Commission set out policy for scholars with respect to Canadian cultural production, it is now scholars who find themselves making funding and policy recommendations to government and even calling for a government commissions to address the concerns of scholarly and cultural production.

Lynne Siemens is exemplary in this regard. Her 2013 report, "Developing Academic Capacity in the Digital Humanities," offers a survey of the DH landscape in Canada and uses the results to argue that DH researchers need three types of support:

> First, given the reliance on technology and computing power, the Digital Humanist needs computers and cyberinfrastructure, accessible from their desk ... Further to this, the researcher also needs access to data in

electronic form and the tools that allow them to analyze, re(interpret) and otherwise visualize that data for new understandings. Of course, this requires more money than the traditional humanities researcher who has been traditionally seen to rely solely on their books and pencils. ... Finally, researchers, particularly those in traditional academic positions, need the support of their peers in order to be able to disseminate their research in discipline-approved venues and ultimately receive tenure.

(2013)

While, more than ten years later, it is questionable whether the majority of DH researchers need more computing power than "the traditional humanities researcher" (who certainly no longer relies "solely on their books and pencils"), Siemens provides a compelling snapshot of DH researchers' experiences that still ring true. Notably, only 20% of her survey respondents reported receiving SSHRC funding, and only 4% of respondents received CFI funds. Many of the concerns that Siemens identifies remain with the community today:

the respondents offered recommendations on the capacity needed to strengthen the DH community. First, they called for more infrastructure such as networks, labs, supply workstations, and computer programming. ... A key component is to ensure adequate research funding to both individuals and universities so that they can "keep digital technologies up-to-date and the infrastructure to support such technologies well into the future—this is the biggest problem at my institution." Finally, there was also a call for maintenance and sustainability. As one stated, "increased funding is an obvious one, but not only for new projects. We need a system in place for ensuring project sustainability." Besides more dollars, some respondents indicate the need to educate grant adjudicators and reviewers to ensure that they have the knowledge needed to effectively evaluate a digital-oriented application.

(2013)

There is a tension inherent in these requests between maintenance (the cost of staying in place) on one hand and innovation (the cost of moving forward) on the other. In a dream world, there would be enough funds for both, but until such time as budgets are unlimited, choices will have to be made.

As this brief discussion has shown, digital humanists in particular—and literary scholars to a lesser degree—are adept at transforming institutions to their needs, working to resist the requirements of research capitalism and bending the frameworks and mandates of those institutions to other ends. While the CFI and the CRC programs are certainly parts of the institutional apparatus of research capitalism, researchers have used those apparatuses to support communities of students and scholars in a range of ways and to expand the definition of *innovation* to promote a range of digital humanities research. As Stephen Slemon notes,

> when we imagine "the institution" as a social force within our usual disciplinary practices, we do so in a way that positions "the institution" as structurally antithetical to something positive, and therefore as something coterminous with the idea of "the obstacle".
>
> *(2007, 73)*

He argues that when

> we habitually envision institutions as obstacles, we commit ourselves a priori to thinking of ways of navigating around them, not to ways of working through them in the project of inflecting the social register. We foreclose on the possibility of institutional forces being redirected towards the emancipative work of social transformation.
>
> *(74)*

This chapter's history demonstrates the ways in which digital humanists have made institutions work for them and their communities by redirecting funding priorities to support diverse research.

As early as 1997, Ray Siemens predicted some of this discussion of the role of the humanities and the value of community in a post on the *Humanist* listserv:

> What I find stunning, and positively so, about this group of individuals is that each person took from HC [Humanities Computing] ... that which they could make use of, or that which they had the suspicion ... they could employ gainfully; once done, it has been my experience that they have contributed back the results of their efforts—be such results work that on the surface does not betray a debt to computing humanism or that which makes a special point of such display, perhaps pushing the boundaries of what we consider the work of the computing humanist to be. It is the work of such individuals, combined with general societal and institutional trends towards computerization, that allow us today to consider even the idea of HC as a field.
>
> *(Siemens 1997)*

Siemens's post demonstrates the robust forms of community building that have dovetailed with efforts to bend institutional priorities to support humanities computing projects. His post appears on the *Humanist* listserv, which emerged from the efforts of early humanities computing scholars to communicate with one another. Siemens would channel his enthusiasm for community into the Digital Humanities Summer Institute (which was always more community than institute), the Implementing New Knowledge Environments Partnership, and a range of other DH initiatives. Siemens's observations bolster Slemon's argument that *institution* need not be synonymous with *obstacle* but can, rather, be transformed to support community and to reimagine shared conceptions of humanities scholarship. As we demonstrate in the next chapter, the bridges between institutions and communities are often built in the labs, centres, and hubs that house digital humanities activity. It is in these spaces that the requirements of institutions are adapted to serve the needs of scholarly communities.

Notes

1 Philip Massolin outlines the humanist philosophy of early twentieth-century Canadian intellectuals, arguing that critics such as Arthur Woodhouse, Watson Kirkconnell, Harold Innis, George Grant, and others responded to the two world wars and the related social transformations with a revised understanding of the humanities and humanism. Massolin writes:

> Amid the apparent "decay of morals" and the "breakdown of international codes," a sense of "personal responsibility" and perspective had been eroded. For the advocates of the university tradition, a rekindling of the arts and humanities was central to the restoration of a stable social order. The academy's role of promoting a moral, socially responsible culture had become essential to a civilization that verged on collapse. Critics of academic modernization thus were convinced of the need for a resurgence of the traditional academy.
>
> *(2015, 108)*

As noted in Chapter 2, many of the early writers in contemporary Canadian literature were students of, and read, these twentieth-century humanists, with Grant, Frye, and Innis making a particular impression on writers such as Margaret Atwood and Dennis Lee. It is worth noting, too, that the humanism of these thinkers was completely indifferent to the dehumanization of Indigenous people, both historical and happening in Canada at the time. Grant, for instance, wrote his humanist polemics from bucolic Dundas, Ontario, while 30 kilometres away Mohawk children were held in the Mohawk Institute Residential School in Brantford.

2 Litt describes how the Massey Commission's recommendation to create the Canada Council was ignored until the death of two Canadian millionaires provided funds that the government itself was unwilling to stump up:

> John Deutsch, secretary of the Treasury Board ... mentioned that the estates of two fabled Canadian millionaires who had died the year before, Izaak

Walton Killam and Sir James Hamet Dunn, promised to yield succession duties of over $100 million. He thought it would be nice if this windfall could be put to some special use instead of simply being absorbed into general revenues.

(Litt 1992, 242)

Deutsch was convinced to help persuade the government to provide $50 million to support universities and an additional $50 million to establish the Canada Council for the Arts.

3 Some of the texts included on the "A" list of best Canadian novels include Adele Wiseman's *The Sacrifice* (1956), Frederick Philip Grove's *Fruits of the Earth* (1956), Martha Ostenso's *Wild Geese* (1925), and Thomas H. Raddell's *The Nymph and the Lamp* (1950). The organizers report that "At least two participants, Eli Mandel and Ronald Sutherland, dissociated themselves entirely from the entire process of the vote" (150). Sutherland voiced his objections in clear terms: "I feel that the ballot to determine the 'hundred best Canadian novels' was an unfortunate and misguided gimmick and that the decision of ECW Press to publicize it further is a disservice to Canadian writing" (Steele 1982, 150–51).

Further reading

Coleman, Daniel, and Smaro Kamboureli, eds. 2011. *Retooling the Humanities: The Culture of Research in Canadian Universities*. Edmonton: University of Alberta Press. https://doi.org/10.1515/9780888646781.

Coombe, Rosemary, Darren Wershler, and Martin Zeilinger. 2014. *Dynamic Fair Dealing: Creating Canadian Culture Online*. Toronto: University of Toronto Press. https://doi.org/10.3138/9781442665613.

Litt, Paul. 1992. *The Muses, the Masses, and the Massey Commission*. Toronto: University of Toronto Press.

Massolin, Philip. 2015. *Canadian Intellectuals, the Tory Tradition, and the Challenge of Modernity, 1939–1970*. Toronto: University of Toronto Press. https://doi.org/10.3138/9781442672246.

Tippett, Maria. 1990. *Making Culture: English-Canadian Institutions and the Arts before the Massey Commission*. Toronto: University of Toronto Press. https://doi.org/10.3138/9781487577537.

Works cited

Blodgett, E. D. 2003. *Five-Part Invention: A History of Literary History in Canada*. Toronto: University of Toronto Press. https://doi.org/10.3138/9781442674950.

Bretz, Andrew, Susan Brown, and Hannah McGregor. 2010. "Lasting Change: Sustaining Digital Scholarship and Culture in Canada." Report of the Sustaining Digital Scholarship for Sustainable Culture Group, December 2010. https://www.alienated.net/wp-content/uploads/2019/09/bretz_brown_mcgregor_lasting_change.pdf.

Brydon, Diana. 2007. "Metamorphoses of a Discipline: Rethinking Canadian Literature within Institutional Contexts." In *Trans.Can.Lit*, edited by Smaro Kamboureli and Roy Miki, 1–16. Waterloo: Wilfred Laurier University Press. https://doi.org/10.51644/9781554581030-003.

CFI. 2016. "Episode One: Fiscal Armageddon." *Our Origin Story*. Canada Foundation for Innovation, September 20, 2016. https://www.innovation.ca/projects-results/research-stories/episode-one-fiscal-armageddon.

Coleman, Daniel, and Smaro Kamboureli, eds. 2011. *Retooling the Humanities: The Culture of Research in Canadian Universities*. Edmonton: University of Alberta Press. https://doi.org/10.1515/9780888646781.

CRKN. n.d. *Canadiana*. Canadian Research Knowledge Network. Accessed June 5, 2024. https://www.canadiana.ca.

CWRC. n.d. *Collaboratory for Writing and Research on Culture*. Accessed July 12, 2024. https://cwrc.ca/.

EMiC. n.d. *Editing Modernism in Canada*. Accessed July 12, 2024. https://editingmodernism.ca/.

Fong, Deanna, and Ryan Fitzpatrick. 2023. "Analogue Thrills, Digital Spills: On the Fred Wah Digital Archive Version 2.0." In *Future Horizons: Canadian Digital Humanities*, edited by Paul Barrett and Sarah Roger, 255–72. Ottawa: University of Ottawa Press. https://doi.org/10.1515/9780776640068-018.

Gaffield, Chad. 2015. "The Surprising Ascendance of Digital Humanities: And Some Suggestions for an Uncertain Future." *Digital Studies / Le champ numérique* 6, no. 1. https://doi.org/10.16995/dscn.2.

Government of Canada. 1951. *Royal Commission on National Development in the Arts, Letters, and Sciences, 1949–1951*. Report. Ottawa: Printer to the King's Most Excellent Majesty. https://www.collectionscanada.ca/2/5/h5-400-e.html.

Government of Canada. 2021. "Tri-Agency Research Data Management Policy." March 14, 2021. https://science.gc.ca/site/science/en/interagency-research-funding/policies-and-guidelines/research-data-management/tri-agency-research-data-management-policy.

Jensen, Graham H. 2023. "Beyond 'Mere Digitization': Introducing the Canadian Modernist Magazines Project." In *Future Horizons: Canadian Digital Humanities*, edited by Paul Barrett and Sarah Roger, 367–88. Ottawa: University of Ottawa Press. https://doi.org/10.2307/jj.17681834.25.

Jensen, Graham, Deseray Manuel, et al. 2022. *Canadian Modernist Magazines Project*. University of Victoria. https://modernistmags.ca.

Kronfeld, Chana. 1992. *On the Margins of Modernism: Decentering Literary Dynamics*. Berkeley: University of California Press. https://doi.org/10.1525/9780520914131.

LINCS. 2024. *Linked Infrastructure for Networked Cultural Scholarship*. https://lincsproject.ca/.

Litt, Paul. 1992. *The Muses, the Masses, and the Massey Commission*. Toronto: University of Toronto Press.

Massolin, Philip. 2015. *Canadian Intellectuals, the Tory Tradition, and the Challenge of Modernity, 1939–1970*. Toronto: University of Toronto Press. https://doi.org/10.3138/9781442672246.

McCarty, Willard, Julianne Nyhan, Anne Welsh, and Jessica Salmon. 2012. "Questioning, Asking and Enduring Curiosity: An Oral History Conversation between Julianne Nyhan and Willard McCarty." *Digital Humanities Quarterly* 6, no. 3. https://www.digitalhumanities.org/dhqdev/vol/6/3/000134/000134.html.

Mount, Nick. 2017. *Arrival: The Story of CanLit*. Toronto: Anansi.

Polster, Claire. 2007. "The Nature and Implications of the Growing Importance of Research Grants to Canadian Universities and Academics." *Higher Education* 53: 599–622. https://doi.org/10.1007/s10734-005-1118-z.

Reder, Deanna, Madeleine Reddon, Alix Shield, Margery Fee, and Susan Glover. n.d. *The People and the Text:* Indigenous Writing in Lands Claimed by Canada. Accessed September 8, 2024. https://thepeopleandthetext.ca/.

Siemens, Lynne. 2013. "Developing Academic Capacity in the Digital Humanities: Thoughts from the Canadian Community." *Digital Humanities Quarterly* 7, no. 1. https://www.digitalhumanities.org/dhq/vol/7/1/000114/000114.html.

Siemens, Ray. 1997. "Disciplined Training // Computing Humanists." *Humanist Listserv*, January 15, 1997. https://dhhumanist.org/archives/Converted_Text/humanist.1996-1997.txt.

Slemon, Stephen. 2007. "Transcanada, Literature: No Direction Home." In *Trans. Can.Lit*, edited by Smaro Kamboureli and Roy Miki, 71–83. Waterloo: Wilfred Laurier University Press. https://doi.org/10.51644/9781554581030-008.

Spinosa, Dani. 2021. "Theft on the Ground Floor." *Anarchist Essays*, March 22, 2021. https://anarchistessays.podbean.com/e/essay-9-dani-spinosa-theft-on-the-ground-floor/.

SSHRC. 2001. "Alternative Wor[l]ds: The Humanities in 2010." Social Sciences and Humanities Research Council of Canada. https://publications.gc.ca/pub?id=9.834503&sl=0.

SSHRC. 2009. "Image, Text, Sound and Technology." Social Sciences and Humanities Research Council of Canada. https://www.sshrc-crsh.gc.ca/funding-financement/programs-programmes/itst/research_grants-subventions_recherche-eng.aspx.

SSHRC. 2021. "Definitions of Terms." Social Sciences and Humanities Research Council of Canada, May 4, 2021. https://www.sshrc-crsh.gc.ca/funding-financement/programs-programmes/definitions-eng.aspx.

SSHRC. 2023. "Guidelines for Effective Knowledge Mobilization." Social Sciences and Humanities Research Council of Canada, November 24, 2023. https://www.sshrc-crsh.gc.ca/funding-financement/policies-politiques/knowledge_mobilisation-mobilisation_des_connaissances-eng.aspx.

Steele, Charles, ed. 1982. *Taking Stock: The Calgary Conference on the Canadian Novel*. Toronto: ECW Press.

Sustaining Digital Scholarship for Sustainable Culture (blog). 2010. https://sustainableknowledgeproject.blogspot.com/.

University of Alberta. 2024. "MA in Digital Humanities." University of Alberta Faculty of Arts. https://www.ualberta.ca/media-technology-studies/programs/digital-humanities/index.html.

Vizenor, Gerald. 2008. *Survivance: Narratives of Native Presence*. Lincoln: University of Nebraska Press.

5
DIGITAL HUMANITIES SPACES
Archives, collaboratories, laboratories, and centres

* * *

As a field so focused on community, it is no surprise that digital humanities blurs the line between the "traditional setting of humanistic work: the private study and the public library, archive, classroom, and meeting space" (Gardiner and Musto 2015, 82). Technology has shifted and so too have the methods and locations of DH work. Institutionally owned, room-sized mainframes have given way to privately owned, portable devices such as laptops and cell phones. As the space taken up by the computers themselves has diminished, digital humanities centres and laboratories have emerged as physical spaces for work that could be dispersed and asynchronous. Meanwhile, archival work that was previously only possible with a special trip can increasingly (although not wholly, given the speed with which digitizing is taking place) be done digitally from anywhere in the world. The digital humanities lab and the digital archive both hold in tension physical presence and virtual manifestation—abstract yet concrete, disconnected yet networked. Just as shifting priorities in institutional and governmental support described in Chapter 4 have influenced concepts of Canadian literature and the emergence of Canadian digital humanities, so too have institutional and domain dynamics played out on the smaller stages of university campuses. This chapter looks at how space has been made for digital humanities in libraries and university departments—specifically in the form of archives and laboratories—as well as how these spaces have shaped DH research in Canada.

DOI: 10.4324/9781003318323-8

Digital archives

Traditionally, an (analogue) archive is a physical collection of related materials. For example, the Thomas Fisher Rare Book Library at the University of Toronto has an archive of Margaret Atwood's papers: writings, artworks, personal correspondence, reviews, and more. Altogether, the archive comprises "717 boxes and items (106 metres)" (TFRBL 2024). End to end, it is longer than the Canadian Parliament's Peace Tower is tall. Thinking about the shelves required alone, it is clear why digitizing might be appealing. There are, of course, other benefits. Physical archives are often gathered by subject or source and arranged temporally: Fisher's Atwood archive groups materials by categories, such as *speeches, essays, and reviews*, and by periods, such as *personal correspondence with Earl Birney, 1970–1971*. By contrast, digital archives—whether they are made up of digitized copies of physical materials or born-digital resources—can be simultaneously arranged in multiple ways. A digital representation of correspondence between Atwood and Birney could appear in (or, more accurately, the relevant files could be pointed at from) categories for both *correspondence* and *Canadian poets* in Atwood's archives, or they could appear in both Atwood's and Birney's archives simultaneously, all while filling a fraction of the space of the physical papers. Digital archives can allow readers to dynamically create and interpret networks of relationships between and within archives. They are thus "a purposeful collection of surrogates ... something that blends features of editing and archiving"—surrogates not simply because digitized files are stand-ins for the physical originals but because the archivist arranges and annotates materials in multiple so that the digital materials benefit from both "the care of treatment and annotation of an edition and the inclusiveness of an archive" (Price 2009).

A danger of digital archives, however, is that they run the risk of losing the materiality (and context) of the archival object. A PDF or high-definition scan of a page is not the equivalent of the original artifact; it is an effective surrogate. Also, researchers may tend to ignore that which cannot be accessed digitally, thus shrinking the field of knowledge (see Chapter 11). Yet, in their field-defining 2004 volume, Susan Schreibman, Ray Siemens, and John Unsworth demonstrate the digital archive's power to contribute meaning to the materials, pointing out that digital archiving is "*a critical and self-conscious activity*, from the choice of what to represent ... [to] the implications of decisions that we make in the use of those tools and the impact they have on analytical processes" (2004, emphasis added). This critical, curatorial activity is also a tenet of *The Digital Humanities Manifesto 2.0*:

> Curation also implies custodial responsibilities with respect to the remains of the past as well as interpretive, meaning-making responsibilities with

respect to the present and future. In a world of perpetual data overload, it implies information design and selectivity: the channelling, filtering, and organization into intelligible and usable information; the digging up of new or long ignored cultural corpora. ... Archives will continue to undergo explosive growth. Digital Humanists must be there, alongside librarians and archivists, to think critically about the challenges and opportunities that such explosive growth provides.

(2009, 9)

The archivist's responsibility is not unique to DH. The distinct field of critical archival studies is dedicated to uncovering and rectifying the injustices embedded in archival practices, both physical and digital. In an editorial that defines (and names) the field of critical archival studies, Michelle Caswell, Ricardo Punzalan, and T-Kay Sangwand note that naming, be it by establishing an academic discipline or creating an archival collection, "is a form of legitimating. Naming is power. Naming is a way of demarcating and defining and delineating and harnessing" (2017). This power is equally true for Canadian literature and digital humanities. It is also true for a dataset, which, in its creation, embeds biases and reifies cultural constructions. Notwithstanding inter- and intra-domain similarities, however, power is especially embedded in digital archiving because it enhances access and facilitates exploration, manipulation, and analysis. Digital archives increase the likelihood of scholarship, which in turn increases the stature of the archival subject.

The term *replatforming* is used, in technological contexts, to describe the act of migrating from an older, unsupported system to a newer, more stable and feature-rich one. The concept of replatforming has been taken on board by digital humanists, first to describe how "the emergence of digital technologies was instrumental in ... reframing, or a replatforming" of humanities domains (Cowan 2018), and more recently to describe the responsibilities implicit in the act providing or increasing access to information (Brown, forthcoming):

> We use the term replatforming to refer to several aspects of providing a platform on which data is disseminated anew, and ... in newly structured ways. Replatforming points to the data's prior life on other platforms; the affordances that platforms can provide for redressing historical under- or misrepresentation by amplifying or reframing data; and the need for critical analysis of the implications of providing a new platform for existing data.
>
> *(Brown et al. 2023, 303)*

This potential for enhanced circulation and reinterpretation exists across DH for both digitized and born-digital materials, as (re)platforming potentially removes geographical, institutional, and credential-based barriers. Disseminating in newly structured and potentially endlessly remixable ways, as in digital archives, comes with both attendant benefits and potential risks (some of which we discuss in Chapters 8–10).[1]

CanLit and the digital archive

As discussed in Chapters 3 and 4, the reification of both CanLit and DH was the result, at least in part, of policies and mandates—forces that also led to an increase in the number of digital CanLit archives:

> Canada was a pioneer in the production of digitized historical literature: the immense and multilingual *Early Canadiana Online* project changed how scholars and students engage with historical literature in Canada, with reference not only to what they read but also how they read and analyze this material. Early resources such as Tom Vincent's CD-ROM-based *Early Canadian Cultural Journals Index* anticipated the production of web-based repositories of early periodical writing. Carole Gerson's *Canada's Early Women Writers Project* recognized the importance of aggregating information about marginal groups of writers in order to better trace their intricate and important connections across social and cultural contexts. The massive bilingual *History of the Book in Canada* project developed practices of communicating knowledge across print and digital platforms. Canada made important contributions to early digital tool development for the humanities through tools such as TACT, a tradition continued through the present in the widely used Voyant Tool suite. Digital platforms such as the Canadian Writing Research Collaboratory (CWRC) enable new ways to organize, analyze, and circulate research on Canadian literary and cultural texts.
>
> *(Brown and Devereux 2017)*

It is not surprising that the longstanding tradition of digital humanists thinking critically about digital archives is matched by one of scholars developing such archives, nor is it surprising that Canada and CanLit have so strong a presence in digital archiving, given both institutional and individual scholarly interest in DH and the dedicated funding streams that have supported this work. *Early Canadiana Online*, for example, was funded by the international Digging into Data Challenge, and its resources and those of the *Early Canadian Cultural Journals Index* have been incorporated into the Canadian Research Knowledge Network's *Canadiana*. The *Canada's Early Women Writers* project received federal support from Social Sciences and Humanities Research Council of Canada (SSHRC) and Canada

Foundation for Innovation (CFI), as well as institutional support from the University of British Columbia and Simon Fraser University. These latter two projects are also now affiliated with the *Collaboratory for Writing and Research on Culture* (CWRC), which is supported by the Digital Research Alliance of Canada (DRAC) and SSHRC. DH developments and support create generative feedback loops:

> The affordances of any given archival organizing platform will have a noticeable impact upon the meaning of the texts it holds, orders, and circulates. The very nature and existence of CanLit—including our perception of its formal and political properties—depends upon such organizing forces.
>
> *(Camlot and McLeod 2019, 9)*

CanLit, as a field of study, is transformed by the practices of archiving it—practices that themselves are informed by a combination of scholarly, political, and financial interests.

Meaning created by and access increased by digital archives also have implications for related fields. For CanLit, there has been a knock-on effect for concepts of national identity: "Digital mediations and representations might enhance the coordination and understanding of formulations of national identity … what becomes digitized will have a bearing on, and will ultimately shape and control, manifestations and interpretations of national identity" (Morra 2019, 47). We are what we archive. Or, perhaps more accurately, what we choose to archive shapes whom we will become. With the effects on national cultural identity looming large, the implications of digital archiving stretch beyond academia and into our political, economic, and creative spaces. To this end, Darren Wershler issues a call for engagement: "we need to work harder on a public version of the deep infrastructure that the cultural preservation community has been calling for repeatedly over the last two decades" (2019, 358).[2] If our archives come to represent who we are, we must build them with intentionality and ethical engagement. Inherent in this call is the democratic potential for any interested party to contribute—be they established scholars or hobby archivists. This idealism, of course, is tempered by the already-discussed reality of political, economic, and institutional interests, which affect what is archived, who has access to the materials, and who is afforded the time and research support to work in the archives once created. To assume that we have the ability to shape archives through our collective will is, perhaps, unrealistically utopian. Like many of the reports on the state of humanism discussed in the previous chapters, Wershler, Morra, McLeod, Brown and others join the chorus calling for a larger, more systematic, approach to Canadian cultural institutional policy suited to the realities of digital culture and research.

Collaboratories

Notwithstanding the potential risks and roadblocks, collaboration offers a route to a public deep infrastructure with the potential to contribute to a shared national identity. Not coincidentally, collaboration is also one of the founding pillars of digital humanities, where its practitioners often view themselves as part of a *community of practice*, as evinced by the number of articles alone that use the term: for example, "Communities of Practice, the Methodological Commons, and Digital Self-Determination in the Humanities" (Siemens 2015), "Building a DIY Community of Practice" (Sanders Garcia et al. 2021), "Expanding Communities of Practice" (Fragaszy Troyano and Rhody 2013), "Facilitating Communities of Practice in Digital Humanities: Librarian Collaborations for Research and Training in Text Encoding" (Green 2014). Originating in the work of Jean Lave and Etienne Wenger, communities of practice are self-sustaining groups that coalesce around a domain and grow their knowledge through shared methods (Wenger-Trayner and Wenger-Trayner, 2015). In theory, all that is needed to gain entry to DH's community of practice is to participate in its activities. Although there are some problems with this everyone-is-welcome, big tent vision (see Chapters 8–10), DH in Canada certainly has many established onramps for those seeking entry to the community, including the collaboratories described in this section, and the laboratories, centres, and training programs discussed in the next.

The digital humanities collaboratory is a gateway to membership in the community. Part digital archive, part virtual laboratory, collaboratories provide access to digitized archival materials, the tools and training to work with them, and often also building blocks for new digital projects and resources:

> Collaboratories extend that dimension of research to distributed groups that may be as small as a work group or as large as an international research community ... They are places ... [to] obtain resources, do work, interact, share data, results, and other information, and collaborate.
> *(Palmer 2004)*

DH projects require the combined efforts of researchers, digitizers, computer programmers, librarians and archivists, and often vast support from students and research assistants; establishing and maintaining a collaboratory is a way of enlisting DH skills in support of the DH community.

In the context of Canadian digital literary studies, there are a few projects that either explicitly name themselves as collaboratories or that function as de facto collaboratories because they serve as training grounds for digital humanists and act as springboards for other digital humanities projects. Below are descriptions of three—the *Collaboratory for Writing and Research on Culture* (CWRC), *Editing Modernism in Canada* (EMiC), and *SpokenWeb*—that function (or, in the case of EMiC, functioned) as communities of practice for Canadian literary digital humanities. All three of these projects were made possible, in part, by federal research funding: CWRC received support from both SSHRC and DRAC, EMiC was funded by a SSHRC Strategic Knowledge Cluster Grant, and *SpokenWeb* was funded by a SSHRC Partnership Grant.

Collaboratory for Writing and Research on Culture

The *Collaboratory for Writing and Research on Culture* (CWRC, pronounced *quirk*) provides a platform for Canadian scholars and scholars studying Canada who are looking to share, connect, create, and preserve research data. Launched in 2016 as the *Canadian Writing Research Collaboratory* (and relaunching under its new name in 2025), CWRC is based at the University of Alberta, where it is led by Susan Brown (director), Mihaela Ilovan (assistant director), and Jeffery Antoniuk (technical lead). Its resources include an online repository for researchers looking to house born-digital materials, digitized texts, images, audiovisual files, and related metadata; open access content shared by CWRC projects; a sizable collection of Canadian cultural content, including the *Early Canadian Cultural Journals Index* and *Canada's Early Women Writers*. With projects contributed by more than one hundred researchers from a range of disciplines, CWRC functions as an access point and hosting infrastructure for historical textual projects with close to 400,000 objects, and more than 1.5 TB of data between them; in 2020, CWRC "served close to 7,000 unique users with access to more than 395,000 cultural objects" (Rockwell et al. 2022). CWRC is a hub for digital humanities Canadian literature projects and is home to many CanLit and CanLit-adjacent projects, such as *Canadian Jewish Women Writers*, *Canadian Women Playwrights Online*, *E. Pauline Johnson's Legends of Vancouver*, *The People and the Text: Indigenous Writing in Lands Claimed by Canada*, *The Digital Page: The Collected Works of P. K. Page*, and *Women's Writing and Reading in Canada from 1950*.

The CWRC platform, built on the Canadian open-source Islandora framework and customized to support collaboration and workflow management, incorporates an extensive range of in-house tools for standards-oriented content creation, management, and publication, which allow projects to build, customize, and maintain their own interfaces. The codebase for both the CWRC platform and a suite of modular editorial tools have been generalized as the *Linked Editing Academic Framework* (LEAF) software for sustainable, open digital humanities projects. LEAF includes custom tools for text encoding, enables users to build their own tools, and extends the CWRC infrastructure to allow for other instances of its *Virtual Research Environment* (VRE) model. LEAF is the product of collaboration between the Canadian CWRC team and international researchers, led by Diane Jakacki (US) and James Cummings (UK). Available via *LEAF Commons*, its tools include the *LEAF-Writer* text editor which provides a graphical user interface for encoding text using TEI (see Chapter 13) and creating linked open data (see Chapter 12), and the *Dynamic Table of Contexts*, a web-based e-reader that uses text encoding to generate an enhanced reading experience.

Editing Modernism in Canada

Based at Dalhousie University, *Editing Modernism in Canada* (EMiC) grew from the belief that digital humanities forms of editorial work, curation, and archiving were particularly well suited to uncovering the history of marginalized and little-known Canadian modernist texts. Running 2007–2015 and led by Dean Irvine, EMiC was a significant force in the expansion of digital humanities methods into Canadian literary scholarship. It was involved in developing the *Routledge Encyclopedia of Modernism* and supported the (now defunct) *Linked Modernisms* project. With respect to CanLit, EMiC held several conferences, including one in 2011 at the TransCanada Institute at the University of Guelph, which resulted in *Editing as Cultural Practice in Canada* (Irvine and Kamboureli 2016). EMiC was also instrumental in the creation of the Canadian Literature Collection at the University of Ottawa Press, a series of Canadian modernist literature and critical works. That EMiC's print publications have outlasted its active, online presence speaks to the ongoing legitimacy afforded print media in academia, the pre-eminence held by physical libraries and archives, and the attendant risks of technology.

As a training ground for DH, the EMiC team organized Textual Editing and Modernism in Canada (TEMiC) at Trent University, and it hosted Digital Editing and Modernism in Canada (DEMiC) as part of the Digital Humanities Summer Institute (DHSI). The *Modernist Commons*, EMiC's online collaboratory, is built on CWRC infrastructure and provides access to archival and critical materials, as well as a space for users to work with their own resources using open-source tools. Although EMiC is no longer in active development, its site continues to function as an archive of Canadian literature and modernist literary cultures. In its time, it was a veritable hub for emerging DH researchers, supporting students across Canada in a uniquely decentralized fashion. Emily Robbins Sharpe and Bart Vautour's *Canada and the Spanish Civil War* (2025), Hannah McGregor's work on early prairie magazines, and Paul Barrett's digital reading of Austin Clarke's literary archive all began as EMiC projects.[3]

SpokenWeb

Founded in 2010, *SpokenWeb* is a literary-historical project that critically engages with Canadian literary sound recordings. Its team consists of nearly one hundred contributors from more than a dozen universities and partner institutions. *SpokenWeb* digitizes and archives audio recordings; it also employs these recordings for research and knowledge mobilization, including for *The SpokenWeb Podcast: Stories about How Literature Sounds* (as of 2024, there have been five seasons and more than fifty episodes). The *SpokenWeb Archive of the Digital Present* documents the research network's own activity, thus contributing back with a living archive of audio recordings that surface "marginalized voices that have not yet been amplified," while also "destabilizing the traditional gatekeeping of the archival process and expanding the collections" (McLeod 2023, 293). *SpokenWeb* replatforms by digitizing tapes that would otherwise be near-impossible for people to discover and access—let alone have the requisite technology to listen to.

SpokenWeb has a wealth of digitized Canadian literary materials. The archives include recordings of and readings of works by Earl Birney, Daphne Marlatt, bpNichol, Roy Miki, Eleanor Wachtel, Fred Wah, and Carolyn Zonailo, among others; they also have recordings of events such as the Sir George Williams Poetry Series (1965–1975) and the Flywheel Reading Series, and archives related to organizations such as the Women and Words Society and the BC Poets and Press. Although *SpokenWeb* does not have an explicitly named collaboratory, its website includes extensive toolkits in areas such as metadata, podcasting, and oral literary history protocols. These resources, plus the public engagement and the project's active invitations to contribute to both the archive and the community, make it a collaboratory in spirit.

CWRC, EMiC, and *SpokenWeb* all attract interested scholars and generate unique communities of practice. All three projects have trained many students in DH research methods and a number of those students, in turn, have developed their own research projects, further expanding the network of DH in Canada.

DH laboratories and centres

If collaboratories provide virtual spaces for DH's communities of practice, laboratories are their physical counterparts. Access to digital resources and virtual collaboration tools may have reduced the need for in-person work (undoubtedly hastened by the COVID-19 pandemic), yet people continue to seek spaces to work together—even when their work is purely digital. Digital humanities laboratories and centres are counted among these spaces. They are places that make visible digital work that can otherwise be difficult to see. If naming and digitizing are forms of legitimating, so too is the granting of physical space on campus. To give digital humanities a room of its own is an endorsement of its place in the academy.

In theory, contemporary digital humanities could function exclusively (or almost exclusively) online. In the early days of humanities computing, this was emphatically not the case since practitioners had to gather where they had access to mainframes and punch-card machines. Even though most students have laptops exponentially more powerful than the room-sized machines used by Father Busa or Sandra Djwa, the impulse to gather still exists—albeit now around large-scale visualization walls and touchscreen monitors instead of in computing centres or Quonset huts. As of 2025, fourteen Canadian universities have digital humanities centres or laboratories in libraries or elsewhere on campus (see Appendix I: digital humanities laboratories and centres at Canadian universities). The uses of these spaces range from collaborative workspaces, individual workstations, lecture halls, and seminar rooms to dedicated studios for activities such as media creation, virtual reality, and gaming. Many centres offer access to (expensive) specialist technologies such as high-performance workstations loaded with technical software, virtual reality (VR) and augmented reality (AR) equipment, 3D printers, multimedia and audiovisual equipment, and gaming devices.

The draw of digital humanities centres is not just the technologies on offer, but also the community support available. Students and scholars who work in DH can find themselves isolated within disciplinary silos, and digital work can be misunderstood or dismissed by those who employ traditional methodologies. In this context, digital humanities centres provide "interdisciplinary 'third places'—a term sociologist Ray Oldenburg has used to identify a social space, distinct from home and workplace. Third places[4] foster important ties and are critical to community life" (Friedlander quoted in Fraistat 2012). These third-place communities are fostered by dedicated staff and the expertise of faculty and librarian leadership.

To fulfil its interdisciplinary, collaborative potential, the DH lab must both welcome those who are new to the discipline and provide for those who are more established. It must function as a place for focused research—both independent and collaborative—but also as a classroom, a knowledge mobilization space such as a lecture hall, conference venue, or project showcase, and even function as a social space. This is a broad mandate:

> Digital humanities centres (or similar research groupings) tend to help build digital collections as scholarly or teaching resources; create tools for authoring, building digital collections, analysing collections, data or research processes and managing the research process; use digital collections and analytical tools to generate new intellectual products; offer digital humanities training, lectures, programs, conferences or seminars on digital humanities topics; have their own academic appointments and staffing; provide collegial support for, and collaboration with, members of other academic departments at the home institution or other academic departments, organizations or projects outside the home institution; conduct research in humanities and humanities computing (such as digital scholarship and publication); create a zone of experimentation and innovation for humanists; serve as an information portal for a particular humanities discipline; serve as a repository for humanities-based digital collections; and provide technology assistance and advice to humanities departments.
>
> *(Berry and Fagerjord 2017, 87)*

To be fair, the breadth of needs is not the exclusive purview of the DH centre, and most of the functions listed above do not actually require a dedicated space. Notwithstanding, when digital humanities stakes a claim to physical space in a university department or library to undertake these activities, the space serves as a marker of the field's concrete reality. At the same time, the expectations for what this reality will bring are clearly high. DH labs and centres are representatives, ambassadors, and advocates for the domain—they are expected to perform as "key sites for bridging the daunting gap between new technology and humanities scholars, serving as the crosswalks between cyberinfrastructure and users," both for better and for worse (Fraistat 2012).

The Canadian centres listed in the appendix have successfully lived up to the weight of these expectations, serving as DH's third places and as meeting spaces for its communities of practice. They organize knowledge mobilization opportunities, provide personalized research support, and offer graduate residencies, fellowships, and other affiliation opportunities. Many are the beneficiaries of institutional and government support for DH in the funding they have received for equipment and programs—and are therefore proof of the good this funding can generate. Many also act as bridges between institutions, by bringing people together for lectures, conferences, and perhaps most successfully, through education and training programs. Several Canadian DH centres run well-attended workshop series, summer schools, or other training programs: for example, the University of Ottawa hosts the Digital Humanities Summer Institute: Technology East (DHSITE), the University of Guelph hosts DH@Guelph, St. Francis Xavier University hosts the Digital Humanities Summer Institute–East, and until 2024, the University of Victoria hosted the DHSI, which has now relocated to Université de Montréal.

DHSI is the best-known and largest gathering of DH scholars not just in Canada but across North America. The first, proto-DHSI courses ran in 2001; in 2002, Ray Siemens and Stéfan Sinclair proposed a second, small group of summer workshops (on "New Media Literacy" and "Humanities Computing in Text Oriented Studies"). While the 2002 courses did not take place, the foundation was still laid for what would become DHSI. By the 2010s, "DHSI began attracting wider and larger participant groups …. Around this same time, the conception of digital humanities as a community of practice emerged, defined in large part by the concept of the *methodological commons*" (Siemens, Arbuckle, and El Khatib 2023, 13, original emphasis)—a term used to refer to the "detailed series of convergence points between many disciplinary groups and ways/clouds of knowing, meeting in and among those things central to the practices of our community" (Siemens 2015). DHSI is a community of practice united by shared methodological approaches and an emerging concern with the social and political implications of DH work. These values are reflected in courses that range from "Race, Social Justice and DH" to "Podcasting"; from "Project Management" to "Databases"; from "Natural Language Processing with Python" to "Surveillance and Critical DH"; from "Linked Open Data and the Semantic Web" to "Deep Learning for Humanists."

In 2023, DH centres and organizations joined forces to offer the Canadian Certificate in Digital Humanities (cc:DH/HN) as a way of recognizing participation in DH's community of practice by providing accreditation for participants of co- and non-curricular DH training. Through certification, the cc:DH/HN formalizes the Canadian digital humanities community of practice, trains the next generation of digital archivists, scholars, and teachers, and paves the way for Canada's continued—and, to quote McCarty, *outsized*—presence in the digital humanities. Like the DH labs that formalize the space for digital humanities within the university, the cc:DH/HN concretizes non-curricular digital humanities learning. The certificate is supported by federal funding (SSHRC), federal research infrastructure (DRAC), and the research community (CSDH/SCHN). To some extent, it formalizes the Canadian DH community of practice via learning opportunities from twenty partner organizations. The cc:DH/HN certificate demonstrates the importance of emerging forms of infrastructure and certification for a new generation of digital humanities scholars. Taken together, the labs, archives, and training opportunities discussed in this chapter signal the increasing formalization and professionalization of digital humanities from a small but mighty group of humanities computing enthusiasts (discussed in Chapter 3) to a stable field with institutional supports, physical hubs of research, and documented and evolving methodologies. In the next chapter, we will see how these institutions and methods have played a role in reshaping ideas of Canadian literature in digital contexts.

Notes

1 With respect to benefits, excellent work has been done on DH's opportunities to and successes in centring the margins. Since much of this work does not engage specifically with Canadian Literature, it is unfortunately beyond the scope of this book. For readers who would like to learn more, see Anne B. McGrail, Angel David Nieves, and Siobhan Senier, eds, *People, Practice, Power: Digital Humanities outside the Center* (Minneapolis: University of Minnesota Press, 2021), and Roopika Risam and Kelly Baker Josephs, eds, *The Digital Black Atlantic* (Minneapolis: University of Minnesota Press, 2021). With respect to risks, see for example, Tara Robertson's "Digitization: Just Because You Can, Doesn't Mean You Should" (2016), where she lays out the problems with digital replatforming in a critique of the unauthorized digitization of *On Our Backs*, a lesbian pornographic magazine.
2 By *deep infrastructure*, Wershler is referring to the "society-wide set of systematic supports ... that will be capable of moving our cultural records into the future *and* managing collective anxieties about this process" in contrast to the current infrastructure, which is "largely relational, emerging out of communities of practice, ... and is mostly invisible until it breaks down at a crucial moment" (2019, 354–55).
3 EMiC criteria for selecting projects and authors focused on canonical authors whose works are out of print, formerly canonical authors whose work is inaccessible, non-canonical authors whose work is unpublished or uncollected, or marginalized or minoritized writers whose work "has not yet been widely recognized as part of modernist literary cultures" (EMiC). The goal of the project was to expand the parameters of modernist literature in several ways.
4 Oldenburg's *third place* refers to spaces that are neither first (home) nor second (work), such as libraries, recreation facilities, religious institutions, and community centres. *Third places* are sites of community and civic engagement. The concept of the *third place* has some similarities to, but predates and is not to be confused with, Homi Bhabha's *third space*, which exists between the oppressor and the subaltern.

Further reading

Camlot, Jason, and Katherine McLeod, eds. 2019. *CanLit Across Media: Unarchiving the Literary Event*. Montréal and Kingston: McGill-Queen's University Press. https://doi.org/10.1515/9780773559813.

Fraistat, Neil. 2012. "The Function of Digital Humanities Centers at the Present Time." In *Debates in the Digital Humanities*, edited by Matthew K. Gold, 281–91. Minneapolis: University of Minnesota Press. https://doi.org/10.5749/minnesota/9780816677948.003.0028.

Pawlicka-Deger, Urszula. 2021. "Laboratory: A New Space in Digital Humanities." In *People, Practice, Power: Digital Humanities Outside the Center*, edited by Anne B. McGrail, Angel David Nieves, and Siobhan Senier. Minneapolis: University of Minnesota Press. https://doi.org/10.5749/9781452968346.

Siemens, Ray. 2015. "Communities of Practise, the Methodological Commons, and Digital Self-Determination in the Humanities." Special issue, *Digital Studies / Le champ numérique* 5, no. 3. https://www.digitalstudies.org/article/id/7291/.

Works cited

Berry, David M., and Anders Fagerjord. 2017. *Digital Humanities: Knowledge and Critique in a Digital Age*. Cambridge: Polity Press.

Brown, Susan. Forthcoming. "Replatforming." In *Critical Infrastructure Studies in Digital Humanities*, edited by Alan Liu, Urszula Pawlicka-Deger, and James Smithies. Minneapolis: University of Minnesota Press.

Brown, Susan, and Cecily Devereaux. 2017. "Introduction: Digital Textualities/Canadian Contexts." *Studies in Canadian Literature / Études en littérature canadienne* 42, no. 2: 145–53. https://id.erudit.org/iderudit/scl42_2art07.

Brown, Susan, Erin Canning, Kim Martin, and Sarah Roger. 2023. "Ethical Considerations in the Development of Responsible Linked Open Data Infrastructure." In *Ethics in Linked Data*, edited by B. M. Watson, Alexandra Provo, and Kathleen Burlingame, 297–324. Sacramento: Library Juice Press.

Camlot, Jason, and Katherine McLeod, eds. 2019. *CanLit Across Media: Unarchiving the Literary Event*. Montréal and Kingston: McGill-Queen's University Press. https://doi.org/10.1515/9780773559813.

Caswell, Michelle, Ricardo Punzalan, and T-Kay Sangwand. 2017. "Critical Archival Studies: An Introduction." Special issue, *Journal of Critical Library and Information Studies* 1, no. 2: 8 pp. https://doi.org/10.24242/jclis.v1i2.50.

Caufield, Catherine. n.d. *Canadian Jewish Women Writers*. Collaboratory for Writing and Research on Culture. Accessed October 10, 2024. https://cwrc.ca/project/canadian-jewish-women-writers.

cc:DH/HN. n.d. *The Canadian Certificate in Digital Humanities / Certificat canadien en Humanités Numériques*. Accessed July 12, 2024. https://ccdhhn.ca/.

Cowan, T. L. 2018. "'Run with Whatever You Can Carry': Cross-Platform Materials and Methods in Performance Studies–Meets–Digital Humanities." *American Quarterly* 70, no. 3 (September): 649–55. https://doi.org/10.1353/aq.2018.0048.

CRKN. 2024. *Canadiana*. Canadian Research Knowledge Network. Accessed June 5, 2024. https://www.canadiana.ca.

CWRC. n.d. *Collaboratory for Writing and Research on Culture*. Accessed July 12, 2024. https://cwrc.ca/.

Demers, Patricia. n.d. *Women's Writing and Reading in Canada from 1950*. Collaboratory for Writing and Research on Culture. Accessed October 10, 2024. https://cwrc.ca/canwwrfrom1950.

DHSI. n.d. *Digital Humanities Summer Institute*. Accessed October 15, 2024. https://dhsi.org/.

The Digital Humanities Manifesto 2.0. 2009. https://jeffreyschnapp.com/wp-content/uploads/2011/10/Manifesto_V2.pdf.

Djwa, Sandra, and Zailig Pollock. n.d. *The Digital Page: The Collected Works of P. K. Page*. Collaboratory for Writing and Research on Culture. Accessed October 10, 2024. https://cwrc.ca/project/digitalpage.

Dynamic Table of Contexts. n.d. Accessed October 15, 2024. https://dtoc.leaf-vre.org/.

EMiC. n.d. *Editing Modernism in Canada*. Accessed July 12, 2024. https://editingmodernism.ca/.

Fragaszy Troyano, Joan, and Lisa M. Rhody. 2013. "Expanding Communities of Practice," *Journal of Digital Humanities* 2, no. 2. https://journalofdigitalhumanities.org/2-2/expanding-communities-of-practice/.

Fraistat, Neil. 2012. "The Function of Digital Humanities Centers at the Present Time." In *Debates in the Digital Humanities*, edited by Matthew K. Gold, 281–91. Minneapolis: University of Minnesota Press. https://doi.org/10.5749/minnesota/9780816677948.003.0028.

Gardiner, Eileen, and Ronald G. Musto. 2015. *The Digital Humanities: A Primer for Students and Scholars*. Cambridge: Cambridge University Press. https://doi.org/10.1017/CBO9781139003865.

Gerson, Carole. n.d. *Canada's Early Women Writers Project*, 2018–2024. Collaboratory for Writing and Research on Culture. Accessed October 10, 2024. https://cwrc.ca/project/canadas-early-women-writers.

Green, Harriett E. 2014. "Facilitating Communities of Practice in Digital Humanities: Librarian Collaborations for Research and Training in Text Encoding," *The Library Quarterly* 84, no. 2: 219–34. https://doi.org/10.1086/675332.

Irvine, Dean J., and Smaro Kamboureli. 2016. *Editing as Cultural Practice in Canada*. Waterloo: Wilfrid Laurier University Press. https://doi.org/10.51644/9781771120937.

Linked Editing Academic Framework. n.d. *Dynamic Table of Contexts*. Accessed October 15, 2024. https://dtoc.leaf-vre.org/.

McGrail, Anne B., Angel David Nieves, and Siobhan Senier, eds. 2021. *People, Practice, Power: Digital Humanities Outside the Centre*. Minneapolis: University of Minnesota Press. https://dhdebates.gc.cuny.edu/projects/people-practice-power.

McLeod, Katherine. 2023. "Sounding Digital Humanities." In *Future Horizons: Canadian Digital Humanities*, edited by Paul Barrett and Sarah Roger, 291–313. Ottawa: University of Ottawa Press. https://doi.org/10.2307/jj.17681834.22.

Morra, Linda. 2019. "CBC Radio's Digital Archives and the Production of Canadian Citizenship and Culture." In *CanLit Across Media: Unarchiving the Literary Event*, edited by Jason Camlot and Katherine McLeod, 35–53. Montréal and Kingston: McGill-Queen's University Press. https://doi.org/10.1515/9780773559813-004.

Palmer, Carole L. 2004. "Thematic Research Collections." In *A Companion to Digital Humanities*, edited by Susan Schreibman, Ray Siemens, and John Unsworth, 384–65. Oxford: Blackwell. https://doi.org/10.1002/9780470999875.

Price, Kenneth M. 2009. "Edition, Project, Database, Archive, Thematic Research Collection: What's in a Name?" *Digital Humanities Quarterly* 3, no. 3. https://www.digitalhumanities.org/dhq/vol/3/3/000053/000053.html.

Risam, Roopika, and Kelly Baker Josephs, eds. 2021. *The Digital Black Atlantic*. Minneapolis: University of Minnesota Press. https://doi.org/10.5749/j.ctv1kchp41.

Robertson, Tara. 2016. "Digitization: Just Because You Can, Doesn't Mean You Should." *Tara Robertson Consulting* (blog), March 21, 2016. https://tararobertson.ca/2016/oob/.

Rockwell, Geoffrey, Matt Huculak, Emmanuel Château-Dutier, Barbara Bordalejo, Kyle Dase, Laura Estill, Julia Polyck-O'Neill, and Harvey Quamen. 2022. "Canada's Future DRI Ecosystem for Humanities & Social Sciences (HSS)." *Digital Research Alliance of Canada*. https://alliancecan.ca/sites/default/files/2022-03/csdh_ndrio_whitepaper.pdf.

Sanders Garcia, Ashley, Lydia Bello, Madelynn Dickerson, and Margaret Hogarth. 2021. "Building a DIY Community of Practice." In *People, Practice, Power: Digital Humanities Outside the Center*, edited by Anne B. McGrail, Angel David Nieves, and Siobhan Senier, 202–22. Minneapolis: University of Minnesota Press. https://dhdebates.gc.cuny.edu/projects/people-practice-power.

Schreibman, Susan, Ray Siemens, and John Unsworth. 2004. "The Digital Humanities and Humanities Computing: An Introduction." In *A Companion to Digital Humanities*, edited by Susan Schreibman, Ray Siemens, and John Unsworth, xxiii–xxvii. Oxford: Blackwell. https://doi.org/10.1002/9780470999875.

Siemens, Ray. 2015. "Communities of Practise, the Methodological Commons, and Digital Self-Determination in the Humanities." Special issue, *Digital Studies / Le champ numérique* 5, no. 3. https://www.digitalstudies.org/article/id/7291/.

Siemens, Ray, Alyssa Arbuckle, and Randa El Khatib. 2023. "The Digital Humanities Summer Institute (DHSI): Community Training Toward Open Social Scholarship." In *Digital Humanities Workshops: Lessons Learned*, edited by Laura Estill and Jennifer Guiliano, 11–23. Abingdon: Routledge. https://doi.org/10.4324/9781003301097-3.

SpokenWeb. 2024. *SpokenWeb*. https://spokenweb.ca/.

TFRBL. 2024. "Manuscript Collection—Margaret Atwood." University of Toronto. Thomas Fisher Rare Book Library. Accessed July 12, 2024. https://discoverarchives.library.utoronto.ca/index.php/margaret-atwood-papers.

Vautour, Bart, and Emily Robins Sharpe, eds. 2025. *Canada and the Spanish Civil War: An Anthology*. Ottawa: University of Ottawa Press.

Wenger-Trayner, Etienne, and Beverly Wenger-Trayner. 2015. "Introduction to Communities of Practice: A Brief Overview of the Concept and Its Uses." June 2015. https://www.wenger-trayner.com/introduction-to-communities-of-practice.

Wershler, Darren. 2019. "The Archive in Motion." In *CanLit Across Media: Unarchiving the Literary Event*, edited by Jason Camlot, and Katherine McLeod, 346–61. Montréal and Kingston: McGill-Queen's University Press. https://doi.org/10.1515/9780773559813-019.

Wilson, Ann, and Dorothy Hadfield. n.d. *Canadian Women Playwrights Online*. Collaboratory for Writing and Research on Culture. https://cwrc.ca/cwpo.

PART III

6
CANADIAN LITERARY CRITICISM AND THE DIGITAL SPHERE

* * *

Canadian novelist Lynn Coady begins her *Who Needs Books? Reading in the Digital Age* (2016) by describing her love of Sesame Street's *The Monster at the End of This Book*. The book consists of Grover repeatedly warning the reader about a monster at the end of the text, a monster that turns out to be Grover himself. Coady uses Grover's parable—we are the monster that we all fear—as an analogy for the monster of the digital feared by authors and readers alike. She summarizes the collective hand-wringing over the state of literature and literacy by noting, "we live in an age where a great many not-young men ... are looking around and making the same complaint" (18), which is that technology has diluted culture and that literature has lost its value. For Coady, the bogeyman of the digital and the anxieties over the transformation of culture are not new. She reminds those not-young men of another not-young man who complained about a new technology upending the social order, lamenting that this new "discovery will create forgetfulness in learners' souls, because they will not use their memories ... they will be hearers of many things and will have learned nothing" (16). The man? Socrates. The technology? writing.[1]

Coady's lecture was given as part of the prestigious Kreisel Lecture series at the University of Alberta's Canadian Literature Centre. Coady is part of a growing number of Canadian authors who are thinking about the relationship between digital technology and literature and how new technologies expand the possibilities for reading and writing. Indeed, Canadian writers have made major contributions to theorizing the relationship

DOI: 10.4324/9781003318323-10

between digital technology and Canadian literature and the ways in which technology changes society. Whereas the previous chapters traced the institutional forces and spaces that shape CanLit and DH, this chapter fills in the relations between Canadian writing, Canadian literary criticism, and digital technology and culture. In what follows, we examine Canadian engagements with theories of DH, digital projects that apply that theory to Canadian literature, and creative experiments that locate DH praxis at the heart of creative work.

Sea change of the digital

In "Survival: Canadian Cultural Scholarship in a Digital Age" (2017), an essay that signals its intentions to wade into the CanLit debate with its Atwood-echoing title, Susan Brown maps the connection between Canadian literary scholarship and digital humanities. She explains,

> Globally, literary scholars are in the midst of a sea change in which culture, publishing, and scholarship are being reshaped in ways that will have massive impacts on how they do their work … Yet to date few Canadianist literary scholars have found their working methods substantially reshaped by this change.
>
> *(2017, 171)*

These comments have their echo in the writing of Edward L. Ayers, for whom

> The articles and books that scholars produce today bear little mark of the digital age in which they are created. Researchers routinely use electronic tools in their professional lives but not to transform the substance or form of their scholarship.
>
> *(2013)*

Brown's aim is to "elucidate the relevance of that elusive field called the 'digital humanities' to the landscape of literary study in Canada" (171), which she does by drawing on her experiences with Canadian DH. In particular, she argues that Canadian scholars have inadequately worked with, and worked to shape, the institutions that will determine future research priorities. She notes that

> The recommendations of a SSHRC-funded Knowledge Synthesis report (Bretz, Brown, and McGregor 2010) on sustaining culture and scholarship note that every major innovation in communications technology

in Canada has prompted a national commission—until now, in the face of the largest shift in modes of communication since the invention of movable type.

(174)

Canadian funding bodies (see Chapter 4) and scholars alike have been slow to respond to this sea change.

Despite the successes we note in the previous chapter and in the projects we describe throughout this book, Brown is still right to say, "Digital texts have proliferated in Canadian lives but sadly not enough in Canadian archives" and "the vast majority of Canada's cultural heritage in print and other paper-based forms awaits transfer into current information formats" (175). There are, of course, many who take seriously the cause of thinking critically about technology. For instance, Maria DiCenzo, writing two years before Brown, reflects on "recent developments and debates in periodical research," and identifies a "divide between the pre- and postdigital worlds ... related to the formation of academic fields and the impact of the large-scale digitization of newspapers, periodicals, and magazines" (2015, 19–20). Similarly, Rosemary Coombe, Darren Wershler, and Martin Zeilinger's *Dynamic Fair Dealing: Creating Canadian Culture Online* (2014) shares Brown's concerns about the effect of digital technology on Canadian cultural production and research. Yet there are others who resist, indifferent to change and likely to persevere with traditional forms of teaching and writing.

Brown cites Atwood's *Survival* (1972) in her argument that

> The survival of Canadian and Quebec writers, of publishers, and of writing seems to be at least as pressing now, as publishing models are being radically disrupted by the advent of digital media, as it did in 1972 in the heyday of cultural nationalism.
>
> *(173)*

As such, Brown contends

> that literary and cultural scholars can and should step up through activism, collaboration, and participation in the reshaping of our discipline and our culture by digital tools in the service of a nationalism committed to an inclusive Canadian cultural record.
>
> *(174)*

This is a call for an inclusive Canadian cultural nationalism attuned to the realities of the digital world—one where digital preservation and access to digital versions of texts are necessary for cultural criticism. As Brown observes, the digital age has had nothing equivalent to the Massey Commission that aims to understand the shifting format of Canadian cultural production. The institutional supports outlined in Chapter 4 have been patchwork and ad hoc and, as a result, the digitization of Canadian cultural material, and the preservation of that material, is haphazard. Frank Davey and Fred Wah's *SwiftCurrent* (1983–1986) "has effectively evaporated" (Schmaltz and Spinosa 2022, 2). The sites for Sachiko Murakami's web-based poetry projects *Figure* (2014) and *Henko* (2012) return only error messages. DH projects such as *The Hypertext Pratt* and *Text Analysis Computing Tools* (TACT) have been lost to time.

Canadian critical interventions

There have been a number of key moments in the history of Canadian literature where critics have endeavoured to theorize the digitization of Canadian culture or to grapple with the sea change of the digital. One such early moment was Northrop Frye's 1989 keynote address[2] at the joint conference for the Association for Computing in the Humanities and the Association for Literary and Linguistic Computing at the University of Toronto. Reflecting on his use of scientific metaphors in the introduction to *Anatomy of Criticism* (1957), Frye notes that such conceptions as "'software programming' and 'computer modelling' were as yet unknown, and if I were writing such an introduction today I should probably pay a good deal of attention to them and talk less about science" (1989, 455). He goes on to generously applaud the use of computation to assist in humanist endeavours while also noting that "the Luddite thesis" (a version of the arguments presented by DH skeptics such as Stephen Marche, Stanley Fish, and Nan Z. Da, to which we turn in Chapter 7) misses "the fact that the most seminal mechanical inventions ever devised—the alphabet, the printing press, and the book—have been in humanist hands for centuries" (457). Frye, perhaps, had read *The Monster at the End of This Book*, published eighteen years prior. He himself does not fear the monster, continuing, "The humanist's preoccupation with the past is concerned with reconstructing that past … The computer can add a fantastic amount of detail to that reconstruction" (458).[3]

These comments demonstrate the views of perhaps the single most influential critic in Canadian literature on the relation between the computational and the humanities, as well as his thoughts on the increased instrumentalism of the university more generally. Frye was an avowed humanist and—given that his later criticism eschewed technological triumphalism and asserted the import of a telos between classical ideas of the humanities and the contemporary university—it is striking that he did not retreat into a very traditional notion of literary interpretation and humanities work. Instead, Frye offers a relatively measured assessment of the possible values and challenges of humanities computing. There is, arguably, something of a budding digital humanist in much of Frye's scholarship, particularly in his desire to understand the structures and systems that animate the imagination and create meaning. *Fearful Symmetry* would make an excellent title for a book on AI.

Frye's willingness to speak to the possibilities of computation might seem at odds with his particular brand of Christian humanism until one recognizes that his literary imagination was shaped by questions of the relationship between technological development, social transformation, and the search for meaning.[4] This intellectual vision was certainly influenced by E. J. Pratt, one of Frye's mentors, whose poetry is filled with images of technology as harbingers of a Janus-faced modernity: the Titanic, the railway, the corporation. This is evident, for example, in Pratt's 1932 poem, "The Man and the Machine," which begins, "By right of fires that smelted ore / Which he had tended years before, / The man whose hands were on the wheel / Could trace his kinship through her steel" (2000, lines 1–4). For Pratt, the relationship between man and machine is both ambivalent and worrying: the "right of fires," in contrast to rites of fire, are equal parts Promethean and hellish. Pratt's work is concerned with the ways in which teleological notions of history produce, and are produced by, new technologies and the manners in which those technologies in turn reconfigure our understanding of community. Frank Davey's "E. J. Pratt: Apostle of Corporate Man" intuits Pratt's attention to the emerging networks of technology and power that would reshape Canadian culture and society. Davey writes that Pratt "makes the network of interaction and interdependency absolutely clear" (60) and that Pratt is "fascinated by power" (Davey 1970, 56). "The Man and the Machine" concludes, "This creature with the panther grace, / This man with slag upon his face" (lines 15–16). Pratt, *à la* Grover, recognizes that in the end the monster is us.

Pratt may have been an early explorer of the transformation of humanity and humans by technology, but the concern with technology, computation, and social change has been a common thread throughout Canadian poetry and literature. Indeed, it is striking just how many Canadian public intellectuals and philosophers are concerned with technology's effects on society. While the 1960s were a key moment in the establishment of Canadian literature (see Chapter 3), the decade was also instrumental in the production of uniquely Canadian reflections on technology and society. Marshall McLuhan and his oracular aphorisms obviously loom large in this context but the work of George Grant is also illuminating. Grant's

Technology & Empire (1969) was published between the *Literary History of Canada* (1965) and Atwood's *Survival* (1972). Atwood's quotation from Grant's work indicates that the debates about technological culture and Canadian literature were intermixed. Grant was a great defender of what he perceived as the humanist tradition, and in *Technology & Empire* and *Lament for a Nation* (1965) he expresses his distress at the erosion of communal and national identity in the face of technological change and American cultural and military imperialism. For Grant, technology represents a great levelling force because the speed and power of communication blend distinct societies into a homogeneous, global culture shaped by the metropolitan centres of power and capital.

Grant's worries about nationhood and Canadian culture became common parlance in Canadian literary circles, finding expression in Atwood's work and other writing from the time, such as Dennis Lee's *Civil Elegies* (1972). Grant wrote, for instance,

> We live then in the most realised technological society which has yet been; one which is, moreover, the chief imperial centre from which technique is spread around the world … the need might seem to press upon us to try to know where we are in this new found land which is so obviously a "terra incognita."
>
> *(1969, 40)*

Some three years later, Atwood adapted this language of newly discovered territory: "Our literature is one such map … We need such a map desperately" (1972, 19). The poets and critics of the 1960s and '70s believed that Canada's position on the peripheries of both British and American empires provided it with a unique perspective on the ways that global communication and emerging forces of capitalism were affecting national and international cultures. (Recognition of Canada's own implication in the power structures of empire was somewhat lacking at the time.) Throughout this period, theorists of technological culture and Canadian literature were at work developing a shared map and vocabulary for the changes to Canadian society and culture.

Early Canadian literatary-digital scholarship

The shared mapping of the space of the nation and the technologies that shape it have also been a constant concern for Canadian literature. The 1955 Canadian Writers' Conference at Queen's University, for instance, included a lengthy talk from CBC producer Robert Weaver on how mass media was transforming the relationship between Canadian writers and the public. William Gibson's *Neuromancer* (1984), perhaps viewed as outside the realm of (at least traditional) Canadian literature, is the ur-text of the cyberpunk genre and responsible for many modern conceptions of networked computing, the Internet, hacker culture, malevolent AI, and the term *cyberspace*. Hugh MacLennan's final novel, *Voices in Time* (1980), depicts a dystopian future in which a sprawling and authoritarian series of bureaucracies—armed with technological and computational power—lead humankind into an increasingly automated existence that ends in apocalypse. More recently, Caitlin Fisher's experiments led to the creation of the hypertext novella and soundscape, *These Waves of Girls* (2001), and to augmented reality (AR) poems and narratives such as *Andromeda* (2008) and *200 Castles* (2009). Fisher's Augmented Reality Lab at York University brings together scholars and students interested in AR, electronic literature, and digital poetry. One could equally conceive of Canisia Lubrin's poetic reimagining of the Mars rover in *Voodoo Hypothesis* (2017) or Liz Howard's exploration of the outer space of the galaxy and the inner space of MRI scanning in *Letters in a Bruised Cosmos* (2021) as subtle engagements with technology's effects on subjectivity. These are but a small selection of how Canadian literature has engaged in critical discussions of the relationship between technology and literature, literature that addresses technological change, and literature that is created using novel experiments with technology.

There are also numerous examples of creative and critical projects that bring together the digital and the humanities in new ways. Paul Hjartarson and Harvey Quamen, for instance, have written about Sheila and Wilfrid Watson's "decade-long dialogue with Marshall McLuhan" (2016, 122) throughout the 1960s that would produce a collaborative play, *From Cliché to Archetype* (1970). Sheila Watson's PhD dissertation on Wyndham Lewis was supervised by McLuhan and there is no doubt that McLuhan's influence is felt throughout her *The Double Hook* (1959). Hjartarson and Quamen observe, "all three writers sought to understand how new media—photography, film, radio, television, and computing—were not only remediating established art forms but also altering day-to-day life" (122).

The Hypertext Pratt

Developed throughout the mid-1990s, Elizabeth Popham and Zailig Pollock's *The Hypertext Pratt* was intended as a digital companion to Pratt's selected poems and letters, acting as a prototype of both a digital edition and a networked approach to understanding Pratt's literary and social worlds. While *The Hypertext Pratt* is, by today's standards, a rudimentary digital archive, it represents an early contribution to digital humanities work in Canadian literature:

> The hypertext Pratt edition was HTML-based, but while we were working on it, it became clear that the future of digital editing was not going to be in HTML. HTML (Hypertext Markup Language) is a presentation-oriented subset of XML (Extensible Markup Language) that focuses on how your text appears on the Web. But XML allows structural and semantic markup as well; it uses stylesheets to transform this structural and semantic information.
>
> *(Pollock 2016, 97–98)*

As the project developed, Pollock discovered the limits of his approach, soon realizing that "all of the encoding I had done was now obsolete" (98). He felt, quite acutely, the painful experience of "what it means to be on the bleeding edge of technological development" (98). In the early days of the Internet, as now, a multi-year project might need to pivot to new technologies in mid-development. Pollock's efforts to develop a bespoke project somewhat independent of Text Encoding Initiative (TEI) standards (see Chapter 13) resulted in several false starts. Reflecting on the project years later, the challenge Pollock faced trying to keep up with shifting technologies is clear:

> For years, I looked back on my sample edition of Pratt as the great failure of my career, the one instance in which I did not complete a job I undertook and did not give SSHRC value for their money. However, in retrospect—and in light of John Unsworth's argument that "if an electronic scholarly project can't fail and doesn't produce new ignorance, then it isn't worth a damn" (n.pag.)—I now look back on it differently—as a prototype that helped me develop a conceptual model for a digital edition that is still valid and useful for me in the work I have continued to pursue. As Galey and Ruecker put it, prototypes "are also theories."
>
> *(98)*

Pollock's supposed failure with *The Hypertext Pratt* will be familiar to any DH practitioner who has worked on a project from the ground up, and his reference to Unsworth's defence of the value of failure is a lesson every aspiring DH researcher must learn. Yet for Pollock, this failure provided a prototype for the eventual success of a subsequent project, *The Digital Page*.

The Digital Page

Developed in the early 2000s, *The Digital Page: The Collected Works of P. K. Page* is, as the project's name suggests, an online repository of P. K. Page's work—the result of a collaboration between Djwa (her first return to the digital humanities since her work on the concordance of Canadian poetry in the 1960s), Pollock, Dean Irvine, Emily Ballantyne, and Page herself. *The Digital Page* navigated a number of technologies for digital editions, including TEI, XSLT (Extensible Stylesheet Language Transformation), and a bespoke interface for working with critical editions. Reflecting on the project years later, Ballantyne and Pollock noted a mirror of their project in the words of Del Jordan, the protagonist of Alice Munro's *Lives of Girls and Women* (1971). Del recalls,

> I would try to make lists. A list of all the stores and businesses going up and down the main street and who owned them, a list of family names on the tombstones in the Cemetery … The hope of accuracy we bring to such tasks is crazy, heartbreaking.
>
> *(1971, 210)*

Del's desire to document, list, and capture the reality of her childhood is, in essence, a model for a humanistic approach to data. In referencing Del's "hope of accuracy," Ballantyne and Pollock gesture on one hand to the impossibility of the completeness of such projects, and on the other hand to the recognition that digital projects are, in part, creative-critical reinterpretations of the original material.

As with *Orlando* (see Chapter 3), *The Digital Page* came out of Pollock's frustration with the limitations of a print edition of Page's *Collected Works* and the accompanying realization that a digital version could accomplish what a print book could not. Page herself, upon learning of the move from print to digital, felt as if, "some kind of miracle has occurred" (Pollock 2016, 101). Ballantyne and Pollock were less enthusiastic, describing it as an unwieldy, "many-headed monster" (2011, 184)—a sentiment that predicts Coady's muppet-metaphored assessment and one which is familiar to many DH scholars.

Both *The Hypertext Pratt* and *The Digital Page* took place at a time when the field of Canadian literature was shifting towards newer writers and university press budgets could not support multi-volume, single-subject publications. It is telling that they focused on Pratt and Page—two writers whose central positions in Canadian literature were no longer assured. By virtue of their supposed minimal financial cost and their anticipated appeal to a wide readership, *The Hypertext Pratt* and *The Digital Page* assert the importance of writers who might otherwise be increasingly overlooked. They offered models of prototyping, iterative design, and collaborative scholarship that went on to inform the next generation of DH scholars and projects.

This process of iteration is especially evident in projects that combine literary scholarship and digital publishing. For example, Dean Irvine's involvement with *The Digital Page* aligned well with his development of *Editing Modernism in Canada* (EMiC), and Graham Jensen's involvement with EMiC subsequently informed his own *Canadian Modernist Magazines Project* (CMMP). Where *The Digital Page* digitizes Page's holograph manuscripts alongside electronic transcriptions, EMiC's *Modernist Commons* has a digital repository of modernist writings alongside a workspace for transcribing, annotating, and collating materials. CMMP extends beyond digitizing and transcribing; in addition to PDF and full-text versions (and forthcoming TEI editions) of the little-known modernist periodicals, CMMP also provides extensive, contextualizing metadata, critical introductions, bibliographies, and teaching materials, thus not just reproducing a corpus (like *The Digital Page*) or providing a space to work with it (like EMiC), but rather expanding the corpus by locating it within theoretical and historical frameworks. There is a direct line of influence and mentorship from *The Digital Page* to EMIC to CMMP, and the shift from the canon to the margins in the subject matter is representative of parallel changes in the field of CanLit.

Contemporary Canadian literary-digital projects

These lines of influence have continued to expand in recent years, leading to the proliferation of innovative digital humanities projects focused on Canadian literature. In what follows we offer a brief overview of two smaller, newer projects (*AMM Bibliography* and *Distant Reading Mennonite Writing*) and two longer-running, larger projects (*Fred Wah Digital Archive* and *The People and the Text*), focusing on both their evolution, affordances and outputs.

AMM Bibliography

Neta Gordon's *AMM Bibliography* records bibliographic and other details related to Ann-Marie MacDonald's writing. Gordon worked in tandem with Brock's Department of Digital Humanities to develop the bibliography and its accompanying digital map of locations that appear in MacDonald's works. The project has evolved from a record of the scholarship relevant to MacDonald's writing to a more complex tracing of the experience of reading her work and an affective mapping of her writing. As Gordon's project has grown, it has come to encompass distant reading, digital collaboration, and data creation (discussed further in Chapter 7).

Distant Reading Mennonite Writing

The *Distant Reading Mennonite Writing* (DRMW) project, led by Robert Zacharias and hosted at the Centre for Transnational Mennonite Studies at the University of Winnipeg, has developed a series of methods for distant reading of Mennonite literature while also creating two datasets relevant to Mennonite studies. Launched in 2020, the project collects records of Mennonite literature and related criticism; its datasets are available via the *Borealis* data repository. In addition to making the data available to researchers, the project also includes extensively documented data models that express the project methodology. The project is dual-focused, in that it serves not only scholars who are seeking materials on Mennonite literature but also opens an otherwise little-known field to both members of Mennonite communities and the broader public.

Fred Wah Digital Archive

The *Fred Wah Digital Archive* is both a bibliography and a repository of Wah's works. It is a longstanding project, which began as a collaboration between Susan Rudy and Wah in 2010, was part of Darren Wershler and Bill Kennedy's now-retired *Artmob* open-source management system, and has since been taken on by Ryan Fitzpatrick and Deanna Fong. Fitzpatrick and Fong bring their expertise in conceptual poetics to read Wah's archives and to reflect on the creative possibilities of digital forms of archiving. Their project attends to the difficulty of archiving Wah's diverse and scattered poetic oeuvre while also thinking about how "the sociality of Wah's poetics have shaped our simultaneous reflections on our own shared labour on his archive" (2023, 256). Fong and Fitzpatrick grapple with the complexity of Wah's archive and his uncomfortable relation to canonical visions of Canadian literature while also reflecting on the labour practices required in the development of such digital archives. Their attention to the difficulties of precariously employed researchers to sustain digital projects nuances Pollock's concerns about impermanence and failure as well as Brown's analysis of the change in scholarly research.

The People and the Text

Deanna Reder (Cree-Métis), Madeleine Reddon (Métis), Alix Shield, Margery Fee, and Susan Glover's *The People and the Text: Indigenous Writing in Lands Claimed by Canada* (*TPatT*) enlists digital archiving practices to argue for the centrality of Indigenous literature in Canada. Their project draws on oral traditions, written texts, multiple forms of autobiography, and interviews to assert Indigenous peoples' literary traditions. The project leads have "brought scholarly attention to understudied or forgotten works; ... prioritized Indigenous literary research methods; ... built a sustainable open-access bibliography of Indigenous texts; ... [and] advocated for systemic change in collection systems and the Indigenization of pedagogical approaches" (Reder et al., n.d.). Like CMMP, TPatT does not limit itself to making resources available (which it does using CWRC infrastructure); it also locates them within their critical and cultural context via edited editions and scholarly texts. For example, Shield's "Rethinking the Paratext: Digital Story-Mapping E. Pauline Johnson's and Chief Joe & Mary Capilano's *Legends of Vancouver*" (2018) demonstrates how DH methods, including "web-based 'story-mapping' and GIS technologies—can inform our ways of rereading twentieth-century Indigenous literature."

Digital poetics, creative praxis

In addition to these explicitly scholarly projects, Canadian poets employ digital technology to reimagine and rewrite literature itself and thereby expand the field of digital humanities. Many of the scholars involved in newer DH projects do not see a contradiction between Canadian literary studies and digital humanities but, rather, bring the digital and the humanities into relation with one another in acts of creative play: for example, electronic literature, digitally inflected poetry, and hypertext. These practitioners put the digital and the humanities into a careful dialogue with questions of power, aesthetics, form, and the archive within Canadian literary studies. Kyle Flemmer's "Cyborg Reading: Transmedial Digital Poetry and the Cyborg Milieu" is exemplary in this regard, opening with his description of a revelatory experience of physically holding "my first poem in 2018 at the Digital Humanities Summer Institute (DHSI) conference in Victoria, BC, a 3D-printed poem by Aaron Tucker, Jordan Scott, and others" (2022, 1). Flemmer's project is demonstrative of the sort of critical and creative work that draws on conceptual poetics to blur the boundaries between creation, criticism, poem, and prototype, using computational and poetic experimentation as the foundation of new forms of interpretation and knowledge.

This computational and poetic experimentation has a long and rich history in Canada. Its origins can be traced to Earle Birney's 1968 "Space Conquest: Computer Poem" and to bpNichol's experimentation with his Apple IIe computer to create *First Screening: Computer Poems* (1984), a series of "kinetic poems" programmed in Apple BASIC. Gregory Betts explains,

> Nichol's experiments with digital poetry began in 1968 and culminated in his iconic suite of digital kinetic poems called *First Screening* in 1984, a date that coincides with the publication of *SwiftCurrent*, the world's first online literary magazine, which featured Nichol and some of [bill] bissett's West Coast peers.
> *(2023, 163)*

First Screening was published by Nichol's own Underwich Editions (in the Underwich Software series) with one hundred disk copies; it has subsequently been recreated in JavaScript and in a series of videos. As Kate Eichhorn points out,

> *First Screening* may have been created by Nichol, but today the work—or the ghosts of the work originally produced by Nichol—points to a much larger collaborative effort, one that exceeds the author's original intentions and any media that Nichol encountered in his lifetime.
> *(2015, 518)*

Nichol was attuned to the experimental and collaborative possibilities afforded by computers, writing in "Some Notes on an Approach to Teaching in Computers" (1985) about the difference between programming as a mode of exploration (open) and as a means of completing a discrete task (closed). He links different modes of programming to different approaches to poetry, arguing that moving between open and closed methods is "what most of [what] even the most fanatic structuralists do (i.e. they have to play with certain commands to see what effects they have before they can incorporate them into their structures)."

Nichol's early reflections on programming and his games with the shifting of authorial identity through transmedia experimentation have echoes in later works. For example, in 1992, poet Nicole Brossard and artist Adriene Jenik collaborated to create a CD-ROM adaptation of Brossard's novel, *Le Désert mauve* (1987). Likewise, Erin Mouré's *Pillage*

Laud (1999) was created, in part, out of the random sentences generated out of her copy of Mac Prose. Describing her work as both "a pillaging and a praising," Mouré "selects from pages of computer-generated sentences to create lesbian love poems—or sex poems" (Book*hug 2011). Nichol, Brossard, Jenik, and Mouré all employ machine writing as part of a poetic-critical practice that "wants us to envision the author as agential within an assembly of subjectivity" (Spinosa 2018, 73).

Around the same time that Nichol was creating kinetic poems using his computer, Frank Davey and Fred Wah were using theirs to publish *SwiftCurrent* (1983–1986), which lays claim to being the first "on-line electronic literary magazine." *SwiftCurrent* ran on UNIX software on a VAX 750 computer at York University. At first, it was a dial-up magazine, before shifting to the Datapac network (a made-in-Canada precursor to the Internet); its "pages" featured writers, mostly those already in Davey and Wah's orbits, from across Canada. *SwiftCurrent* attempted to take advantage of the software by letting users customize their reading experience, for example, by allowing them to delete authors from their particular instance of the magazine. For Davey, "*SwiftCurrent* represents a fundamental alteration to the ways in which literary texts have been distributed in our culture" (Davey and Wah 1986, 112). He had hoped that readers would also use the platform to collaborate on work, but this potential sadly went unrealized. Notwithstanding this unfulfilled potential, *SwiftCurrent* still represents a "digitally-oriented avant-garde with a utopian vision for periodical publication" (Schmaltz and Spinosa 2022, 2). *The SwiftCurrent Anthology*, the only analogue published issue to emerge from the magazine, features work from Davey, bpNichol, Lissa Paul, Eli Mandel, and others. It also includes a user's manual for those eager to read the online edition, although this manual is now redundant because the digital content of the site has been lost.[5]

Some thirty years later, Davey continued to experiment with networked computers and data. His *Bardy Google* (2010) is a series of poems stitched together from the text of Google search results. He writes, "Each of the texts in this book was constructed through the use of specifically devised Internet searches" and the poems are "part of my ongoing work to the [sic] use the sentence as the basic structural unit of poetry—to create poetic texts, as they have always been created, out of the materials of prose" (2010, 7). The collection includes self-reflective (and ironizing) poems such as "New Turning Points for Canadian Literature" and "Surviving the Paraphrase," as well as several parodies of online discourse. About the method of construction used for *Bardy Google*, Davey says,

Because the content of the Internet, and the search-engine priorities assigned to that content, change continuously, these texts are unique and unrepeatable. The same search protocols used in a later month or year could produce quite different results from those assembled here—or distressingly similar ones.

(2010)

Davey's comment aligns with Dani Spinosa's observation that "all poetry written in the last half-century—especially, but not exclusively, experimental poetry—is influenced by the radical potentials and McLuhanian obsolescences of technology and the technologization of poetry" (2018, xxix). The obsolescence that Spinosa refers to is what makes Davey's poems impossible to recreate, has disappeared the digital *SwiftCurrent*, and even makes Davey's own *Bardy Google* barely Googleable (since Google chose the name *Bard* as the name for its first AI chatbot, launched in 2023 and now renamed *Gemini*). In the lines they blur, these poetic works are also examples of how digital affordances have flattened the distinctions between the critical, the experimental, and the poetic.

In *Anarchists in the Academy: Machines and Free Readers in Experimental Poetry* (2018), Spinosa theorizes a relationship between conceptual poetry, machine writing, the digital humanities, and post-anarchist politics. These politics can also be seen in the works of poets and critics such as Wayde Compton and Kaie Kellough, both of whom employ digital forms of poetic and musical production to challenge received ideas of what counts as poetry, sound, and criticism within Canadian contexts. Compton's engagement with turntablism, remix, and digital sound technology constitutes a largely unexamined dimension of digital engagements with the humanities and the human. For example, his "Turntable Poetry, Mixed-Race, and Schizophonophilia" (2010) expands the rubric of the digital humanities by opening the field to a tradition of Black creative and critical practices. Compton's work critically interrogates how digital technologies, through their logics of reproduction and difference, remix and transformation, can reinterpret history's script from the vantage of the Black diaspora. His critical and creative writing engenders the question of why Black engagements with technology have remained invisible to white DH scholars. For example, Compton's collection of short stories, *The Outer Harbour* (2014), riffs on his critical work and includes stories about cyborgs and digital avatars projected into the real world as a form of disinformation and crowd control; its avant-garde artistic practices raise questions about Canadian history, digital simulation, and diasporic identity all within a postmodern, digital imaginary. Like Compton, Kellough's short stories, poems, and musical performances blend digital forms of technology and music to reimagine the text of history sonically via notions of tidalectics, call and response, and remix. For Kellough, the musical cultures of the Black Atlantic, jazz, dub, hip-hop, and experimental electronic music offer ways to re-read history anew. Like Compton's works, Kellough's are forms of digital experimentation that fall outside of recognized, institutionalized visions of digital humanities but that draw attention to the construction of the human subject within the humanities in a way that enriches DH scholarship.

These are but a few examples of the history of poetic-critical experiments with computers and digital technology. As Spinosa, Fan, Eichhorn, and others have all shown, conceptual poets are often at the forefront of experimenting with digital technology in their challenges to notions of authorship, criticism, and literature. Contemporary experimental poets such as Rasiqra Revulva and MLA Chernoff satirize the forms of subjectivity, gender, and power that circulate online and on social media. Fan and Spinosa argue that "Digital reading and writing permeates the literary and academic fields across … Canada," while also recognizing that "it is clear that networked technologies are not treated as central to the understanding of literature itself, as the 'Can-Lit' community writ large still tends to prioritize print books" (2021). They draw attention, for instance, to the lack of crossover between the Electronic Literature Organization's 2018 conference in Montréal and the Koncrete Kanada conference held in Ottawa that same year. They note that despite the thematic similarities, there was little connection between the two, thus affirming the "persistent disciplinary silos … in Canadian scholarship" (2021). Like Brown, Fan and Spinosa call on Canadian scholars to seriously engage with digital text and technology, because electronic literature, poetic production, and criticism all offer rich sites for theorizing the relationship between Canadian literature and the digital.

As this chapter has demonstrated, there is a substantial history of Canadian critics employing digital methods in their scholarly work and of Canadian writers using digital methods in their creative practices. While a great number of these latter projects have escaped the notice of DH scholars in Canada, their work expands definitions of digital humanities with a more robust engagement of how subjectivity is remade within digital creative forms. The next chapter extends this discussion to examine how Canadian literary critics have theorized the digital humanities and, specifically, digital forms of reading.

Notes

1 Alex Good's *Revolutions: Essays on Contemporary Canadian Fiction* (2017) is exemplary of these not-young men's fear of the destructive power of the digital and their lament for an Arcadian literary past. After several complaints about the state of Canadian literature (with representative chapter titles such as "Shackled to a Corpse: The Long, Long Shadow of CanLit"), Good's final chapter, "The Digital Apocalypse," reaches new heights of hyperbole. He writes that "E-books reduce literature to the status of Tetris" (253), and wonders,

> What will happen when people come to see *Pride and Prejudice* no longer as a novel, or even a book, but only as a worthless file to be diced, sliced, mashed-up, manipulated and (mostly) ignored? ... How will such texts be "read" when they appear on a digital page framed by a toolbar and links with embedded videos, pop-ups, and banner ads?.
>
> *(255)*

One wonders how a book can be "ignored" while also being "diced, sliced, mashed-up" and "manipulated" and, for that matter, what company would want their banner ad associated with a "worthless file." For Good, however, these concerns are less urgent than his final worry as expressed in the final paragraph of his collection. He concludes with a meditation on

> the analogy that has sometimes been drawn between the Internet and the atomic bomb ... Humanity might not survive such a disaster ... The sole necessary survivor would be the Internet itself, a force we should be able to recognize now as the true destroyer of worlds.
>
> *(262)*

The monster of the digital, indeed.

2 Many DH scholars will feel seen by Frye's speculation that "There are still many scholars who would be frightened by the thought of a computer scanning all the editions on machine time, perhaps leaving them less able to answer the stock idiot's question, How do you manage to get through so long a summer with nothing to do?" (1989, 454).

3 While recognizing the limits of his own technological imagination, Frye does

> hope that within a few years the most mind-numbing of humanist activities, the marking of undergraduate essays, would disappear as the essays were fed into a machine that would not guess at the mark, would not be affected by prejudice or exasperation, and would not respond to the protests of failed students. It would also, of course, have a complete file of the essays written in the fraud factories, and when it was received, one would start bellowing the name of the student who had bought it over a public address system. I should also hope to see the end of the conception of "productive scholar," with its nineteenth-century industrial over-tones, and "creative scholar" put in its place.
>
> *(Frye 1989, 458)*

4 Frye's essays on Canada are replete with images of technologies that have transformed society. In his "Humanities in a New World," Frye writes "just as we have engineering and other forms of applied science, so there is a vast area of what we may call verbal technology, the use of words for practical or useful purposes" (1958, 72).

5 Poetic snarkiness survived the move from digital to analogue forms as evinced by Davey and Wah's comments, in their introduction, that "Some users, particularly those in Kingston, Ont., have been unable to recall the login names they have selected for themselves, or to distinguish upper from lower case letters in those names" (1986, 8).

Further reading

Betts, Gregory, and Christian Bök, eds. 2019. *Avant Canada: Poets, Prophets, Revolutionaries*. Waterloo: Wilfrid Laurier University Press. https://doi.org/10.51644/9781771123532.

Compton, Wayde. 2010. *After Canaan: Essays on Race, Writing, and Region*. Vancouver: Arsenal Pulp Press.

Spinosa, Dani. 2018. *Anarchists in the Academy: Machines and Free Readers in Experimental Poetry*. Edmonton: University of Alberta Press. https://doi.org/10.1515/9781772124057.

Works cited

Atwood, Margaret. 1972. *Survival: A Thematic Guide to Canadian Literature*. Toronto: Anansi.

Ayers, Edward L. 2013. "Does Digital Scholarship Have a Future?" *Educause Review* 49, no. 4: 24–34. https://er.educause.edu/articles/2013/8/does-digital-scholarship-have-a-future.

Ballantyne, Emily, and Zailig Pollock. 2011. "Respect des fonds and the Digital Page." In *Archival Narratives for Canada: Retelling Stories in a Changing Landscape*, edited by Kathleen Garay and Christl Verduyn, 184–200. Halifax: Fernwood.

Betts, Gregory. 2023. "saga uv th relees uv human spirit from compuewter funckshuns." In *Future Horizons: Canadian Digital Humanities*, edited by Paul Barrett and Sarah Roger, 161–80. Ottawa: University of Ottawa Press.

Birney, Earlie. 1968. "Space Conquest: Computer Poem." *Gronk2*. Toronto: Ganglia Press.

Book*hug. 2011. "*Pillage Laud* by Erin Mouré." *Book*hug Press*. https://bookhugpress.ca/shop/books/poetry/pillage-laud-by-erin-moure/.

Bretz, Andrew, Susan Brown, and Hannah McGregor. 2010. "Lasting Change: Sustaining Digital Scholarship and Culture in Canada." Report of the Sustaining Digital Scholarship for Sustainable Culture Group, December 2010. https://www.alienated.net/wp-content/uploads/2019/09/bretz_brown_mcgregor_lasting_change.pdf.

Brown, Susan. 2017. "Survival: Canadian Cultural Scholarship in a Digital Age." *Studies in Canadian Literature / Études en littérature canadienne* 42, no. 2: 171–200. https://id.erudit.org/iderudit/scl42_2art09.

Coady, Lynn. 2016. *Who Needs Books? Reading in the Digital Age*. Edmonton: University of Alberta Press. https://doi.org/10.1515/9781772121438.

Compton, Wayde. 2010. *After Canaan: Essays on Race, Writing, and Region*. Vancouver: Arsenal Pulp Press.

Coombe, Rosemary, Darren Wershler, and Martin Zeilinger. 2014. *Dynamic Fair Dealing: Creating Canadian Culture Online*. Toronto: University of Toronto Press. https://doi.org/10.3138/9781442665613.
Davey, Frank. 1970. "E. J. Pratt: Apostle of Corporate Man." *Canadian Literature* 43: 54–66.
Davey, Frank. 2010. *Bardy Google*. Vancouver: Talonbooks.
Davey, Frank, and Fred Wah. 1986. *The SwiftCurrent Anthology*. Toronto: Coach House Press.
DiCenzo, Maria. 2015. "Remediating the Past: Doing 'Periodical Studies' in the Digital Era." *English Studies in Canada* 41, no. 1: 19–39. https://doi.org/10.1353/esc.2015.0000.
Djwa, Sandra, and Zailig Pollock. n.d. *The Digital Page: The Collected Works of P. K. Page*. Collaboratory for Writing and Research on Culture. Accessed October 10, 2024. https://cwrc.ca/project/digitalpage.
Eichhorn, Kate. 2015. "The Digital Turn in Canadian and Québécois Literature." In *The Oxford Handbook of Canadian Literature*, edited by Cynthia Sugars, 512–23. Oxford: Oxford University Press. https://doi.org/10.1093/oxfordhb/9780199941865.001.0001.
EMiC. n.d. *Editing Modernism in Canada*. Accessed July 12, 2024. https://editingmodernism.ca/.
Fan, Lai-Tze, and Dani Spinosa. 2021. "Introduction: Decoding Canadian Digital Poetics." *electronic book review*, July 2, 2021. https://doi.org/10.7273/8hbe-rv49.
Flemmer, Kyle. 2022. "Cyborg Reading: Transmedial Digital Poetry and the Cyborg Milieu." MA thesis, University of Calgary.
Fong, Deanna, and Ryan Fitzpatrick. 2023. "Analogue Thrills, Digital Spills: On the Fred Wah Digital Archive Version 2.0." In *Future Horizons: Canadian Digital Humanities*, edited by Paul Barrett and Sarah Roger, 255–72. Ottawa: University of Ottawa Press. https://doi.org/10.1515/9780776640068-018.
Fong, Deanna, and Ryan Fitzpatrick. 2024. *Fred Wah Digital Archive*. https://fredwah.ca/.
Frye, Northrop. 1958. "Humanities in a New World." In *Northrop Frye's Writings on Education*, edited by Jean O'Grady and Goldwin French, 69–85. Toronto: University of Toronto Press. https://doi.org/10.3138/9781487595623-002.
Frye, Northrop. 1989. "Literary and Mechanical Models." In *The Secular Scripture and Other Writings on Critical Theory: 1976–1991*, edited by Joseph Adamson and Jean Wilson, 451–62. Toronto: University of Toronto Press. https://doi.org/10.3138/9781442627550.
Good, Alex. 2017. *Revolutions: Essays on Contemporary Canadian Fiction*. Windsor: Biblioasis.
Gordon, Neta. 2023. *AMM Bibliography*. https://www.ammbibliography.com/.
Grant, George. 1969. *Technology and Empire: Perspectives on North America*. Toronto: Anansi.
Hjartarson, Paul, Harvey Quamen, and EMiC RA. 2016. "Editing the Letters of Wilfrid and Sheila Watson, 1956–1961: Scholarly Edition as Digital Practice." In *Editing as Cultural Practice in Canada*, edited by Dean Irvine, 121–37. Waterloo: Wilfrid Laurier Press. https://doi.org/10.51644/9781771120937-010.
Jensen, Graham, Deseray Manuel, et al. 2022. *Canadian Modernist Magazines Project*. University of Victoria. https://modernistmags.ca.

Klinck, Carl F., Alfred G. Bailey, Claude Bissell, Roy Daniells, Northrop Frye, and Desmond Pacey, eds. 1967. *Literary History of Canada*. Toronto: University of Toronto Press.

Munro, Alice. 1971 (2014). *Lives of Girls and Women*. Toronto: Penguin.

Nichol, bp. 1985. "Some Notes on an Approach to Teaching Computers." *bpnichol.ca*. https://bpnichol.ca/sites/default/files/archives/document/Teaching Computers.pdf.

Pollock, Zailig. 2016. "The Material and Cultural Transformation of Scholarly Editing in Canada." In *Editing as Cultural Practice in Canada*, edited by Dean Irvine, 93–104. Waterloo: Wilfrid Laurier Press. https://doi.org/10.51644/9781771120937-008.

Pratt, E. J. 2000. "The Man and the Machine." In *Selected Poems: E. J. Pratt*, edited by Sandra Djwa, W. J. Keith, and Zailig Pollock, 77. Toronto: University of Toronto Press. https://doi.org/10.3138/9781442679719.

Reder, Deanna, Madeleine Reddon, Alix Shield, Margery Fee, and Susan Glover. n.d. *The People and the Text: Indigenous Writing in Lands Claimed by Canada*. Accessed September 8, 2024. https://thepeopleandthetext.ca/.

Schmaltz, Eric, and Dani Spinosa. 2022 "Where in the Web Is *SwiftCurrent*?" Paper presented at the Electronic Literature Organization Annual Conference, May 31, 2022.

Shield, Alix. 2018. "Rethinking the Paratext: Digital Story-Mapping E. Pauline Johnson's and Chief Joe & Mary Capilano's *Legends of Vancouver*." BC Studies, 197: 107–21. https://doi.org/10.1515/9781772840193-004.

Spinosa, Dani. 2018. *Anarchists in the Academy: Machines and Free Readers in Experimental Poetry*. Edmonton: University of Alberta Press. https://doi.org/10.1515/9781772124057.

Zacharias, Robert. 2024. *Distant Reading Mennonite Writing*. Accessed October 10, 2024. https://ctms.uwinnipeg.ca/projects/drmw/.

7
CANADIAN LITERATURE AS DATA

* * *

Canadian author and critic Stephen Marche's "Literature Is Not Data: Against Digital Humanities" (2012) is one of many jeremiads against the digital humanities, a genre of complaint capitalized upon by Stanley Fish, Nan Z. Da, Daniel Allington, Sarah Brouillette, and David Golumbia, among others. Marche's argument recalls Lynn Coady's parable about the monster of the digital outlined in Chapter 6. Like Fish, Marche tends to conflate computational literary studies (CLS) and digital humanities, even though the former is generally understood to be a subset of the latter.[1] Marche also neglects to address the numerous digital projects and methods that are not concerned with literature, thus betraying an ignorance of the composition of digital humanities work. Yet, at the heart of Marche's argument is a "deeper problem with digital humanities in general"—his perceived incompatibility between literature and data and "a fundamental assumption that runs through all aspects of the methodology and which has not been adequately assessed in its nascent theory. Literature cannot meaningfully be treated as data" (2012). In this chapter, we survey the theoretical framing and critiques of *reading* literature as data and examine how Canadian critics and writers have responded to these concerns.

Marche's argument is simple: "Literature is not data." It is also, at times, hyperbolic. Consider, for example, his claim that "Google Books, in its way, represents an even more profound shift than the printing press" (2012). For literary digital humanities scholars, however, the problem is more nuanced, as reading literature as data gives rise to additional complexities of meaning, interpretation, provenance, and context.

DOI: 10.4324/9781003318323-11

The transformation of literature into machine-processable formats comes with obvious advantages: being able to use digital tools, engage in distant reading, develop concordances, and more. Yet it also raises methodological, theoretical, and practical challenges—challenges that can be seen as threats or opportunities. John B. Smith's "Computer Criticism" (1978) and Rosanne G. Potter's "Literary Criticism and Literary Computing: A Difficult Synthesis" (1989) cast the challenges of transforming literature into data as methodological questions for literary criticism, as it requires researchers to strike a balance between making literary data machine-readable while also retaining literature's complex layers of meaning.

These ongoing, global debates extend well beyond Canada and Canadian literature. Fish, for instance, sees no "difficult synthesis" nor dilemma concerning computational literary studies, arguing, instead, that digital humanities projects "crank up a huge amount of machinery in order to produce something that was obvious from the get go" and digital humanities researchers "dress up garden variety literary intuition in numbers" (2019). Quoting Da's infamous critique of CLS, Fish argues that "The antidote to the whole puffed-up thing" of the digital humanities is to "just read the texts" (2019). For DH scholars working with literature, the notion of just reading is either methodologically naïve or disingenuous. One foundational truism of literary criticism is that one cannot *just read* but, rather, that every reading presupposes a methodology and a series of significant features that the reading aims to uncover. Ironically, this is a point that Fish spent a large part of his career making.

Adam Hammond, for instance, argues that "What the digital age has accomplished, above all else, is to defamiliarize the act of reading" (2016, 4). This is a mischaracterization of the accomplishments of the digital age, to be sure, but Hammond is right to recognize that the notion of reading has been transformed by the digital, even for projects well outside of DH. One challenge of digital humanities projects is that they typically require an explicit statement of methodology. The *SpokenWeb* website is replete with discussions of method and procedure; project documentation provides rich methodological context for the metadata, collections, archives, recordings, and archival best practices. Likewise, *The Endings Project* explicitly and comprehensively defines the concept of data and sets out the principles around which the project is organized. The *Linked Infrastructure for Networked Cultural Scholarship* (LINCS) not only provides extensive documentation for the technical processes of creating linked open data, but it also explains the principles guiding the data's ontological structures. These kinds of explicit definitions of terms, processes, methodologies, and epistemologies are commonplace in digital humanities research.

It is incumbent upon DH projects to ask the difficult questions: What does it mean to read in the context of a digital project? How do we navigate Potter's "difficult synthesis"? How do we render our texts as data? What information is considered relevant and what is discarded? How was the data collected, curated, and analyzed? Grappling with these and other questions, DH practitioners are likely to find that, while any desired final synthesis remains elusive, the questions are worth asking all the same. As Jim Egan explains,

> DH appeals to me for precisely the same reason as theory ... DH and theory each ask those interested in the humanities to ask themselves why we do what we do the way we do it. What do we learn when we close-read a literary text? What assumptions about our goals, aims, and values are embedded within the methods of close-reading? What relationship does history bear to literature—what, after all, is the difference between the categories of history and literature, if any, and what ends do these distinctions serve? Indeed, why do we have literature departments at all?
>
> *(2013)*

Egan understands that the representation of literature as data is neither impossible nor a death knell for the humanities but rather a methodological challenge and an opportunity to explicitly state not just the principles of digital work but also the humanistic principles that a given project endorses.

Yet while Fish, Marche, Da, and others repeat their mantra that "literature is not data," such a limited definition of data will likely be unsatisfactory to most digital humanities scholars. The *Oxford English Dictionary* definition of data as "Related items of (chiefly numerical) information considered collectively, typically obtained by scientific work and used for reference, analysis, or calculation" and as "Quantities, characters, or symbols on which operations are performed by a computer" only begins to capture the various meanings of data and the uses to which it is put. For the developers of *The Endings Project*, data is "the expression of the source information, knowledge, and expertise of our researchers"—an expansive, generous, community-oriented definition (2024). Literary scholars have puzzled over the distinction between text and data with no satisfactory resolution. (For more on definitions of data in a practical sense, see Chapters 11–12.)

Methodological opportunities

Digital humanities research "consists in repeatedly coadjusting human concepts and machine technologies until ... the two stabilize each other in temporary postures of truth that neither by itself could sustain" (Liu 2013, 416). The explicit expression of those temporary postures—and a continued negotiation between the interpretation of cultural objects and the construction of data—is at the heart of digital humanities work and extends beyond mere questions of process to DH's broader social and cultural contexts. This reflection on DH methodologies requires, in turn, an investigation of the humanities more broadly. As Len Findlay notes,

> the humanities remain ... surprisingly opaque to themselves—both as purveyors of useful knowledge and as pursuers of knowledge for its own sake—and worse than opaque to many of their possible or actual external constituencies ... The humanities need, therefore, to be translated both inside and outside their ever-shrinking or self-instrumentalizing academic domain.
>
> *(2011, 41–42)*

DH provides an opportunity to investigate the humanities' opacity and to translate humanities work to a wider public.

Many of the critiques of DH from the aforementioned critics posit what Jamie Skye Bianco terms a "retro-humanism" that itself remains "surprisingly opaque" and relevant only to an "ever-shrinking" constituency of cloistered practitioners (2012). By contrast, DH can participate in the active translation of humanities questions into public concerns by explicitly requiring expressions of methodology, by interrogating the vision of the humanities the project endorses (in the manifest ways in which that question can be framed), and in the relationship between the project and broader social, cultural, and public contexts.[2]

The methodological and conceptual challenges of encoding cultural objects as data are a concern for each of the projects outlined in the previous chapters. When Mary Vipond argues that historians "continue to assume that the media by which [cultural] meanings are often transmitted need not to be factored into the analysis of cultural practices" (2003, 8), she anticipates the questions at the heart of most digital humanities projects: How are cultural objects remediated, or transformed, into data? What modes of analysis are made possible and foreclosed upon in the process of that transformation? How does that shift in the media affect acts of interpretation, and what is the materiality of data? Put simply, digitization changes a text and allows new ways of reading while foreclosing others.

Johanna Drucker argues that the reduction of cultural objects to data represents

> the hallmark of realist models of knowledge and needs to be subjected to a radical critique to return the humanistic tenets of constructed-ness

and interpretation to the fore. Realist approaches depend above all upon an idea that phenomena are *observer-independent* and can be characterized as *data*.

(2011, original emphasis)

Yet, for Drucker, the answer is not simply that "literature is not data" nor is it to abandon the valuable processes of computationally aided cultural analysis. Instead, she argues, "we reconceive of all data as capta" (2011, original emphasis). Drucker explains that "*Capta* is taken actively while *data* is assumed to be a 'given' able to be recorded and observed. From this distinction, a world of differences arises." That distinction requires recognizing that humanistic inquiry is always situated and partial.

If *data* implies an objective and complete recording of some phenomena, *capta* offers a more nuanced framework for understanding—and working with—cultural objects because it affirms the social construction of those objects, the contexts in which their meaning is produced, and the role of the observer in producing that meaning. For Drucker, capta offers a way of conceiving of data according to humanistic principles, including the understanding,

> that the humanities are committed to the concept of knowledge as interpretation, and, second, that the apprehension of the phenomena of the physical, social, cultural world is through constructed and constitutive acts, not mechanistic or naturalistic realist representations of preexisting or self-evident information. Nothing in intellectual life is self-evident or self-identical, nothing in cultural life is mere fact, and nothing in the phenomenal world gives rise to a record or representation except through constructed expressions.
>
> *(2011)*

These humanistic principles also structure Julia Flanders and Trevor Muñoz's attention to data curation. Like capta, data curation, distinct from data collection, stresses the selection, transformation, and observation of data while foregrounding humanistic principles and the role of the researcher in that process of curation; in this regard, data curation has much in common with critical archival practices. Data is not merely there (wherever *there* is) after it is collected; it is selected, transformed, stored, catalogued, and represented by a researcher according to their needs.

According to Flanders and Muñoz,

> A key aspect of data curation is thus to ensure that the representation of objects of study in the humanities functions effectively as data: that they are processable by machines and interoperable such that they are

durably processable across systems and collections whiles still retaining provenance and complex layers of meaning.

(2013)

Data's provenance refers to both the process by which the data was created and how it was encoded, whereas the complex layers of meaning refer to the social, historical, cultural, and other contexts relevant to the data. While these processes might appear, at first glance, to be intuitive, the acts of curating data—from the initial stages of collection to the construction of metadata to the means of storage and the processes of analysis—are all nontrivial tasks imbued with questions of humanistic analysis. As such, data "Curation encompasses gathering material, making it discoverable by describing and organizing it, placing it in a context of related information, supporting its use for diverse intellectual purposes, and ensuring its long-term survival" (Muñoz and Renear 2011).

Flanders and Muñoz stress the need for researchers to plan for, and be involved in, the "active and ongoing management" (Flanders and Muñoz 2013) of their data, ensuring that it can migrate across platforms, remain accessible to interested parties, and is usable in contemporary forms of data analysis. Humanistic data curation extends the FAIR principles which require that data be Findable, Accessible, Interoperable, and Reusable (see Chapters 11–12 for further discussion of data curation, cleaning, and management according to FAIR and other principles). This is no small task given the rate at which platforms, technologies, and file formats evolve, often rendering yesterday's data inaccessible with today's technology. Indeed, numerous projects outlined throughout this book, from the *Collaboratory for Writing and Research on Culture* (CWRC) to *The Hypertext Pratt*, have all struggled with the difficulties of shifting data formats and migrating across platforms. Flanders and Muñoz direct readers to the consortia and institutions concerned with data curation including the Digital Curation Centre (UK) and the National Digital Information Infrastructure and Preservation Program (US). In Canada, the Digital Research Alliance of Canada (DRAC) has produced a series of data curation guides for researchers. It is one thing, of course, to acknowledge the need for careful data curation and vigilance in updating formats and platforms, and another thing altogether to actually support that work—not only recognizing it as essential, valuable work, but also perhaps even regarding it as an opportunity to expand paradigms of research in the humanities to include digitization and curation.

Thus, in the curation of their data and the composition of their capta, in their methodological decisions about how to render literature machine-processable, and in the creation of metadata, digital humanities researchers engage complex questions concerning the relation between the digital and the humanities. Susan Brown imagines this relation as the *gap* between the two spaces of DH work:

> I invoke the gap to acknowledge these continuities with our present situation while insisting that it is imperative that humanities scholars not be put off by the digital-humanities divide. The broader scholarly community must address it by engaging with the development of digital tools and methods for teaching, conducting research, and disseminating its results, despite the advertised risks. ... From the insight that humans and artifacts are mutually constituted, we must recognize that work underway now in information and communication technologies will reshape incalculably how work in the humanities will be conducted.
> *(2007, 205–7)*

The gap between the digital and the humanities offers an opportunity for researchers to theorize their engagement with both, to "make explicit the priorities and categories that inform their work, and what they 'mean' ... in new and challenging ways" (218). Brown's gap evokes Potter's "difficult synthesis" and Julie Thompson Klein's notion of DH as a kind of "boundary work ... a composite label for the claims, activities, and structures by which individuals create, maintain, break down, and reformulate boundaries between knowledge units" (Klein 2015). Alan Liu agrees with Brown and Klein, arguing that the gap between the digital and the humanities produces a "meaning problem," wherein "It is not clear epistemologically, cognitively, or socially how human beings can take a signal discovered by a machine and develop an interpretation leading to a humanly understandable concept" (2013, 414). For Brown, Liu, and others, the acts of data curation, the construction of capta, and the gap between humanistic knowledge and digital humanities are key considerations in both the theory and practice of DH research. Yet, the metaphor of the gap requires revisiting as the relationship between the two becomes increasingly complex. For example, the division between the digital and the textual is hard to discern in texts such as Joshua Whitehead's *Jonny Appleseed* (see Chapter 10), where the protagonist constructs their identity through their social media accounts, or in Rupi Kaur's Instapoetry, in which poetry is shaped by Instagram's algorithm and platform. Given the lengthy history of computer-assisted poetry and e-lit (see Chapter 6) in Canada, the space between the textual and the digital has long been hazy.

Project goals, methodological challenges

Virtually every DH project we have described has, with varying degrees of intentionality, grappled with data curation in some form. Projects such as

The Hypertext Pratt (see Chapter 6) wrestled with data management and shifting data standards. Larger projects such as CWRC (see Chapter 5) and LINCS (see Chapter 11) have made creation, access, and preservation key dimensions of their work. Where these larger projects often have staff dedicating time to data collection, curation, and storage—and therefore the capacity to implement standards and ensure best practices—smaller projects can find themselves under-resourced or ill-equipped to proceed with intentionality.

When it comes to data creation and management, the *Canadian Modernist Magazines Project* (CMMP) is exemplary in this regard. "Dedicated to digitizing, sharing, and facilitating the study of modernist and proto-modernist literary magazines of historical and cultural significance that were published in Canada between approximately 1900–1950," the CMMP highlights the importance of little magazines in Canadian modernism. In "Beyond 'Mere Digitization': Introducing the Canadian Modernist Magazines Project," project lead Graham Jensen explains that the "undervalued work of digitization ... is of theoretical as well as practical significance; it involves processes that translate both humanities materials *and* methodologies into the digital realm" (2023, 367). In particular,

> Because we are aware of the potential methodological and literary-critical problems of forcing modernist periodicals into pre-existing bibliographic ontologies and digital frameworks, we have attempted, as much as possible, to encode only metadata essential for navigational and basic research purposes. Even the seemingly straightforward task of assigning genre (is this text a "manifesto," an "editorial," or an "essay"?) involves editorial choices that risk imposing bibliographic interpretations and structures on magazines so as to materially reconstruct them—and therefore undermine the extent to which they function as faithful witnesses to modernist projects of self-fashioning.
>
> *(369)*

Jensen's project navigates a range of challenges to acquire the relevant material, digitize it, and structure it as data. In the very collection of data, he needed to develop a working definition of his "broad view of modernism" to decide which magazines to include; he subsequently designed his metadata to ensure that he was neither foreclosing interpretive possibilities nor imposing generic categorizations on his corpus. The curation of paratextual materials required an opening up to possible interpretive futures as Jensen considered how to work with accompanying paratextual material such as advertisements and marginalia.

Our own research project, *Canadians Read*, echoes a number of Jensen's observations about data management, curation, and processing. *Canadians Read* examines Canadian literary discourse on social media to trace how Canadians write about, discuss, and engage literature online, and also how social media affects public discussions of literature. We collected datasets of Twitter posts using hashtags such as #CanadaReads and #CanLit as well as a smaller, related set of Instagram posts. What began as a relatively straightforward process of data collection required substantial cleaning and curation based on careful decisions about what constitutes public discourse and even Canadian literature. The seemingly banal process of filtering out spam and irrelevant tweets led to considerations of where the borders lie between, for example, spam, authorial self-promotion, and legitimate conversation. The inherently memetic quality of hashtags and the retweeting system created extra layers of consideration, as we had to determine what to exclude from our analysis. Additionally, the bilingual nature of Canadian literary discourse also required grappling with data (and hashtags) in both English and French. These processes involved the transformation of raw captured data into a carefully curated set of capta. Our own experiences have emphasized how, as Jensen observes, there is far more to data curation than *mere digitization*.

Expanding DH's rubric

Beyond the bounds of explicit digital humanities projects, Canadian literature also has a long history of representing and challenging ideas of data and its epistemological neutrality. The historical *Book of Negroes* is an example of the confluence of cultures of data, the complexities and contradictions of ideas of race, as well as representations of history. The original *Book of Negroes*, compiled in 1783, was a record of the more than 3,000 enslaved and free Black people who fled from the United States to Canada during the American Revolution. The two copies of the *Book* (one recorded by the British officers, another by American officers) included information about the individuals' age, sex, point of arrival, a statement about their perceived racial qualities, and a description of the individual. The book is a rich yet flawed record of Black presence in America and Canada in the eighteenth century, replete with denigrating and objectifying descriptions of Black people, reading more like an inventory sheet than an account of people and their lives. It was created to track Black people and to preserve systems of slavery in the US and white supremacy in Canada. The book is also an early form of data that affirms a racist worldview through the naturalization of categories of observation and metadata.

In the creation of the original *Book of Negroes*, the authors employed metadata and data curation to record Black lives. In doing so, their dataset reifies notions of race, gender, labour, ability, and other categories of identity. In the historical reinterpretation of that data, scholars have read the book against the grain to discern the complexity of the lives that the data both represents and obscures. The reinterpretations of the data draw attention to the racist forms of observation and control built into the data's construction. As Jessica Marie Johnson argues, and as we discuss in Chapter 9,

> The archive of Atlantic slavery—images, numbers, and texts ... haunts efforts to render black people as human ... the study of black life and culture must also accompany an ethical and moral concern with sustaining black life and shaping black futures.
>
> *(2018, 65)*

As we discuss in Chapter 9, Johnson raises crucial ethical questions concerning data's capacity to record and reproduce violence while also calling for a methodology that reads data in order to interpret the historical archive anew. In this respect, Lawrence Hill's *The Book of Negroes* (2007), a celebrated Canadian novel that reimagines some of the lives behind the historical document, can be seen as an attempt to creatively reimagine the original data. Hill's novel is an example of Saidiya Hartman's "critical fabulation" (2008, 11), whereby Black writers write against the silence and violence of the past by imagining the vibrant, joyous, and complex lives of those who are rendered mere data in the archive. Hill foregrounds the blood and violence in the historical archive while also using his literary imagination to create a story of Black joy and perseverance that makes the original data signify otherwise. His novel draws on the data to tell a story, but it is not restrained by the immanent categories that the original *Book* imposes upon its subjects. Following Hill's example, DH projects should seek out ways to work with data that do not decontextualize or reduce but rather bring it to life.

As with the original *Book of Negroes*, data has too often been employed by those in power to encode and subsequently reify oppressive categories of identity. In the next section, we turn to projects that work in the gap between the digital and the humanities to challenge the oppressive and reductive uses of data through their creative and critical practices.

Notes

1 The authors of *Digital_Humanities* argue that "Digital Humanities projects can be described by sketching their structure at several levels," including, but not limited to "design, computation, processing, digitization, classification,

description, metadata, organization, navigation, curation, analysis, editing, modeling, prototyping" (Burdick et al. 2012, 4). Katherine Bode, meanwhile, suggests, "Da's idiosyncratic definition of CLS is partly a product of problematic divisions within digital literary study" but also insists that Da's definition "omits what I'd call digital literary scholarship: philological, curatorial, and media archaeological approaches to digital collections and data" (2019).

2 Matthew Jockers's explication of his term *macroanalysis* is representative of the kinds of methodological questions that pervade digital humanities research, and it offers a more complex examination of the meaning of reading than Fish or Marche's critiques of DH. Jockers writes,

> By way of an analogy, we might think about interpretive close readings as corresponding to microeconomics, whereas quantitative distant reading corresponds to macroeconomics. Consider, then, the study of literary genres or literary periods: are they microanalytic? Say, for example, a scholar specializes in early-twentieth-century poetry. Presumably, this scholar could be called upon to provide sound generalizations, or "macroreadings," of twentieth-century poetry based on a broad familiarity with the individual works of that period. This would be a type of "macro" or "distant" reading. But this kind of macro-reading falls short of approximating for literature what macroeconomics is to economics, and it is in this context that I prefer the term *analysis* over *reading*. The former term, especially when prefixed with *macro*, placed the emphasis on the systematic examination of data, on the quantifiable methodology. It de-emphasizes the more interpretive act of "reading". This is no longer reading that we are talking about.
>
> *(2013, 25)*

Further reading

Barrett, Paul and Sarah Roger, eds. 2023. *Future Horizons: Canadian Digital Humanities*. Ottawa: University of Ottawa Press. https://doi.org/10.2307/jj.17681834.

Burdick, Anne, Johanna Drucker, Peter Lunenfeld, Todd Pressner, and Jeffrey Schnapp. 2012. *Digital_Humanities*. Baltimore: The MIT Press. https://doi.org/10.7551/mitpress/9248.001.0001.

Gold, Matthew, and Lauren F. Klein, eds. 2023. *Debates in the Digital Humanities 2023*. Minneapolis: University of Minnesota Press. https://dhdebates.gc.cuny.edu/projects/debates-in-the-digital-humanities-2023.

McGrail, Anne B., Angel David Nieves, and Siobhan Senier, eds. 2021. *People, Practice, Power: Digital Humanities Outside the Centre*. Minneapolis: University of Minnesota Press. https://dhdebates.gc.cuny.edu/projects/people-practice-power.

Works cited

Barrett, Paul, and Sarah Roger. n.d. *Canadians Read*. Accessed October 10, 2024. https://canadiansread.ca/.

Bianco, Jamie Skye. 2012. "This Digital Humanities Which Is Not One." In *Debates in the Digital Humanities*, edited by Matthew K. Gold, 96–112. Minneapolis: University of Minnesota Press. https://doi.org/10.5749/minnesota/9780816677948.003.0012.

Black Loyalists: Our History, Our People. The Book of Negroes. n.d. Accessed September 4, 2024. https://blackloyalist.com/cdc/documents/official/book_of_negroes.htm.

Bode, Katherine. 2019. "Computational Literary Studies: A Critical Inquiry Online Forum." *In the Moment* (blog), *Critical Inquiry*, April 1, 2019. https://critinq.wordpress.com/2019/03/31/computational-literary-studies-a-critical-inquiry-online-forum/.

Brown, Susan. 2007. "Don't Mind the Gap: Evolving Digital Modes of Scholarly Production Across the Digital-Humanities Divide." In *Retooling the Humanities: The Culture of Research in Canadian Universities*, edited by Daniel Coleman and Smaro Kamboureli, 203–32. Edmonton: University of Alberta Press. https://doi.org/10.1515/9780888646781-013.

Burdick, Anne, Johanna Drucker, Peter Lunenfeld, Todd Pressner, and Jeffrey Schnapp. 2012. *Digital_Humanities*. Baltimore: The MIT Press. https://doi.org/10.7551/mitpress/9248.001.0001.

CWRC. n.d. *Collaboratory for Writing and Research on Culture*. Accessed July 12, 2024. https://cwrc.ca/.

Drucker, Johanna. 2011. "Humanities Approaches to Graphical Display." *Digital Humanities Quarterly* 5, no. 1. https://www.digitalhumanities.org/dhq/vol/5/1/000091/000091.html.

Egan, Jim. 2013. "Review of *Macroanalysis: Digital Methods and Literary History*, by Matthew Jockers." *College Literature* 40, no. 2: 196–203.

The Endings Project. 2024. *The Endings Project*, July 7, 2024. https://endings.uvic.ca/.

Findlay, Len. 2011. "Extraordinary Renditions: Translating the Humanities Now." In *Retooling the Humanities: The Culture of Research in Canadian Universities*, edited by Daniel Coleman and Smaro Kamboureli, 41–58. Edmonton: University of Alberta Press. https://doi.org/10.1515/9780888646781-005.

Fish, Stanley. 2012. "Mind Your P's and B's: The Digital Humanities and Interpretation." *Opinionator* (blog), *The New York Times*, January 23, 2012. https://archive.nytimes.com/opinionator.blogs.nytimes.com/2012/01/23/mind-your-ps-and-bs-the-digital-humanities-and-interpretation/.

Fish, Stanley. 2019. "Afterword: Computational Literary Studies: Participant Forum Responses, Day 3." *In the Moment* (blog), *Critical Inquiry*, April 3, 2019. https://critinq.wordpress.com/2019/04/03/computational-literary-studies-participant-forum-responses-day-3-5/.

Flanders, Julia, and Trevor Muñoz. 2013. "An Introduction to Humanities Data Curation." *DH Curation Guide*. https://curationexperts.com/introduction-to-humanities-data-curation.

Hammond, Adam. 2016. *Literature in the Digital Age: A Critical Introduction*. Cambridge: Cambridge University Press. https://doi.org/10.1017/CBO9781107323551.

Hartman, Saidiya. 2008. "Venus in Two Acts." *Small Axe* 26, no. 2: 1–14. https://doi.org/10.1215/-12-2-1.

Jensen, Graham H. 2023. "Beyond 'Mere Digitization': Introducing the Canadian Modernist Magazines Project." In *Future Horizons: Canadian Digital Humanities*, edited by Paul Barrett and Sarah Roger, 367–88. Ottawa: University of Ottawa Press. https://doi.org/10.2307/jj.17681834.25.

Jensen, Graham, Deseray Manuel, et al. 2022. *Canadian Modernist Magazines Project*. University of Victoria. https://modernistmags.ca.
Jockers, Matthew L. 2013. *Macroanalysis: Digital Methods and Literary History*. Urbana: University of Illinois Press. https://doi.org/10.5406/illinois/9780252037528.001.0001.
Johnson, Jessica Marie. 2018. "Markup Bodies: Black [Life] Studies and Slavery [Death] Studies at the Digital Crossroads." *Social Text* 36, no. 4: 57–79. https://doi.org/10.1215/01642472-7145658.
Klein, Julie Thompson. 2015. *Interdisciplining Digital Humanities: Boundary Work in an Emerging Field*. Ann Arbor: University of Michigan Press. https://doi.org/10.3998/dh.12869322.0001.001.
LINCS. 2024. *Linked Infrastructure for Networked Cultural Scholarship*. https://lincsproject.ca/.
Liu, Alan. 2013. "The Meaning of the Digital Humanities." *PMLA* 128, no. 2: 409–23. https://doi.org/10.1632/pmla.2013.128.2.409.
Marche, Stephen. 2012. "Literature Is Not Data: Against Digital Humanities." *Los Angeles Review of Books*, October 28, 2012. https://lareviewofbooks.org/article/literature-is-not-data-against-digital-humanities/.
Muñoz, Trevor, and Allen Renear. 2011. "Issues in Humanities Data Curation." *Proceedings of the American Society for Information Science and Technology* 48, no. 1: 1–4.
Oxford English Dictionary. 2024. "Data (n.)." *Oxford English Dictionary Online*. Accessed October 15, 2024.
Potter, Rosanne G. 1989. "Literary Criticism and Literary Computing: A Difficult Synthesis." In *Literary Computing and Literary Criticism: Theoretical and Practical Essays on Theme and Rhetoric*, edited by Rosanne G. Potter, 93–106. Philadelphia: University of Pennsylvania Press.
Smith, John B. 1978. "Computer Criticism." *Style* 12, no. 4: 326–56.
SpokenWeb. 2024. *SpokenWeb*. https://spokenweb.ca/.
Vipond, Mary. 2003. "The 2003 Presidential Address of the CHA: The Mass Media in Canadian History: The Empire Day Broadcast of 1939." *Journal of Canadian Historical Association / Revue de la Société historique du Canada* 14, no. 1: 1–21. https://doi.org/10.7202/010317ar.

PART IV

8
INTERSECTIONAL DIGITAL HUMANITIES

* * *

Digital humanities is often referred to as a *big tent* not just because of its disciplinary and methodological breadth but also because of the stated diversity of its community. This diversity is, however, more aspiration than reality: "One would be forgiven, for example, after coming away from the annual international conference of the Alliance of Digital Humanities Organizations (ADHO) conference assuming DH were a parade of white men quantifying literary text" (Eichmann-Kalwara, Jorgensen, and Weingart 2018). Across the next three chapters, we explore how digital humanists have been working to right this balance: from a feminist and LGBTQ+ vantage here in Chapter 8, from the perspective of race in Chapter 9, and from an Indigenous standpoint in Chapter 10. While our focus is the juncture of Canadian literature and digital humanities, and while there has been a welcome and well-overdue diversification in CanLit in recent years, the project of transforming CanLit is just beginning. To that end, we have broadened our scope across this section to include some work being done in the Canadian DH community on non-Canadian literature and DH projects in literary-adjacent fields.

According to Nickoal Eichmann-Kalwara, Jeana Jorgensen, and Scott B. Weingart's analysis of ADHO DH conference programs from 2000 to 2015, women represent roughly one-third of presenters overall—less when it comes to single-authored papers. Yet, despite this imbalance, there is "anecdotal awareness that many of the most respected role models and leaders in the community are women," a tension that can be explained by the "pink collar work" of community building, collaboration, and mentorship disproportionately taken on by women. A network analysis by Jin Gao et al. similarly showed that while, across fifty years of articles in three well-known DH journals, two-thirds of the authors were male, females were "significantly more important ... in forming the co-authorship network" (2022). This homogeneity is not limited to gender. ADHO's global status belies the composition of its conference attendees, with more than 70% from Europe and North America in the first fifteen years since 2000. The only year that saw more than 30% of attendees from outside Europe or North America, the conference took place in Australia. During this period, authors with names common in the US passed ADHO peer review 72% of the time, while authors with other (read: non-English) names had a success rate of only 61% (Eichmann-Kalwara, Jorgensen, and Weingart 2018). Anecdotal evidence from conferences and publications supports this conclusion: DH is a very white field.

As the ADHO conference programs did not have any information about gender, the authors of their analysis added it to the data themselves—an approach they acknowledge was neither straightforward nor uncontroversial, given that they relied on a combination of personal knowledge and assumptions. Their approach still provides a useful "preliminary lens to view gender diversity" (Eichmann-Kalwara, Jorgensen, and Weingart 2018). To focus the lens further, Barbara Bordalejo (in 2024, the current president of CSDH/SCHN) developed a survey to "address directly those issues that Weingart [and his collaborators] had found elusive" by asking members of the DH community to anonymously provide information about themselves (2018). The 438 responses she received demonstrate not only that "digital humanists are binary, white, affluent, and Anglophone," but also that this bias becomes more pronounced as DH scholars move up the institutional ranks. Nearly 80% of Bordalejo's respondents were white—a disparity that rose to 88% for full professors. Similarly, while those who identified as male or female were matched early in their careers, males outnumber females three to two at the rank of associate professor and above. Correlation does not equal causation, but 37% of females identified themselves as a primary caregiver at home, compared to only 29% of males. It seems that females are disproportionately responsible for community and caregiving in both their personal and professional lives.

Bordalejo's most revealing results came from the comments respondents provided. One noted, "ethnicity is a trivial accident of birth and not connected to the truly great heritage I enjoy from the other earlier humans who were not my direct ancestors." Another listed his invisible disability as "Being a stupid asshole." A third indicated, "All in All, a pretty fucking stupid survey." With more generosity than is warranted, Bordalejo says that these comments—and the many others she quotes, all of which are similarly absurd—

> occurred only with data provided by scholars who identified themselves as heterosexual men, which suggests that the main representatives of the heteronormative patriarchy are also the victims of society that has created them and made them oblivious to the situation of others.

A call to (intersectional) action

Considering both the "disturbing ... level of aggression and vitriol" in the comments that Bordalejo received and the quantitative evidence supporting biases in DH, it is no surprise that myriad calls have been issued for digital humanities to change. For example,

> DH can and must do more to directly address issues faced by those who are marginalized—not despite the fact that, but precisely because, digital fields have long been problematic spaces for those who live life otherwise. For much of their history, these fields (such as computer science, video games, and humanities computing) have been implicitly structured as white, male, heteronormative spaces.
> *(Ruberg, Boyd, and Howe 2018)*

> [I]f we are to have a more just feminist digital humanities, we must attend to the ways that academic practices and digital spaces and tools are being leveraged by those with power—very often to limit marginalized people and at the most extreme in order to consume or promote violence against women, people of color, and trans people.
> *(Wernimont 2015)*

> Gender, race, sexuality, class, and disability might then be understood not as things that can simply be added on to our analyses (or to our metadata), but instead as operating principles of a different order, always already coursing through discourse and matter.
> *(McPherson 2014, 181)*

> Finding ways of bridging Black women's lived realities while also attempting to articulate some guidelines for doing the work of Black DH (and embracing the phrase, "the personal is political") is worthy

of discussing and debating further, but only as to those next, actionable steps. Inaction is not acceptable. "Pearl clutching", hand-wringing, and talking things to their untimely demise can no longer be the default.

(Nieves 2022)

Overlapping sites of discrimination and disadvantage have resulted in a homogeneous DH community, and clearly, there is a collective appetite for the discipline to "critically investigate structures of power, like race and gender" (Posner 2015). That this even needs to be said in 2024 feels somewhat dispiriting, even before we acknowledge that it has been being said for the past ten plus years. The pace of change has been slower than many—ourselves included—would have liked.

If there ever were a domain ripe for change, DH seems to be it. As Bonnie Ruberg, Jason Boyd, and James Howe note, while "many of the data-driven initiatives that have earned DH its most visible accolades eschew rather than engage topics of difference and identity," this need not be so (2018). DH is well placed to effect change, since "technology, while imbued with problems of discrimination and difference, can ... become a powerful platform for critiquing dominant norms"; if deployed correctly, "the digital humanities can speak directly to intersectional concerns of social justice" (2018). Writing from the perspective of queer studies, Ruberg, Boyd, and Howe argue that DH is simpatico with subaltern critiques of power, the homogeneity of its community notwithstanding. They point specifically to DH's "common ethos: a commitment to exploring new ways of thinking and to challenging accepted paradigms of meaning-making," and a long history and ongoing practice of using emerging technologies to play with—and to break—codes of meaning and representation (2018).

Ruberg, Boyd, and Howe's above-mentioned *intersectional concerns* are a reference to intersectional feminism, a framework that considers the compounding effects of overlapping, concurrent inequalities and privileges. Intersectionality comes from the legal scholarship of Kimberlé Crenshaw, where she uses it to explain the convergent and compounding effects of race, class, and gender in the subordination of Black women:

> Discrimination, like traffic through an intersection, may flow in one direction, and it may flow in another. If an accident happens in an intersection, it can be caused by cars traveling from any number of directions and, sometimes, from all of them.
>
> *(1989, 149)*

Although Crenshaw was writing from a Black feminist perspective—and her ideas about intersectionality can be traced to the works of scholars such as

W. E. B. Du Bois and bell hooks—intersectionality has subsequently expanded to refer, in Patricia Hill Collins's words, to "the critical insight that race, class, gender, sexuality, ethnicity, nation, ability, and age operate not as unitary, mutually exclusive entities, but as reciprocally constructing phenomena that in turn shape complex social inequalities" (2015). Although not without problems of dilution and appropriation, this opening up of intersectionality to include additional sites of subordination is in keeping with Crenshaw's original argument: "there is more to gain by collectively challenging the hierarchy rather than by each discriminatee individually seeking to protect her source of privilege within the hierarchy" (1989, 145). Yet, it is worth noting that anti-racist feminists have been clear that intersectional analyses do not attempt to equate all forms of inequity but, rather, demonstrate how interrelated and distinct forms of power and oppression shape subjectivities and social positions in complex and uneven ways.

Kara Keeling's "Queer OS" offers something of an early framework for thinking about the relationship between queerness, race, new media, and digital humanities. Keeling argues that "the materiality, rhetorics, forms, and ontologies of new media readily lend themselves to a theoretical encounter with queer theory" (2014, 152). Her notion of Queer OS is premised on understanding how "race, gender, class, [and] citizenship" are "mutually constitutive with sexuality and with media and information technologies" (153) to offer a robust and historicized vision of queerness. Keeling resists a narrow vision of queerness as singularly concerned with sexuality and instead conceives of it as a framework for difference more generally. She

> understands *queer* as a naming orientation towards various and shifting aspects of existing reality and the social norms they govern, such that it makes available pressing questions about, eccentric and/or unexpected relationships in, and possible alternatives to those social norms.
>
> *(153, original emphasis)*

This argument aligns with Tara McPherson's work (see Chapter 9) to describe the ideological connections between the development of computing technologies and US racial inequalities. For both Keeling and McPherson, critical digital humanities can challenge social structures by unearthing the connections between social inequality and technological developments. Indeed, Keeling argues that one of queer theory's key insights is that the segmentation of cultural and political life into discrete categories obscures connections that have significant effects on people's lives.

Keeling's vision of a queer DH necessarily grounds queer theory in the historical experiences of queer people's struggle for liberation. As Ruberg,

Boyd, and Howe argue, "moving toward a queer digital humanities means valuing queer lives and embracing a queer ethos but also addressing the actionable, concrete ways that queerness can shift how the work of DH is done" (109). Shifting the work of DH can range from focusing on previously ignored histories and communities to challenging binary categories of data that erase queer life, to resisting the gendered language of computational technology, and to foregrounding the materiality of digital scholarship. Queer DH thus employs the lessons of queer theory to develop new modes of working with data, digital culture, and digital labour.

In "Man and His Tool, Again?" (2015), Jamie Skye Bianco embeds Keeling's arguments for a queer digital praxis in the form of a digital essay. Readers move through Bianco's text by clicking the hypertext sections; each click reveals a new section of the essay. The text unfolds and expands unevenly, making a linear mode of reading virtually impossible. Instead, reading becomes unexpected and unfamiliar as the text generates queer modes of play and exploration. Bianco's essay demonstrates that "texts and technologies are not neutral conduits for meaning, but are actively produced in their readers, viewers, and users" (Starosielski 2015). By forcing the reader into an unusual relationship to the text, Bianco foregrounds the digital interface and—by punning on male scholars' obsession with their tools—it requires readers to actively think about their orientation in relation to the text. The essay challenges notions of orientation not just in terms of physically navigating the text but also in terms of gender and sexual orientation and the perspective (and modes of play) the user adopts as they move through the text. As Nicole Starosielski explains in her response to Bianco's essay:

> There is a play with visibility here, one that builds on a long history of feminist and queer reading practices. To merely click through the quotations, one would literally fail to see the argument. The piece forces the reader to pause, to move her indexical pointer away from the quotations in order to reveal the feminist analysis. This not only instantiates a particular politics of visibility, in which we must unearth voices hidden beneath, but requires an active and embodied reader to move through the work, clicking each fragment to move the narrative along.
>
> *(2015)*

Bianco's essay couples a relatively straightforward quantitative analysis of digital humanities work (engaging in textual word counts) with a playful and queer rendering of her argument to challenge the very possibility of a *straightforward* reading. Bianco's playful essay reminds readers of a key lesson of queer and feminist forms of digital humanities work: all knowledge is partial, situated, and informed by social codes of sexuality and gender.

As Bianco's and Keeling's essays demonstrate, intersectional thought offers the potential for much-needed redress of tech and academia's long history of ignoring marginalized identities. As we show in this chapter and the two that follow, intersectional thinking has been taken up by DH practitioners who use their projects to "[resist] binary logic, [encourage] complex analysis, and [foreground] difference" (Risam 2015). These thinkers refuse binary thought in their work, often beginning by subjecting DH to scrutiny and critique from queer, antiracist, and anti-colonial perspectives. To achieve these ends, however, requires a deep transformation of both theory and praxis. For lasting change to be made, we must take care to centre intersectionality, rather than treating it as an afterthought; it is not enough to make token attempts at inclusion for optics' sake, or to limit ourselves to "common sense advice" and "practical tweaks" (Risam 2015).

Subjects and subjectivity

Although a given project's relationship to questions of power may be explicitly stated (in a *methodology* or *project goals* section, for instance) or may be implicit in a project's design, the ideological stakes are often not immediately apparent, leading Jacqueline Wernimont to ask,

> Are digital archives feminist because the content is by women, or because the modes of production are feminist, or because the technologies themselves are feminist or used to feminist ends? Is it all three? Do we have to account for both the historical and social contexts from which particular archives arise when thinking about the nature of their feminism? What tools might be helpful in thinking through the sense that tools like XML are neutral?
>
> *(2013)*

Given the complexities of identity and the problems inherent in categorization, we cannot assume intent behind projects, nor can we presume to know how those who created them identify. Self-identification can go some of the way to filling this gap: for example, by using FemTechNet's "Women, Enby [nonbinary], Gender Queer and Other Gender Minorities in DH" (names, Twitter handles, pronouns, scholarly fields, and more for those listed) and The Colored Conventions Project's "Black Digital

Humanities Projects & Resources" (titles of and links to DH projects, online resources, and related events). While lists that collate projects and communities are informative, it is reductive to rely on information about individual projects or people; a wholesale change in methodologies and ideologies would be far more productive.

DH practitioners must therefore grapple with the modes of production, the social contexts, the intended ends, and the (non)neutrality of tools as they develop their projects. Kaylin Land's 2020 study, "Predicting Author Gender Using Machine Learning Algorithms: Looking Beyond the Binary," demonstrates the problem with the assumed neutrality of archive, methodology, and machine. In considering DH projects that use machine learning algorithms to predict—or make generalizations about literary style based on—author gender, Land notes that patterns spotted by the computers (and the researchers interpreting the data they generate) do not tell us anything about how women write. Instead, they tell us about computational biases, researcher assumptions, and the oppressive expectations faced by and market forces shaping the output of women writers. Land reminds us, "it is critical to ask questions that refute the easy conclusion that women are inherently different than men" (2020). The sad truth is that a purely technical, decontextualized analysis of the author gender reifies social categories rather than scrutinizing how gender is socially constructed. The fact that Land even finds reductive so-called analyses on which to base her own research tells us as much about inequalities in DH as the comments Bordalejo received on her survey.

Fortunately, in the Canadian DH landscape, there are groups dedicated to asking the difficult questions that Wernimont and Land pose. York University's Feminist Digital Methods Research Cluster supports "Collaborative and transnational feminist digital projects" and works with "Intersectional approaches to feminist digital methods" (Centre for Feminist Research, n.d.). The University of Guelph's DH@Guelph Interdisciplinary Feminisms series fosters "interdisciplinary, intersectional … conversations about gender and sexuality" (DH@Guelph, 2023). The qCollaborative intersectional feminist design research lab, with nodes at the University of Waterloo and Mount Royal University, "is committed to challenging and changing unjust behaviours, such as racism, colonialism, (cis)sexism, homophobia, transphobia, ableism, classism, and xenophobia wherever they occur, including in academia, in social justice movements, and in ourselves" (Weins et al. 2020, 2–3). The Transgender Media Lab at Carleton University is dedicated to preserving and sharing the audiovisual work of trans, Two Spirit, nonbinary, intersex, and gender-nonconforming people through its *Transgender Media Portal* and its mailing list for amplifying work related to intersectional, feminist, queer, and trans digital humanities.

These programs are among those that locate intersectional feminist theory and practice at the heart of their work, and many of the projects that are described in the next section have come out of—or are affiliated with researchers who are members of—these groups.

Projects

Projects that aim to challenge oppression must reconsider theoretical models, the application of these models in research, the affordances built into our datasets, tools, and interfaces, and the community-centred practices enlisted. This section looks at a number of feminist, queer, intersectional digital humanities projects engaging with (Canadian) literature and undertaken by Canadian teams.

The Orlando Project

When it comes to understanding how feminist principles might be put into practice, the place to start is *The Orlando Project*, the ur-project for Canadian, intersectional, feminist digital humanities. *Orlando*'s express purpose is to "[harness] the power of digital tools and methods to advance feminist literary scholarship," which it achieves through its textbase of born-digital, critical-biographical writing about women writers: their lives and works—and the social, political, and historical contexts that shaped them (*Orlando* 2024). The *Orlando* team

> sees gender as an indispensable tool for historical analysis that helps to shape the questions we ask about the production, reception, and features of written texts and about the ways in which these have been understood throughout the history of women's writing.
>
> *(Orlando 2023)*

Orlando's custom-built system for tagging (or encoding) its vast quantity of material, so that it can be searched, browsed, and endlessly recombined, demonstrates the ways in which the lives and literatures of women are the product of complex, interlinked, situated contexts.

Among *Orlando*'s text tags, the team's custom-created *cultural formation* tag and its associated sub-tags stand out for their ability to capture intersectional identities in all their subjective, historical complexities. Cultural formation refers to "social identity and subjectivity, such as race, ethnicity, nationality, religion, gender, sexuality, class, and political allegiance," but also the "different combinations and interactions of these for different writers" (*Orlando* 2023); by using tags for identities, *Orlando* makes space for the ways in which they overlap and are discursive, historically grounded, socially constructed, and mutable. The tags also situate identity within time and space, "with attributes to capture information about such issues as current alternative terms for particular categories and whether authors self-defined with them" (Holland and Brown 2018). Intersectional to its core, *Orlando* uses cultural formations "to forestall simplistic interpretation" by revealing how "such identities are culturally produced and embedded in discourse" (*Orlando* 2023). Even gender, which is foundational to the project's focus on women's writing, is understood to be a contextual, cultural construct rather than an inherent, independent, or fixed entity—a view that may seem common sense to readers of this volume but is sadly not the case in some circles even today, and certainly was not as widely accepted when *Orlando* began.

LGBTQ+ and feminist archives

Where *Orlando* is concerned with writing *about* women writers, there are also projects that publish historical and literary works themselves. For example, *Women Writers Online*, a full-text collection of women's writing from 1526 to 1850, plug gaps in the archive, albeit only for works that are in the public domain. *The ArQuives: Canada's LGBTQ+ Archives* is not explicitly DH, but it is a major collection of queer histories, images, narratives, and videos. Similarly, the *LGBTQ Oral History Digital Collaboratory*, led by Elspeth Brown (who is also director of the Critical Digital Humanities Initiative at the University of Toronto), is a hub for digital projects focused on queer life and history and provides a platform for stories from disability activists, oral histories of queer life in Canada, and the queer history of Hanlan's Point, Toronto's only nude beach; it also provides a home for projects such as the *Pussy Palace Oral History Project*, *Queer and Disabled Activisms in Tkaronto Documentary Project*, and the *Trans Activism Oral History Project*. The *Transgender Archives*, led by Aaron Devor (chair in Transgender Studies at the University of Victoria), is the largest Trans+ archive in the world, with enough materials to fill over 160 metres of shelves (more than one and a half times the size of the Margaret Atwood archive mentioned in Chapter 5). Its collection includes both digitized and born-digital materials. The *Collaboratory for Writing and Research on Culture* (CWRC), directed by Susan Brown (Canada Research Chair in Collaborative Digital Scholarship at the University of Guelph) and Mihaela Ilovan also plays host to feminist and intersectional digital archives. Its collections include projects on Canadian women's writing, such as *Canada's Early Women Writers*, *Canadian Jewish Women Writers*, *Canadian Women Playwrights Online*, *English-Canadian Women's*

Poetry to 1867, the *Feminist Caucus Living Archives*, and *Women's Writing and Reading in Canada from 1950*. It also hosts projects about individual Canadian women writers, including Winnifred Eaton, L. M. Montgomery, P. K. Page, and E. Pauline Johnson. Additional intersectional and diversity-focused CWRC projects include *Digital Diversity: Writing | Feminism | Culture* and *The People and the Text: Indigenous Writing in Lands Claimed by Canada*.

Yellow Nineties 2.0

There are also smaller, more focused projects that combine full-text access with contextual information and critical-research outputs in the vein of projects like Graham Jensen's *Canadian Modernist Magazines Project* discussed in the previous chapter. The *Yellow Nineties 2.0*, led by Lorraine Janzen Kooistra at Toronto Metropolitan University, offers access to digitized versions of late-Victorian little magazines, supplemented by extensive scholarly context, including overviews, critical introductions, and essays on selected contributors; an additional personography built using linked open data "makes visible the creative productions of women and other historically marginalized persons" who constitute the magazines' networks of contributors (Hedley and Janzen Kooistra 2018). The *Yellow Nineties* project applies a critical, queer, feminist lens in its personography by treating identity as "fluid and contingent." This is essential to the project's task of breaking down the normative, homogeneous tendencies inherent in prosopographical work,[1] thus undercutting the generalization that the magazines' contributors were "middle-aged, British, Caucasian male[s] who studied at Oxbridge"—a group that sounds not all that dissimilar to the average ADHO presenter invoked by Eichmann-Kalwara, Jorgensen, and Weingart (Hedley and Janzen Kooistra 2018). Like *Orlando*, the *Yellow Nineties* "rather than flattening ambiguities, highlight[s] the noncorrelative by showing the politics of gender and sex at work ... [and] self-reflexively highlighting the contingent nature of the data ... as well as supporting feminist inclusivity in our digital humanities praxis" (Hedley and Janzen Kooistra 2018). The structure of the personography and the affordances of the linked data tools used to build it, both of which reject binary categorizations, are what makes this specificity possible.

Lesbian and Gay Liberation in Canada

Lesbian and Gay Liberation in Canada (LGLC), led by Constance Crompton (University of Ottawa) and Michelle Schwartz (Toronto Metropolitan University), is a digital archive of lesbian, gay, bisexual, and transgender history in Canada, 1964–1981. The project uses TEI (see Chapter 13) to transform a digitized version of Don McLeod's two-volume *Lesbian and Gay Liberation in Canada* (1996) into a searchable, linked database that invites users to explore events and figures in the history of gay liberation in Canada. Out of this database, Crompton and Schwartz have generated a series of network graphs that show links between people, places, events, and publications that would be otherwise difficult to discern. Like *Orlando* before it, LGLC emerges from the limits of print-based scholarship and uses digital technology to complicate our understanding of the histories the project documents:

> In addition to broadening the book form, we are investigating the interoperability of the existing modelling and knowledge-capture systems, including TEI, MARC, and graph databases ... We are investigating how data exchange formats and database structures shape how we record information and, as a result, what we can know about cultural history and the people who forged that history, when it and they are represented as data.
>
> *(Schwartz and Crompton 2015)*

By using markup, the project creators are able to generate visualizations that demonstrate relationships between actors in the history of Canadian lesbian and gay liberation. The affordances of DH have proven to be particularly valuable for subaltern histories where documentation is sparse and actors often had to conceal their involvement for fear of reprisal. LGLC's

> graph database with the text of each event as well as a network of whom appeared in events with whom, how gay activists deployed pseudonyms, how queer community groups, publishers, and bars moved around their home cities over time, and which archival sources act as documentary witnesses,

recalls the multiplicity of ways that users can traverse *Orlando*'s textbase to explore the situated contexts of women writers (Schwartz and Crompton 2015); like the *Yellow Nineties*, the LGLC team is working with the *Linked Infrastructure for Networked Cultural Scholarship* to create linked open data to allow for even more nuanced exploration. The extensive, interlinked, contextualized history provided by—and the ongoing data augmentation work of—LGLC would be impossible within the limits of a print book.

Principles and practices

All of the projects described above have archival aspects to them. They either assemble primary-source collections or they gather information about the creators or subjects of said materials. Archives are always expressions of power. For Alana Cattapan, "activism and the archive are often one and the same," and "digital humanities has worked to blur the boundaries of who gets to name, create, and define the archive, and what it means to house a collection" (2017). DH's tools and techniques make it possible to create an archive even with limited resources and minimal (or nonexistent) institutional support—circumstances all too familiar to many working on materials that have been shunted to the margins, and also sadly too familiar to scholars who themselves have found themselves marginalized. *HistSex*, for example, offers a catalogue of archives, digital projects, and publications of LGBTQ+ research and an interactive timeline of the history of sexuality (Watson 2024). Built using *Omeka S*, a free, web-based publishing platform for cultural heritage data, *HistSex* is exemplary of how a group—in this case, sex educators, historians, and librarians, led by B. M. Watson (University of British Columbia)—can produce a resource that fills a gap in the mainstream archival landscape.

HistSex and many of the other projects described above are forthright about their ideologies and often about their teams' identities, thus emphasizing the alignment between subject matter and intention and also highlighting the central role that methodology plays in developing projects such as these. Perhaps because of the risks of having an ideology ascribed to the work by others, some DH projects subvert this by explicitly foregrounding their ideologies. This can take the form of fulsome documentation, as with the collaborative work of *Orlando* and CWRC to explicitly define their "ontology's most significant terms, such as those for social identities, and to provide definitions for categories and key terms that cannot be sourced from external ontologies" (Brown 2020, 169). It can also take the form of clear and well-defined terms, such as those provided by *Homosaurus: An International LGBTQ+ Linked Data Vocabulary*. Or it can take the form of comprehensible and navigable relationships of the sorts created by *Yellow Nineties* and LGLC. These are all examples of applying DH for specific, intersectional ends.

Alongside embedding ideology in methods, there are also explicit calls for intersectional commitment. For example, "The Feminist Data Manifest-No" recognizes historical and ongoing systemic harms embedded in data practices, and it calls for individuals and communities—especially those of "embodied difference"—to refuse exploitation and reclaim autonomy (Cifor et al. 2019). The "cyberfeminist praxis" FemTechNet calls for its members to "recognize digital and other technologies can both subvert and reinscribe oppressive relations of power" and to "work to make these complex relations of power transparent" through accountability, collaboration, collectivity, and care (FemTechNet). Similarly, the eighteen "Feminist Principles of the Internet" include a call to "reclaim technology as a platform for creativity and expression, as well as to challenge the cultures of sexism and discrimination in all spaces" (Association for Progressive Communication, n.d.). According to these projects, it is incumbent upon DH practitioners to refuse the harmful practices de facto in mainstream technology and on the web.

Brown, Clements, and Grundy argue that we must ensure that we are "not just *consumers* of technology, but *producers* of technological tools that suit our aims and methodologies" (Brown, Clements, and Grundy 2006, 318; original emphasis). Wernimont, meanwhile, notes that even "those who cannot make" (read: not *producers*) need not find ourselves "in subordinated, devalued, 'user' positions" (2013). Those who engage in "Research that mobilizes and centres data by and for Indigenous, Black, poor, uncitizened, transgender, disabled and other minoritized, over-researched and underserved people" can intervene directly in the archives and in the code (Cifor et al. 2019). We can repurpose existing systems to express and explore identities in new ways. In doing so, we can engage in what Zach Blas calls "disidentifying as a hacker strategy" (2008, 16). Like intersectionality, disidentification highlights overlapping sites of marginalization; like hacking, disidentification has the potential to disrupt the system from within:

> Instead of buckling under the pressures of dominant ideology (identification, assimilation) or attempting to break free of its inescapable sphere (counter identification, utopianism), this "working on and against" is a strategy that tries to transform a cultural logic from within, always laboring to enact permanent structural change, while at the same time valuing the importance of local or everyday struggles of resistance.
>
> *(Muñoz 1999, 148)*

Disidentification neither submits to nor refuses the system. Instead, it looks for opportunities to "compute queerly … to make central those externalities—exploits, bugs, breakdown, abuse, and misuse—of our digital culture that, while pervasive, we nonetheless disavow" (Gaboury 2018, 485). It must be remembered that just as subjects rarely choose to succumb to the logic of ideology, not all subjects are able to easily disidentify from that same logic. Yet, this chapter is rife with examples of *working on* and *working against*—of transforming cultural logics from within. Even the analyses of DH conference attendees and journal article authors referenced at the start of this chapter are examples of DH turning its tools on its own outputs to uncover biases of gender and race. Similarly, Land's textual analysis highlights the illogic of generalizing gender based on authors' writing. *Orlando* subverts binary logic to develop a tagging system that allows for multiple, overlapping, and even conflicting identities. *Yellow Nineties* and LGLC work within the rigid structures of databases to draw nuanced pictures of marginalized communities.

As we shall see in the next two chapters, disidentification as a strategy of resistance is often limited by the material structures of power that affect racialized and Indigenous people differently. Those systems of power cannot always be hacked as easily as Blas suggests. As a result, racialized and Indigenous DH practitioners have developed new strategies for thinking about difference, power, and agency in their projects. We survey these theories and strategies to explore how DH can be used to both antiracist (Chapter 9) and anti-colonial (Chapter 10) ends.

Note

1 A *prosopography* is a collective biography of a group of people, often focused on their social, political, and familial contexts. A *personography* is akin to a bibliography, but instead of providing structured information about books, it provides structured (biographical) information about individuals. As Hedley and Janzen Kooistra explain, "Personography has its origins in prosopography—a traditional historiographic method that develops a collective biography of a population by flattening out differences and anomalies to create a typical subject" (2018). Where a prosopography generalizes, a personography is sensitive "to non-normative identities and relationships."

Further reading

Bianco, Jamie Skye. 2012. "This Digital Humanities Which Is Not One." In *Debates in the Digital Humanities*, edited by Matthew K. Gold, 96–112. Minneapolis: University of Minnesota Press. https://doi.org/10.5749/minnesota/9780816677948.003.0012.

Cifor, Marika, Patricia Garcia, T. L. Cowan, Jasmine Rault, Tonia Sutherland, Anita Say Chan, Jennifer Rode, Anna Lauren Hoffmann, Niloufar Salehi, and Lisa Nakamura. 2019. "Feminist Data Manifest-No." https://www.manifestno.com/.

D'Ignazio, Catherine, and Lauren F. Klein. 2023. *Data Feminism*. Cambridge: The MIT Press. https://doi.org/10.7551/mitpress/11805.001.0001.

Losh, Elizabeth, and Jacqueline Wernimont. 2018. *Bodies of Information: Intersectional Feminism and Digital Humanities*, edited by Elizabeth Losh and Jacqueline Wernimont. Minneapolis: University of Minnesota Press. https://dhdebates.gc.cuny.edu/projects/bodies-of-information.

Risam, Roopika. 2015. "Beyond the Margins: Intersectionality and the Digital Humanities." *Digital Humanities Quarterly* 9, no. 2. https://www.digitalhumanities.org/dhq/vol/9/2/000208/000208.html.

Wernimont, Jacqueline. 2013. "Whence Feminism? Assessing Feminist Interventions in Digital Literary Archives." *Digital Humanities Quarterly* 7, no. 1. https://www.digitalhumanities.org/dhq/vol/7/1/000156/000156.html.

Works cited

The ArQuives: Canada's LGBTQ+ Archives. n.d. Accessed August 26, 2024. https://arquives.ca/.

Association for Progressive Communication. n.d. "Usage." *Feminist Principles of the Internet*. Accessed September 8, 2024. https://feministinternet.org/en/principle/usage.

Beverley, Andrea. n.d. *Feminist Caucus Living Archives*. Collaboratory for Writing and Research on Culture. Accessed October 10, 2024. https://cwrc.ca/project/feminist-caucus-living-archives.

Bianco, Jamie Skye. 2015. "Man and His Tool, Again? Queer and Feminist Notes on Practices in the Digital Humanities and Object Orientations Everywhere." *Digital Humanities Quarterly* 9, no. 2. https://www.digitalhumanities.org/dhq/vol/9/2/000216/000216.html.

Blas, Zach. 2008. *Gay Bombs: User's Manual*. Queer Technologies Inc. https://zachblas.info/works/queer-technologies/.

Bordalejo, Barbara. 2018. "Minority Report: The Myth of Equality in the Digital Humanities." In *Bodies of Information: Intersectional Feminism and Digital Humanities*, edited by Elizabeth Losh and Jacqueline Wernimont, 320–43. Minneapolis: University of Minnesota Press. https://doi.org/10.5749/j.ctv9hj9r9.21.

Brown, Elspeth, and Alisha Stranges. 2024. *LGBTQ Oral History Digital Collaboratory*. https://lgbtqdigitalcollaboratory.org/.

Brown, Susan. 2020. "Categorically Provisional." *PMLA* 135, no. 1: 165–74. https://doi.org/10.1632/pmla.2020.135.1.165.

Brown, Susan, Patricia Clements, and Isobel Grundy. 2006. "Sorting Things In: Feminist Knowledge Representation and Changing Modes of Scholarly Production." *Women's Studies International Forum* 29, no. 6: 317–25. https://doi.org/10.1016/j.wsif.2006.04.010.

Cattapan, Alana. 2017. "Notes on the Digital Humanities and (Canadian) Feminist Archives." *Field Guide* (blog), *Media Commons*, April 12, 2017. https://mediacommons.org/fieldguide/question/what-role-digital-humanities-future-archive/response/notes-digital-humanities-and-canadian-.

Caufield, Catherine. n.d. *Canadian Jewish Women Writers*. Collaboratory for Writing and Research on Culture. Accessed October 10, 2024. https://cwrc.ca/project/canadian-jewish-women-writers.

Centre for Feminist Research. n.d. "Feminist Digital Methods." York University. Accessed September 8, 2024. https://www.yorku.ca/cfr/feminist-digital-methods/.

Cifor, Marika, Patricia Garcia, T. L. Cowan, Jasmine Rault, Tonia Sutherland, Anita Say Chan, Jennifer Rode, Anna Lauren Hoffmann, Niloufar Salehi, and Lisa Nakamura. 2019. "Feminist Data Manifest-No." https://www.manifestno.com/.

Collins, Patricia Hill. 2015. "Intersectionality's Definitional Dilemmas." *Annual Review of Sociology* 41: 1–20. https://doi.org/10.1146/annurev-soc-073014-112142.

The Colored Conventions Project. n.d. "Black Digital Humanities Projects & Resources." Accessed August 26, 2024. https://bit.ly/Black-DH-List.

Crenshaw, Kimberlé. 1989. "Demarginalizing the Intersection of Race and Sex: A Black Feminist Critique of Antidiscrimination Doctrine, Feminist Theory and Antiracist Politics." *The University of Chicago Legal Forum*: 139–68.

Crompton, Constance, and Michelle Schwartz. n.d. *Lesbian and Gay Liberation in Canada*. Accessed September 5, 2024. https://lglc.ca/.

Demers, Patricia. n.d. *Women's Writing and Reading in Canada from 1950*. Collaboratory for Writing and Research on Culture. Accessed October 10, 2024. https://cwrc.ca/canwwrfrom1950.

Devereux, Cecily. n.d. *English-Canadian Women's Poetry to 1867*. Collaboratory for Writing and Research on Culture. Accessed October 10, 2024. https://cwrc.ca/project/english-canadian-women's-poetry-1867.

DH@Guelph. 2023. "Interdisciplinary Feminisms Series." University of Guelph. https://www.uoguelph.ca/arts/dhguelph/thinc/if.

Digital Diversity: Writing | Feminism | Culture. n.d. Collaboratory for Writing and Research on Culture. Accessed October 10, 2024. https://cwrc.ca/project/digital-diversity.

Digital Transgender Archive. 2024. *Homosaurus: An International LGBTQ+ Linked Data Vocabulary*. https://homosaurus.org/.

Djwa, Sandra, and Zailig Pollock. n.d. *The Digital Page: The Collected Works of P. K. Page*. Collaboratory for Writing and Research on Culture. Accessed October 10, 2024. https://cwrc.ca/project/digitalpage.

Eichmann-Kalwara, Nickoal, Jeana Jorgensen, and Scott B. Weingart. 2018. "Representation at Digital Humanities Conferences (2000–2015)." In *Bodies of Information: Intersectional Feminism and Digital Humanities*, edited by Elizabeth Losh and Jacqueline Wernimont, 72–92. Minneapolis: University of Minnesota Press. https://doi.org/10.5749/j.ctv9hj9r9.9.

FemTechNet. n.d.-a. *FemTechNet*. Accessed August 26, 2024. https://www.femtechnet.org/.

FemTechNet. n.d.-b. "Women, Enby, Gender Queer and Other Gender Minorities in DH." Accessed August 26, 2024. https://docs.google.com/spreadsheets/d/1pPscJX7I7Vvuc4YIBbd38nbWgIjp-0FiI5yZ1sxG6Vk/edit?gid=0#gid=0.

Gaboury, Jacob. 2018. "Critical Unmaking: Toward a Queer Computation." In *The Routledge Companion to Media Studies and Digital Humanities*, edited by Jentery Sayers, 483–91. London: Taylor and Francis. https://doi.org/10.4324/9781315730479-50.

Gao, Jin, Julianne Nyhan, Oliver Duke-Williams, and Simon Mahony. 2022. "Gender Influences in Digital Humanities Co-authorship Networks." *Journal of Documentation* 79, no. 7: 327–50. https://doi.org/10.1108/JD-11-2021-0221.

Gerson, Carole. n.d. *Canada's Early Women Writers Project, 2018–2024*. Collaboratory for Writing and Research on Culture. Accessed October 10, 2024. https://cwrc.ca/project/canadas-early-women-writers.

Hedley, Alison, and Lorraine Janzen Kooistra. 2018. "Prototyping Personography for *The Yellow Nineties Online*: Queering and Querying History in the Digital Age." In *Bodies of Information: Intersectional Feminism and Digital Humanities*, edited by Elizabeth Losh and Jacqueline Wernimont, 157–72. Minneapolis: University of Minnesota Press.https://doi.org/10.5749/j.ctv9hj9r9.13.

Holland, Kathryn, and Susan Brown. 2018. "Project | Process | Product: Feminist Digital Subjectivity in a Shifting Scholarly Field." In *Bodies of Information: Intersectional Feminism and Digital Humanities*, edited by Elizabeth Losh and Jacqueline Wernimont, 409–33. Minneapolis: University of Minnesota Press. https://doi.org/10.5749/j.ctv9hj9r9.25.

Janzen Kooistra, Lorraine. n.d. *Yellow Nineties 2.0*. Accessed July 12, 2024. https://1890s.ca/.
Jensen, Graham, Deseray Manuel, et al. 2022. *Canadian Modernist Magazines Project*. University of Victoria. https://modernistmags.ca.
Keeling, Kara. 2014. "Queer OS." *Cinema Journal*, 52, no. 2: 152–57. https://doi.org/10.1353/cj.2014.0004.
Land, Kaylin. 2020. "Predicting Author Gender Using Machine Learning Algorithms: Looking Beyond the Binary." *Digital Studies / Le champ numérique* 10, no. 1. https://doi.org/10.16995/dscn.362.
L. M. Montgomery Collection. n.d. Collaboratory for Writing and Research on Culture. Accessed October 10, 2024. https://cwrc.ca/lmmontgomery.
McPherson, Tara. 2014. "Designing for Difference." *Differences: A Journal of Feminist Cultural Studies* 25, no. 1: 178–88. https://doi.org/10.1215/10407391-2420039.
Muñoz, José Esteban. 1999. *Disidentifications: Queers of Color and the Performance of Politics*. Minneapolis: University of Minnesota Press.
Nieves, Angel David. 2022. "'For the Master's [DH] Tools Will Never Dismantle the Master's House': An Alternative Primer for a Critical Black DH Praxis." *Digital Humanities Quarterly* 16, no. 3. https://www.digitalhumanities.org/dhq/vol/16/3/000633/000633.html.
Orlando. 2023. *The Orlando Project*. https://orlando.cambridge.org/.
Orlando. 2024. "The Orlando Project: Feminist Literary History and Digital Humanities." *The Orlando Project*. https://www.artsrn.ualberta.ca/orlando/.
Posner, Miriam. 2015. "What's Next: The Radical, Unrealized Potential of Digital Humanities." *Miriam Posner* (blog), July 27, 2015. https://miriamposner.com/blog/whats-next-the-radical-unrealized-potential-of-digital-humanities/.
Reder, Deanna, Madeleine Reddon, Alix Shield, Margery Fee, and Susan Glover. n.d. *The People and the Text: Indigenous Writing in Lands Claimed by Canada*. Accessed September 8, 2024. https://thepeopleandthetext.ca/.
Risam, Roopika. 2015. "Beyond the Margins: Intersectionality and the Digital Humanities." *Digital Humanities Quarterly* 9, no. 2. https://www.digitalhumanities.org/dhq/vol/9/2/000208/000208.html.
Ruberg, Bonnie, Jason Boyd, and James Howe. 2018. "Toward a Queer Digital Humanities." In *Bodies of Information: Intersectional Feminism and Digital Humanities*, edited by Elizabeth Losh and Jacqueline Wernimont, 108–28. Minneapolis: University of Minnesota Press. https://doi.org/10.5749/j.ctv9hj9r9.11.
Schwartz, Michelle, and Constance Crompton. 2015. "Lesbian and Gay Liberation in Canada: Representing the Dyke Dynamo." *Digital Studies / Le champ numérique* 5, no. 3. https://doi.org/10.16995/dscn.27.
Shield, Alix. n.d. *E. Pauline Johnson's Legends of Vancouver*. Collaboratory for Writing and Research on Culture. Accessed October 10, 2024. https://cwrc.ca/project/e-pauline-johnson's-legends-vancouver.
Starosielski, Nicole. 2015. "Orientation: 'Man and His Tool, Again?'" *Digital Humanities Quarterly* 9, no. 2. https://www.digitalhumanities.org/dhq/vol/9/2/000211/000211.html.
Transgender Media Portal. 2024. *Transgender Media Portal*. Accessed October 30, 2024. https://www.transgendermediaportal.org/.

University of Victoria. n.d. *Transgender Archives*. Accessed September 8, 2024. https://www.uvic.ca/transgenderarchives/index.php.

Watson, B. M. 2024. *HistSex*. https://histsex.org/.

Weins, Brianna, Stan Ruecker, Jennifer Roberts-Smith, Milena Radzikowska, and Shana MacDonald. 2020. "Materializing Data: New Research Methods for Feminist Digital Humanities." *Digital Studies / Le champ numérique* 10, no. 1. https://doi.org/10.16995/dscn.373.

Wernimont, Jacqueline. 2013. "Whence Feminism? Assessing Feminist Interventions in Digital Literary Archives." *Digital Humanities Quarterly* 7, no. 1. https://www.digitalhumanities.org/dhq/vol/7/1/000156/000156.html.

Wernimont, Jacqueline. 2015. "Introduction to Feminisms and DH Special Issue." *Digital Humanities Quarterly* 9, no. 2. https://www.digitalhumanities.org/dhq/vol/7/1/000156/000156.html.

Wilson, Ann, and Dorothy Hadfield. *Canadian Women Playwrights Online*. Collaboratory for Writing and Research on Culture. https://cwrc.ca/cwpo.

Women Writers Online. n.d. Brown University. https://www.wwp.brown.edu/.

9
RACE, POWER, AND DIGITAL CULTURE

* * *

Race and data are inextricable. Casual racist thinking and the formal systems of racial classification can both be used to divide people into categories. For example, IBM's role in designing databases for the Nazi regime to track Jewish people across Europe (Beatty 2001) and its customized software designed for apartheid South Africa have both been well documented. Similarly, Canada's Indian Pass system functioned as an early form of bureaucratic colonial management designed to preserve a system of apartheid. The *Book of Negroes* (discussed in Chapter 7) is a case study in an effort to project incoherent racial classifications onto a diverse population, as demonstrated by the text's absurd attempts to codify people using racist and ableist terms such as "quadroon," "mulatto," and "idiot"—terms that reveal both the contradictions of racial thinking and racism's reliance on data to try to overcome those contradictions (Black Loyalists, n.d.). This chapter hones the discussion of intersectionality and power in Chapter 8 to focus on how DH research and histories of data have reified or challenged notions of race.

Bureaucratic systems of racial control rely on the ideas of race and the ability to measure and track the application of this idea within a population. Lisa Lowe's *The Intimacies of Four Continents* (2015) reads British colonial archives to identify sites of racial difference as well as unlikely forms of intimate knowledge that connect people despite colonial apartheid. Likewise, Caitlin Rosenthal reads the archives of plantation slavery to study plantation owners' "obsession with data" (2018, 2)—the crude

DOI: 10.4324/9781003318323-14

record-keeping and accounting practices they used to manage the system of plantation slavery. Lily Cho (2021) demonstrates the role of data in the management of Chinese migrants to Canada in the late nineteenth and early twentieth century, when CI 9 forms were used by Canadian immigration officials to track Chinese immigrants and to enforce the racist Chinese Head Tax policy. Cho argues that the production of this data did more than merely affirm racial difference: it was part of the "mass capture" of Chinese subjects in Canada, identifying, tracking, and managing the population, in order to construct migrant Chinese people as non-citizen subjects (2021, 27). Even as they lived in Canada, Chinese migrants were constantly reminded of their exclusion. Like the *Book of Negroes* years before, CI 9 forms represent a form of data designed to exclude racialized people from the nation, as do the countless instances of appropriated and weaponized uses of Indigenous data in Canada. Systems of racial management produce vast archives of material that both enact and document racial repression and violence. Researchers in a range of disciplines read that data as both a tool and effect of racist policies and governance and, more recently, Indigenous people have created their own datasets as part of acts of historical recovery and contemporary resistance (see Chapter 10).

Data oppression is widespread even today, including (but not only) at the intersection of racial discrimination, big data, and emerging technologies of artificial intelligence. Safiya Noble's *Algorithms of Oppression* (2018) examines how racist discourse is promoted—and naturalized—by digital tools and online discourse, and, for example, how search engines naturalize and reproduce racist discourse. Cathy O'Neil's *Weapons of Math Destruction* (2016) traces the use of big data to perpetuate race, class, and gender inequality. O'Neil's thesis is that although big data claims to merely observe people's behaviour, it shapes it by reifying discrimination using algorithms that present social constructions as scientific facts. Noble and O'Neil both demonstrate how artificial intelligence systems and big data algorithms interpret the world based on training data and are thereby at risk of reproducing and solidifying the social inequities that their training data reflects. The selection of training data, the design of algorithms, the composition of programming and design teams, and the oppressive identities that data can reflect all contribute to data oppression.

Wendy Hui Kyong Chun traces the origins of these forms of oppression to concepts that originate with British eugenicists, who were eager to predict and shape the future by manipulating observable variables in the population. These eugenicists enlisted linear regression to achieve their ends; linear regression is also one of the key mathematical concepts underpinning the predictive models used by big data today. Chun asks,

> To what extent has eugenics reemerged—if it has—not simply or directly through the proliferation of genetic testing and manipulation, but also through biometric methods and predictions? And how have data analytics and machine learning been used to found a revised form of eugenics, in which discriminatory pasts, presents, and futures coincide?
>
> *(2024, 58)*

These are urgent questions, particularly as large language models and other forms of machine learning generate outputs that remain opaque to the programmers that design them, even as we accept them readily into our daily lives. In 2024, Google Gemini's image-generating chatbot, when asked to produce images of white couples, claimed it was "unable to generate images of people based on specific ethnicities and skin tones … to avoid perpetuating harmful stereotypes and biases," yet it churned out historically anomalous images of Black soldiers in Nazi-era uniforms (Grant 2024). As AI systems are increasingly integrated into our decision-making processes, including criminal sentencing, credit score assessment, university acceptances, and more, they must be subject to intense scrutiny to ensure that they do not reproduce—or, worse, amplify—existing inequities.

Digital humanities and (the absence of) race

While there is a lengthy history of the relationship between race and data, digital humanities research, projects, and datasets have been slow to take race into account. DH's careful attention to the construction of data offers opportunities to interrogate how race is represented as data, yet for most of the discipline's history, race has been an afterthought—if considered at all. It is striking, given DH's focus on methodology, how little digital humanities scholars have been concerned with questions of difference.[1] Tara McPherson's "Why Are the Digital Humanities So White?" (2012) argues that the race-blind approach to DH applies a "lenticular logic" that separates the world of technology from broader social and political contexts. McPherson demonstrates that programming concepts such as modularity (the idea that every program should perform a single operation), pipes (the UNIX command for linking modular programs), and modular data "clearly work in the service of new regimes of security"; in a broader sense, these functions collude to prevent the kind of analysis that would put technology into meaningful conversation with racial politics. McPherson's argument places the history of the rise of networked computing in service of military interests alongside the concurrent civil rights and feminist movements, and she asks how the racial dimensions of DH, and computing more generally, become legible when these histories are conceived in relation. She argues that "technological formations are deeply bound up with racial formations," particularly as they "both represent a move towards modular knowledges." In response, McPherson calls for a wider historical view that sees the numerous links between race and data.

As the discussion of intersectionality in the previous chapter demonstrates, a broader understanding of computation in the context of social change and resistance to oppression demonstrates both technology's culpability in oppression and its capacity to help people improve their conditions. Yet, too often this work falls to those who have been on the receiving end of these forms of (technological) subjugation. Furthermore, when DH practitioners discuss race, they often gesture vaguely towards notions of diversity or multiculturalism. For antiracist critics, these gentle, inclusive terms are less incisive than the clearer, critical language of antiracism. For critics of the celebratory imagery of the big tent, fuzzy (meaning both *vague* and *warm*) concepts such as diversity and multiculturalism offer a means of sidestepping meaningful engagement with how digital projects and data cultures contribute to systems of discrimination.[2] These critics reject the portrayal of DH as having overcome the challenges of difference in favour of an incisive, productive digital humanities praxis that puts the entanglements of race and DH front and centre.

Roopika Risam stresses the need for an intersectional approach to data as a key component of critical digital humanities. She calls on DH scholars to "identify the layers of difference" within data and digital humanities methods "and use that knowledge as a basis for project design" (2015). This call for *layers of difference* is echoed in Alan Liu's theory of a "diversity stack" (2020, 135), his term for the kind of methodological infrastructure suited to diverse forms of DH. Liu's theory adapts Internet protocol design as a metaphor for how all DH projects must layer into their design considerations of multilingualism, multimedia, diversity of representation, worldviews and assumptions about history and temporality, and finally, concerns with identity. Liu's theory is compelling in its effort to pull DH away from monolingual and monocultural forms of scholarship, yet his attempt to generalize engagements with difference under the broad language of diversity—and to conceive of diversity as a technical problem— loses the sharpness of more pointed language of antiracism. Liu's theory also raises the question of whether DH engagements with differences may, in fact, be generalizable to the kind of infrastructural template he proposes. It may be the case that serious engagement with racial, gender, class, and other forms of difference each require unique models of scholarship and are not reducible to a single framework.

Christina Boyles, meanwhile, draws attention to the management of data, arguing that "postcustodial approaches to data collection" (2021)—the notion that, instead of physically acquiring data and records, archivists must support those to whom the data belongs (equally valuable for thinking about Indigenous data, as in Chapter 10)—can serve as a basis for intersectional DH methods. Boyles proposes an approach that foregrounds the roles of people and communities by asking two questions: "'How can we develop an ethical framework that is focused on our relationship to people rather than data?' and 'How would this transform our work with our communities and institutions?'" (2021). Catherine D'Ignazio and Lauren F. Klein's *Data Feminism* (2023) is an example of the first question put into practice; they employ Black feminist Patricia Hill Collins's notion of "the matrix of domination" (1990) to explain how systems of power and oppression operate in structural (laws and policies), disciplinary (police and judiciary), hegemonic (circulation of ideas), and interpersonal (individual experiences and interactions) dimensions of society. Collins's intersectional feminist approach to understanding power offers a rich language for assessing the construction of race, gender, and other forms of difference across social spaces.

Attempts to answer Boyles's second question form the core of work by scholars such as Chun (2024), Virginia Eubanks (2018), Kim Gallon (2016), Noble (2018), and Katherine McKittrick (2021)—all of whom draw on the lessons and practices of Black studies and critical race theory to generate new modes of analyzing race's engagement with technology. McKittrick's *Dear Science and Other Stories* (2021) traces the relationships between Black life and Black methodologies with the design of technological systems, algorithms, and soundscapes, arguing that "blackness and race are implicit to mathematical codes, discourses, and problems" (104). Her analysis of the algorithms that attempt to predict criminality and Black death demonstrates that—rather than beginning from a place of Black life—these algorithms reinscribe Black people's death as part of a cycle of rational discrimination and violence. For example, she describes the results of "an algorithm that scanned juvenile detention and school attendance records, as well as test scores, and used these archives to prognosticate the preventable death of youths" (103), which, among others, identified the risks faced by Davonte Flennoy, one of ten people shot and killed in low-income neighbourhoods in Chicago over a four-day period in June 2012 (Reel 2014):

> the algorithm mathematically refused all aspects of his livingness. Flennoy's archive—his records, his test scores—were culled and collated, and he was

determined to be highly killable, or "ultra-high-risk." The algorithm was granted more energy and vitality—through the act of application—than Flennoy (the object and outcome of the mathematical analysis). After the predictive system algorithmically anticipated his death, and measures were taken to prevent his death, Flennoy was killed in June 2012.

(McKittrick 2021, 103–4)

The algorithm and the software design, complete with complex academic networks of funding and support, offer nothing by way of liberating Black people; instead, they render Black life mere data to be measured, recorded, observed, predicted, and—ultimately—discarded. McKittrick's essay implicitly asks what responsibilities such projects have to the communities they claim to serve. She shows "not simply that the results" of algorithms "are racist … but that the work of administrating algorithms … requires biocentric methods and methodologies that can only produce dehumanizing mathematical results" (111). The reduction of Flennoy's life to a series of data points dehumanizes him via an encoded paradigm of white supremacy and racism: "What we have is a system wherein black people are dehumanized in advance, and this dehumanization is hardened and made objective by mathematical codes" (113–14).

Although Flennoy is American, the challenges McKittrick poses are both universal and also particularly relevant for us (and McKittrick) as Canadians. She concludes her story (her term for the critical and personal essay form she practices throughout *Dear Science*) with a series of questions designed to open our thinking about digital culture:

> What happens to our questions if we insist our methodologies are, in themselves, forms of black well-being? What happens if the nonmeasurability-noncomputability of black life is indicative of, necessary to, our analytics? What if we are not seeking outputs, answers, conclusions that end with only describing racism within our present system of knowledge? What if the answers that emerge from our colonial and plantocratic blueprints are not good enough? What if there is not a learning outcome? What if we taught and wrote not as problem solvers who count and assess variables (and creative texts can, at times, be theorized as variables) but as intellectuals who, with all our hearts, believe in opacity and giving on and with rather than finding, grasping, and having?
>
> *(117)*

McKittrick and other Black and racialized scholars working on digital culture and technology urge us to go beyond merely observing how technology, algorithms, and digital culture encode racism and white supremacy, to (as we explore in the next section) using technology to transform systems and to imagine alternative futures.

A call to action

While there have been many calls to reclaim technology from its inherently oppressive power structures, the most clearly articulated of these charges have come from scholars working in Black DH. It is to them, therefore, that we turn to offer an example of how digital humanities can analyze and transform tools of oppression. In particular, we look at how Black digital humanities scholars employ methodologies from Black studies to articulate new terms, new frameworks, and new ways of thinking about Black resistance and Black life. Saidiya Hartman explains,

> The intention here isn't anything as miraculous as recovering the lives of the enslaved or redeeming the dead, but rather laboring to paint as full a picture of the lives of the captives as possible. This double gesture can be described as straining against the limits of the archive to write a cultural history of the captive, and, at the same time, enacting the impossibility of representing the lives of the captives precisely through the process of narration.
>
> *(2008, 11)*

It is with Hartman's "double gesture" in mind that Gallon writes,

> Recovery rests at the heart of Black studies, as a scholarly tradition that seeks to restore the humanity of black people lost and stolen through systemic global racialization. It follows, then, that the project of recovering lost historical and literary texts should be foundational to the black digital humanities.
>
> *(2016)*

The DH project *(Un)Silencing Slavery* is exemplary in this regard. The project's title simultaneously points to the erasure at the heart of slavery's archive while also demonstrating DH's potential to speak back to those silences—a potential the project achieves by resurfacing the lives of individuals who were enslaved at Rose Hall Plantation, Jamaica. The project describes itself as

> a memorial, as a site of mourning and grieving, as a gesture of gratitude and appreciation, and as a catalyst for the ongoing recognition,

exploration, and presentation of the enslaved persons ... conceived in recognition of, and resistance to, what continues to be silenced about them and the institution of slavery today.

(Naylor et al. 2022)

(Un)Silencing Slavery demonstrates what Gallon identifies as the potential latent at "the intersection between Black studies and digital humanities" to transform "concept into corporeal reality while lending language to the work of the black digerati inside and outside of the academy" (2016). Achieving this material reality requires the privileging of "Black knowledge production [by] seeking to reach Black people where they are and acknowledging 'the different ways of knowing' they produce" (Frazier, Hyman, and Green 2023).

The need to centre Black people as researchers and participants is a regular refrain for those working in the Black digital humanities (and, by corollary, all minority and intersectional groups). In "All the Digital Humanists Are White, All the Nerds Are Men, but Some of Us Are Brave,"[3] which appeared in the very first issue of the *Journal of Digital Humanities*, Moya Z. Bailey asserts, "There is still a need to challenge the 'add and stir' model of diversity, a practice of sprinkling in more women, people of color, disabled folks and assuming that is enough to change current paradigms" (2011). Bailey's statement is just as relevant today as it was fifteen years ago; so too is her prescient question, "What counts as a digital humanities project?" which anticipates contemporary DH's failure to recognize how Black (and other minority) digital scholarship meaningfully transforms digital humanities. In practical terms, this means scholars engaging in research that serves, rather than observes, their own communities and that makes race an organizing consideration from the outset. It also means drawing on broader challenges put forward by Black and other minority scholars to the institutional structures of the university and its categories of knowledge, instead seeking out alternative ways of producing intellectual work.

For Bailey, Gallon, McKittrick, and others, the alternative to *add and stir* is making race the central principle around which DH projects are organized and using DH methods to understand how racialized people resist racist dehumanization. A fully realized centring of Black scholars and Black scholarship entails Black scholars leading projects, as well as projects drawing on Black studies and critical race theory as the basis of their methodologies; the same is true for any of the marginalized (and intersectional) groups we identify in Chapter 8 and for the Indigenous DH projects we discuss in Chapter 10. A truly anti-racist, intersectional digital humanities requires projects that factor in race from the outset, that are conversant with critical race theory, and whose teams include a diverse membership, including leadership from and participation of members of the communities they study. They also require wider changes to dismantle the structures of power and privilege that serve as barriers keeping some from participating in—and directing—DH projects.

There are myriad ways for this to be achieved. For example, in her work, Jessica Marie Johnson surveys historians' use of statistical and quantitative methods (broadly speaking, this is referred to as *cliometrics*) to offer a precise accounting of the slavery's realities; alongside, she explores the outrage that some historians express at the prospect of turning the horrors of slavery into quantitative measurement—a parallel practice of both using and interrogating DH methods. For Johnson, the application of DH methods to her material is more than just a way of generating analysis. Rather, it is fundamental to the work itself. She argues that researchers must conceive of "the term *data* transhistorically to gesture to the rise of the independent and objective statistical fact as an explanatory ideal party to the devastating thingification of black women, children, and men" (2018, 58). Johnson's work "undisciplines" notions of data (and digital humanities more generally) by showing how allegedly neutral definitions exclude data's entanglement with race, for example, by linking the rise of quantitative methodologies to the development of the *Trans-Atlantic Slave Trade Database* (first on CD-ROM and then online in 2008). Johnson suggests that despite the database's laudable aims,

> metrics in minutiae neither lanced historical trauma nor bridged the gap between the past itself and the search for redress. Computation could not, it seemed, capture the violent quandary that was the nation's history of and relationship to human bondage.
>
> *(62)*

Johnson's work provides a sobering reminder of how quantitative data, when inadequately framed and contextualized, impoverishes scholarship. In her assertion that "There is no bloodless data in slavery's archive" (70), Johnson, like McKittrick, and like those who study the Chinese Head Tax data, challenges the use of data that merely records—and therefore reproduces—historical violence.

Both McKittrick's and Johnson's work calls on digital humanities researchers to take questions of race seriously, not merely as a means of identifying the racial dimensions of a project but rather as a way of questioning whether the project does more than merely count, since enumerating alone "haunts efforts to render black people as human" (Johnson 2018, 65). Instead, DH practitioners must use their tools and methods to contextualize the archive and connect it to present-day concerns. For example, the digital *Map of White Supremacy's Mob Violence* connects the documentation of lynchings and racial murder in the United States to sociologist Monroe Work's advocacy work: "In the end facts will help eradicate prejudice and misunderstanding ... for facts are the truth and the truth shall set us free" (PlainTalkHistory, n.d.). The project makes users participants in the archive by asking them to determine what counts as racially motivated violence; their choices affect the digital map that the site generates. By combining historical facts with digital rhetoric and audience participation, the project highlights the constructed nature of the map as a form of knowledge and data, and it calls into question historical representation itself. In this regard, the project aligns with Gallon's and Bailey's insistence that Black digital projects must combine quantitative analyses with historical contextualization and an understanding of Black life; akin to Hartman's "double gesture," it is "straining against the limits of the archive."[4] Like the queer mapping projects discussed in the previous chapter, and many of the Indigenous DH projects discussed in the next chapter, the *Map of White Supremacy's Mob Violence* encodes historical data on a map while asking users to reflect on the assumptions implicit in both the construction of the map and the dataset.

Race, literature, and culture

Just as scholars use DH to engage in recovering, reanimating, and transforming *histories* of the oppressed, they also use DH to recover, reanimate, and transform the *stories* of the oppressed with projects that focus on creative and contemporary works by Black and racialized writers. The *Black Book Interactive Project*, launched in 2010, is one of the earliest such examples; its team employs text mining and other DH methodologies of reading to highlight marginalized texts by Black writers:

> Based on our collection of some 2000 novels, most of which are neither widely read not taught, we see the digital medium as a way to provide new levels of access, consolidate a large amount of data and invite new questions. What patterns exist among book titles, word count, and chapter structure of the novels? What are the terms and examples ... authors use to describe race and racial tension, and how does this shift over time?
>
> *(The Black Book Interactive Project, n.d.)*

Richard Jean So's book, *Redlining Culture: A Data History of Racial Inequality and Postwar Fiction* (2020), similarly takes a data-driven approach to interpreting the racial composition of American fiction. So argues, "scholars of U.S. literature have partly misread its postwar history by failing to recognize ... unchanging racial inequality [and] cultural redlining because our available methods, such as close reading and historicism, are not well equipped to discern such patterns" (6). The combination of natural language processing and text mining allows So to draw out patterns of redlining in American literature, demonstrating how a small group of African American authors were valorized in a field otherwise dominated by white authors.

Scholars have also investigated how online spaces serve as locations for community building, discussion, and activism; they have also explored how race is imagined online. For example, Sarah J. Jackson, Moya Z. Bailey, and Brooke Foucault Welles's *#HashtagActivisim: Networks of Race and Gender Justice* theorizes the labour and interventions of Black and trans people in online spaces. They enlist social media network analysis to trace how marginalized people use social media to speak back to dominant discourse—and how, in doing so, they participate in the work of creating "raced and gendered counterpublics" (2020, xxxv). Similarly, Long Le-Khac, Maria Antoniak, and Richard Jean So's "BLM Insurgent Discourse, White Structures of Feeling and the Fate of the 2020 'Racial Awakening'" employs a distant reading of Twitter data to argue that "#BLM in 2020 ... challenges the theories and methods that cultural studies brings to the analysis of cultural change, racial ideology, and hegemony" (2022, 668). These projects, like the *Lesbian and Gay Liberation in Canada* project described in the previous chapter, employ a combination of distant reading and affect studies to understand the lived experiences of marginalized communities.

As these projects suggest, Black DH is predominantly theorized by American scholars working on American history and slavery studies. This is due, in no small part, to the large number of Black Studies programs at American universities (especially in comparison to their Canadian counterparts) and to financial support for DH from US funders (such as the Mellon Foundation) and private universities—a pattern akin to that which shaped the emergence of DH and CanLit (see Chapter 4). While American projects are certainly important, they are demonstrative of what Sayan Battacharyya (himself a professor at Yale University) describes as the "Epistemically Produced Invisibility" of DH scholars and projects in the global south (2022).[5] Battacharyya draws on Gayatri Spivak's famous question, "Can the Subaltern Speak?" (1988) to suggest that within DH, epistemological frames and material systems of funding are constructed by those in the global north. Scholars in Europe and North America have their power and presence solidified through funding and support that colleagues in other parts of the world typically cannot access, a process the editors of *Global Debates in the Digital Humanities* refer to as *epistemicide*: "Applied to DH, epistemicide refers to the way academic institutions, publishers, values, norms, traditions of thought, technologies, and standards have been used to render invisible the knowledge produced by communities of the epistemic South" (Fiormonte, Ricaurte, and Chaudhuri 2022, xii). Like the racial biases we discussed above, the same problems have worked their way right into the system: Arjun Ghosh, in his assessment of the cultural bias of machine learning tools, argues, "Anglo-American institutions work to use their advantage in the balance of knowledge distribution to maintain their hegemonic position" (2024, 1). Ghosh's view is affirmed by the University of Toronto's *The Knowledge G.A.P.* project, which uses DH methodologies to explore the "unequal and under representation of academic content produced in and by 'Global South' researchers" (*Knowledge G.A.P.*, n.d.)—an example of turning the digital humanities lens on the field itself to understand what causes (and perpetuates) the uneven intersections of race, class, and subalternity.[6]

In Canada, DH projects have both sought to recover histories of racialized people and to connect those histories to ongoing struggles for racial justice. For example, librarians and archivists Alan Cho and Sarah Zhang have analyzed the *Register of Chinese Immigrants to Canada, 1886–1949* database in an effort to read the lives, the communities, and the patterns of migration that the database records. Cho and Zhang use the database to reread this data in an attempt to understand what Lily Cho calls the forms of "mass capture" that such datasets represent (Cho and Zhang 2023). Their work uses DH methods to consider the racial dimensions of Canadian citizenship and to understand an important moment in Chinese Canadian history. Meanwhile, *The Black Past in Guelph: Remembered and Reclaimed*, led by Jade Ferguson with support from the Guelph Black Historical Society, combines historical archival work, maps, and narrative descriptions in "Mapping Black Lives" under headings such as "Quotidian Lives," "Wayward Lives," and "Aspirational Lives." Contributors to the archive combine historical research with Hartman's critical fabulation to bring these historical figures to life. The site is a rich resource that depicts the vibrancy of Black histories in Canada by connecting the narratives to a carefully researched map of the Queen's Bush settlement, an early Black settlement in Ontario.

A number of nascent digital projects in Canada also promise to make original contributions to the study of race in Canada. For example, Claudine Bonner's work on Black migration to Canada, 1880–1930, combines digital humanities with archival studies, Black studies, and labour studies. She enlists digital methods to interpret the archives at the Canadian

Museum of Immigration in Halifax, NS, taking a holistic approach by coupling data with critical interpretation and historical context to understand Black people's movement between the Maritimes and the Caribbean. At Toronto Metropolitan University, Cheryl Thompson has recently launched the *Mapping Ontario's Black Archives* project which aims to collate the numerous digital archives of Black history in Ontario. Similarly, the digital teaching site, *Race, Migration and the Canadian Nation* (Varadharajan et al., n.d.), offers a series of digital modules designed to help students understand the historical construction of race in Canada through podcasts, videos, and digital texts.

Many of the above-mentioned projects do not identify as DH despite making use of DH methodologies. This speaks to the limits of theories of DH when it comes to engaging with racialized, marginalized, and intersectional communities and scholars, or perhaps to the possibility that the big tent is not as welcoming as some of those inside might believe, or even to the possibility that the work done by those who are marginalized is illegible to the DH community. Projects that do not explicitly identify as DH include *The Family Camera Network*, an online repository of digitized photographs meant to challenge notions of the family for queer and racialized people in Canada, and the *Northside Hip Hop Archive*, a digital archive of Canadian hip hop including recordings, promotional flyers, interviews, magazines, an accompanying curriculum, and more. *Northside* frames itself as being epistemically rooted in Black studies in Canada, not DH.

Kelly Baker Josephs theorizes the possibility of a distinct way of being in the digital for projects such as these that either self-identify or are seen by others as being on the margins. In "Digital Yards: Caribbean Writing on Social Media and Other Digital Platforms," she proposes the *digital yard* (2021): a network of communication and cultural expression that extends Kamau Brathwaite's statement that "Caribbean arts ... begin in the yard" (1996, 3) to digital spaces. For Josephs, the web functions as a "yard-like space for connecting people ... as well as for generating, circulating, and preserving the Caribbean arts" (2021, 219). When Canadian writers such as Kaie Kellough and Wayde Compton engage in digital scholarly and artistic experimentation outside the terminology of digital humanities, they are working in the digital yard (see Chapter 6). For example, Kellough—along with Canadian scholars and artists Ronald Cummings and Nalini Mohabir—organized a "digital wake" for Barbadian poet and theorist Kamau Brathwaite. The event gathered people via the @Kamauremix Twitter account, with posts aggregated and connected via the #KamauBrathwaite and #40NightsofTheVoice hashtags (Prater 2020).

Challenging the *human* in digital humanities

New spaces, such as the one that Josephs proposes, are a start, but it is possible (indeed, likely) that a radical overhaul is required for a true anti-racist reframing of DH. The work of Sylvia Wynter is central to such a project, particularly her challenging of the discursive-political category of Man (her term for the European construction of the human), which—in contrast to Black, Indigenous, and racialized others—has been posited as the enlightenment subject *par excellence*. For Wynter, "the struggle of our new millennium will be one between the ongoing imperative of securing the well-being of our present ethnoclass (i.e., Western bourgeois) conception of the human, Man, which overrepresents itself as if it were the human itself" (2003, 260). While Wynter's work is complex (in both style and content), her incisive critique of humanism provides the grounds for a reassessment. Whereas critiques of the digital humanities have often focused on the perceived incompatibility of the digital and the humanities (see Chapter 2), Wynter challenges us to interrogate the relationship between the humanities and the human, particularly in terms of how our shared conception of Man has become naturalized through humanist—and humanities—discourse.

Taking up the challenges posed by Wynter's work, Gallon raises digital humanities' engagement with the human by suggesting,

> Ultimately, the task of black digital humanities is to ask "What aspect of the digital humanities might be made more 'humanistic' if we were to look at them from the perspective of blackness?" The black digital humanities raises the question, "How can digital tools and processes such as text mining and distant reading be justified when there is so much to do in reconstituting what it means to be human?"
>
> *(2016)*

Such questions do not deny the value of these digital humanities tools and methods but, rather, seek to locate them in the contexts of race and humanism. An emerging cohort of DH scholars and students are insisting DH work be put into a critical dialogue with Black studies, critical race theory, postcolonial studies, and feminist studies. This group of digital humanities scholars have shifted the focus of DH both to include a broader range of projects and to demand that such projects ethically engage with the communities that they study. In the next chapter, we extend this examination of power, difference, and race to discuss how Indigenous scholars, DH practitioners, and communities have employed digital technology to challenge colonialism on epistemological and material grounds and have challenged the digital humanities' own participation in ongoing colonial systems of power.

Notes

1 One of the fiercest critiques of DH in the 1990s and early 2000s is that it gained prominence at a time when humanities research and teaching was reckoning with race, gender, sexuality, and other forms of difference. Critics accused DH of being a depoliticized field of research that offered refuge from the intense political debates occurring in other parts of the humanities (see Allington, Golumbia, and Brouillette 2016).
2 In a Canadian context, Sunera Thobani argues that "the adoption of multiculturalism helped stabilize white supremacy by transforming its mode of articulation in a decolonizing era" (2007, 146). Likewise, Stephen Lewis argues for the need to specifically attend to anti-Black racism in his "Report on Race Relations in Ontario" (1992). Lewis was asked to comment on "race relations" by Ontario's then-premier, Bob Rae. After interviewing hundreds of racialized people in Canada, Lewis strikingly eschews the safe language of race relations common to government reports and, instead, explicitly addresses the unique forms of discrimination that Black people in Canada experience:

> First, what we are dealing with, at root, and fundamentally, is anti-Black racism. While it is obviously true that every visible minority community experiences the wounds and indignities of systemic discrimination ... it is the Black community which is the focus. It is Blacks who are being shot, it is Black youth that is unemployed in excessive numbers, it Black students who are being inappropriately streamed in schools, ... Just as the soothing balm of "multiculturalism" cannot mask racism, so racism cannot mask its primary target.
>
> *(1992, 2)*

3 The title of Bailey's essay is a callback to Akasha Gloria Hull, Patricia Bell-Scott, and Barbara Smith's classic Black feminist anthology, *All the Women Are White, All the Blacks Are Men, But Some of Us Are Brave* (1982).
4 These are but a small sample of the excellent historical-archival DH projects that engage with slavery's historical archive. Although further discussion of these projects is beyond the scope of this book, we encourage readers to explore this area independently. Some projects to start with include the *Digital Archaeological Archive of Comparative Slavery*, a complex and detailed digital archive of archaeological sites, and *SlaveVoyages*, which features interactive maps, 3D reconstructions of ships, timelines, a video introduction by Henry Louis Gates Jr., and lengthy methodology section that explains the decision making in the database construction and site design.
5 Roopika Risam argues that "the question at the heart of decolonization and digital humanities is how we can use technologies to undo the technologies of colonialism" (2018, 80–81). This is a significant question for scholars concerned with how technology and digital humanities reproduce global inequities. Richard Asiedu, Michelle Stewart, and Sfundo Cele argue, "Decolonization involves a paradigm shift from a culture of denial to creating space for indigenous political philosophies and knowledge systems, thereby shifting cultural perceptions and power relations in real ways" (2024, 1). Their attention to the *real* (material) ways of creating space for Indigenous African epistemologies and perspectives offers a more robust vision of how digital technology can be used in the process of decolonization.
6 North American and European hegemony in DH has been challenged by projects that are transnational in the composition of their team and focus on

diasporic work that questions the centrality of the nation in framing racialized people's lives. Risam and Kelly Baker Josephs's *The Digital Black Atlantic* aims "to consider what 'Black Atlantic' as a formulation offers the study of Blackness and digital cultures, while articulating the challenges that approach offers to digital humanities" (2021). In addition to shifting the grounds of Blackness beyond the United States, the notion of the Black Atlantic offers,

> a method for incorporating and foregrounding transnationality and cross-temporality; a framework for addressing these concerns in relation to race, enslavement, and colonialism; a challenge to the European periodization of history and culture; a decentering of whiteness; a critique of fictive "universal" epistemology for digital humanities; and an articulation of the necessity of interdisciplinarity.

The concept of the Black Atlantic draws on the work of sociologist Paul Gilroy, who conceives of Black cultural production in transnational and cross-national terms rather than as contained within national borders—an idea that is also present in the boundary-troubling work of Indigenous DH (see Chapter 10). Organized according to *Memory*, *Crossings*, *Relations*, and *Becomings*, the volume includes contributions from scholars from around the globe, and the sections indicate a dual attention to historical and future visions of Blackness, difference, and transnationality.

Further reading

Browne, Simone. 2015. *Dark Matters: On the Surveillance of Blackness*. Durham: Duke University Press. https://doi.org/10.1515/9780822375302.

McKittrick, Katherine. 2021. *Dear Science and Other Stories*. Durham: Duke University Press. https://doi.org/10.1215/9781478012573.

Noble, Safiya. 2018. *Algorithms of Oppression*. New York: NYU Press. https://doi.org/10.18574/nyu/9781479833641.001.0001.

Risam, Roopika, and Kelly Baker Josephs. 2021. *The Digital Black Atlantic*. Minneapolis: University of Minnesota Press. https://doi.org/10.5749/j.ctv1kchp41.

Steele, Catherine Knight, Jessica H. Lu, and Kevin C. Winstead. 2023. *Doing Black Digital Humanities with Radical Intentionality: A Practical Guide*. New York: Routledge. https://doi.org/10.4324/9781003299134.

Works cited

Allington, Daniel, David Golumbia, and Sarah Brouillette. 2016. "Neoliberal Tools (and Archives): A Political History of the Digital Humanities." *Los Angeles Review of Books*, May 1, 2016. https://lareviewofbooks.org/article/neoliberal-tools-archives-political-history-digital-humanities/.

Asiedu, Richard, Michelle Stewart, and Sfundo Cele. 2024. "Investigating the Role of Digital Arts in Decolonizing Knowledge and Promoting Indigenous Standpoints." *Journal of the Digital Humanities Association of Southern Africa* 5, no. 1: 13 pp. https://doi.org/10.55492/dhasa.v5i1.5016.

Bailey, Moya Z. 2011. "All the Digital Humanists Are White, All the Nerds Are Men, but Some of Us Are Brave." *Journal of Digital Humanities* 1, no. 1.

Battacharyya, Sayan. 2022. "Epistemically Produced Invisibility." In *Global Debates in the Digital Humanities*, edited by Domenico Fiormonte, Sukanta Chaudhuri, and Paola Ricaurte, 3–14. Minneapolis: University of Minnesota Press. https://doi.org/10.5749/9781452968919.
Beatty, Jack. 2001. "Hitler's Willing Business Partners." *The Atlantic*, April 2001. https://www.theatlantic.com/magazine/archive/2001/04/hitlers-willing-business-partners/303146/.
Black Book Interactive Project. n.d. Accessed September 4, 2024. https://iopn.library.illinois.edu/omeka/s/BBIP/page/welcome.
Black Loyalists: Our History, Our People. The Book of Negroes. n.d. Accessed September 4, 2024. https://blackloyalist.com/cdc/documents/official/book_of_negroes.htm.
Boyles, Christina. 2021. "Intersectionality and Infrastructure: Toward a Critical Digital Humanities." In *People, Practice, Power: Digital Humanities Outside the Centre*, edited by Anne B. McGrail, Angel David Nieves, and Siobhan Senior, 99–117. Minneapolis: University of Minnesota Press. https://doi.org/10.5749/9781452968346.
Brathwaite, Kamau. 1996. "Note(s) on Caribbean Cosmology." *River City* 16, no. 2: 1–17.
Cho, Alan, and Sarah Zhang. 2023. "A Legacy of Race and Data: Mining the History of Exclusion." In *Future Horizons: Canadian Digital Humanities*, edited by Paul Barrett and Sarah Roger, 389–405. Ottawa: University of Ottawa Press.
Cho, Lily. 2021. *Mass Capture: Chinese Head Tax and the Making of Non-Citizens*. Montréal and Kingston: McGill-Queen's University Press. https://doi.org/10.1515/9780228009320.
Chun, Wendy Hui Kyong. 2024. *Discriminating Data: Correlation, Neighborhoods, and the New Politics of Recognition*. Cambridge: The MIT Press. https://doi.org/10.7551/mitpress/14050.001.0001.
Collins, Patricia Hill. 1990. *Black Feminist Thought: Knowledge, Consciousness, and the Politics of Empowerment*. Boston: Unwin Hyman.
D'Ignazio, Catherine, and Lauren F. Klein. 2023. *Data Feminism*. Cambridge: The MIT Press. https://doi.org/10.7551/mitpress/11805.001.0001.
Eubanks, Virginia. 2018. *Automating Inequality: How High-Tech Tools Profile, Police, and Punish the Poor*. New York: Macmillan.
The Family Camera Network. n.d. https://familycameranetwork.org.
Ferguson, Jade. n.d. *The Black Past in Guelph: Remembered and Reclaimed*. Accessed October 10, 2024. https://blackpastinguelph.com.
Fiormonte, Domenico, Paola Ricaurte, and Sukanta Chaudhuri. 2022. "Introduction." In *Global Debates in the Digital Humanities*, edited by Domenico Fiormonte, Paola Ricaurte, and Sukanta Chaudhuri, ix–xxxviii. Minneapolis: University of Minnesota Press.
Frazier, Nishani, Christy Hyman, and Hilary N. Green. 2023. "Black Is Not the Absence of Light: Restoring Black Visibility and Liberation to Digital Humanities." In *Debates in the Digital Humanities 2023*, edited by Matthew K. Gold and Lauren F. Klein, 140–65. Minneapolis: University of Minnesota Press. https://doi.org/10.5749/9781452969565.

Gallon, Kim. 2016. "Making a Case for the Black Digital Humanities." In *Debates in the Digital Humanities 2016*, edited by Matthew K. Gold and Lauren F. Klein, 42–49. Minneapolis: University of Minnesota Press. https://doi.org/10.5749/j.ctt1cn6thb.7.

Ghosh, Arjun. 2024. "Recovering Knowledge Commons for the Global South." *Journal of the Digital Humanities Association of Southern Africa* 5, no. 1. https://doi.org/10.55492/dhasa.v5i1.5011.

Grant, Nico. 2024. "Google Chatbot's A.I. Images Put People of Color in Nazi-Era Uniforms." *New York Times*, February 22, 2024. https://www.nytimes.com/2024/02/22/technology/google-gemini-german-uniforms.html.

Hartman, Saidiya. 2008. "Venus in Two Acts." *Small Axe* 26, no. 2: 1–14. https://doi.org/10.1215/-12-2-1.

Hull, Gloria T., Patricia Bell Scott, and Barbara Smith. 1982. *All the Women Are White, All the Blacks Are Men, But Some of Us Are Brave*. New York: Feminist Press.

Jackson, Sarah J., Moya Bailey, and Brooke Foucault Welles. 2020. *#Hashtag Activism: Networks of Race and Gender Justice*. Cambridge: The MIT Press. https://doi.org/10.7551/mitpress/10858.001.0001.

Johnson, Jessica Marie. 2018. "Markup Bodies: Black [Life] Studies and Slavery [Death] Studies at the Digital Crossroads." *Social Text* 36, no. 4: 57–79. https://doi.org/10.1215/01642472-7145658.

Josephs, Kelly Baker. 2021. "Digital Yards: Caribbean Writing on Social Media and Other Digital Platforms." In *Caribbean Literature in Transition, 1970–2020*, edited by Ronald Cummings and Alison Donnell, 219–34. Cambridge: Cambridge University Press. https://doi.org/10.1017/9781108564274.016.

Le-Khac, Long, Maria Antoniak, and Richard Jean So. 2022. "#BLM Insurgent Discourse, White Structures of Feeling and the Fate of the 2020 'Racial Awakening.'" *New Literary History* 53, no. 4: 667–92. https://doi.org/10.1353/nlh.2022.a898325.

Lewis, Stephen. 1992. "Report on Race Relations in Ontario." Government of Ontario. https://ia903104.us.archive.org/22/items/stephenlewisrepo00lewi/stephenlewisrepo00lewi.pdf.

Liu, Alan. 2020. "Towards a Diversity Stack: Digital Humanities and Diversity as Technical Problem." *PMLA* 135, no. 1: 130–51. https://doi.org/10.1632/pmla.2020.135.1.130.

Lowe, Lisa. 2015. *The Intimacies of Four Continents*. Durham: Duke University Press. https://doi.org/10.1515/9780822375647.

McKittrick, Katherine. 2021. *Dear Science and Other Stories*. Durham: Duke University Press. https://doi.org/10.1215/9781478012573.

McPherson, Tara. 2012. "Why Are the Digital Humanities So White?" In *Debates in the Digital Humanities*, edited by Matthew K. Gold, 139–60. Minneapolis: University of Minnesota Press. https://doi.org/10.5749/9781452963754.

Naylor, Celia E., Kristen Akey, Madiha Zahrah Choksi, Alex Gil, Moacir P. de Sá Pereira, and Monique J. S. Williams. 2022. *(Un)Silencing Slavery: Remembering the Enslaved at Rose Hall Plantation, Jamaica*, August 6, 2022. https://rosehallproject.columbia.edu.

Noble, Safiya. 2018. *Algorithms of Oppression*. New York: NYU Press. https://doi.org/10.18574/nyu/9781479833641.001.0001.
Northside Hip Hop Archive. n.d. *Northside Hip Hop Archive*. Accessed October 10, 2024. https://www.nshharchive.ca/.
O'Neill, Cathy. 2016. *Weapons of Math Destruction*. Largo: Crown Books.
PlainTalkHistory. n.d. Monroe and Florence Work Today. Accessed June 20, 2024. https://plaintalkhistory.com/monroeandflorencework/welcome/?u=2.
Prater, Tzarina T. 2020. "Always Together: A Digital Diasporic Essay." *archipelagos* 5. https://archipelagosjournal.org/issue05/prater-elegy.html.
Reel, Monte. 2014. "Chronicle of a Death Foretold: Predicting Murder on Chicago's South Side." *Harper's Magazine*, March 2014. https://harpers.org/archive/2014/03/chronicle-of-a-death-foretold-2/.
Risam, Roopika. 2015. "Beyond the Margins: Intersectionality and the Digital Humanities." *Digital Humanities Quarterly* 9, no. 2. https://www.digitalhumanities.org/dhq/vol/9/2/000208/000208.html.
Risam, Roopika. 2018. "Decolonizing the Digital Humanities in Theory and Practice." In *The Routledge Companion to Media Studies and Digital Humanities*, edited by Jentery Sayers, 78–86. New York: Routledge.
Risam, Roopika, and Kelly Baker Josephs. 2021. *The Digital Black Atlantic*. Minneapolis: University of Minnesota Press. https://doi.org/10.5749/j.ctv1kchp41.
Rosenthal, Caitlin. 2018. *Accounting for Slavery*. Cambridge: Harvard University Press. https://doi.org/10.4159/9780674988590.
SlaveVoyages Consortium. 2021. *SlaveVoyages*. https://slavevoyages.org.
So, Richard Jean. 2020. *Redlining Culture: A Data History of Racial Inequality and Postwar Fiction*. New York: Columbia University Press. https://doi.org/10.7312/so--19772.
Spivak, Gayatri Chakravorty. 1988. "Can the Subaltern Speak?" In *Marxism and the Interpretation of Culture*, edited by Cary Nelson and Lawrence Grossberg, 271–313. Basingstoke: Macmillan.
The Knowledge G.A.P. n.d. Accessed August 10, 2024. https://knowledgegap.org/.
Thobani, Sunera. 2007. *Exalted Subjects: Studies in the Making of Race and Nation in Canada*. Toronto: University of Toronto Press.
Thomas Jefferson Foundation. 2024. Digital Archaeological Archive of Comparative Slavery. https://daacs.org.
Thompson, Cheryl. n.d. *Mapping Ontario's Black Archives*. Accessed October 15, 2024. https://mobaprojects.ca/.
Varadharajan, Asha, Sedef Arat-Koç, Paul Barrett, Laura Madokoro, and Vinh Nguyen. n.d. *Race, Migration, and the Canadian Nation*. Accessed September 8, 2024. https://racemigrationcanada.com.
Wynter, Sylvia. 2003. "Unsettling the Coloniality of Being/Power/Truth/Freedom: Towards the Human, After Man, Its Overrepresentation—An Argument." *CR: The New Centennial Review* 3, no. 3: 257–37. https://doi.org/10.1353/ncr.2004.0015.

10
INDIGENOUS DIGITAL HUMANITIES

* * *

In *Cybertypes: Race, Ethnicity, and Identity on the Internet*, Lisa Nakamura identifies a divide between those for whom "the master's tools can never dismantle the master's house" and those for whom "getting online" is the only way to "bring about 'genuine change' in the often imperialistic images of race that exist online" (2002, 30). Jennifer Wemigwans (Anishnaabekwe, Ojibwe/Potawatomi) encountered this tension firsthand when seeking support for her Indigenous digital project, *FourDirectionsTeachings.com*: "Half of the Indigenous arts council would say, 'This is audacious and who does she think she is?' And the other half would say, 'This is really innovative and shows a lot of promise'" (Sharma and Wemigwans 2022, 209). The pull in Indigenous communities between resisting and embracing technology is understandable. On one hand, there is a longstanding history of colonial systems using data for control. Digital humanities has, too often, observed and described Indigenous peoples from a colonial perspective, and transformation of either the digital or the humanities (let alone the two in conjunction) has resisted serious consideration of Indigenous epistemologies and histories. On the other hand, DH offers opportunities to go beyond Eurocentric ideas to realize the potential in the affordances of the digital for projects looking to assert autonomous Indigenous histories, stories, and epistemologies.

Building on the previous chapter's discussion of the relationship between DH and race, this chapter explores Indigenous conceptions of—and the protocols for respectful engagement with—data. It also offers some examples of

DOI: 10.4324/9781003318323-15

digital humanities projects created *with* and *by* Indigenous communities *for* Indigenous communities. We note that this is a very limited discussion: the diversity of Indigenous methodologies and epistemologies is matched by the diversity of Indigenous peoples. We cannot cover everything and therefore want to signal that this discussion is not comprehensive; we encourage readers to learn directly from the Indigenous scholars and DH practitioners we mention by reading their works and visiting their projects. In acknowledging this multiplicity, we follow the lead of Cree scholar Willie Ermine and his notion of the ethical space of engagement. Ermine rejects the possibility of a shared perspective in favour of respecting—and maintaining—each culture's "own distinct and autonomous view," which inheres in the

> space between two entities, as a space between the Indigenous and Western thought worlds. The space is initially conceptualized by the unwavering construction of difference and diversity between human communities. These are the differences that highlight uniqueness, because each entity is moulded from a distinct history, knowledge tradition, philosophy, and social and political reality.
>
> *(2007, 194)*

With Ermine's words in mind, we have chosen to present a range of projects and perspectives without trying to unify them into a single, false, pan-Indigenous notion of digital humanities.

We also acknowledge that our own position as settler scholars, our personal and scholarly contexts, inevitably inform our relationship to the Indigenous works we reference. In doing so, we learn from Susan Hill's (Haudenosaunee) conception of "two-row or decolonizing research," which resonates with—but, it must be stressed, is distinct from—Ermine's ethical space, and which holds in tension the relation of and distinction between epistemologies, histories, and peoples:

> As Sotsitowahkenha (the late John Mohawk) would repeat, the core questions for any Haudenosaunee analysis are, What is the thinking? Is the thinking right? This directs the scholar to consider not only events and interests but also principles and objectives. How a people behave is influenced by what they believe—and what they believe is in turn a reflection of what they have been taught about who they are, how they should live, and what their purpose is.
>
> *(2009, 486)*

These are not trivial questions for us (as they should not be for any scholars in the digital humanities), nor can these questions be reduced to any broad notion of *methodology*. They require us to speak to our own relation to the communities and forms of knowledge we study and to consider whose voices are being centred and whose needs are being served by our research. They call on us to recognize the biases implicit in our research questions and embedded in their digital tools. They also call on DH to think about how place and geography shape knowledge. They oblige us to consider whether data should be open, shared, or protected and require that researchers take seriously the ethical stakes of their work. In this chapter, we engage with Hill's questions and the principles they engender by allowing Indigenous projects to speak for themselves, resisting the Western, totalizing tendency to unify them into a singular argument.

We also follow the lead of David Gaertner, who, in "Why We Need to Talk about Indigenous Literature and the Digital Humanities," proposes some concrete actions that DH settler scholars (ourselves included) can take. We take seriously not just our ongoing engagement with reconciliation but also the need to learn from our Indigenous colleagues without placing upon them the burden of directing our participation in reconciliation—a balance we think Gaertner's recommendations strike, and therefore quote here at length:

> Settler scholars in DH can facilitate these conversations by addressing the historical and colonial contexts of their own work and by citing Indigenous new media theorists in their conference talks and publications. Even better, we can find ways to centre Indigenous scholars in technology conferences, and we can stop tokenizing Indigenous presenters and presentations. We can make sure that Indigenous collaborators are paid fairly for their work and we can recognize the privilege, social and financial, that allows us to work in the fields of technology studies. We can attend to the ways in which technology has historically contributed to the displacement of Indigenous communities and the ways it continues to do so and we can call to account the colonialist metaphors that pervade in technology and technology studies. We can put ourselves in service to community, not with a research agenda in mind, not with the hope to test drive a new project, but as a point of access to resources and expertise, if the need/desire for them is there. We can be critical of things like open access and the notion of the commons it rests on. We can work *with* and *for* instead of *on*. We can stop trying to figure out how to get more Indigenous folks to DH gatherings and start showing up and supporting Indigenous poetry readings, book launches, and podcasts.
>
> *(2017)*

The above-listed recommendations require ongoing effort. Just as they are not tasks to be completed once and ticked off a list, so too it is not enough to confine engagement with Indigenous scholarship, literature, and ways of knowing to a single chapter of this book. To this end, we have problematized the idea of Canada throughout, with particular attention to the political and cultural forces at play in the construction (and deconstruction) of CanLit. We also note that many of Gaertner's recommendations are not specific to Indigenous-settler relations in DH, but rather speak to both the strength of community in DH and the problems that trouble it. For example, fair pay and fair recognition for work, recognizing privilege, and calling to account colonialist and other systems of power that pervade technology are at the core of intersectional DH. Working in service to a community is fundamental to communities of practice. Critical engagement with—rather than blanket acceptance of—open access is built into FAIR data principles (see Chapter 12). Our obligations with respect to Indigenous DH are, in many ways, our obligations to the domain and to each other more generally.

Data sovereignty and data management

Gaertner's first recommendation is for settler scholars to address the contexts of their own work. This is difficult to do, in that it asks us to consider the genealogy of our thinking, it troubles our relationship with the land on which we live as guests, and it requires us to grapple with our role in perpetuating colonial projects. The acknowledgement process is even more difficult in DH. Unlike a conference paper, journal article, or book, which are typically the work of a single person or a small team residing in a limited number of spaces, DH projects are more expansive. Consider, for example, the *Linked Infrastructure for Networked Cultural Scholarship* (LINCS) project, whose researchers and project staff are spread from Halifax to Victoria, and which is hosted on decentralized resources provided by the (federally funded) Digital Research Alliance of Canada. The footer on its website includes the following text:

> While members of LINCS gather together on-line from all across North America and beyond, our servers, which are also on Indigenous territories, produce the worlds we create and meet in. In particular we want to acknowledge that our servers are situated on the traditional lands of the WSÁNEĆ (Saanich), Lkwungen (Songhees), and Wyomilth (Esquimalt) peoples.
>
> *(2024)*

There is a balance to be struck between the physical places in which DH projects occur, the seemingly non-space of cyberspace, and the land-extractive practices required to build and power the machines we use (see the introduction, where we place our own work in context and discuss environmental toll of digital humanities).

Acknowledging how seemingly intangible digital works are rooted in—and dependent upon—place is a step towards Gaertner's "call to account the colonialist metaphors that pervade in technology and technology studies" and to "be critical of things like open access and the notion of the commons it rests on" (2017). There is a long, well-known history of colonial extraction and consumption, not only with respect to natural resources but also of Indigenous culture, information, and knowledge via "the vast store of materials in Western museums, archives, libraries, and personal collections that were not voluntarily given, and would not generally meet the standards of prior informed consent" and the "variety of spaces that have violated indigenous peoples' rights by defining their collective works as 'folklore' and excluding their protection via copyright system" (Christen 2012, 2889). This pattern persists on the Internet, where Indigenous information[1] is decontextualized and recirculated. As Judy Iseke-Barnes and Deborah Danard explain,

> Cyberspace and information technology are limitless in their potential as the modes of transmission for the dominant society to continue colonization practices. Information accessed through the Internet has no context in which to position it and is distanced from the indigenous peoples that it purports to represent.
>
> *(2007, 33)*

Indigenous communities know all too well that the principle of *terra nullius*—the "legal and moral justification for colonial dispossession of sovereign Indigenous Nations, including First Nations in what is now Canada"—is dangerous, whether applied to physical space or cyberspace (Assembly of First Nations 2018, 2).

Recent years have seen pushback against practices of consumption and appropriation. The Indigenous data sovereignty movement has emerged to protect against

> loss of access to ancestral knowledge, loss of control over proper care of heritage, diminished respect for the sacred, commercialization of cultural distinctiveness, uses of special or sacred symbols that may be dangerous to the uninitiated, replacement of original tribally produced

work with reproductions, threats to authenticity and loss of livelihood, among other things.

(Brown and Nicholas 2012)

In Canada, the movement is led by the First Nations Information Governance Centre / Centre de gouvernance de l'information des Premières Nations (FNIGC), an independent body established by a special mandate from the Assembly of First Nations Chiefs-in-Assembly. The FNIGC advocates for community- and Nation-based information governance via its First Nations Principles of OCAP, first articulated in 2009:

- **Ownership** refers to the relationship of First Nations to their cultural knowledge, data, and information. This principle states that a community or group owns information collectively in the same way that an individual owns his or her personal information.
- **Control** affirms that First Nations, their communities, and representative bodies are within their rights to seek control over all aspects of research and information management processes that impact them. First Nations control of research can include all stages of a particular research project—from start to finish. The principle extends to the control of resources and review processes, the planning process, management of the information and so on.
- **Access** refers to the fact that First Nations must have access to information and data about themselves and their communities regardless of where it is held. The principle of access also refers to the right of First Nations' communities and organizations to manage and make decisions regarding access to their collective information. This may be achieved, in practice, through standardized, formal protocols.
- **Possession** While ownership identifies the relationship between a people and their information in principle, possession or stewardship is more concrete: it refers to the physical control of data. Possession is the mechanism by which ownership can be asserted and protected.

(FNIGC 2024)

The FNGIC emphasizes that these principles can only serve as a starting point, as each First Nation has its own worldview, its own customs, and its own relationships—within its community and also between its community and others. There is no single approach to data governance that works for all, and just as minority scholars have called for with respect to race-based data (see Chapter 9), all work with data by and about First Nations (and all Indigenous) communities must be community-values led.

Alongside OCAP principles, there are other Indigenous data protocols, such as the Nindokiikayencikewin Indigenous Knowledges & Data Governance Protocol (2021), published by the federal government-funded Indigenous Innovation Initiative. The most widely used principles are the international CARE Principles for Indigenous Data Governance, created by the Global Indigenous Data Alliance (GIDA). Founded in 2019, GIDA's mission is to advance data rights as set out by the United Nations Declaration on the Rights of Indigenous Peoples (UNDRIP), which asserts, "Indigenous peoples have the right to revitalize, use, develop and transmit to future generations their histories, languages, oral traditions, philosophies, writing systems and literatures, and to designate and retain their own names for communities, places and persons" (United Nations 2007). The CARE principles are:

- **Collective Benefit**: Data ecosystems shall be designed and function in ways that enable Indigenous Peoples to derive benefit from the data.
- **Authority to Control**: Indigenous Peoples' rights and interests in Indigenous data must be recognized and their authority to control such data be empowered. Indigenous data governance enables Indigenous Peoples and governing bodies to determine how Indigenous Peoples, as well as Indigenous lands, territories, resources, knowledges and geographical indicators, are represented and identified within data.
- **Responsibility**: Those working with Indigenous data have a responsibility to share how those data are used to support Indigenous Peoples' self-determination and collective benefit. Accountability requires meaningful and openly available evidence of these efforts and the benefits accruing to Indigenous Peoples.
- **Ethics**: Indigenous Peoples' rights and wellbeing should be the primary concern at all stages of the data life cycle and across the data ecosystem.

(GIDA 2019)

The CARE principles were developed as a counterpart to the FAIR data principles (Findable, Accessible, Interoperable, and Reusable), which, as GIDA notes, "primarily focus on characteristics of data that will facilitate increased data sharing among entities while ignoring power differentials and historical contexts" (2019). Although the FAIR principles, which we later discuss in the context of data management (see Chapter 12), facilitate technical interoperability and uniform application of standards, they are sometimes also (inaccurately) invoked with reference to the idea that information should be allowed to circulate openly and freely. The arguments both for and against open information are manifold and beyond the scope of this book, but with respect to Indigenous data sovereignty, GIDA emphasizes, "greater data sharing alone creates a tension for Indigenous Peoples who are also asserting greater control over the application and use of Indigenous data and Indigenous Knowledge for collective benefit" (2019).

The movement for Indigenous data sovereignty is connected to the broader call for intersectional information rights (as discussed in Chapter 8). For example, the "Feminist Data Manifest-No" includes a refusal of "coercive settler colonial logics of knowledge and information organization" in favour of "tribal nation sovereignties and Indigenous information management that values Indigenous relationality, the right to know, and data sovereignty" (Cifor et al. 2019). The "Manifest-No" also draws a connection between harms perpetuated by colonialism, and it calls for the "lifting up, mobilizing, and celebrating their knowledges in building a data methodology of the oppressed," particularly for those who are "Black, Indigenous, and people of color." A data methodology of the oppressed has the potential for collective benefit, for example by addressing problems with the widely used yet inadequate Library of Congress Subject Headings (LCSH), which are rife with colonialist and heterosexist terms, among them "Indians of North America," "Eskimo," and "Butch and Femme (Lesbian culture)" (Brown 2020, 227). When we use these historical terms, we contribute to entrenching their biases: "Wrong, misleading, derogatory, or offensive metadata … gets continually and endlessly circulated once … digitized, put online, and then scraped up by aggregators" (Christen quoted in *Humanities for All* 2024).

Unsurprisingly, the problem runs deeper than nomenclature. The very way in which data is constructed often consigns Indigenous people to minor, marginalized, historical positions. Again, the LCSH are demonstrative of this:

> The call numbers E51–61 … include works on "Pre-Columbian America. The Indians" and from E71, "North America," move to E73–74 the "Mound Builders." From that point on until E99, which provides classifications based on tribes, there is, apparently, room for everything "Indian." And after that? E101–135, "Discovery of America and Early Explorations." *The implication is temporal: Indigenous nations and histories exist in the past, before the establishment of current political systems.*
>
> (Reder and Fee 2022, 296–97; emphasis added)

These categories reinforce oppressive, colonial epistemologies that "will prevail well into the future unless we work toward more permeable, capacious, and dynamic alternatives" (Brown 2020, 227). The pursuit of well-informed and carefully considered alternatives has been taken up by several groups. For example, the National Indigenous Knowledge & Language Alliance / Alliance nationale des connaissances et des langues autochtones (NIKLA-ANKLA) is currently building a *Respectful Terminology Platform*. Led by Camille Callison (Tāltān Nation) and Stacy Allison-Cassin (Métis Nation of Ontario), the platform will facilitate the creation and use of "a dynamic, multilingual set of terminologies applied to Indigenous Peoples, places, heritage, tradition, knowledge and cultures … [to] replace outdated and inappropriate terminologies used currently in cultural memory sectors such as museums, libraries, archives centers and galleries" (NIKLA, n.d.). Until the NIKLA platform is available, resources such as *The "Use Our Words" Toolkit* provide guidance for individual projects and cultural heritage institutions looking for alternatives to problematic terminologies (Bourdages and Caporiccio 2020).

Both the OCAP and CARE principles assert the right to self-representation; they also both insist on self-determination when it comes to access and reuse. One way of enabling agency is through tools and platforms that have been designed to accommodate Indigenous ways of knowing. For example, *Traditional Knowledge* (TK) *Labels* provide a standardized, interoperable way to place clear conditions on the use and circulation of information. "Developed through sustained partnership and testing within Indigenous communities across multiple countries," the labels are adaptable to "local and specific conditions for sharing and engaging in future research and relationships in ways that are consistent with already existing community rules, governance, and protocols for using, sharing, and circulating knowledge and data." For example,

- **Provenance Labels** identify the group or sub-group which is the primary cultural authority for the material, and/or recognizes other interest in the materials (attribution, clan, family, multiple communities, community voice, and creative).
- **Protocol Labels** outline traditional protocols associated with access to this material and invite viewers to respect community protocols (verified, non-verified, seasonal, women general, men general, men restricted, women restricted, culturally sensitive, secret/sacred).
- **Permission Labels** indicate what activities the community has approved as generally acceptable. Other uses require direct engagement with primary cultural authorities (open to commericalization, non-commercial, community use only, outreach, open to collaboration).

(Local Contexts 2024)

TK Labels were initially designed to be used in *Murkutu CMS* (content management system), a free, open-source digital platform for Indigenous cultural heritage management. Created by members of the Warumungu Aboriginal community (central Australia) in collaboration with Kimberly Christen and Craig Dietrich, the platform takes its name from a Warumungu word for *dilly bag*—a safe keeping place for sacred materials:

> Warumungu elder, Michael Jampin Jones chose Mukurtu as the name for the community archive to remind users that the archive, too, is a safe keeping place where Warumungu people can share stories, knowledge, and cultural materials properly using their own protocols.
> *(Centre for Digital Scholarship and Curation 2024)*

Now maintained by a team based at Washington State University, *Murkutu* is widely used, including by many of the projects mentioned in this chapter. It allows users to define and control access levels based on community-driven cultural protocols and values. It also allows the creation and connection of multiple records for a single item to capture overlapping layers of knowledge: for example, an object's description can be both physical and cultural. Data and metadata gathered in or created using *Murkutu* can be transferred to other platforms and used in other contexts without any information being lost. This is essential to ensure that digital archives are dialogical rather than extractive, and it allows Indigenous communities to retain control—and make the best use of—their information.[2]

Projects

If we were to draw a Venn diagram of Indigenous work, digital humanities, and Canadian literature, a substantial amount of work would sit at the intersection of Indigenous projects and digital humanities, just as a decent amount would sit at the intersection of digital humanities and Canadian literature. Identifying work to place in the middle of the diagram, however, would be more challenging, since Indigenous epistemologies often problematize the very categories of both Canada and literature.[3] Indigenous DH cannot be subject to the organizing logic of national borders; there are many communities whose territories and connections predate and problematize these lines. To apply a third-party (rather than self-selected) label of *Canadian* to an Indigenous project is to engage in colonial, appropriative logics. In the case of literature, Daniel Heath Justice (Cherokee) points out that "assumptions about what is or is not 'literary' are used to privilege some voices and ignore others" (2018, xvii). Deanna Reder (Cree-Métis) and Margery Fee similarly reject Eurocentric literary conventions that distinguish "between reality and fantasy, between the experiences of the physical and the experiences of the magical or spiritual [that] does not exist in Cree storytelling traditions" (2022, 299). They instead advocate for "a definition of writing that allows us to read all expressions of particular cultures as multimodal communicative practice" (2022, 226). This multimodality calls to mind Wemigwans's conception of the Internet, with its "visual, oral, and textual modes of presenting information in a way that supports cultural perspectives" (Nakata quoted in Wemigwans 2018, 23). The projects described in this section highlight some of the these "multimodal communicative practices" in Indigenous (literary) digital humanities—from community-led oral history to collaborative scholarly archives, from decolonizing maps to poetry that centres the colonial legacy of digitized literature.[4]

Voices of the Land

Voices of the Land is a digital public project that provides a space for Indigenous communities to collect and share stories and to contextualize those stories in Indigenous epistemologies and traditions. Based in Alberta but with contributions from further afield, it provides resources for creating the audio and video it hosts on its custom platform. User-created content covers topics ranging from kinship to territory, art to governance—a breadth captured by videos featuring oral histories, language tutorials, cooking lessons, book reviews, and more. *Voices of the Land* has been developed through a process of community consultation and rooted in the "7 Sacred Teachings," which act as an explicitly stated methodological-epistemological framework for the site and also serve as an ethical framework that centres the project in love, respect, courage, honesty, wisdom, humility, and truth. Because the site hosts community-created content, it provides robust information about both Indigenous protocols and digital practices related to information sharing, copyright, and permissions; each story's page includes a clearly stated community protocol to indicate whether access is open or restricted to a particular group, as well as a Creative Commons license (if applicable). The site also makes use of the conventions of trigger warnings, flagging content on topics such as residential schools, day schools, and the Sixties Scoop; clearly marking this material and including a link to a page with personal support resources is exemplary of the project's community-centred ethics of care.

FourDirectionsTeachings.com

Voices of the Land places a limit on who can access the materials, which have been created with specific communities in mind. By contrast,

FourDirectionsTeachings.com (2012) is open to—and has been made for—a much broader audience:

> Originally conceived as a national Aboriginal educational initiative, FourDirectionsTeachings.com was developed so that Indigenous communities across the country, both on and off reserve, could benefit from its content. The idea was to provide a culturally sensitive pedagogical aid that could be accessed easily by Indigenous educators, front-line workers in literacy and community wellness programs, and non-Indigenous people working with Indigenous students or teaching Indigenous-themed curricula to all kinds of learners. Today the website has reached far beyond the original target audience and is seen and utilized by Indigenous and non-Indigenous people in many different contexts as a valuable resource for introducing Indigenous Knowledge.
>
> *(Wemigwans 2018, 22)*

The recordings of oral Indigenous knowledge and philosophy on *FourDirectionsTeachings.com* have accompanying, custom-created animations to teach the process of "listening with intent" (13), and the site also provides resources for teachers looking to incorporate Indigenous culture and knowledge in their classrooms. Unlike *Voices of the Land*, which is an open platform, *Four Directions* features curated contributions from Dr. Reg Crowshoe and Geoff Crow Eagle (Blackfoot teaching), Mary Lee (Cree teaching), Lillian Pitawanakwat (Ojibwe teaching), Tom Porter (Mohawk teaching), and Stephen Augustine (Mi'kmaq teaching)—all of whom were approached by a National Advisory Committee of Indigenous People for the protection and promotion of Indigenous Knowledge. About the experience of working with this committee, Wemigwans says,

> the advisory group gave me the confidence to proceed ... because I thought not only that I was working for the community but also that the community was involved in the project. ... the presence of an advisory committee and the referrals that came from it assured Elders and Traditional Teachers that a community-based process was being undertaken and that a sense of accountability was in place.
>
> *(22)*

Although the intentionality of Wemigwans' process seems, at first glance, to be the opposite of a platform like *Voices of the Land*, both work towards the same goal: knowledge created by those who are accountable to a community.

Kiinawin Kawindomowin / Story Nations

Oral history and the written word are also combined in projects that bring together past and present, Indigenous and settler. *Kiinawin Kawindomowin / Story Nations* is a multimedia collaboration between members of Rainy River First Nations, Anishinaabe consultants, and researchers at the University of Toronto. Starting with the diary of Frederick Du Vernet, an Anglican missionary who visited the Ojibwe people of Manidoo Ziibi (Rainy River) in 1898, the project joins a digitized and transcribed diary with multimedia resources including narrative audio, a text-linked glossary, a map gallery, and supplementary critical and creative materials. Videos created for the project feature members of Rainy Rivers First Nations, who share their own history and describe their connection to place.

Native Land Digital and Whose Land

There are also a number of significant Indigenous mapping projects, such as *Native Land* and *Whose Land*, with the latter built using data from the former. Maps are, in their own way, an act of storytelling—"a two-dimensional mosaic of storied relations on the land" (Justice 2018, 197). Digital maps tell stories not just on the page, but also by using technological affordances to bring place into dialogue with people. *Native Land* invites community-contributed oral histories, written documents, and maps, which it uses to update its content; *Whose Land* provides landing pages for community-generated videos, stories, and supplementary information. With the options to toggle between views—the same space shown according to features such as territories, communities, languages, or treaties—the digital mapping projects also foster conversations with and among non-Indigenous audiences:

> Native Land Digital creates spaces where non-Indigenous people can be invited and challenged to learn more about the lands they inhabit, the history of those lands, and how to actively be part of a better future going forward together.
> *(Native Land Digital 2024)*

> [*Whose Land*] is intended to be used as an educational tool to create dialogue around reconciliation. It is a starting point for conversations between Indigenous and non-Indigenous citizens across this country about land, territorial recognition and land acknowledgement.
> *(Whose Land, n.d.)*

There are, of course, problems inherent in digital mapping, which relies either directly or indirectly on tools that have their origins in colonial projects and the military-industrial complex. There is a longstanding history of erasing Indigenous histories and presences with maps that naturalize settler visions of space and nation (see, for example, Hunt and Stevenson 2016, Pereira and Sletto 2024), and digital maps run the risk of reproducing colonial visions of nation-state as the natural unit of political and cultural organization. Indigenous-led mapping projects (*Native Land* is the work of a Canadian not-for-profit) push back on this history by, as Lisa Brooks argues, using digital maps as tools of "memory and survival" for "helping people to comprehend that there are different ways of seeing the land and its history, and different ways to center places" (2018, 277). In doing so, digital mapping projects offer us a model for how digital humanities methods can be used in support of Indigenous epistemologies that work towards "decolonizing geographies of power" (Hunt and Stevenson 2016).

Terrastories

Maps are also often incorporated as an element of story-based DH projects, as seen in both *Voices of the Land* and *Kiinawin Kawindomowin*. *Terrastories* is a free, open-source application designed for Indigenous communities to create and connect audio and video content to locations on a map. Features include the ability to set permissions that limit access to a community, the option to add community-generated custom filter terms specific to a community, and a design that facilitates translations, so that communities can create and access interfaces in their own languages. The Haudenosaunee community at the Six Nations Reserve of the Grand River has created an interactive *Terrastories* map for their *Ohneganos Ohnegahdę:gyo Water Research Program*, led by Dawn Martin-Hill (Mohawk, Wolf Clan). Pins on the *Ohneganos Ohnegahdę:gyo* map lead to location-specific audio and video recordings, historical documents, and contemporary photographs on topics ranging from ecology to medicine, ceremony to history.

The People and the Text

Where mapping projects use place as their organizing principle, digital archives gather around categories such as people, objects, or time. When it comes to the intersection of DH, Indigenous literature, and digital archives, foremost is *The People and the Text: Indigenous Writing in Lands Claimed by Canada* (TPatT) (also discussed in Chapter 6). This project "aims to research and recover lost texts in what is now called Canada, up until

1992" (Reder and Fee 2022, 293). Its database includes full text, digitized primary source works, audio recordings of author interviews, and—in collaboration with the *Collaboratory for Writing and Research on Culture*—an extensive, open-access bibliography of Indigenous texts and related secondary materials, including original research, interviews, and videos. By prioritizing "Indigenous literary research methods that consider our responsibilities to relevant Indigenous communities and individuals," the TPatT team has "brought scholarly attention to understudied or forgotten works" (Reder et al., n.d.).

Great Lakes Research Alliance for the Study of Aboriginal Arts & Cultures

TPatT is an example of a digital archive of both community and scholarly interest.[5] Another project that sits at this intersection is the archive held by the Great Lakes Research Alliance for the Study of Aboriginal Arts & Cultures (GRASAC 2024a). A multi-disciplinary network, GRASAC's focus is the histories, languages, and cultures of the Anishinaabe, Haudenosaunee, and Huron-Wendat cultures of the Great Lakes region. Since 2005, the network's community has been building the *GRASAC Knowledge Sharing Platform* (2024b), a collaboratively generated database that provides permissions-based, password-protected access to digital records for over 5,000 *relatives* (the project's term for *heritage items*) and 17,000 Anishinaabemowin and Cayuga words. The database brings together "record sets for material culture, archival documents, historic photographs and language in order to reveal the interrelationships of these different forms of expressive culture" (Bohaker, Corbiere, and Philips 2015, 46).

Wikipetcia Atikamekw Nehiromowin

There are also archives made for (and by virtue of their very design are only for use by) members of an Indigenous community. *Wikipetcia Atikamekw Nehiromowin*, an Atikamekw instance of Wikipedia has been created by high school students in the Atikamekw community of Manawan. The site was developed in partnership with elders and with support from language specialists, project leaders, and Wikimedia Canada. Although *Wikipetcia* has its origins in a scholarly project that was looking for ways to rectify the complete absence of Atikamekw-language materials online, the result is far more than a language-learning resource. It also represents "cultural maintenance, pedagogical achievements, revaluation of the Atikamekw values, and philosophy and lessons learned from the collaboration of teachers, pupils, local language experts, other local voluntary contributors, and academics." *Wikipetcia* exists solely for the community who created it, since its content, exclusively in Atikamekw, "creates a safeguard to protect sensitive cultural knowledge." The site is also subject to community-generated rules: for example, "oral sources are allowed, following the local tradition, while articles about medical use of plants and secret ceremonies are forbidden" (Stoner 2023).

#HonouringIndigenousWriters

Wikipetcia makes excellent use of an established public platform, as does *A Year of #HonouringIndigenousWriters*. Every day in 2016, Daniel Heath Justice (Cherokee), professor of First Nations and Indigenous Studies and English, tweeted the name of an Indigenous writer, plus as much additional information as he could fit in 140 characters. Starting with Beth Brant/Degonwadonti (Bay of Quinte Mohawk) on January 1, 2016, and ending with Mary Kathryn Nagle (Cherokee Nation) on December 31, 2016, Justice celebrated a sliver of the vast, growing archives of Indigenous literature. Reflecting on his list, Justice notes that he succeeded in "foregrounding Indigenous women and queer/two-spirit writers," but also that "transgender Indigenous writers are woefully underrepresented" as are "Black Indian writers and Indigenous writers from Africa," and there was "a complete absence of Freedmen writers" in his list (215); although there is plenty to celebrate, Justice acknowledges there is also a lot of work yet to be done—especially when applying an intersectional lens to Indigenous literature. All 366 tweets appear at the end of his book, *Why Indigenous Literatures Matter* (2018, 216–40). The list and its hashtag subsequently spawned a Wikipedia edit-a-thon, started by David Gaertner and Erin Fields at the University of British Columbia in 2018, and which has expanded to include in-person and online readings and events (Gaertner 2023).

Literary interventions

Towards the end of *Why Indigenous Literatures Matter* (2018), Justice issues a call for Indigenous writers to "knit the jagged edges of our histories across the woundings of time, space, and experience" (184). Both Jordan Abel (Nisga'a) and Joshua Whitehead (Oji-Cree) heed this call to darn stories frayed by colonialism and the passage of time, which they achieve by enlisting digital technology and experimental writing in radical new ways. Finding the conventional tools at their disposal lacking, both use "digital language to define an existence that cannot be communicated solely through writing conventions in English, Cree, or computer code" (Martínez 2018, 627). Like the DH projects described above, Abel and Whitehead's work wrests control of "digital technologies to offer mediated sites of kinship, connection, and survivance that extend notions of place-based sovereignty into notions of ideological and identity-based sovereignty" (Cooper 2020, 493).

In *Un/inhabited* (2015) and *Injun* (20136), Jordan Abel blurs the boundaries between criticism, conceptualism, and poetry using *Project Gutenberg's* collections: he erases, distorts, and remakes the colonial archive in order to express colonialism's ongoing violence. Employing forms of digital textual analysis, he rereads pulp western novels to challenge the voice of empire. Abel explains,

> *Injun* was constructed entirely from a source text comprised of 91 public domain western novels with a total length of just over ten thousand pages. Using CTRL+F, I searched the source text for the word "injun," a query that returned 509 results. After separating out each of the sentences that contained the word, I ended up with 26 print pages. I then cut up each page into a section of a long poem. Sometimes I would cut up a page into three- to five-word clusters. Sometimes I would cut up a page without looking. Sometimes I would rearrange the pieces until something sounded right. Sometimes I would just write down how the pieces fell together. *Injun* and the accompanying materials are the result of these methods.
>
> *(2013, 83)*

By constructing poems from public domain texts, themselves based on reductive portrayals of Indigenous peoples, Abel reverses the direction of extraction, creating pastiche from an archive beset by misrepresentation. He also challenges the notion that open-source repositories are inherently good. Abel draws attention to *Project Gutenberg*'s role in perpetuating settler colonial violence by reprinting—and therefore replatforming (see Chapter 5)—material rife with problematic language, imagery, and ideology. In doing so, he poses a challenge to *Project Gutenberg*'s own assertions that it "is powered by ideas, ideals, and by idealism" and that "Everyone is welcome here at Project Gutenberg" (Hart 2007). As McDougall suggests, "If we consider cyberspace in this context of *terra nullius*, then in making these novels available in the 'public domain,' *Project Gutenberg* reinstates, through both literary and digital spaces, colonial narratives of inhabitance, ownership, violence, and territory" (2019).

Abel's work asks tough questions about the inheritance of Canadian literature and the digital humanities alike. His poetics of transformation reveals new ways to both reread and rewrite the colonial literary archive, such that readers come away from Abel's work asking,

> Who is the public that these digital repositories are supposed to represent? What are the ethics of the preservation of fundamentally racist texts? How does the uncontested preservation of these texts contribute to or deter from the quality of life for Indigenous persons? How do the memories embedded within these electronic texts, or e-texts, build toward a decolonized future, if at all?
>
> *(Schmaltz 2019)*

Adding to the effect of the digital, even Abel's technical practices challenge the colonial narrative. There is a parallel between data mining—the use of digital tools to extract that which is useful for research from a corpus—and colonial and settler resource extraction:

> data mining embodies colonial practices of land excavation in that to "mine" something is to engage directly with land and territory. The emphasis on extraction of raw data for the sake of "useful" delivery is reminiscent of colonial tendencies to mine raw resources from stolen land to actualize utilitarian productions and capitalist aims.
>
> *(McDougall 2019)*

Abel's work troubles the metaphor and practices of data mining, and it also challenges the techno-utopian ideology of open-source text repositories.

In "Cartography," the second section of *Un/inhabited*, Abel overlays cut-outs on the source text to generate images that conjure the impression of maps. The shapes the poems take on the page are at once familiar and unfamiliar, both connecting the reader to and breaking their relationship with the land. In this regard, the experience of reading the poems is not dissimilar to viewing the *Native Land* maps: while the lines representing Indigenous territories intersect and overlap, more familiar geopolitical boundaries are nowhere to be seen. The map is (un)familiar—compelling yet unsettling. Eric Schmaltz explains, in the same way "The poems represent shorelines upon which colonial forces landed, moved inward, and claimed the land as they advanced," so too the novels out of which the poems are made are "one of the ways that colonizers articulated and shaped their relationship to the land and their memories of it" (2019). In her commentary on *Un/inhabited*, Kathleen Ritter recalls Grant's and Atwood's cartographic metaphors, arguing that the collection

> is more akin to reading a map ... Abel has disrupted the reading process so that a straight path through the work is impossible, and instead

invites the reader to discover other ways of understanding and deriving meaning from a text.

(2014, xviii)

Abel employs digital methods to rewrite his source material and thereby redraw colonialism's conceptual map. He thus writes new maps using the settlers' own language, reminding readers that "the language writers use to describe the material world can significantly impact the world and its cultural and social values, and political systems" (Schmaltz 2019).

Like Abel, Whitehead's poetry is also an act of reclaiming—one that challenges readers to reconsider the relationship between embodiment, Indigenous and queer identities, and digital technology. Many of the poems in *full-metal indigqueer* (2017) open with installation sequences, loading the literary interlocutor whose works Whitehead sets about disrupting and dismantling. A list of sources at the end of the volume runs from *Seinfeld* to *The Faerie Queen* by way of superhero movies, children's books, top forty hits, and contemporary Canadian literature. Both *full-metal indigiqueer* and Whitehead's *Jonny Appleseed* (2018) also feature digitally mediated protagonists: Zoa, a Two-Spirit, Indigiqueer, cyber-literary-trickster, and Jonny, a technologically disembodied cyber-sex worker. Yet, despite their on-screen presentations, both are also "embodied, Indigenous, biological" (Cooper 2020, 492). Jonny is a real (fictional) person both on and off camera; Zoa may be what Gaertner describes as "a disembodied singularity" (Gaertner 2019), but as Whitehead's own video game avatar, Zoa has allowed him "to break barriers & defy expectations, to re-augment myself through language & find myself in the most unexpected places" (Whitehead 2017, 115). Zoa is simultaneously a digital representation of Whitehead and a trickster mediator that plays in the space between author and poetic voice, mimesis and reality.

While Abel challenges the mantra of open access by reappropriating historical texts that reduce Indigenous history to stereotype and Indigenous personhood to silence, Whitehead with his consumption and reclaiming of classical European and contemporary Western popular culture uses his writing to challenge those who seek to consume the contemporary Indigenous body. He reminds us that the colonial desire to collect and exploit Indigenous identities, stories, and data is ongoing—not just a holdover from the days of Abel's reclaimed westerns:

> I am often mistaken for Jonny himself (several interviewers, while asking me questions, have called me Jonny; and I have encountered this confusion in brief romantic encounters as well). One of the perplexing things that interests me in the contemporary consumption of BIPOC

and queer writing is that our texts are readily misread as confession, non-fiction, memoir, boudoir.

(2022, 71)

Whitehead's words may be aimed, in part, at contemporary Canadian literature's desire to claim any and all BIPOC writers—as a penance for past wrongs—through a kind of tokenism and appropriation. His language of confession and of boudoir suggests the desire for bared souls and forced intimacy that he perceives in his readers' response to his work; as he suggests elsewhere, "writing autobiography is akin to literary voyeurism in the form of extraction through confession" (2022, 44). A reader who interprets fiction as confession also presumes that the author lacks literary skill. Thus, the playful and disruptive figures of Zoa and Jonny offer creative ways of challenging readers' assumptions. Whitehead continues, "I have become tired and bothered by these classifications, which I read as boundary and border," echoing the decolonial pushback on the settler logics of mapping (2022, 72). It is not for nothing that the first eighteen pages of *full-metal indigiqueer* show a gradually expanding white circle on an otherwise black page, the text at the centre declaring "H3R31M" [here I am] (Whitehead 2017, 17).

Whitehead rejects boundary and border as an imposed misreading of author and text, instead situating his writing in "a digital space that can be reprogrammed to achieve decolonization" (Martínez 2018, 628). This is not an attempt to suture some rupture of the past, to "knit the jagged edges of our histories" to again quote Justice (2018, 184), or to recover from historical violence, but, rather, a forward-looking contextualization, a reimagining of a technologically facilitated future that has yet to arrive. In "mihkokwaniy," Whitehead holds a conversation with the murdered grandmother[6] he never knew:

> what would life have been like
> if you had lived beyond thirty-five [questionmark] …
> would i be able to speak cree
> without having to google translate
> this for you [questionmark].
>
> *(101; square brackets in original)*

By coupling suppositions about the life that could have been to the life that was, the imagined future contrasting with his grandmother's murder, "mihkokwaniy" evokes the possibility of a life given shape in poetry alongside the real violence of the world Whitehead inhabits. The powers of the digital, represented here by *Google Translate*, are equivocal: if *Google*

Translate were able to translate Cree (which, as of 2024, it cannot), it would make communication possible, but as technologically mediated and distanced it would be wholly inadequate. Like Abel's dynamic transformation of the archive of colonial literature, Whitehead's work is steeped in the context and relationality of the time and place of the telling, of the identities of speaker and listener both: oratory "cascades into infinite register across time, space, and geographies" (2022, 73). There are some places that can be reached only by art, not by technology.

Oral stories are "an entry point into community enrichment and the building of futures through the interlacing of our histories" with "a key role in the development, empowerment, and futurity of Indigenous peoplehoods" (Whitehead 2022, 74, 75). For both Abel and Whitehead, digital technology can enable the forms of interlacing of unlikely histories and rewriting of a violent history of dispossession into glimpses of Indigenous survivance and joy. In *Making Love with the Land* (2022), Whitehead meditates on the relations between queer and Indigenous life, colonial violence, writing, and digital culture, among other topics. In "The Year in Video Gaming," for example, he describes two "cousin-siblings" who, in mourning a family death, seek "escapism, entertainment, and social enrichment. Their medium of choice? *Fortnite*" (57). He contextualizes their actions with his own teenage experience of online gaming, where—embodied by his avatar Zoa—he/they would

> lounge around in the digital pastures of the game's idylls, taking pictures, talking about our personal lives, and sharing stories. This, to me, was a sovereign way of owning a body I had been taught to distrust because I was queer, Indigenous, and fat. I re-created myself as an imagined embodiment of pixels: here I was a muscle queen, a femme Orc with a red mohawk … I was powerful, haughty, righteous in my beings.
> *(2022, 60)*

Whitehead's ambivalence towards digital spaces is offset by the potential he recognizes in them. They are unable to return to him his grandmother; they offer respite from daily oppression and violence; they are latent with potential for transforming both self and landscape; they are seductive forms of story; they are a model for and an inescapable component of Whitehead's own creative practice.

When Justice says, "Indigenous literatures are a vital expression of … imaginative commitment, righting—and writing—relations across time and space" (2018, 116), he could well be describing the dynamism inherent in Whitehead's resistance to narrative calcification and Abel's reanimation of the colonial archive, both of which demonstrate the ways in which Indigenous writers use digital technology to make their literature matter anew. Justice explains:

> In reflecting on why Indigenous literatures matter, I've never considered literature to be simply that body of creative expression on a bookshelf or electronic device. Our literatures are the storied archives—embodied, inscribed, digitized, vocalized—that articulate our sense of belonging and wonder, the ways of meaning-making in the world and in our time. Sometimes those literatures are the stories we tell around the kitchen table or the songs shared at the ceremonial ground; sometimes they're spoken at a microphone at the back of a crowded coffee house or read in solitary silence at the end of a long day; sometimes they're discussed with vigour in a classroom or whispered softly over a lover's damp skin.
>
> *(2018, 186)*

Justice's words stress both the formal variety of Indigenous literatures as well as the import of those literatures to the communities they serve. Indigenous literatures and digital projects are forms of expressing and encouraging belonging, expressions at the wonder of Indigenous survivance and resistance, and forms of Indigenous meaning-making that challenge the colonial archive. The obligation to community and nation, in the many forms it takes, is one of the hallmarks of Indigenous literature and Indigenous digital humanities.

Abel's and Whitehead's works, like many of the projects discussed in this chapter, call on DH practitioners to expand their understanding of DH and to account for how Indigenous people continue to use digital technology to assert their own individual and community identities. It is telling how little Indigenous concerns are factored into self-identifying digital humanities projects and how few of the projects outlined in this chapter, as with the projects in Chapter 10, are identified as digital humanities despite their goals, methods, and outcomes all being squarely DH in nature. This is cause for concern in the theorizing of digital humanities as it demonstrates a lacuna in the field. Still, to look for a unifying framework into which all Indigenous DH work could be placed would be a mistake. Many of the interventions discussed in this chapter push back against the notion of a single, shared culture or against the inherent virtues of digital tools—with their pseudo-utopian, settler-colonial logics—as a means of circulating cultural knowledge.

Notes

1 We are using the more general phrase *Indigenous information* in preference to the more specific *Indigenous knowledge* to refer to all information that is by, for, about, or in any way related to Indigenous individuals and communities. We are limiting our use of *Indigenous knowledge* to refer to knowledge systems and epistemologies. Our phrasing choices are guided by the Indigenous scholars

whose works we reference, and we have retained individuals' preferred terms in quotations throughout.

2 It bears noting that *Murkutu* projects are subject to the same resource and labour demands and the attendant problems related to compensation, credit, and maintenance that we have described elsewhere:

> Hosting a Mukurtu site requires the technical means to host the site as well as the human resources to maintain it, make decisions about how it will be used, and manage the collections. "This is one piece of the puzzle," Christen says. "The technology is something that launches us into relationships. It doesn't create the relationships. It doesn't sustain them. It doesn't negate the need for labor and infrastructure".
>
> *(Machaluk 2020)*

3 Although our focus is on the intersection of CanLit and DH, we include projects that take place outside the geographical bounds of Canada and that fall within a broader realm of storytelling, such as oral history projects. We encourage readers to consult *Reviews in Digital Humanities*, an online peer-reviewed journal for digital humanities projects. Its registry includes the option to search for projects by field of study, including those categorized as *First Nations and Digital Studies*.

4 We have opened this section to a broader range of digital projects than those covered in other chapters, and although we refuse Western canonical boundaries in defining Indigenous literature, we are also aware of the harms that can be perpetuated when we dismiss mythological stories as fiction or assume a one-to-one relationship between the story being told and the storyteller telling it—a "failure to recognize the borders and boundaries ... [and] a wider refusal to engage with Indigenous literatures as sovereign entities," which "symbolizes a deeper failure to overcome the colonial reading practices that occlude or appropriate Indigenous voices" (Gaertner 2023).

5 There are many archives that are nominally based in the northern contiguous US, which we mention to push back against the organizing logic of national borders. These include *Stolen Relations: Recovering Stories of Indigenous Enslavement in the Americas* and the *Native American Women Playwrights Archive*. Archives built using *Murkutu CMS* include the *Plateau People's Web Portal Project*, the *Chugachmiut Heritage Library & Archive*, the *Genoa Indian School Digital Reconciliation Project*, the *Huna Heritage Digital Archives*, and the *Passamaquoddy Peoples' Knowledge Portal*.

6 Introducing the poem on *Indigenous Arts & Stories*, Whitehead says:

> I wrote this piece in commemoration of the kokum I never met who was murdered in the sixties. The poem is an act of what Gerald Vizenor calls, survivance. It is survival and it is resistance; it is bringing the historical into the present to disrupt the everyday. I want people to stop, think, and know that this is a historical reality that continues today. This poem is for all MMIWG2S peoples.
>
> *(2016)*

At the end of "mihkokwaniy" Whitehead includes a photograph of his grandmother, Rose Whitehead, under which appears the following text:

> i dedicate this poem to all missing & murdered Indigenous women, girls & two-spirit peoples; for their families, friends, loved ones & kin. we are a collective trauma that demands to be examined, reconciled, resolved & healed.
> today we survive; tomorrow we resist.
>
> *(104)*

Further reading

Christen, Kimberly. 2012. "Does Information Really Want to Be Free? Indigenous Knowledge Systems and the Question of Openness." *International Journal of Communication* 6: 2870–93. https://ijoc.org/index.php/ijoc/article/view/1618.
FNGIC. 2024. "The First Nations Principles of OCAP®." The First Nations Information Governance Centre. https://fnigc.ca/ocap-training/.
GIDA. 2019. *CARE Principles for Indigenous Data Governance*. The Global Indigenous Data Alliance. Research Data Alliance International Indigenous Data Sovereignty Interest Group. https://www.gida-global.org/care.
Reder, Deanna, and Margery Fee. 2022. "The People and the Text: An Inclusive Collection." In *Collection Thinking: Within and Without Libraries, Archives and Museums*, edited by Jason Camlot, Martha Langford, and Linda M. Morra, 293–305. London: Routledge. https://doi.org/10.4324/9781003282303-24.
Wemigwans, Jennifer. 2018. *A Digital Bundle: Protecting and Promoting Indigenous Knowledge Online*. Regina: University of Regina Press. https://doi.org/10.1515/9780889775527.

Works cited

Abel, Jordan. 2013. *Injun*. Vancouver: Talonbooks.
Abel, Jordan. 2014. *Un/inhabited*. Vancouver: Talonbooks.
Assembly of First Nations. 2018. "Dismantling the Doctrine of Discovery." January 2018. https://afn.ca/wp-content/uploads/2018/02/18-01-22-Dismantling-the-Doctrine-of-Discovery-EN.pdf.
Bohaker, Heidi, Alan Ojiig Corbiere, and Ruth B. Phillips. 2015. "Wampum Unites Us: Digital Access, Interdisciplinarity and Indigenous Knowledge—Situating the GRASAC Knowledge Sharing Platform." In *Museum as Process: Translating Global Knowledges*, edited by Raymond Silverman, 45–66. Abingdon: Routledge.
Bourdages, Lauren, and Kassandra Caporiccio. 2020. *The "Use Our Words" Toolkit*. Accessed September 8, 2024. https://indigenouslis.ca/the-use-our-words-toolkit/.
Brooks, Lisa. 2018. "Awikhigawôgan ta Pildowi Ôjmowôgan: Mapping a New History." *The William and Mary Quarterly* 75, no. 2: 259–94. https://doi.org/10.5309/willmaryquar.75.2.0259.
Brown, Deidre, and George Nicholas. 2012. "Protecting Indigenous Cultural Property in the Age of Digital Democracy: Institutional and Communal Responses to Canadian First Nations and Māori Heritage Concerns." *Journal of Material Culture* 17, no. 3: 307–24. https://doi.org/10.1177/1359183512454065.
Brown, Susan. 2020. "Categorically Provisional." *PMLA* 135, no. 1: 165–74. https://doi.org/10.1632/pmla.2020.135.1.165.
Centre for Digital Scholarship and Curation. 2024. *Murkutu CMS*. Pullman: Washington State University. Accessed September 5, 2024. https://mukurtu.org/.
Christen, Kimberly. 2012. "Does Information Really Want to Be Free? Indigenous Knowledge Systems and the Question of Openness." *International Journal of Communication* 6: 2870–93. https://ijoc.org/index.php/ijoc/article/view/1618.

Chugachmiut Heritage Library & Archive. 2024. https://archive.chugachmiut.org/.
Cifor, Marika, Patricia Garcia, T. L. Cowan, Jasmine Rault, Tonia Sutherland, Anita Say Chan, Jennifer Rode, Anna Lauren Hoffmann, Niloufar Salehi, and Lisa Nakamura. 2019. "Feminist Data Manifest-No." https://www.manifestno.com/.
Cooper, Lydia R. 2020. "A Future Perfect: Queer Digital Sovereignty in Joshua Whitehead's *Jonny Appleseed* and *full-metal indigiqueer*." *Contemporary Literature* 60, no. 4: 491–514. https://doi.org/10.3368/cl.60.4.491.
Digital Democracy. 2024. *Terrastories*. https://terrastories.app/.
Edmonton Public Library. 2024. *Voices of the Land*. https://voicesoftheland.org/.
Ermine, Willie. 2007. "The Ethical Space of Engagement." *Indigenous Law Journal* 6, no. 1: 193–203. https://tspace.library.utoronto.ca/bitstream/1807/17129/1/ILJ-6.1-Ermine.pdf.
FNIGC. 2024. "The First Nations Principles of OCAP®." The First Nations Information Governance Centre. https://fnigc.ca/ocap-training/.
Gaertner, David. 2017. "Why We Need to Talk about Indigenous Literature and the Digital Humanities." *Novel Alliances* (blog), January 26, 2017. https://novelalliances.com/2017/01/26/indigenous-literature-and-the-digital-humanities-2/.
Gaertner, David. 2019. "Indigenous Digital Poetics: Joshua Whitehead's *full-metal indigiqueer*." *Novel Alliances* (blog), November 28, 2019. https://novelalliances.com/2019/11/28/the-road-to-reconciliation-is-paved-with-g-dintentions-lack-as-resistance-in-joshua-whiteheads-full-metal-indigiqueer-2/.
Gaertner, David. 2023. "#HonouringIndigenousWriters: Visiting with and through Indigenous Literatures in the 'Digital Turn'." *Transmotion* 9, no. 1: 147–78. https://doi.org/10.22024/UniKent/03/tm.1107.
Genoa Indian School Digital Reconciliation Project. n.d. *Genoa Indian School Digital Reconciliation Project*. Accessed September 8, 2024. https://genoaindianschool.org/home.
GIDA. 2019. *CARE Principles for Indigenous Data Governance*. The Global Indigenous Data Alliance. Research Data Alliance International Indigenous Data Sovereignty Interest Group. https://www.gida-global.org/care.
GRASAC. 2024a. *Great Lakes Research Alliance for the Study of Aboriginal Arts & Cultures*. https://grasac.artsci.utoronto.ca/.
GRASAC. 2024b. *GRASAC Knowledge Sharing Platform*. https://gks.artsci.utoronto.ca/.
Hart, Michael S. 2007. "The Project Gutenberg Mission Statement." *Project Gutenberg*. https://www.gutenberg.org/about/background/mission_statement.html.
Hill, Susan M. 2009. "Conducting Haudenosaunee Historical Research from Home: In the Shadow of the Six Nations-Caledonia Reclamation." *American Indian Quarterly* 33, no. 4: 479–98. https://doi.org/10.1353/aiq.2009.a362022.
Humanities for All. 2024. "Murkutu CMS: An Indigenous Archive and Publishing Tool." Accessed September 5, 2024. https://humanitiesforall.org/projects/mukurtu-an-indigenous-archive-and-publishing-tool.
Huna Heritage Foundation. 2024. *Huna Heritage Digital Archives*. https://archives.hunaheritage.org/.
Hunt, Dallas, and Shaun A. Stevenson. 2016. "Decolonizing Geographies of Power: Indigenous Digital Counter-Mapping Practices on Turtle Island." *Settler Colonial Studies* 7, no. 3: 372–92. https://doi.org/10.1080/2201473X.2016.1186311.

Indigenous Innovation Initiative. 2021. *Nindokiikayencikewin: Indigenous Knowledges and Data Governance Protocol*. Toronto: Indigenous Innovation Initiative. www.indigenousinnovate.org.

Invert Media. 2012. *FourDirectionsTeachings.com*. https://www.fourdirectionsteachings.com/.

Iseke-Barnes, Judy, and Deborah Danard. 2007. "Indigenous Knowledges and Worldview: Representations and the Internet." In *Information Technology and Indigenous People*, edited by L. E. Dyson, 27–29. Hershey: Information Science Pub. https://doi.org/10.4018/978-1-59904-298-5.ch003.

Justice, Daniel Heath. 2018. *Why Indigenous Literatures Matter*. Waterloo: Wilfred Laurier University Press. https://doi.org/10.51644/9781771121774.

Kiinawin Kawindomowin / Story Nations. n.d. Accessed September 8, 2024. https://storynations.utoronto.ca/.

LINCS. 2024. *Linked Infrastructure for Networked Cultural Scholarship*. https://lincsproject.ca/.

Local Contexts. 2024. *Traditional Knowledge Labels*. https://localcontexts.org/labels/traditional-knowledge-labels/.

Machaluk, Erin. 2020. "Mukurtu: A Digital Platform That Does More Than Manage Content." *Humanities: The Magazine of the National Endowment for the Humanities* 41, no. 4. https://www.neh.gov/article/mukurtu-digital-platform-does-more-manage-content.

Martin-Hill, Dawn. n.d. *Ohneganos Ohnegahdę:gyo*. Accessed September 5, 2024. https://explore.terrastories.app/community/ohneganos.

Martínez, Shanae Aurora. 2018. "*full-metal indigiqueer* by Joshua Whitehead." *The Georgia Review* 72, no. 2: 627–35.

McDougall, Aislinn Clare. 2019. "The Decolonization of Print, Digital, and Oral Spaces in Jordan Abel's Injun." *Canadian Literature* 239: 87–106.

Nakamura, Lisa. 2002. *Cybertypes: Race, Ethnicity, and Identity on the Internet*. New York: Routledge. https://doi.org/10.4324/9780203953365.

Native American Women Playwrights Archive. 2024. https://spec.lib.miamioh.edu/home/nawpa.

Native Land Digital. 2024. *Native Land*. https://native-land.ca/.

NIKLA. n.d. *Respectful Terminology Platform Project*. National Indigenous Knowledge & Language Alliance. Accessed September 5, 2024. https://www.nikla-ancla.com/respectful-terminology.

Passamaquoddy Community. n.d. *Passamaquoddy Peoples' Knowledge Portal*. Accessed September 5, 2024. https://passamaquoddypeople.com/.

Pereira, Davi, and Bjørn Sletto. 2024. "Indigenous Cartographies." In *The Routledge Handbook of Cartographic Humanities*, edited by Tania Rossetto and Laura Lo Presti, 254–60. Abingdon: Routledge. https://doi.org/10.4324/9781003327578-33.

Plateau People's Web Portal Project. n.d. Accessed September 5, 2024. https://plateauportal.libraries.wsu.edu/.

Reder, Deanna, Madeleine Reddon, Alix Shield, Margery Fee, and Susan Glover. n.d. *The People and the Text: Indigenous Writing in Lands Claimed by Canada*. Accessed September 8, 2024. https://thepeopleandthetext.ca/.

Reder, Deanna, and Margery Fee. 2022. "The People and the Text: An Inclusive Collection." In *Collection Thinking: Within and Without Libraries, Archives and Museums*, edited by Jason Camlot, Martha Langford, and Linda M. Morra, 293–305. London: Routledge. https://doi.org/10.4324/9781003282303-24.

Ritter, Kathleen. 2014. "Ctrl-F: Reterritorializing the Canon." In *Un/inhabited*, edited by Jordan Abel, vii–xix. Vancouver: Talonbooks.

Schmaltz, Eric. 2019. "Politics of Memory: Digital Repositories, Settler Colonialism, and Jordan Abel's Un/inhabited." *English Studies in Canada* 45, no. 4: 123–42. https://doi.org/10.1353/esc.2019.0020.

Sharma, Sarah, and Jennifer Wemigwans. 2022. "Toward a Media Theory of the Digital Bundle: A Conversation with Jennifer Wemigwans." In *Re-understanding Media: Feminist Extensions of Marshall McLuhan*, 209–24. Durham: Duke University Press. https://doi.org/10.2307/j.ctv2drhchc.17.

Stolen Relations: Recovering Stories of Indigenous Enslavement in the Americas. n.d. Accessed September 8, 2024. https://indigenousslavery.org/.

Stoner, Melissa S. 2023. "Wikipetcia Atikamekw Nehiromowin." *Reviews in Digital Humanities* 4, no. 10. https://doi.org/10.21428/3e88f64f.b8080e14.

United Nations. 2007. "United Nations Declaration on the Rights of Indigenous Peoples." https://www.un.org/development/desa/indigenouspeoples/wp-content/uploads/sites/19/2018/11/UNDRIP_E_web.pdf.

Wemigwans, Jennifer. 2018. *A Digital Bundle: Protecting and Promoting Indigenous Knowledge Online*. Regina: University of Regina Press. https://doi.org/10.1515/9780889775527.

Whitehead, Joshua. 2016. "mihkokwaniy," Indigenous Arts & Stories. http://www.our-story.ca/winners/writing/5518:mihkokwaniy.

Whitehead, Joshua. 2017. *full-metal indigiqueer*. Vancouver: Talonbooks.

Whitehead, Joshua. 2018. *Jonny Appleseed*. Vancouver: Arsenal Pulp Press.

Whitehead, Joshua. 2022. *Making Love with the Land*. Toronto: Knopf.

Whose Land. n.d. Accessed September 5, 2024. https://www.whose.land/en/.

Wikipetcia. 2024. *Wikipetcia Atikamekw Nehiromowin*. https://atj.wikipedia.org/wiki/Otitikowin.

PART V

11
DATA ACQUISITION

* * *

Data acquisition may, at first glance, appear to be the most banal of digital humanities processes, but it is the foundation on which many DH projects are built. While obtaining data has certainly become easier—thanks to digitization support from university librarians, access to powerful scanners, and even the ability to capture high-quality images with a phone—the data acquisition and management processes still have many labour- and resource-intensive steps. Additionally, every step from cleaning the data (see Chapter 13) to analyzing it (see Chapters 13 and 14) and managing it (see Chapter 12) adds opportunities for the interpretation and analysis that are at the core of DH. Creating or collecting data is, inevitably, more than just a process of accumulation; it is an act by which you can "reveal properties and traits not evident when the artifact was in its native form" (Schreibman, Siemens, and Unsworth 2004). As Stefan Higgins, Lisa Goddard, and Shahira Khair explain,

> datasets are not merely a haphazard agglomeration of "stuff," but created, organized, and delimited data that are thereafter put to the work of analysis and interpretation. How a dataset is organized influences what we can learn from data, and datasets therefore require purposeful *design*. Data and dataset design allow researchers to use data for "reference, analysis, and calculation." In other words, they allow data … to be put to *work*. This work is diverse: historical (and even ancient) practices from weaving to notching to knotting to quilting

(insofar as they involve patterning, calculation, and even accounting) are data work, involving reference, analysis, and accounting, and are not reducible in meaning to the numerical .... That is, data work is not reducible only to a spreadsheet of numbers or what a researcher does with those numbers thereafter; it is, instead, by definition, a humanities practice, too.

(2004; original emphasis)

The authors gesture towards the humanities considerations of history, representation, agency, and more that go into designing a dataset. From the objects of study to the categories of knowledge, the design of the dataset has knock-on effects on the research itself. Acquiring data is not, therefore, a precursor to a digital humanities project, but rather already a step of delineation, interpretation, and analysis. In this chapter, we offer a guide to seeking out data for DH projects, both born-digital and already-digitized resources. In subsequent chapters, we explain how to manage and store data (Chapter 12) and how to work with it in a range of ways (Chapters 13–15).

Before turning to where to find data, however, we would like to think critically about the specificities of digital data. In this domain, historians have a lot to teach us. The authors of *Exploring Big Historical Data: The Historian's Macroscope* (2015) explain,

> For historians, as we work with digitized primary sources, we need to always consider the quality of the text. How was it constructed? Was it double-blind entered, like the *Old Bailey Online*? Or did commercial OCR algorithms, intended for law firms and applied to this job for which they were not designed, scan it? ... Citing the digital matters, both for intellectual honesty as well as recognizing the algorithms that underlie these databases.
>
> *(Graham et al. 2022, 49)*

Digitizing can add context and meaning through factors such as methodology, metadata, and quality of the digital version. Digitization can also strip away context and undercut meaning. For example, OCR can incorrectly identify words, spreadsheets can be missing data, audio recordings can have sections that are inaudible, users can inadvertently insert mistakes or even alter or cherry-pick data to bring an argument into focus; the methods of digitization or data acquisition can fundamentally affect analyses and conclusions. Graham et al. remind us that digitization is a process whereby relevant information is both added to and removed from the original object; the method of digitization affects the meanings associated with the data. As such, Canadian historians who work with digitized versions of the *Book of Negroes* (the record of Black Loyalists who escaped to Nova Scotia during the American Revolution, available from the Nova Scotia Archives and *Black Loyalists: Our History, Our People*; see Chapter 7) or the *Register of Chinese Immigrants to Canada, 1886–1949* (Ward and Yu 2008) (records related to the head tax paid by Chinese immigrants to Canada, available from UBC Library Open Collections; see Chapter 9) should include as part of the research process an overview of their methods for working with these digital materials and archives. How, for instance, would these projects deal with terms in the data that are racist and offensive? How would these projects grapple with multiple languages in the dataset? These are just a few of the questions that data acquisition raises. In the digital humanities, it is always worth asking "what it is that the digitization is aiming to capture?"—a question not simply about how information has moved from page to screen, but also about surrounding contexts, meanings, intentions, and biases that have also been acquired and created (Deegan and Tanner 2004). File structures, metadata, and access rights, among other things, all add layers of meaning to the dataset.

Finding data

When it comes to Canadian literature, primary source materials already available for DH work range from scans of holograph manuscripts to digitized full-text versions of published works. Extensive data derived from secondary and supplementary materials are also available: archives of an author's personal and professional correspondence, related media such as interviews and book reviews, and ephemera such as book covers and social media content. The breadth and volume of material available depend on the author or text in question: digitized manuscripts are more likely to be available for public domain works of authors of substantial standing; social media content is largely (although not exclusively) available for contemporary authors—and typically younger ones, at that.[1]

If you are looking for material to serve as the basis for a digital humanities project, you have plenty of options. For one, you can choose to work with only the primary source material. For example, a digital textual analysis could be done on the poetry of Bliss Carman by downloading his poems from *Project Gutenberg*, a free online repository of literature in the public domain (discussed below). For another, you could choose to combine literary texts with the materials that scaffold them. Not only are E. Pauline Johnson's stories and poetry available as public domain, full-text digitizations but so too are scans of some of her letters and photographs. A DH project could combine this material with substantial supplementary information, from sources ranging from an existing DH project that maps her *Legends of Vancouver* (Graham 2017) to her entry in the *Dictionary of Canadian Biography* (Rose 1998).

When seeking digitized materials, it is worth remembering that the line between digital archival material and interpretive digital project is hazy. If you were interested in *Anne of Green Gables* (1908) you could download the text from *Project Gutenberg* but equally you could read a digitized version of L. M. Montgomery's holograph manuscript, supplemented with additional information and accompanying photographs and audio notes, made available by *The Anne of Green Gables Manuscript: L. M. Montgomery and the Creation of Anne*. This feature-rich version is not a straight reproduction; it adds an interpretive gloss via the supplementary and scholarly materials provided. The questions about construction, methodology, and intention that we have asked throughout this book are reminders to think critically about the meanings embedded in a digital resource as part of the process of using it.

Each project is different. Some will rely on preexisting data whereas others will need to create their own bespoke datasets. What follows are some examples of where and how you can acquire data. Given the ever-changing landscape of digital humanities and technologically dependent resources, the resources we describe are meant only to give a sense of the breadth available for the study of Canadian literature. Before working with any dataset, we encourage you to confirm that the materials are, indeed, available for reuse and also to consider the ethics of using them.

Large-scale text repositories

Downloadable, full-text materials are largely limited to works that are in the public domain; this means, at the time of writing, works published in or before 1971.[2] The dearth of out-of-copyright Canadian literary texts has "been an impediment to establishing substantial sets of digitized Canadian texts for analysis and to sharing such datasets for the purposes of being able to evaluate claims, replicate results, and build upon prior work" (Brown and Devereux 2017). Even within what is available, not all of the material is worthy of our regard, as Jordan Abel's critical reworkings of public domain westerns show (see Chapter 10). Notwithstanding, there are several well-established digital archives with Canadian content. *Project Gutenberg* and the *HathiTrust Digital Library* are the two best known. *Project Gutenberg* has a library of 70,000 free texts, including a large collection of works by Canadian authors such as Sara Jeannette Duncan, E. Pauline Johnson, Louis Hémon, Archibald Lampman, Stephen Leacock, L. M. Montgomery,[3] Susanna Moodie, Catharine Parr Traill,

John Richardson, and Robert Service. Individual works can be saved to a computer from a web browser or via the Gutenberg API (see Chapter 14), which allows users to pull material directly into tools, programming environments, or data stores.

Like *Project Gutenberg*, the *HathiTrust Digital Library* provides access to public domain Canadian literature and literary criticism. It has an extensive collection of documents such as reports from the Canada Council and other funding organizations, and it includes sizable contributions of materials from Canadian universities, for example, York University, Western University, and Toronto Metropolitan University. *HathiTrust*'s more than 18 million individual texts can be downloaded as PDF or plain-text files or through its API (which is, unfortunately, functionally more limited than *Gutenberg*'s).

Aggregators and specialized archives

Alongside repositories that provide direct access to material, there are sites that act as aggregators for smaller digital archives. *Humanities Data* is a website that points at web-hosted digital humanities data (albeit not all Canadian) (Lavin, n.d.); *Borealis* is a repository supported by universities across Canada (albeit not all humanities). The Canadian Research Knowledge Network's (CRKN) *Canadian National Digital Heritage Index* (CNDHI) catalogues materials from more than 1,500 collections, over fifty of which have CanLit content. The CNDHI links outwards to archives at Canadian universities, libraries, and heritage institutions; authors represented include George Elliott Clarke, Irving Layton, W. O. Mitchell, Pamela Mordecai, Richard Outram, Anne Szumigalski, and Yves Thériault. Also represented are thematic collections on topics such as Inuit literature, Canadian science fiction and fantasy, Canadian folklore, and Canadian comic books. Specialized digital archives include the Canadian poetry section of *Representative Poetry Online* (the history of which is discussed in Chapter 3), which features a selection of poems by hundreds of Canadian poets alongside biographies, bibliographies, and other information. Many Canadian universities also have subject- and author-specific literary archives, although their digital materials are often limited to finding aids.

Existing digital humanities projects are also excellent sources of aggregated or specialized data. Some projects provide direct access to materials. For example, the *Canadian Modernist Magazines Project* has digitized editions of four Canadian magazines—*Neith* (1903–1904), *Le Nigog* (1918), *Preview* (1942–1945), and *First Statement* (1942–1945)—browsable by volume, contributor, and text. Others act as aggregators, such as the *AMM Bibliography*, which provides a database of criticism on and reviews of Ann-Marie MacDonald's work. Users can search by text, topic, and type of publication, and they can also contribute back to the database. Other projects provide not just access to materials but also tools or even spaces to work with them, as in the collaboratories (CWRC, EMiC, and *Spoken-Web*) discussed in Chapter 5. Funders such as SSHRC encourage open access and emphasize the importance of good research data management practices, with the result being that many researchers have made their data available for reuse via an institutional repository, a federal repository such as *Borealis*, an international repository such as *Zenodo*, or by other means. Currently, there is no resource that aggregates or directs researchers to data generated by SSHRC-funded projects.

There is also a great deal of disaggregated materials available. These resources can be frustratingly difficult to locate, but once identified, they can be excellent—especially because so many of them are previously untapped research resources. For example, if you are interested in contemporary literature, you can download content directly from journals such as *Canadian Literature*, *The Tamarack Review*, *The Ex-Puritan*, and others. These do-it-yourself forms of data collection may require you to do substantial amounts of data cleaning and curation to make the data usable for analysis, but this sort of hands-on work can produce valuable, focused research datasets. Note also that this material is often still under copyright, so although it can often be used for research purposes, you should take care to obtain permission before extensively quoting from the material or sharing either full-text versions or data derived from the texts.

Supplementary materials

Bringing together primary and supplementary materials is one of the many things that digital humanities projects do particularly well. For comparative, supplementary, and historical Canadian materials to augment literary texts or to provide the basis for contextualizing research, *Canadiana* is an excellent source, including over 80,000 monographs, 95,000 periodical issues, 10,000 government publications, 22,000 maps, and a range of other sources. *Canadiana* is searchable and texts can be saved as PDFs for further analysis. The *Érudit* platform provides access specifically to Canadian humanities, social science, and cultural heritage resources, including open-source journal articles, books, conference proceedings, and other research materials. The Canadian federal government runs *Open Government* (2023), which includes datasets relevant to Canadian government operations accessible via the Web or via their API. Likewise, Library and Archives Canada (LAC) has accessible datasets, some via the *Open Government* site and others via LAC directly. Canadian university libraries also offer excellent historical datasets and other materials. UBC Libraries, for instance, have developed an API for their collection of more than 200,000 images, dissertations, texts, maps, and other unique cultural objects. You can search the collection via the *UBC Open Collections* (University of British Columbia 2008) website via the UBC Open Collections API. Similarly, research search services also provide datasets. For example, using *Constellate* you can search JSTOR, Portico, and other databases to create a dataset of relevant scholarly metadata (ITHAKA 2024).

Born-digital and emerging resources

In addition to digitized materials, there are also those that are born digital. Susan Brown and Cecily Devereux point to the emergence of born-digital literature as a genre with great digital humanities potential:

> The exploration of diversity of form, identity, content, and medium within what we might consider not simply CanLit but CanDigLit itself, in the work of Jordan Abel, J. R. Carpenter, Sachiko Murakami, and Kate Pullinger, to name but a few, can help to push digital literary studies in the direction of [a broader] cultural critique.
>
> *(2017)*

Earlier waves of Canadian digital poetics are also a great source of digitized materials. For example, Jim Andrews et al. have made available an emulated version of *First Screening*, the kinetic poems bpNichol created on an Apple IIe using BASIC (see Chapter 6). Frustratingly, Frank Davey and Fred Wah's *SwiftCurrent* electronic literary magazine cannot be found online; instead, a Google search leads to the Simon Fraser University Special Collections' analogue archival fonds related to Davey and Wah.

Social media is also a useful source of textual data, particularly public discourse. However, where social media was once relatively straightforward (and free) to acquire, the cost in both time and money to get data from organizations like Facebook and Twitter is now prohibitive, thus rendering this form of research all but impossible, while also challenging the rhetoric of free speech with which these platforms justify their existence. Reddit makes its data available to users via an API. There are also many useful data repositories online, such as *Kaggle*.

From corpus to curation

Once you have worked out what data you want and where you will get it, the next step is to actually acquire it. This can be done in one of two ways: you can either work with materials that have already been digitized and collected, or you can gather or create them. For gathering materials, you can use Internet-scraping tools such as *Wget*[4]; for creating new content, you can generate digital text from scans, PDFs, or word processing files. Regardless of the starting point, text analysis works best on plaintext. Converting files to plaintext is the third and final step, and a quick search online will yield plenty of tools (both free and paid) that can be used for this purpose.

Regardless of whether the data has all come from one place or has been assembled from many different ones, the next step is to curate the corpus. A corpus is a collection of digital, textual materials, which is often organized around a central theme, be it the same author, a shared genre, or a shared period. Assembling a corpus is already an interpretive act in that you are choosing what is included in your analysis and what is not; you are also influencing the shape and scale of analysis possible with your choices. For example, working on a corpus of poetry collections, you may wish to remove introductions and supplementary material. This is best done in the text file you will be using for your analysis. While there are specialty text editing programs (experienced users often prefer *Notepad*++), free programs that come preloaded on most computers, such as *Notes* or *TextEdit* (on a Mac) or *Notepad* (on a PC), will suffice for most users. Curation can be done in many ways, ranging from the use of complex programming languages to GUI-tool-based systems to using familiar methods such as the in-built search and filter functions in word processing and spreadsheet software.

In what follows, we describe the process of curating a literary corpus to be used for textual analysis. This is not the only way to work with digital (literary) materials, but rather an example for one way to get started. Your first step in curating the corpus is to remove any irrelevant metadata from the text. Books from *Gutenberg*, for example, will include headers, footers, and other metadata that will not be relevant to most analyses. Depending on the source of the textual data, you may also need to remove non-alphanumeric characters. The process of converting a PDF to plaintext can, for example, introduce unwanted text (where, for instance, a pen mark on a page is interpreted as a comma), which might need removing. This can be done via a *find and replace* command in your text editor or with more accuracy and sophistication using a programming language (see Chapter 14).

Your next step may be to remove the stop words. Stop words are those that appear so often in text that they are irrelevant to, or can interfere with, textual analysis. If stop words are not removed, they will obscure the kinds of interesting results that computational analysis can help with; in other words, they can produce *noise*, which makes it hard to spot the *signal*. A typical stop word list begins with something like the following: [I, the, and, for, from, to, he, her, in, of, it, yes, you, who, when, where, has, she, our, not, ...] (see Chapter 14 for more information about stop words, including the full list of 127 words in the *Natural Language Toolkit* English-language list). Which stop words to remove, however, depends on your corpus and your research questions. For example, you can expand your stop words list to exclude frequently occurring character names, location names, or common phrases. Or your list can retain words that are often excluded; for example, pronouns could be kept if you were undertaking a gender-inflected analysis. The choices you make about stop word lists may also depend on the period, genre, and other factors: an analysis of early modern drama will likely include *thou* as a stop word, whereas you might want to keep it in an analysis for contemporary texts. The concluding sentences of Joyce's *Ulysses* include the word *yes* eleven times (and it is the final word in the novel); although *yes* often appears on stop words lists, removing it from an analysis of *Ulysses* changes the meaning of that final section. Canadian texts sometimes include words in both French and English (not to mention other languages, regional vocabularies, and dialects), which your stop word list might need to accommodate.

After removing stop words, your next step may be to undertake more complex curation via stemming and lemmatizing. Stemming is the process of removing the morphological variants (suffixes) of words to reduce the words to their stems such that a series of similar words all converge on the same word: for example, *amortizing*, *amortized*, and *amortizes* all transform into *amortize*. Lemmatizing engages in a similar process but uses a combination of stemming and substitution to group together similar words: *corpora* and *corpuses* become *corpus*, while *better* becomes *good*. Following stemming and lemmatizing, the next step is tokenizing the text. This is the process by which a text is broken up from a morass of text into machine-processable units, known as tokens. A token is a designated unit of analysis for the purpose of digital textual interpretation. Typically, when working with prose, each token represents a single word in the text. This can change, however, and depending on your research question, tokens may be comprised of entire sentences or even paragraphs. When dealing with poetry, for instance, your tokens may be a word or a line in a poem.

The process of data curation is not only lengthy but also often iterative. Careful curation of data is necessary to locate the signal among all the potential noise, and no one process will suit all purposes. Consequently, data is often curated in several rounds. Your first attempts at analyzing the corpus can yield areas for further curation, for example, you may find more stop words to remove or more noise to filter. This process recalls Drucker's argument for *capta* as it captures how data is shaped by research questions and principles of humanistic inquiry. One research question can also give rise to another: a text that is tokenized into lines to answer one question may later be re-tokenized into words to answer another. A major advantage of working computationally is that you may find going back to make these sorts of adjustments relatively straightforward, especially if your preceding files have been carefully saved. Once your data is collected, curated, and shaped in a manner suited to the research questions, you will find additional challenges in the form of developing metadata, storing data, and preserving research results. Regardless of where your materials have come from, once they have been assembled as your corpus, they constitute a new research dataset you must manage in its own right with robust research data management practices. The next two chapters offer a starting point for addressing these concerns: Chapter 12 discusses storing and managing data and Chapter 13 introduces concepts in the analysis of textual data.

Notes

1 Of course, age and appetite for joining the public conversation may be no barrier to entry, as Zach Schonfeld explains in "No, Alice Munro Has Not Joined Twitter" in an October 9, 2013, article in *The Atlantic*.
2 Whereas an author's work previously entered the public domain in Canada fifty years after their death, as of 2022, this changed to seventy years. No new works will join the public domain until 2043, but researchers who are willing to wait until then will be spoiled for CanLit choices, as authors such as Morley Callaghan, Marian Engel, Northrop Frye, Margaret Lawrence, Hugh MacLennan, Marshal McLuhan, bpNichol, and Gabrielle Roy will all enter the public domain that year.
3 As of July 2024, Montgomery is the only Canadian author to make it into the hundred most-downloaded books on *Project Gutenberg*, with *The Blue Castle* in ninth (47,526 downloads) and *Anne of Green Gables* in fifty-second (9,832 downloads).
4 A tool such as *Wget* requires some degree of technical knowledge but is effective for downloading the entire contents of a single website and can allow you to use web scraping to develop a dataset. Online tutorials can guide new users in *Wget* basics.

Further reading

Deegan, Marilyn, and Simon Tanner. 2004. "Conversion of Primary Sources." In *A Companion to Digital Humanities*, edited by Susan Schreibman, Ray Siemens, and John Unsworth, 488–504. Oxford: Blackwell. https://doi.org/10.1002/9780470999875.

Drucker, Johanna. 2011. "Humanities Approaches to Graphical Display." *Digital Humanities Quarterly* 5, no. 1. https://www.digitalhumanities.org/dhq/vol/5/1/000091/000091.html.

Drucker, Johanna. 2021. *The Digital Humanities Coursebook: An Introduction to Digital Methods for Research and Scholarship*. Abingdon: Routledge. https://doi.org/10.4324/9781003106531.

Graham, Shawn, Ian Milligan, Scott B. Weingart, and Kimberley Martin. 2022. *Exploring Big Historical Data: The Historian's Macroscope*, 2nd ed. London: Imperial College Press. https://doi.org/10.1142/12435.

Works cited

Andrews, Jim, Geof Huth, Lionel Kearns, Marko Niemi, and Dan Weber. 2007. "First Screening: Computer Poems." Accessed October 31. https://www.vispo.com/bp/introduction.htm.

Black Loyalists: Our History, Our People. The Book of Negroes. n.d. Canada's Digital Collections Program, Industry Canada. Accessed September 4, 2024. https://blackloyalist.com/cdc/documents/official/book_of_negroes.htm.

Borealis. n.d. *Borealis: The Canadian Dataverse Repository*. Accessed July 12, 2024. https://borealisdata.ca/.

Brown, Susan, and Cecily Devereux. 2017. "Introduction: Digital Textualities/Canadian Contexts." *Studies in Canadian Literature / Études en littérature canadienne* 42, no. 2: 145–53. https://id.erudit.org/iderudit/scl42_2art07.

CRKN. 2024. *Canadiana*. Canadian Research Knowledge Network. Accessed June 5, 2024. https://www.canadiana.ca.

CRKN. n.d. *Canadian National Digital Heritage Index*. Canadian Research Knowledge Network. Accessed July 12, 2024. https://www.cndhi-ipnpc.ca/en.

CWRC. n.d.. *Collaboratory for Writing and Research on Culture*. Accessed July 12, 2024. https://cwrc.ca/.

Deegan, Marilyn, and Simon Tanner. 2004. "Conversion of Primary Sources." In *A Companion to Digital Humanities*, edited by Susan Schreibman, Ray Siemens, and John Unsworth, 488–504. Oxford: Blackwell. https://doi.org/10.1002/9780470999875.

EMiC. n.d. *Editing Modernism in Canada*. Accessed July 12, 2024. https://editingmodernism.ca/.

Érudit Consortium. 2024. *Érudit*. Accessed October 15, 2024. https://www.erudit.org/en/.

Gordon, Neta. 2023. *AMM Bibliography*. https://www.ammbibliography.com/.

Government of Canada. 2023. *Open Government*. November 23, 2023. https://open.canada.ca/en.

Graham, P. J. 2017. *Legends of Vancouver* (website). https://www.legendsofvancouver.net/.

Graham, Shawn, Ian Milligan, Scott B. Weingart, and Kimberley Martin. 2022. *Exploring Big Historical Data: The Historian's Macroscope*, 2nd ed. London: Imperial College Press. https://doi.org/10.1142/12435.

HathiTrust. 2024. *HathiTrust Digital Library*. https://www.hathitrust.org/.

Higgins, Stefan, Lisa Goddard, and Shahira Khair. 2024. "Research Data Management in the Humanities: Challenges and Opportunities in the Canadian Context." *Digital Studies / Le champ numérique* 14, no. 1: 1–22. https://doi.org/10.16995/dscn.9956.

ITHAKA. 2024. *Constellate*. https://constellate.org/.

Jensen, Graham, Deseray Manuel, et al. 2022. *Canadian Modernist Magazines Project*. University of Victoria. https://modernistmags.ca.

Lavin, Matthew J. n.d. *Humanities Data*. Accessed July 12, 2024. https://humanities data.com/.
Project Gutenberg. n.d. Accessed September 8, 2024. https://www.gutenberg.org/.
Representative Poetry Online. n.d. Accessed July 12, 2024. https://rpo.library.utoronto.ca/.
Rose, Marilyn J. 1998. "Johnson, Emily Pauline." In *Dictionary of Canadian Biography*, vol. 14. University of Toronto / Université Laval, 2003. https://www.biographi.ca/en/bio/johnson_emily_pauline_14E.html.
Schonfeld, Zach. 2013. "No, Alice Munro Has Not Joined Twitter." *The Atlantic*, October 9, 2013. https://www.theatlantic.com/culture/archive/2013/10/no-alice-munro-has-not-joined-twitter/310159/.
Schreibman, Susan, Ray Siemens, and John Unsworth. 2004. "The Digital Humanities and Humanities Computing: An Introduction." In *A Companion to Digital Humanities*, edited by Susan Schreibman, Ray Siemens, and John Unsworth, xxiii–xxvii. Oxford: Blackwell. https://doi.org/10.1002/9780470999875.
SpokenWeb. 2024. *SpokenWeb*. https://spokenweb.ca/.
Ward, Peter W., and Henry Yu. 2008. "Register of Chinese Immigrants to Canada, 1886–1949." University of British Columbia Open Collections. Updated August 31, 2012. https://doi.org/10.14288/1.0075988.
Woster, Emily, ed. 2024. *The Anne of Green Gables Manuscript: L. M. Montgomery and the Creation of Anne*. https://annemanuscript.ca/.

12
DATA MANAGEMENT

* * *

The idea of having an explicit plan for managing research data may seem an odd proposition for the humanities. Traditionally, humanities materials are either already managed by someone else (e.g., published works and materials from archives) or they are not subject to any requirements for how they are handled (e.g., personal notes). However, when humanities data is expanded to include the "plurality of objects that researchers put to work in order to know how humans articulate meaning," the amount of material to be managed increases dramatically (Higgins, Goddard, and Khair 2024). Take, for example, this list of answers given to a survey question asking researchers about the types of data they had, and which from a SSHRC-sponsored 2021 event, Research Data Management for Digitally Curious Humanists:

> text; audio files; video files; image files; physical archival records; medieval texts; library catalogue data; policy papers and records; VHS; 8 mm film; camcorder tapes; community relations (impact, contributions, feedback); religion in the 20th century; social movements in the 20th century; organizational memberships, budgets, bureaucratic documents; paper correspondence; interviews; maps; cultural analytics (e.g., Wikipedia links); programming languages; software; geodata; book history; literature (across genres, styles, and historical periods); culture and cultural objects (e.g., toys, games, clothing, foods); translations; radio tapes; prosopography; historical artefacts (and images of artefacts);

DOI: 10.4324/9781003318323-18

state and private financial records (e.g., grant records); text corpora; ephemera like clippings, photos, journals, logs; web usage and analytics; CSV files.

(Higgins, Goddard, and Khair 2024)

Only some of the things researchers mentioned are data in the traditional sense (library catalogue data, web analytics, and CSV files). Many others (toys, games, clothing, and food) seem more like objects from a museum collection, but they are still objects that need storing and managing.

Research data management (RDM) is the term used to describe both the managing objects of study and the things that are generated in the processes of collecting, organizing, and analyzing them. Metadata—information about the objects—is often created to help with the data management process, and RDM is then used to manage both data and the metadata about it. Management can also be used for anything created to work with the data (e.g., code written to analyze text files), built to share research findings (e.g., a project website or platform), or anything that has been made to facilitate work more generally, such as DH tools and interfaces.

A data management plan (DMP), which describes how researchers plan to store their digital research data, metadata, and related code is a requirement of Canadian federal funders, as set out in the "Tri-Agency Research Data Management Policy" (2021).[1] According to the Tri-Agency, data management is necessary to ensure that research "makes good use of public funds" and that "data collected through the use of public funds" is, where possible, "available for reuse by others" (SSHRC 2024). Institutions without RDM strategies can find their (and their researchers') funding eligibility blocked. Of course, RDM is more than just an obligation: it is also an opportunity to think critically about objects of study, to interrogate the ethical dimensions of creating and circulating information, to anticipate potential future uses of research, and to preserve and make the most of one's own research materials. To these ends, this chapter looks at RDM from both practical and theoretical perspectives, building on our earlier discussions of data. There are two sides to RDM: the practical aspects of creating a plan and the research- and field-shaping questions that emerge from it. We start with some information about how you can create a DMP before turning to the big-picture questions.

RDM planning basics

There are many examples to draw on as a basis for your DMP. Some researchers have made their plans available via repositories such as *Borealis* and *Zenodo*. The Digital Research Alliance of Canada's (DRAC) *Data*

Management Plan Assistant has an extensive collection of publicly available plans, and if you create an account, you can see plans shared by researchers at your own institution (DRAC 2024a).[2] The *DMP Assistant* also has a plan builder, which can guide you through the process of creating a document that covers the following areas:

- **Data collection**: Will data be collected, created, or both? How will the data be gathered or made?
- **Documentation and metadata**: How will the data be documented? What metadata standards will be used? What data formats will be used?
- **Storage and backup**: How and where will the data be stored during the project?
- **Preservation**: How and where will the data be stored after the project is finished? What are the long-term preservation plans?
- **Sharing and reuse**: Will others be able to reuse the data? How will they access it? Will limits be placed on how the data can be reused?
- **Responsibilities and resources**: Who is responsible for the data, for the project, and for ensuring the long-term preservation of both?
- **Ethics and legal compliance**: Who owns the data? Is the data subject to any ethical guidelines or legal requirements? How will these be adhered to?

If you are new to the process, many of the *DMP Assistant's* sections have links to resources that offer guidance on practical aspects of data management, including ethics, heritage value, and sharing and reuse.

When creating a DMP, you may find that you need to go back to basics. It is hard to institute a long-term plan without establishing first principles, such as a classification system for organizing materials, naming conventions for digital files, or a process for versioning work. While file management is outside the scope of this book, the potential benefits of establishing some protocols will be obvious to anyone who has tried to navigate a folder's worth of drafts with confusing file names. While it may seem counterintuitive to decide how to manage files or whether to use a content management system such as *Omeka* (Digital Scholar, n.d.) or *Collective Access* (Whirl-i-Gig 2024) before starting to gather your data, spending some time on these questions at the start can save you time down the road. DMPs are meant to be living documents, which means they can evolve across the lifecycle of your project.

A great place to start to understand the value of DMPs is *Research Data Management in a Canadian Context: A Guide for Practitioners and Learners* (Thompson et al. 2023), which has been created by Canadian research librarians and is geared specifically to Canadian requirements and available data management infrastructure. DH-specific resources are also useful where the *DMP Assistant*'s degree of detail may be excessive. For example, *The Digital Documentation Process* has been built specifically for DH projects (Fostano and Morreale 2019); its project itinerary wizard provides step-by-step instructions for documenting and archiving your project.

A DMP requires somewhere for you to put the data. *Borealis: The Canadian Dataverse Repository* provides archival services to researchers affiliated with participating Canadian universities and research organizations, a list of which can be found on its website. A search of the open-source (free-to-use) materials archived in *Borealis* also yields results related to RDM, including sample DMPs and a guide to publishing materials in *Borealis*. The *Federated Research Data Repository* (FRDR; DRAC 2024b), meanwhile, is available to faculty, librarians, and researchers affiliated with Canadian post-secondary institutions or any other organization eligible for Tri-Agency funding. FRDR datasets receive external review (or *curation*) before being approved for publication. Unlike *Borealis*, which accepts everything from slide decks to workshop materials, FRDR is only for more traditionally defined, large research datasets. If you do not want to or cannot use *Borealis* or FRDR, there are free services such as *Zenodo*, *GitHub*, and *GitLab*. Other options include institution-specific storage (e.g., at your university library) or joining forces with other DH projects and platforms, such as CWRC (see Chapter 5).

Although DMPs are usually created at the beginning of a project and are designed to manage data from acquisition through to archiving, the SSHRC-funded *The Endings Project*, based at the University of Victoria, encourages you to think about their project from finish to start as well. Thinking about how your project will end is a great way to plan for long-term accessibility and stability, since "it is much easier to design a project from scratch with longevity in mind than it is to rescue or re-work an old project which has been active for a long time" (Endings 2024). The "Endings Principles for Digital Longevity" cover data, documentation, processing, products, and release management, which are not coincidentally many of the same elements that appear in a DMP. Endings-compliant projects are published in a static format (no dependencies, required support, or backend software requirements) and securely archived. *The Endings Project* is itself endings compliant, and its site has links to other exemplary projects, open-source code for programmers to use to test and support their own projects' compliance, and resources related to the theory and practice of DH project preservation.

Best practices through FAIR data

The push for good data management practices has arisen, in part, in response to what happens when data and projects go unmanaged. Given the speed with which technology advances and the ease with which digital data can be erased, there is a very real risk that digital resources will be fleeting. For example, the University of Manitoba's *Canadian Literature Archive* (CLA)—online since 1994, last updated in 2006—disappeared from the web at some point during the time in which we were writing this book. Meanwhile, the website for the Canadian Literature Centre (CLC) currently points to a website promoting Canada as a location for international students.[3] The CLC's actual content has been acquired by the American-owned EBSCO Information Services and is now behind a paywall.[4] The CLA and CLC sites represent the worst and second-worst scenarios: data that disappears or is scooped up by commercial interests.

By far a better scenario would be data that is preserved and for which access, once granted, is maintained. Even better still, the best scenario would be data that is easy to find and easy to use. This type of gold-standard data is commonly referred to using the acronym FAIR (Findable, Accessible, Interoperable, and Reusable), which refers to four principles for data creation and management (GO FAIR Initiative, n.d.):

- **Findable:** index clearly and robustly to facilitate both human- and machine-based searching; unique persistent identifiers unambiguously distinguish the content
- **Accessible:** use free, open, standardized protocols; materials may be behind paywalls, but are no other barriers to access
- **Interoperable:** use formal, shared resources such as data structures, vocabularies, and references to organize the data
- **Reusable:** can be replicated wholesale or recombined with other materials for new uses; license and credit information is clearly stated

While creating and maintaining data that is truly FAIR is more complex than required for most DMPs, the principles can guide good data management. We therefore look at the criteria for FAIR to think about data management more broadly. It is worth noting that many of the FAIR conditions can be achieved by working with established data management systems and organizations.

Findable data

Data is findable when it has clear, robust metadata and makes use of persistent identifiers (PIDs); this section looks at both in turn. Metadata is structured data about data. Data that is structured is standardized—it fits into clear categories, such as *author* or *title*. Metadata that is deployed digitally can be used in all kinds of complex, interesting, productive ways. Consider, for example, the *Fred Wah Digital Archive*. The project's metadata-rich bibliography contains all the basic details that users would expect in a library catalogue (author, publisher, release date), but also additional information such as who is named in a book's acknowledgements, who wrote the cover blurb, who of note is mentioned in the text, what other works are related, and so on. This additional information fans out across the archive such that users can click on hyperlinked terms to follow paths from one work or contributor to the next.

The metadata described above is known as *descriptive* metadata because it describes what is in the data. Other types of metadata include *operational* metadata, which captures things like file formats and access protocols, and *administrative* metadata, which contains information about creators, owners, and rights. Although operational and administrative metadata do not conjure a sense of the data in the same way that descriptive metadata does, both are still very valuable. For one, anyone who wants to use data created by someone else will need information about how to access the data and what the conditions are for reuse. For another, knowing who created the dataset, when, why, and how can tell us a lot about what is in the data, what might be missing from it, and what ideologies may underpin it, among other things. Knowing the intentions of and conditions set by the data creators, as made possible for Indigenous information using *Traditional Knowledge Labels* (see Chapter 10) can also help us determine whether we have the right to access it. There is therefore potentially a lot to capture in metadata; when creating your own, it is up to you to decide how much to gather and with what specificity.

If the metadata is to be FAIR, it needs to be machine readable, which typically requires that it be structured using an established, standardized metadata system. Even if you are not aspiring to the high bar of FAIR, you would be well served to look into these standardized systems, since their familiarity and consistency can make them easier to implement and easier to use, both within and between datasets. For example, libraries often use the MARC 21 Format for Bibliographic Data (MAchine Readable Cataloging), which is why the information in catalogues is consistent across institutions (LoC 2024). DH projects might consider using Dublin Core metadata—one of the most widely used standards—as it is both clear and specific, yet also has broadly generalizable fields.

The second component of findable data is that it uses PIDs. A PID is a unique, long-lasting label or code that can be used to reliably identify a person, place, or thing. A familiar, broadly used PID is the International Standard Book Number (ISBN) for published books. Since the ISBN is unique to this book, entering it into a library catalogue or search engine will always only direct you to this book and nothing else. Being able to unambiguously point at something specific is useful, as anyone with a commonly occurring name would know. The Paul Barrett who co-wrote this book is not, sadly, the Paul Barrett who is an expert in aerosol-cloud interactions nor the Paul Barrett paleontologist after whom the dinosaur *Vectipelta barretti* was named.

FAIR metadata uses PIDs to unambiguously distinguish who or what is being referred to. Winnifred Eaton's Virtual International Authority File (VIAF, a PID for authors) connects records for Onoto Watanna, Winnifred Eaton, and Winnifred Eaton Babcock—all of whom are the same person—so that anyone who searches for one will find information pertaining to all three. There are also PIDs specifically for academics and their objects of study. Open Researcher and Contributor IDs (ORCID) are PIDs that point at records pages researchers can populate with publications, grants, and more. Where ORCIDs are for people, Digital Object Identifiers (DOI) are for things: anything from physical or digital objects to abstract concepts. Each DOI is a unique number, which can be used in a database or as part of a URL. Scholarly publications often have DOIs assigned to them at publication, and datasets are given DOIs when archived in repositories.

PIDs are useful because they can authoritatively and uniquely identify (or disambiguate) the things to which they are applied, and because they can be interlinked. An ORCID record for a researcher can contain the DOIs for the researcher's publications, as well as other identifiers, such as those from the Research Organization Registry (ROR), which are used for institutional affiliations. When the information held by the various registration agencies is pulled together, users can traverse the information: for example, you could travel from the DOI for this book to Paul Barrett's ORCID and onward to *Future Horizons: Canadian Digital Humanities* using DOIs or the University of Guelph using RORs; if you started from a different Paul Barrett's ORCID, you could follow the PIDs to articles about dinosaurs in *Nature* and the Natural History Museum in London, UK. Since PIDs are machine-readable, a computer could also traverse this information. Using a query service that pulls information from the agencies that manage PIDs, you could ask for a list of every academic author who has published in a journal issue or edited collection that also included Paul Barrett; the resulting list of people could be the starting point for drawing a network of researchers working at the intersection of Canadian Literature and digital humanities (and, depending on your query, possibly also dinosaurs).

Accessible data

Accessible data is retrievable using a free and open protocol such as the Hypertext Transfer Protocol (HTTP), which is the system used to move information across the web. All the data storage repositories recommended in this chapter are accessible in FAIR's sense of the word.

FAIR also advocates for metadata that remains accessible beyond the lifespan of the data. Metadata is much less resource intensive than data itself; it takes a lot less space to store details about who created a dataset and what it contained than to store the actual data that the metadata describes. GO FAIR explains,

> Datasets tend to degrade or disappear over time because there is a cost to maintaining an online presence for data resources. When this happens, links become invalid and users waste time hunting for data that might no longer be there. Storing the metadata generally is much easier and cheaper. ... Even if the original data are missing, tracking down people, institutions or publications associated with the original research can be extremely useful.
>
> *(GO FAIR Initiative, n.d.)*

Using PIDs, which are, by definition, persistent, is a great way to meet this criterion.

There is another possible meaning of accessible, that access to the data is freely given, which is not a criterion for FAIR data:

> This is a key, but often misunderstood, element of FAIR. The "A" in FAIR does not necessarily mean "open" or "free". Rather, it implies that one should provide the exact conditions under which the data are accessible. Hence, even heavily protected and private data can be FAIR.
>
> *(GO FAIR Initiative, n.d.)*

Best practices describe *how* data is accessed; *whether* the data is available for use is a different and more complicated matter. There are many good arguments in favour of data that is open or free. First, when projects share their data, they make it possible for others to validate, extend, or respond to their work. Second, showing the inner workings of a project demonstrates the labour involved. Third, sharing data builds bridges between researchers and projects. SSHRC encourages—although does not require—researchers to make data available for reuse by others and also reusable by others, so that researchers can benefit from and build upon work that has come before. This sort of data is accessible in both senses of the word. Access terms for datasets and publications can be specified using a Creative Commons license. Terms for software and code can be set using licenses such as those provided by the Open Source Initiative; popular choices include the MIT and GNU licenses.

Of course, there are many problems with sharing data and therefore plenty of compelling arguments for limiting access. For one, a great deal of Canadian cultural material remains under copyright and cannot be shared. Furthermore, as discussed in Chapter 10, some Indigenous information is designated only for use within a community. Kimberly Christen points out that

> Western intellectual property regimes are hostile to and dismissive of indigenous claims and worldviews, ... [and] digital tools aimed at sharing and exchanging cultural information are also ill-equipped to deal with the diverse social structures, cultural protocols, and histories of exploitation and exclusion of indigenous peoples globally.
>
> *(2012)*

Some data cannot be shared ethically, and universal open access can be inattentive to particular community needs and even a form of digital colonialism.

Interoperable data

Data is interoperable when it can be read by humans or interpreted by machines. For example, Dublin Core (discussed above) and the Text Encoding Initiative (TEI) (see Chapter 13) both have schemas that make them interoperable. When it comes to the digital humanities, the best way for you to facilitate interoperability is by using well-established, widely used data schemas, ontologies (which define categories, properties, and relationships within data), and vocabularies (which select terms to describe data). Higgins, Goddard, and Khair point to the CWRC ontology and *Linked Infrastructure for Networked Cultural Scholarship* (LINCS) vocabularies as two Canadian contributions with particular use for digital humanities projects (2024). The Canadian Heritage Information Network (CHIN) is also an excellent source of interoperable standards, particularly its *Data Dictionaries* (which can be used to define the categories in a database) and its *Nomenclature for Museum Cataloguing* (which is both a classification system and a vocabulary). Other resources include the VIAF for authors, *Homosaurus* for LGBTQ+ terms (Digital Transgender Archive 2024) and the suite of *Getty Vocabularies*, including the *Art & Architecture Thesaurus*. NIKLA's *Respectful Terminology Platform*, still under development, will be an invaluable resource once launched (see Chapter 10). While interoperability is the gold standard, it can be hard to achieve; ontologies and vocabularies are complex and digital humanists may struggle to make use of them with the degree of precision required to facilitate true interoperability. Currently, topics such as data modeling, structured vocabularies, and ontologies are taught only in DH workshops or specialist programs such as Master of Library and Information Sciences (MLIS) degrees. We recommend you ask for help from your institution's librarians or digital humanities centre staff.

The second obstacle to interoperability is that even if all digital humanists were au fait with both theory and application, the available structures are often ill-suited to their needs. As Miriam Posner notes, "I've been struck by how often it seems that what the scholar *really* needs is data-modeling advice" (2015). There are some humanities-specific schemas, models, and vocabularies, but most resources are intended for use in the cultural heritage sector at best and in the sciences at worst. For example, many data standards can specify a time with pinpoint accuracy, but few can handle imprecise timespans. It is easy to create interoperable metadata for an event with an exact date, for example, women gaining the right to vote in Canada (May 24, 1918). It is much harder to create interoperable metadata for an event where the boundaries are less clear, for example, the Sixties Scoop (which, despite its name, covers a period from the 1950s to the 1980s).

Posner also notes that off-the-shelf data solutions rarely have space for nuance, alternative epistemologies, or structures of power. For example, Wikidata captures "sex or gender" in a single property that conflates everything from sex assigned at birth to gender identity and gender expression. The historical metadata properties for Indigenous peoples in Library of Congress and Canadian Subject Headings are not just inaccurate but racist.[5] Working with data in the humanities can therefore mean taking things "which were not at all created for our purposes ... and working against their grain or reinventing them to try and tease out the things we think are really interesting" (Posner 2015). It can also mean creating something new and fit for purpose, a task not to be undertaken lightly and one that raises challenges for interoperability. For example, the custom markup schema designed for *The Orlando Project*: none of the off-the-shelf options were suitable for "a feminist theory of subjectivity in which women's identities and writing are understood to be multiple, substantial, historically and materially contingent, and at times unknown or incongruous with the concepts of language in our time" (Holland and Brown 2018), and it took the project team nearly three years to create a resource that met their needs.

Reusable data

Reusable does not mean that the data must be available for reuse, but rather that it has been constructed in a way that facilitates its reuse. To make data reusable, GO FAIR recommends that creators ensure that they provide enough information about the data to make it possible for others to decide if it suits their needs. This means well-structured metadata that describes what is in the dataset, where it came from, how it was gathered and processed, who was involved, and so on. It also means clearly stating what forms of reuse are possible, so that others do not decline to use the data out of an abundance of caution. You can achieve this by using a widely used license, such as those provided by Creative Commons or the Open Source Initiative, and by clearly indicating who should be credited if the data is reused. Finally, to enhance the likelihood of reuse, your data should "meet domain-relevant community standards" which means that you should adhere to norms specific to your research field (GO FAIR Initiative, n.d.).

Linked open data as a model for best practice

To return to the beginning, RDM requires plans for collecting and creating data, documenting and describing it, storing and preserving it, sharing it for reuse, caring for it in the long term, and ensuring that it is handled in a manner that is both legal and ethical. While each of these elements can be planned for individually, frameworks such as FAIR provide structures within which to design a project that has good data management practices built in from the start. One of the best ways to ensure that your data is properly managed is to make use of existing infrastructure that adheres to best practices. Publishing data in *Borealis* or FRDR is a good way to ensure accessibility; connecting your published dataset to your ORCID record and obtaining a DOI for the dataset both help make your dataset findable.

Another route to gold-standard data is to create linked open data (LOD). The *Linked Infrastructure for Networked Cultural Scholarship* (LINCS), led by Susan Brown, brings together a suite of tools for digital humanists to make interlinked, contextualized data. LOD uses Resource Description Framework (RDF), a standard type of structured data, and Uniform Resource Identifiers (URI), which uniquely identify the things to which the data refers. PIDs such as ORCIDs and DOIs are URIs; the vocabularies mentioned in the section on interoperability (above) all use URIs to unequivocally identify each of their terms. By connecting PIDs and leveraging the information they contain, LOD can produce very rich metadata. All the components in the structured data are then related to each other using an ontology, which provides a model that governs how the components connect. For example, in a dataset about authors, the ontology would let us say Dionne Brand wrote *What We All Long For*, but it would not let us say the inverse (since authors write books, but not vice versa); the use of URIs would let us connect up with other information about Brand, such as the contents of her VIAF record, which has details about her publications, or her Wikidata record, which has seventy-one pieces of information about her, ranging from who preceded and succeeded her as the poet laureate of Toronto, where she went to school, and what awards she has received. Because LOD uses PIDs and standardized structures, has rich metadata and a high degree of interoperability, and is machine-readable, LOD is also usually FAIR data.

Although LOD sounds both rigid and technical at first, it has many benefits both for RDM and for the ways in which it enriches data by linking it up with other datasets and making it searchable, browsable, and queryable. Linked open data excels at creating network graphs (see Chapter 13); it can also draw together data across DH projects and digital resources, thus leveraging the contributions of entire communities and breaking down data silos. LINCS has a suite of tools and training resources to support researchers interested in creating LOD.[6] A partnership between LINCS and CWRC (as well as ongoing work with other research projects) means tools from CWRC-affiliated LEAF (the *Linked Editing Academic Framework*) such as *LEAF-Writer* support the creation of LOD, and there will soon be a wealth of CanLit LOD available for researchers to connect up with their own datasets.

The costs of data management

Managing research data is a lot of work, regardless of whether you maximize interoperability by creating LOD, aspire to best practices by working towards data that is FAIR, ensure your project's long-term sustainability by becoming Endings Compliant, or just adhere to a basic DMP. Much has been written about the problem of (invisible, uncredited) labour in the digital humanities in general (e.g., see Graban et al. 2019; Nowviskie 2011; Risam 2020; Smith and Whearty 2023). Well-managed data can be the result of contributions from many corners—from the librarians who advise on data structures through to (unpaid) students who input reams of meticulous metadata—and academic structures that use the lead researcher's name as shorthand for the entire team make it hard to ensure that the breadth of the work and the number of individuals involved are acknowledged.[7] To rectify this, we need to adopt "systems of reward that don't just value the new, but find nobility in activities like metadata enhancement, project maintenance, and forward migration" (Nowviskie 2015), and we need to give fair credit for everyone "from researchers developing DMPs, to data librarians setting institutional data policies, to data or technical support officers assisting or leading the technical execution of RDM" (Higgins, Goddard, and Khair 2024). It is for these reasons that, throughout this book, we have tried to name the people who create and maintain the projects and tools and who run the laboratories and DH centres—people whose contributions are essential to Canadian DH, both past and future.

Notes

1 Referred to collectively as the Tri-Agency funders, these are the Social Sciences and Humanities Research Council of Canada (SSHRC), the Natural Sciences and Engineering Research Council of Canada (NSERC), and the Canadian Institutes of Health Research (CIHR).
2 At the time of writing, the *DMP Assistant* had fifteen templates: two general (one long-form and one for simplified for funding applications), one for "Research in History and the Humanities," and one for "Arts-Based Research." Of the remainder, there were a handful of hyper-specific science templates, including ones for "Water Quality Research," "Neuroimaging in the Neurosciences," and "Studying Molecular Interactions." It is perhaps unsurprising that a DRAC-led tool leans towards the sciences; in their most recent report on RDM—"The Current State of Research Data Management in Canada: An Update to the LCDRI Data Management Position Paper" (Khair et al. 2020)—the humanities is mentioned a mere six times in 110 pages.
3 The text on the website of the supposed Canadian Literature Centre opens, "What reason would you have for pursuing upper-level education in Canada?" A good question indeed, although perhaps not one the Canadian Literature Centre would pose.
4 Canadian Literature Centre resources behind a paywall on the EBSCO site include, among others, *The Annotated Bibliography of Canada's Major Authors*, *Brick: A Literary Journal*, *Canadian Literature*, *Room*, and *University of Toronto Quarterly*.
5 Some successes have been made to rectify these problems. However, Wikidata is a community initiative and change-driving consensus across contributors can be difficult. Both the Library of Congress in the US and Library and Archives Canada, meanwhile, are in the process of slowly updating their metadata terms. To learn more, check out the Wikidata Gender Diversity group (Metilli et al. 2022), *The "Use our Words" Toolkit*, and the work being done by the National Indigenous Knowledge & Language Alliance / Alliance nationale des connaissances et des langues autochtones (NIKLA-ANCLA).
6 Many of the CanLit projects mentioned throughout this volume are working with LINCS to create LOD, including *HistSex*, *Lesbian and Gay Liberation in Canada*, *The Orlando Project*, *The Yellow Nineties 2.0*, and projects that sit under the umbrella of CWRC.
7 The entry for *labor* in the MLA's *Digital Pedagogy in the Humanities: Concepts, Models, and Experiments*, problematizes student contributions to DH projects:

> Students' exposure to digital production in the classroom often takes the form of performing labor on a faculty project without credit or compensation ... Their labor is invisible and easily taken for granted. With apologies to Marx and Engels, if there is a spectre haunting digital pedagogy, it is labor.
> *(Keralis and Andrews 2020)*

It also refers readers to the UCLA Center for Digital Humanities' "A Student Collaborators' Bill of Rights" (2015) best practices for student-scholar collaborations, and it advocates for students to receive acknowledgement, meaningful learning opportunities, and financial remuneration for their work.

Further reading

Digital Preservation Coalition. 2015. *Digital Preservation Handbook*, 2nd ed. https://www.dpconline.org/handbook.

Flanders, Julia, and Trevor Muñoz. 2013. "An Introduction to Humanities Data Curation." *DH Curation Guide*. https://archive.mith.umd.edu/dhcuration-guide/guide.dhcuration.org/glossary/intro/index.html

Higgins, Stefan, Lisa Goddard, and Shahira Khair. 2024. "Research Data Management in the Humanities: Challenges and Opportunities in the Canadian Context." *Digital Studies / Le champ numérique* 14, no. 1: 1–22. https://doi.org/10.16995/dscn.9956.

Thompson, Kristi, Elizabeth Hill, Emily Carlisle-Johnston, Danielle Dennie, and Émelie Fortin, eds. 2023. *Research Data Management in the Canadian Context: A Guide for Practitioners and Learners*. London: Western University Libraries.

Works cited

Barrett, Paul, and Sarah Roger, eds. 2023. *Future Horizons: Canadian Digital Humanities*. Ottawa: University of Ottawa Press. https://doi.org/10.2307/jj.17681834.

Borealis: The Canadian Dataverse Repository. Accessed July 12, 2024. https://borealisdata.ca/.

Bourdages, Lauren, and Kassandra Caporiccio. 2020. *The "Use Our Words" Toolkit*. https://indigenouslis.ca/the-use-our-words-toolkit/.

Canadian Heritage Information Network. 2023. *Data Dictionaries*, November 6, 2023. https://app.pch.gc.ca/application/ddrcip-chindd/description-about.app?lang=en.

Canadian Heritage Information Network. 2024. *Nomenclature for Museum Cataloging*, October 23, 2024. https://page.nomenclature.info/apropos-about.app?lang=en.

Christen, Kimberly. 2012. "Does Information Really Want to be Free? Indigenous Knowledge Systems and the Question of Openness." *International Journal of Communication* 6: 2870–93. https://ijoc.org/index.php/ijoc/article/view/1618.

Creative Commons. n.d. *Creative Commons*. Accessed October 10, 2024. https://creativecommons.org/.

CWRC. n.d. *Collaboratory for Writing and Research on Culture*. Accessed July 12, 2024. https://cwrc.ca/.

Digital Scholar. n.d. *Omeka*. Accessed July 12, 2024. https://omeka.org/.

Digital Transgender Archive. 2024. *Homosaurus: An International LGBTQ+ Linked Data Vocabulary*. https://homosaurus.org/.

DRAC. 2024a. *Data Management Plan Assistant*. Digital Research Alliance of Canada. https://dmp-pgd.ca/.

DRAC. 2024b. *Federated Research Data Repository*. Digital Research Alliance of Canada. https://www.frdr-dfdr.ca/repo/.

Dublin Core Metadata Initiative. 2024. *Dublin Core*. https://www.dublincore.org/.

EBSCO. 2024. "The Canadian Literature Centre." EBSCO Information Services. https://www.ebsco.com/products/research-databases/canadian-literary-centre.

The Endings Project. 2024. *The Endings Project*, July 7, 2024. https://endings.uvic.ca/.

Fong, Deanna, and Ryan Fitzpatrick. 2024. *Fred Wah Digital Archive*. https://fredwah.ca/.

Fostano, Katherina, and Laura K. Morreale. 2019. *The Digital Documentation Process*, January 31, 2019. https://digitalhumanitiesddp.com/.

The Getty Research Institute. n.d. *Getty Vocabularies*. Accessed October 10, 2024. https://www.getty.edu/research/tools/vocabularies/.

GO FAIR Initiative. n.d. *FAIR Principles*. Accessed July 12, 2024. https://www.go-fair.org/fair-principles/.

Graban, Tarez Samra, Paul Marty, Allen Romano, and Micah Vandergrift. 2019. "Introduction: Questioning *Collaboration*, *Labor*, and *Visibility* in Digital Humanities Research." *Digital Humanities Quarterly* 13, no. 2. https://www.digitalhumanities.org/dhq/vol/13/2/000416/000416.html.

Higgins, Stefan, Lisa Goddard, and Shahira Khair. 2024. "Research Data Management in the Humanities: Challenges and Opportunities in the Canadian Context." *Digital Studies / Le champ numérique* 14, no. 1: 1–22. https://doi.org/10.16995/dscn.9956.

Holland, Kathryn, and Susan Brown. 2018. "Project | Process | Product: Feminist Digital Subjectivity in a Shifting Scholarly Field." In *Bodies of Information: Intersectional Feminism and Digital Humanities*, edited by Elizabeth Losh and Jacqueline Wernimont, 409–33. Minneapolis: University of Minnesota Press. https://doi.org/10.5749/j.ctv9hj9r9.25.

Janzen Kooistra, Lorraine. n.d. *The Yellow Nineties 2.0*. Accessed July 12, 2024. https://1890s.ca/.

Keralis, Spencer D. C., and Pamela Andrews. 2020. "Labour." *MLA Digital Pedagogy in the Humanities*. https://digitalpedagogy.hcommons.org/keyword/Labor/.

Khair, Shahira, Rozita Dara, Susan Haigh, Mark Leggott, Ian Milligan, Jeff Moon, Karen Payne, Elodie Portales-Casamar, Ghilaine Roquet, and Lee Wilson. 2020. "The Current State of Research Data Management in Canada: An Update to the LCDRI Data Management Position Paper." Digital Research Alliance of Canada, November 2020. https://alliancecan.ca/sites/default/files/2022-03/rdm_current_state_report-1_1.pdf.

LoC. 2024. *MARC 21 Format for Bibliographic Data*. Library of Congress Network Development and MARC Standards Office, June 2024. https://www.loc.gov/marc/bibliographic/.

LGLC. n.d. *Lesbian and Gay Liberation in Canada*. Accessed September 5, 2024. https://lglc.ca/.

LINCS. 2024. *Linked Infrastructure for Networked Cultural Scholarship*. https://lincsproject.ca/.

Linked Editing Academic Framework. n.d.-a. *Linked Editing Academic Framework–Virtual Research Environment*. Accessed September 8, 2024. https://www.leaf-vre.org/.

Linked Editing Academic Framework. n.d.-b. *LEAF-Writer*. Accessed September 8, 2024. https://leaf-writer.leaf-vre.org.

Local Contexts. 2024. *Traditional Knowledge Labels.* https://localcontexts.org/labels/traditional-knowledge-labels/.
Metilli, Daniele, Chiara Paolini, Marta Fioravanti, and Beatrice Melis. 2022. "Research: Wikidata Gender Diversity." https://meta.wikimedia.org/wiki/Research:Wikidata_Gender_Diversity.
NIKLA. n.d. *Respectful Terminology Platform Project.* National Indigenous Knowledge & Language Alliance. Accessed September 5, 2024. https://www.nikla-ancla.com/respectful-terminology.
Nowviskie, Bethany. 2011. "Where Credit Is Due." *Bethany Nowviskie* (blog), May 31, 2011. https://nowviskie.org/2011/where-credit-is-due/.
Nowviskie, Bethany. 2015. "Digital Humanities in the Anthropocene." *Digital Scholarship in the Humanities* 30, no. 1 (December): i4–i15. https://doi.org/10.1093/llc/fqv015.
OCLC. 2024. *Virtual Information Authority File.* https://viaf.org/.
Open Source Initiative. n.d. *Open Source Initiative.* Accessed October 10, 2024. https://opensource.org/.
ORCID. n.d. *Open Researcher and Contributor ID.* Accessed October 10, 2024. https://orcid.org/.
Posner, Miriam. 2015. "Humanities Data: A Necessary Contradiction." *Miriam Posner* (blog), June 25, 2015. https://miriamposner.com/blog/humanities-data-a-necessary-contradiction/.
Risam, Roopika. 2020. "The Stakes of Digital Labor in the Twenty-First-Century Academy: The Revolution Will Not Be Turkified." In *Humans at Work in the Digital Age,* edited by Shawna Ross and Andrew Pilsch, 239–49. London: Routledge. https://doi.org/10.4324/9780429244599-18.
Smith, Astrid J., and Bridget Whearty. 2023. "All the Work You Do Not See: Labor, Digitizers, and the Foundations of Digital Humanities." In *Debates in the Digital Humanities 2023,* edited by Matthew K. Gold and Lauren F. Klein, 27–46. Minneapolis: University of Minnesota Press. https://doi.org/10.5749/9781452969565.
SSHRC. 2021. "Tri-Agency Research Data Management Policy." Social Sciences and Humanities Research Council of Canada, March 14, 2021. https://science.gc.ca/site/science/en/interagency-research-funding/policies-and-guidelines/research-data-management/tri-agency-research-data-management-policy.
SSHRC. 2024. "Guide to Preparing a Data Management Plan." Social Sciences and Humanities Research Council of Canada, June 5, 2024. https://www.sshrc-crsh.gc.ca/funding-financement/apply-demande/guides/guide_preparing_data_management_plan-guide_preparation_plan_gestion_donnees-eng.aspx.
Thompson, Kristi, Elizabeth Hill, Emily Carlisle-Johnston, Danielle Dennie, and Émelie Fortin, eds. 2023. *Research Data Management in the Canadian Context: A Guide for Practitioners and Learners.* London: Western University Libraries. https://doi.org/10.5206/ZRUV7849.
Watson, B. M. 2024. *HistSex.* https://histsex.org/.
Whirl-i-Gig. 2024. *Collective Access.* Accessed July 12, 2024. https://www.collectiveaccess.org/.

13
STEPS TOWARDS ANALYZING TEXT

* * *

Once your corpus is collected (Chapter 11) and your data management plan is in place (Chapter 12), you are ready to start analyzing your data. Textual analysis is often a starting point for literary-minded researchers starting out in DH. Analyzing text with some help from a computer is intuitively analogous to traditional forms of literary analysis; it also has a relatively low bar to entry. There are many free, web-based tools with intuitive interfaces, and you can even do sophisticated textual analysis with relatively little computational power or programming knowledge. Gone are the days of arcane concordance programs such as PRORA or complex tools like TACT (see Chapter 3). Novice DH practitioners instead are getting their start via user-friendly interfaces such as *Voyant Tools*, which makes it easy to play with a corpus, or *LEAF-Writer*, which makes it easy to search through and mark up a text.

Minding the gap

Concealed within the ease of this play, however, are questions about the implications of DH methods for meaning and interpretation. Answering such questions requires a deeper understanding of what is going on under the hood. To be able to draw meaningful, informed conclusions, we need to understand how a program or tool functions. A major challenge of digital humanities is, as we have reiterated throughout this volume, bridging this gap between tools and outputs, methods and meanings. For example,

DOI: 10.4324/9781003318323-19

while network graphs and word clouds are attractive, rigorous scholarship that uses them needs to explain both what they mean and how they were created. To make things more complicated, these explanations must address both humanities and computational concerns. Geoffrey Rockwell and Stéfan Sinclair, the creators of *Voyant Tools*, acknowledge that meeting the needs of both groups can be challenging:

> Papers drawing on computer-assisted text analysis, with their long lists of word counts and their complicated discussions of statistical methods, can be hard to read [however] … Authors of articles that draw on computational methods might feel damned if they do (include enough information about the technical methods) and damned if they don't (include enough to make sense of their computed claims).
>
> *(2016, 15)*

As a DH scholar, you can find yourself in a difficult position. Not only do you need to bring together the quantitative measures of the computer with the forms of interpretation standard in most traditional forms of textual analysis, but you also need to be able to explain these methods to (sometimes skeptical) others.[1] This added complexity of DH work represents both a methodological challenge and a significant amount of additional labour.

Teasing out these tangled questions of concealed workings, interpretation, meaning, and value has shadowed digital textual analysis since its inception. Indeed, in an interview where she reflects on her career, DH pioneer Susan Hockey says that the question at the root of digital textual analysis has always been "how do you represent interpretation" (Nyhan and Flinn 2016) via computational methods? Alan Liu calls this "the meaning problem" in DH, observing that "It is not clear epistemologically, cognitively, or socially how human beings can take a signal discovered by a machine and develop an interpretation leading to a humanly understandable concept" (2013, 414). While this problem, which plagues human-computer interaction more generally, feels prescient in the emerging AI age, the meaning problem at the intersection of DH and literary analysis asks us how we move from word counts, assessments of vocabulary complexity, and other forms of quantitative measurement to compelling arguments concerning the meaning of a text.[2]

Although there are many for whom turning any part of literary analysis over to a computer is a non-starter (see the comments from Stanley Fish and Stephen Marche in Chapter 7), it is worth emphasizing that digital textual analysis is not simply a matter of a scholar handing the work over to a computer and then waiting for the results. As Thomas Rommel notes, it is

> one of the particular strengths of most electronic studies of literature that the criteria used in the process of analysis are situated in a theoretical model of textuality that is based on a critical examination of the role of the critic and the specific properties of the text.
>
> *(2004)*

Critic and text come first, and as Hugh Craig argues, the technology simply provides a jumping-off point: "stylistic analysis is open-ended and exploratory. It aims to bring to light patterns in style which influence readers' perceptions and relate to the disciplinary concerns of literary and linguistic interpretation" (2004).

Some DH scholars take these ideas even further, arguing that there is no true separation between human thought and computational processing—the two are interdependent and intertwined. Katherine Bode argues that DH work must be "Attuned to the coconstitution of computational methods and objects—with each other, and with literary subjectivities and textualities" (2023, 508); for Bode, there is no final distinction between "computation and literary phenomena" (507). As Julia Flanders, Syd Bauman, and Sarah Connell explain, computational work is shot through with analytic, interpretive interventions:

> It is analytical, in identifying a set of components into which the text can be meaningfully broken and whose relationship can be represented through the markup ... is strategic, in that text encoding is always aimed ... at some intellectual or practical goal ... And ... interpretive, in that the act of encoding will always take place through a connection between an observing individual and a source object.
>
> *(2016, 105)*

Their definition of text encoding as the "process of creating a digital model of a textual source using markup" suggests that how text is encoded inevitably depends on the kinds of analysis that the researcher wants to perform. Every act of textual analysis involves converting a textual object into data, removing extraneous features, and preparing the encoded object for analysis; these are all steps that both add layers of interpretation to and remove layers of interpretation from the text.

Computational interventions into a text may always be human-informed, but they are not all equal. There are many DH methodologies for text analysis, ranging from using computers to facilitate word- or even character-level analysis through to processing quantities of text so vast that no one person could ever read them. On the micro end, *textual encoding* typically refers to a kind of markup, or identifying, of the salient features of a text—often done using an encoding standard such as the one created by the Text Encoding Initiative (TEI) (see below). On the macro end, *distant reading* is the term used to describe computational analyses of large textual corpora (reading at a distance); it is typically contrasted with the traditional, scholarly practice of close reading. Alongside distant reading, Tanya Clement advocates for *differential reading*: a method of interpretation that moves adroitly between close and distant readings to put computational and humanistic modes of analysis in dialogue. Textual analysis can, therefore, take on a range of forms and degrees of complexity from excavating meaning from details as small as a single, distinctive punctuation choice (facilitated by text encoding) to using statistical learning to discern the topics or themes of a corpus (courtesy of distant reading).

Analyzing the corpus using GUI-based tools

Textual analysis proper can take a variety of forms and use a variety of tools. An excellent starting point is the Canadian-made *Text Analysis Portal for Research 3* (TAPoR 3). TAPoR began as a project in 2004 at McMaster University and has grown, in its third version, into a major resource for textual analysis. TAPoR is not a text analysis tool, but rather a starting point for scholars looking for resources in organizational categories such as analysis, annotating, gathering, interpretation, organizing, search, storage, and visualization—the breadth of which is demonstrative of the wide range of scholarly activities that fall under the umbrella of textual analysis. TAPoR can be used to

> discover text manipulation, analysis, and visualization tools; read tool reviews and recommendations; learn about papers, articles and other sources about specific tools; tag, comment, rate, and review collaboratively; and browse lists of related tools in order to discover tools more easily.
>
> *(TAPoR, n.d.)*

TAPoR's curated tool lists combine tried-and-tested tools with innovative ones, grouped by tasks such as sentiment analysis and web scraping; the "Easy tools to start with" list is great if you are new to text analysis. TAPoR is currently co-led by Rockwell and Milena Radzikowska, and previously also by Sinclair.

Voyant Tools, also the product of a Rockwell-Sinclair collaboration, is one of the most-used DH GUI-based tools worldwide: "The most popular DH tools on Compute Canada infrastructure are Voyant (voyant-tools.org), a web-based reading and analysis environment for digital texts that has had over 1 million visitors since 2018" (Rockwell et al. 2022). *Voyant* bundles together, via a clear and user-friendly interface, a number of textual analysis resources and visualizations. It allows users to work with a selection of preloaded literary corpora or to upload their own corpora in plaintext or PDF format. Users can visualize and analyze their corpora directly within *Voyant*'s web interface, which provides more than thirty tools for textual analysis. Upon first loading, the interface opens five default windows—a word cloud, a reader, a plot of most frequent terms across the corpus, a summary of the corpus, and keywords in context. For each of these windows and all thirty tools, users can customize their results, for example, by changing the stop word list, the number of relevant terms, and other variables.

There are as many ways to use *Voyant* as there are combinations of tools within its interface. Rockwell and Sinclair (2016) have used *Voyant* to identify trends in the corpus of the *Humanist* listserv (see Chapter 3) while Kiera Obbard (2024) has used *Voyant* to survey the Facebook papers leaked to the press in 2021. Research published in *Digital Studies / Le champ numérique* uses *Voyant* for studies of everything from gothic literature to autoethnography to video games (see, for example, Iantorno 2020; Sapach 2020; Wikle 2020). Figure 13.1 depicts a *Voyant* analysis of eleven issues of *Canadian Literature*, which formed the basis of Paul Barrett's "Paraphrasing the Paraphrase OR What I Learned from Reading Every Issue of *Canadian Literature& SCL / ÉLC*" (2016).

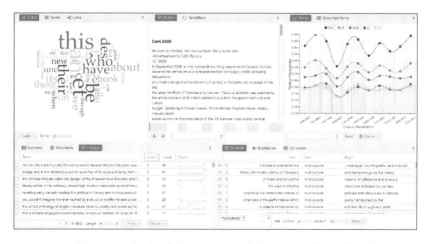

FIGURE 13.1 *Voyant* analysis of eleven issues of the journal *Canadian Literature*.

While *Voyant* is an extremely powerful and effective way to begin working with textual analysis, its visualizations can be deceptively simple. In this respect, they constitute a form of capta (see Chapter 7), insofar as the user is not able to wholly scrutinize what goes into the making of the charts, plots, and graphs. Users of *Voyant*—or indeed of any DH tool or interface—would be mindful not to interpret the outputs as verified fact but rather to extend the analysis and scrutiny to the tools and visualizations themselves, as they are but one of many lenses through which to view the corpus. It is also worth noting that *Voyant* is restricted to relatively small corpora compared to what is possible with a programming language, and it also places limits on your abilities to adjust the settings of its various tools. Discussion of these limitations is not meant to undermine *Voyant*'s effectiveness but, rather, ensure that you approach it—and indeed any tool—with an understanding of both its power and its limits.

In addition to feature-rich, DH-specific resources like *Voyant*, there are opportunities for text analysis built into other familiar interfaces. For example, the *Google Ngram Viewer* and the *HathiTrust Bookworm* both offer an effective means of searching for n-grams. An *n-gram* is any phrase of 'n' words; n = 2 is a bi-gram ("Two Solitudes"), n = 3 is a tri-gram ("The Polished Hoe"), n = 4 is a quad-gram ("Lullabies for Little Criminals"), and so forth. Both tools let users search for any n-gram across their large collections of digitized texts. While the *Google Books* corpora is slightly larger than *HathiTrust's* (limited to a mere seventeen million books), *Bookworm* offers a slight advantage in that it also lets you see the texts in which the n-gram appears—an obvious benefit for contextualizing the prevalence of a given phrase.

Voyant, *Bookworm*, and the *Ngram Viewer* are all great starting points for textual analysis. Users who are seeking more control over the methods of their analysis of their work may, however, wish to explore their texts programmatically. As the two graphs in Figure 13.2 demonstrate, the distinct (yet overlapping) corpora yield different results. The algorithms used to search the corpora are not transparent, and comparing the two graphs reminds us that these results are capta, not data (see Chapter 7). The presentation of the data can also have a significant impact on interpretation. For example, the scale used for the y-axis in the *Bookworm* graph makes the increase in the use of *multiculturalism* since 2012 seem far more dramatic than is perhaps warranted. These tools may therefore be best suited as starting points for generating a hypothesis and thinking about a topic, rather than as sources for conclusive evidence.

Analyzing the corpus programmatically

If you want more control over the analysis than is possible with the existing tools, you would be well served by working directly with code. Working in

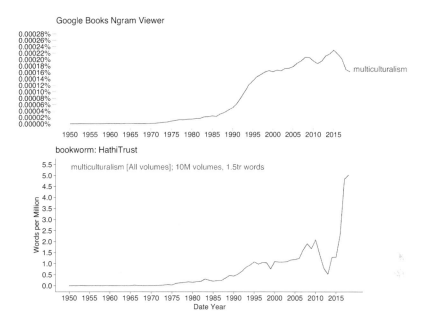

FIGURE 13.2 Search for multiculturalism in *Google Ngram Viewer* and *HathiTrust Bookworm*.

a programming language such as Python or R ensures that you can control the conditions of your analysis, and that you are not subject to the decisions made by the programmers who designed the interfaces. In addition, you can generate a robust and detailed textual analysis if you are able to scrutinize both the method of analysis and the results themselves. Chapter 14 introduces the preliminary steps for programming for textual analysis. This section sets the stage for that discussion by providing an overview of the forms of digital textual analysis you might apply. These include (but are not limited to) text encoding, natural language processing, computational stylistics, sentiment analysis, and distant reading.

Text encoding

One of the primary ways to bring together corpus and code is via text encoding, a process of using markup to describe both the content and layout of a text. This idea may already be familiar if you have used HTML to lay out a webpage, for example, or if you have used Markdown to format text. Digital humanities lets us take things one step further by using markup not just to designate appearance but also, for example, to capture semantics using the guidelines and standards such as those of the Text Encoding Initiative (TEI), which was developed specifically to encode humanities textual data. From the earliest days of humanities computing, scholars have used computers to create digital editions of texts—a task that functions best if done using standardized methods. The first "Guidelines for Electronic Text Encoding and Interchange" (TEI) were released in 1994; today, the term TEI refers both to (1) the organization responsible for developing and evolving guidelines for textual markup and (2) the set of principles designed to universalize the digital encoding of texts. As Ide and Sperberg-McQueen explain, TEI provides "encoding conventions for describing the physical and logical structure of many classes of texts, as well as features particular to a given text type or not conventionally represented in typography" (1995, 7). The TEI conventions strike a balance between providing guidelines and standards on one hand and ensuring flexibility for a range of disciplinary practices, project goals, and theoretical frameworks on the other.

TEI can be used to tag the layout of a text on a page—useful, for example, for capturing the distinctive elements of the works of poetry. It can also be used to flag languages, which would be immensely helpful for computational analysis of texts that switch back and forth between languages, such as Heather O'Neill's *The Girl Who Was Saturday Night* (2014). Tags can be applied to elements referred to in the text, such as names of people or places, and can even be used to unify multiple, distinct references to the same thing. For example, the description of Barbados in Austin Clarke's work as "Barbados," "Bimshire," "Bim," "B'does" and "little England." When working with drafts, TEI can be used to capture additions and deletions, as done in *The Winnifred Eaton Archive*, which uses TEI in its encoding of Eaton's written material. TEI is an invaluable resource for tagging and structuring documents encoded for the web (Chapman and Cole 2024).

The best places to start with TEI are the *TEI Guidelines* and online tutorials, such as those from *TEI by Example*. For those who prefer a GUI-based tool, *LEAF-Writer*, from the *Linked Editing Academic Framework* (LEAF) is an excellent resource that combines TEI with linked open data to mark up texts. *LEAF-Writer* is also developing named entity recognition, which will make it possible for users to partially automate the process of identifying and annotating people, places, and organizations in a document. *LEAF-Writer*'s user-friendly interface lets users toggle between tagged and text-only views, which also makes it an excellent option for those who are looking for an onramp to working with encoded materials; texts tagged in *LEAF-Writer* can be exported and uploaded to sites such as CWRC or tools such as the *Dynamic Table of Contexts*, where they can be shared, worked with, and explored further.

Text analysis using Python

Until tools like *LEAF-Writer* can perform named entity recognition, the work must be done programmatically. In Chapter 14, we discuss the Python programming language in more detail; below we survey the methods one might use for textual analysis in Python. Python libraries are collections of code blocks designed to achieve specific tasks; programmers share their libraries so that others can benefit from—and build on—their work. There are more than 100,000 Python libraries available, for everything from working with tabulated data (*Pandas*), machine learning algorithms (*SpaCy*), and web data collection and retrieval (*Beautiful Soup*). For text analysis, the *Natural Language Toolkit* (NLTK 2023) and *tidytext* libraries are two of the most popular. NLTK includes tools for analyzing everything from individual characters (e.g., a single letter or punctuation mark) to strings of words (e.g., a series of any length in consecutive order) to entire texts. It can be used to remove stop words, for stemming and lemmatizing, for tokenizing, and for named entity recognition. It can also perform a range of additional functions, such as:

- **Keyword in Context (kwic)**: identify keywords and locate them within surrounding words for context
- **Collocations**: identify words that frequently appear in proximity regardless of consecutive order
- **Parts of Speech (POS) Tagging**: identify and tag words by type (e.g., noun, verb, preposition, adjective, pronoun, numeral)
- **Word Frequency Distribution**: identify the location of a term across a corpus, and create a graphical distribution of frequency of use (akin to the *Google Ngram Viewer*)

If you were interested in understanding, for instance, Michael Ondaatje's use of geographic locations, you might use named entity recognition to find all proper nouns, which could then be checked for locations. You might also use parts of speech tagging to find all words tagged as geographical names. Likewise, if you were interested in the use of the term *diaspora* in Canadian literature or criticism, you could use a word frequency distribution on a selection of texts to see who uses the term, where, when, and in what contexts. Note that these functions and many other functions are available via the in-built commands in the NLTK library, but they can also be executed using *Voyant* or the tools listed in TAPoR; if you do not need the degree of control that working programmatically provides, or you are more comfortable working with a user-friendly interface rather than in the command line, it is worth looking around for a tool, as you are likely to find one that performs the function you want.

Sentiment analysis

Sentiment analysis lets you assess (via a numerical score) the *sentiment*—or more accurately, the affect—of a corpus. It works by assigning numerical ratings based on perceived positivity, negativity, and neutrality on a scale of 1 (highest) to –1 (lowest). For instance, the statement "*What We All Long For* is an excellent novel" is clearly a positive statement and might score 0.7 positive (for it to receive a 1.0 would require that kind of gushing praise Canadianists eschew). By contrast, the statement "Canadian literature is a dumpster fire" would be scored as very negative. Sentiment analysis could be used, for example, on a corpus of reviews in the *Literary Review of Canada* to contrast reviews of books by writers of colour with reviews of those by white writers.

Note that sentiment analysis works best on shorter texts. It is better suited to a study of the sentiment of social media posts commenting on Canadian literature than to gauging the overall tone of Rohinton Mistry's *A Fine Balance* (736 pages) or Ann-Marie MacDonald's *Fall On Your Knees* (566 pages). This is intuitive given that a shorter text will tend to have a smaller number of expressed sentiments than a larger, more complex one. Unfortunately, sentiment analysis is not particularly adept at identifying nuance or irony. Where a human would detect that a statement like "This writer thinks he is the best thing since sliced bread" is sarcastic, a sentiment analysis algorithm would have difficulty doing so. There are a number of sentiment analysis Python libraries, including one that is built into the NLTK library. If you are looking to experiment with this method of textual analysis, we recommend the *Vader* library for its combined ease of use and efficacy.

Network analysis

Network analysis is the creation and analysis of the networks of relationships both within and beyond a text. Within a text, these networks can be characters who speak to one another, characters that are mentioned on the same page of a text, and so on. Outside a text, these can be authors who share editors and publishers, known literary influences, users on social media who interact with one another, and so on. Networks are not limited to being about people—fictional or factual—they can also be used to draw connections between places, genres, themes, and more. Network graphs visualize relationships as a collection of nodes and edges: the nodes represent each of the individuals (often represented by circles) and the edges represent the connections (often represented by lines linking the nodes to each other). Nodes and edges are sometimes, but not always, labelled. Network graphs are useful because they let us create quick visual representations of relationships that might otherwise escape our notice. The density or diffusion of the network graph can show us how a field of discourse or a narrative operates: who or what is at the centre and who or what is an outlier. This measure of network centrality can provide an indication of primary actors and outliers within a given network. For example, *SpokenWeb*'s *Archive of the Digital Present* (2022) records online literary events in Canada during the COVID-19 pandemic; its network analysis illustrates the relationships and connections between participants in the events.

Topic modeling

Topic modeling is one of the most complex forms of computational textual analysis. Developed by statistician and computer scientist David Blei, it is a hypothesis-free statistical method for *discovering* the topics of a given corpus. Whereas the previous examples begin with a research question or hypothesis—for example, when did *multiculturalism* become prominent in the discussion of Canadian literature, or in what contexts do characters refer to *diaspora* in contemporary Canadian fiction—topic modeling works without a specific research question. Instead, topic modeling attempts to discover the underlying (hidden) topical structure of a given collection of texts. In this regard, it is the most computationally dependent of the analytic methods we discuss. While most of the other methods could be accomplished manually, albeit with varying degrees of difficulty, topic modeling places much more faith in the machine.

Topic modeling begins with the intuition that any corpus includes a select number of topics. If one were to imagine a corpus consisting of the entirety of the *Globe and Mail*, the topics would roughly align with the sections of the newspaper: sports (with a large section devoted to hockey), business, theatre, literature (when the paper covered literature in any meaningful way), and so on. Digging deeper, topics for a corpus limited to the past twenty years would probably include Indigenous peoples, Middle East conflict, Anglophone-Francophone relations, and so forth. Topic modeling starts from the view that statistical methods can independently intuit these topics. If we were to topic model the entirety of Canadian literature, or some subset of that collection of texts (say, articles about Francophone authors writing in English or about first-generation Asian writers in Canada), we might find that the model identified topics across the corpus that had not been spotted by—or perhaps even ran counter to the generally accepted views of—scholars. Topic modeling is, therefore, a distant reading method for both identifying patterns that might have escaped the observation of the individual reader and for discerning links between texts in a corpus. Or, as Blei explains, "the goal of topic modeling is to automatically discover the topics from a collection of documents … This can be thought of as 'reversing' the generative process—what is the hidden structure that likely generated the observed collection?" (2012, 79).

Topic modeling uses statistical methods for identifying relationships between words and documents, often using a method called the Latent Dirichlet Allocation (LDA). The mathematical basis for LDA and topic modeling requires a graduate-level understanding of statistics; in this respect, it is another version of the same problem of black-box code concealing the workings of digital humanities research and tools. A select few may understand how it works, but the vast majority will have to take it in good faith that it does.

There are several methodological questions raised by topic modeling. It is unclear whether the topic modeling algorithm *discovers* the topical structure of a corpus or if we, in our configuration of the algorithm, *assert* that topical structure. In other words, is the algorithm finding a list of topics that exists in the corpus, or is it interpreting the corpus according to our instructions and thereby finding that set of topics? This complex question cuts not only to the heart of the debates about topic modeling's efficacy to produce meaningful results but also more generally to a point that we have been making throughout: every step in a digital humanities process is an interpretive act. This question of interpretative intervention is particularly complex with respect to topic modeling given that we are the ones who specify the number of topics that the algorithm should discover. We instruct the topic modeling algorithm to find X topics in the corpus where X is some number. So, topic modeling is only partially hypothesis-free as we shape the results by the value of X.[3] In addition, topic modeling requires us to choose a number of settings (called *hyperparameters*) that will affect the fit of the model to the documents. The number of topics, the selection of parameters, the curation of data, and the selection of the algorithm will each affect our eventual discovery of topics.

Furthermore, what is a topic in the context of literature? Is it a theme or something different? From a computational perspective, a topic is a statistical distribution over a corpus; this is a definition that is sure to leave most literary scholars dissatisfied (if not confused). When we think of a topic, we likely think of a single word or phrase (as in *Indigenous peoples* or *Anglophone-Francophone relations* in our newspaper example), but topic modeling does not actually generate topics with this degree of precision. Instead, it produces a collection of words that tend to co-occur (as a statistical distribution) and calls that a topic. So, we would not get *Indigenous peoples* as a topic but, rather, clusters of words like "Indigenous, reconciliation, residential, colonialism, resistance, language, Catholic" and so forth. It remains for the individual user to discern a topic among the collection of terms that topic modeling generates. This recalls Sandra Djwa's computational concordance of Canadian poetry in the 1960s (see Chapter 3); her early intuitions about the use of computers to analyze literary themes have been proven true.

Reservations about topic modeling are reasonable. However, the possibilities it offers for distant reading a corpus make it a textual analysis tool worthy of exploration for anyone interested in understanding trends and links across a corpus. For example, Lauren F. Klein's "Dimensions of Scale: Invisible Labor, Editorial Work, and the Future of Quantitative Literary Studies" (2020) employs topic modeling to discern the invisible labour of Mary Ann Shadd and Lydia Maria Child; both were editors of abolitionist journals, and Shadd was the first woman publisher in Canada. Klein writes, "topic modeling becomes a meaningful analytical tool indeed: it not only enables a view from a distance but also helps bring to light certain invisible aspects of knowledge production" (27). In Canadian contexts, Barrett's (2016) work on topic modeling Canadian literature theorizes its value as a form of paraphrase and as a hypothesis-generating method for exploring a corpus. Tanya Clement's notion of "differential reading" (2013) is a particularly useful framework for topic modeling, as it offers a methodology for moving between close and distant reading practices, for example, by using topic modeling to return to the texts armed with new questions in mind. Rather than conceiving of topic modeling as a method for discovering some dimension of a corpus, differential reading enables scholars to use it as a basis for new close readings. In the next chapter, we delve even further into the technical side of digital literary analysis by introducing the Python programming language and introductory concepts in programming for digital humanities projects.

Notes

1 Rockwell and Sinclair address the problem by proposing "an alternative approach: the hybrid essay, an interpretive work embedded with hermeneutical toys that can be explored for technique" (2016, 17). Their *hermeneutica* approach combines the exploratory and playful power of *Voyant* and the essays collected in their *Hermeneutica* (2016) book. *Jupyter Notebook* (Chapter 14) and *Voyant*'s *Spyral Notebook* offer similar forms of hybrid essay, which combines code, explanation, and methodological framing.
2 The inverse problem is that technically adept contributors, such as developers with a background in computer science, struggle with the humanities lines of inquiry at the heart of DH projects. Perhaps because DH knowledge

mobilization originates from humanities ways of thinking, this problem is less well documented.
3 There are mathematical methods for evaluating and measuring a topic's relative clarity (what computer scientists call *semantic coherence*) and consistency (see Mimno et al. 2011; Wallach et al. 2009). These methods will not be entirely satisfactory to a literary critic. Indeed, the notion of topical coherence upon which topic modeling depends is at odds with the kinds of formal experimentation, linguistic discordance, and poetic play that constitute a great deal of experimental literature. The pursuit of topical coherence presumes that a given corpus has coherent topics; this is not necessarily a given.

Further reading

Barrett, Paul. 2016. "Paraphrasing the Paraphrase OR What I Learned from Reading Every Issue of *Canadian Literature* & *SCL / ÉLC*." *Canadian Literature* 228/229 (Summer): 208–29. https://doi.org/10.14288/cl.v0i228-9.187589.

Flanders Julia, Syd Bauman, and Sarah Connell. 2016. "Text Encoding." In *Doing Digital Humanities: Practices, Training, Research*, edited by Constance Crompton, Richard Lane, and Ray Siemens, 104–22. London: Routledge. https://doi.org/10.4324/9781315707860.

Rockwell Geoffrey, and Stéfan Sinclair. 2016. *Hermeneutica: Computer-Assisted Interpretation in the Humanities*. Cambridge: The MIT Press. https://doi.org/10.7551/mitpress/9780262034357.001.0001.

TEI by Example. 2020. Centre for Scholarly Editing and Document Studies, Royal Academy of Dutch Language and Literature and Centre for Data, Culture and Society, University of Edinburgh. https://teibyexample.org/exist/.

Works cited

Barrett, Paul. 2016. "Paraphrasing the Paraphrase OR What I Learned from Reading Every Issue of *Canadian Literature* & *SCL / ÉLC*." *Canadian Literature* 228/229 (Summer): 208–29. https://doi.org/10.14288/cl.v0i228-9.187589.

Blei, David. 2012. "Statistical Topic Models." *Communications of the ACM* 55, no. 4: 77–84. https://doi.org/10.1145/2133806.2133826.

Bode, Katherine. 2023. "What's the Matter with Computational Literary Studies?" *Critical Inquiry* 49, no. 4: 507–29. https://doi.org/10.1086/724943.

Chapman, Mary, and Jean Lee Cole, eds. 2024. *The Winnifred Eaton Archive*. Version 2.0, February 3, 2024. https://winnifredeatonarchive.org.

Clement, Tanya. 2013. "Text Analysis, Data Mining, and Visualizations in Literary Scholarship." In *Literary Studies in the Digital Age: An Evolving Anthology*, edited by Kenneth M. Price and Ray Siemens. https://doi.org/10.1632/lsda.2013.8.

Craig, Hugh. 2004. "Stylistic Analysis and Authorship Studies." In *A Companion to Digital Humanities*, edited by Susan Schriebman, Ray Siemens, and John Unsworth, 271–88. Oxford: Blackwell. https://doi.org/10.1002/9780470999875.ch20.

Dynamic Table of Contexts. n.d. Accessed October 15, 2024. https://dtoc.leaf-vre.org/.

Flanders, Julia, Syd Bauman, and Sarah Connell. 2016. "Text Encoding." In *Doing Digital Humanities: Practices, Training, Research*, edited by Constance Crompton, Richard Lane, and Ray Siemens, 104–22. London: Routledge. https://doi.org/10.4324/9781315707860.
Google. n.d. *Google Ngram Viewer*. Accessed September 8, 2024. https://books.google.com/ngrams/.
HathiTrust. n.d. *HathiTrust Bookworm*. Accessed September 8, 2024. https://bookworm.htrc.illinois.edu/develop/.
Iantorno, Michael. 2020. "GameSound, Quantitative Game Analysis, and the Digital Humanities." *Digital Studies / Le champ numérique* 10, no. 1. https://doi.org/10.16995/dscn.319.
Ide, Nancy, and C. M. Sperberg-McQueen. 1995. "The TEI: History, Goals, and Future." *Computers and the Humanities* 29: 5–15. https://doi.org/10.1007/BF01830313.
Klein, Lauren F. 2020. "Dimensions of Scale: Invisible Labor, Editorial Work, and the Future of Quantitative Literary Study." *PMLA* 135, no. 1: 23–39. https://doi.org/10.1632/pmla.2020.135.1.23.
Linked Editing Academic Framework. n.d.-a. *Dynamic Table of Contexts*. Accessed October 15, 2024. https://dtoc.leaf-vre.org/.
Linked Editing Academic Framework. n.d.-b. *LEAF-Writer*. Accessed September 8, 2024. https://leaf-writer.leaf-vre.org.
Liu, Alan. 2013. "The Meaning of the Digital Humanities." *PMLA* 128, no. 2: 409–23. https://doi.org/10.1632/pmla.2013.128.2.409.
Mimno, David, Hanna Wallach, Edmund Talley, Miriam Leenders, and Andrew McCallum. 2011. "Optimizing Semantic Coherence in Topic Models." *Proceedings of the 2011 Conference on Empirical Methods in Natural Language Processing*, July 27–31, 2011, 262–72. https://dl.acm.org/doi/10.5555/2145432.2145462.
NLTK Project. 2023. *Natural Language Toolkit*. Version 3.8.1, January 2, 2023. https://www.nltk.org/.
Nyhan, Julianne, and Andrew Flinn. 2016. *Computation and the Humanities: Towards an Oral History of the Digital Humanities*. New York: Springer. https://link.springer.com/book/10.1007/978-3-319-20170-2.
Obbard, Kiera. 2024. "The Instagram Effect." PhD diss., University of Guelph, August 27, 2024.
Rockwell, Geoffrey, Matt Huculak, Emmanuel Château-Dutier, Barbara Bordalejo, Kyle Dase, Laura Estill, Julia Polyck-O'Neill, and Harvey Quamen. 2022. "Canada's Future DRI Ecosystem for Humanities & Social Sciences (HSS)." *Digital Research Alliance of Canada*. https://alliancecan.ca/sites/default/files/2022-03/csdh_ndrio_whitepaper.pdf.
Rockwell Geoffrey, and Stéfan Sinclair. 2016. *Hermeneutica: Computer-Assisted Interpretation in the Humanities*. Cambridge: The MIT Press. https://doi.org/10.7551/mitpress/9780262034357.001.0001.
Rommel, Thomas. 2004. "Literary Studies." In *A Companion to Digital Humanities*, edited by Susan Schreibman, Ray Siemens, and John Unsworth, 88–96. Oxford: Blackwell. https://doi.org/10.1002/9780470999875.

Sapach, Sonja. 2020. "Tagging My Tears and Fears: Text-Mining the Autoethnography." *Digital Studies / Le champ numérique* 10, no. 1. https://doi.org/10.16995/dscn.328.

SpokenWeb. 2022. *Archive of the Digital Present.* https://adp.spokenweb.ca.

TAPoR. n.d. *Text Analysis Portal for Research 3.* Version 3.0. Accessed July 10, 2024. https://tapor.ca/home.

TEI by Example. 2020. Centre for Scholarly Editing and Document Studies, Royal Academy of Dutch Language and Literature and Centre for Data, Culture and Society, University of Edinburgh. https://teibyexample.org/exist/.

TEI. 2023. *Text Encoding Initiative.* https://tei-c.org.

Wallach, Hanna M., Iain Murray, Ruslan Salakhutdinov, and David Mimno. 2009. "Evaluation Methods for Topic Models." *Proceedings of the 26th International Conference on Machine Learning*, June 14–18, 2009, 1105–12. https://doi.org/10.1145/1553374.1553515.

Wikle, Olivia. 2020. "Listening at a Distance: Reading the Sound World of Gothic Literature with Topic Modelling and Text Analysis." *Digital Studies / Le champ numérique* 10, no. 1. https://doi.org/10.16995/dscn.333.

14
PROGRAMMING

* * *

For those who want to move beyond prebuilt tools and customize their textual analysis, working in a programming language is the best choice. Yet programming comes with some difficulty as users must grapple with complex technical concepts, arcane terminology, and intimidating levels of technical expertise. Case in point: Susan Hockey begins her *A Guide to Computer Applications in the Humanities* (1980) with a discussion of the joys of computer programming in the arcane language SNOBOL, a language that was specifically designed for working with text. She introduces her readers to programming with the following code segment:

```
      &TRIIM = 1
      &ANCHOR = 1
      LETTERS = 'ABCDEFGHIJKLMNOPQRSTUVWXYZ'
      WORDPAT = BREAK(LETTERS) SPAN(LETTERS) . WORD
MORE  CARD = INPUT                :F (PRINT)
AGAIN CARD WORDPAT =              :F (MORE)
      IDENT(WORD, 'AND')          :F (AGAIN)
      COUNT = COUNT + 1           : (AGAIN)
PRINT OUTPUT = COUNT
END
```

After presenting the reader with this intimidating wall of complex code, Hockey comments, "Learning to program a computer is not at all difficult. On the contrary, it can be an amusing intellectual exercise" (1980, 11). Generations of unamused DH scholars and programmers will disagree

DOI: 10.4324/9781003318323-20

with Hockey's assessment, particularly those who have spent frustrating hours attempting to get an apparently simple computer program to function. For many, a wall of indecipherable code is enough to send them running. Thankfully, things have changed for the better since the days of SNOBOL: code is far easier to work with and far simpler to read (although code, and computers in general, have become more complex). There are online communities dedicated to helping new programmers. Coding can even be an enjoyable challenge, largely thanks to the satisfaction experienced when the code finally works.

Programming has always been a part of digital humanities—at least for some. For many years, the field was divided along the lines of "hack" and "yack" (Nowviskie 2014), where *hack* refers to those with technical skills and *yack* refers to those who engage in discussions of DH's merits and methods. These debates concerning programming and making more generally are informed by a gendered vision of DH, where (often masculine-coded) technical expertise is valued over (often female-coded) humanistic inquiry (see Chapter 8). As earlier chapters on the history of humanities computing have demonstrated (and as captured in the above example from Hockey's programming manual), this coding of technical expertise as the domain of men is incorrect. And, as we have argued throughout the book, this paradigm presents a false division between making and thinking in DH. The hack/yack paradigm has thankfully been largely dismantled, and most DH practitioners recognize the value (and interdependence) of a range of DH approaches.

Partly due to the decline of the hack/yack debate, and partly due to the increasing availability of digital humanities tools with user-friendly interfaces,[1] it is not at all required that DH scholars be familiar with programming languages or concepts. There are many excellent tools that require no understanding of programming, and programming is a small subset of the range of possible work in DH. However, learning to program does enable you to customize tools, work more closely with the machine, encode methodology, and develop unique digital projects. It also frees you from relying on expensive products designed by large corporations. Furthermore, programming requires systematic, algorithmic thinking, which can be beneficial for breaking a complex project into smaller, more manageable parts. If you want to learn how to program, there are many approaches to choose from. Python is DH's language of choice for many reasons, including its extensive collection of libraries, readable code, and its suitability for textual analysis. R is another popular language, although more so in the social sciences and statistics than in digital humanities.[2] Other programming languages also have a home in DH. For example, *Spyral Notebook*, which is interoperable with *Voyant Tools*, uses JavaScript.

Python is highly human-readable. For scholars who are used to being able to make meaning from the characters on the page (or screen), this is no small advantage. Consider the following code to achieve the same common programming task, printing the phrase "Hello world" (or, in this case, a slightly more Canadian "Bonjour le monde") in three programming languages: Java, C++, and Python:

Java
```
public class Java_is_hard {
    public static void main (String[] args) {
        System.out.println("Bonjour le monde");
    }
}
```

C++
```
#include <iostream>
using namespace std;
int main()
{
    cout << "Bonjour le monde";
    return 0;
}
```

Python
```
print("Bonjour le monde")
```

The Python code is the shortest, most intuitive, and easiest to read. Another advantage of Python is that it is one of the programming languages that can be written via a web browser—no need to download additional software. To get started with Python, we recommend the use of free, online development environments such as *Jupyter Notebook* or *Google Colab*, a Google-hosted *Jupyter Notebook* service. Once you are ready to move on to complex programming or working with large sets of files, you will need to install Python on your computer; for most introductory purposes, a browser-based tool will suffice.

There are several useful guides to getting started in digital humanities work in Python. We recommend Melanie Walsh's excellent *Introduction to Cultural Analytics & Python* (2021). Walsh's interactive textbook is designed for novices, assumes no prior knowledge, and is available for free online. It starts with the absolute basics of how to read code and work with texts as computer files, and it is specifically geared towards digital humanities. *Programming Historian* is also a great online resource for programmers (and DH users) of all skill levels. It features over one hundred lessons in English (plus a smaller selection in French, Spanish, and Portuguese).

Programming Historian's extensive Python programming lessons cover everything from basics to complex forms of plotting, mapping, textual analysis, and machine learning. The lessons are created by a team of volunteers, the majority of whom have a digital humanities background. Geoffrey Rockwell and Stéfan Sinclair's *Hermeneutica* (2016) is a great resource for high-level textual analysis and Nick Montfort's *Exploratory Programming for the Arts and Humanities* (2021) is also an excellent introductory text to DH Python programming and includes useful exercises for honing one's Python skills. If you are looking for something less self-directed, there are plenty of in-person and online opportunities, including those offered as part of the Canadian Certificate in Digital Humanities. Given this range of great resources (not to mention the limited amount of space available here), our goal in this chapter is to provide a gentle, page-based introduction to coding. The intention is not to replace hands-on learning, but rather to walk through some human-readable code as a way of demystifying programming and demonstrating some of its potential DH uses.

Building blocks

The very first step in beginning to code is understanding that code is essentially a set of instructions that you are asking the computer to execute; if the computer is making maple syrup, the computer code is the recipe and the digitized materials are the bucketfuls of maple sap. Likewise, an algorithm is a specific set of instructions designed to complete a discrete task, usually as quickly and efficiently as possible; to extend the cooking analogy, an algorithm is the recipe's steps, such as "fill the pot with maple sap and set it over the fire to boil." Novice programmers are routinely frustrated by the specificity with which code must be written, but computers require the same amount of precision in code as we expect in scholarly writing—sometimes more. The computer would fail to cook anything using our syrup recipe, since lighting the fire is implied but not stated. Recall the perennial comment left by instructors in the margins of undergraduate essays: "I think I know what you are *trying* to say, but I can only mark what you have *actually* written." Computers are the same: a computer cannot infer what a programmer wants to do; it can only do what is written in the code. Consequently, the smallest mistake in computer code can lead to unpredictable results. For instance, Python is case-sensitive, so the `print` command is not the same as the `Print` command. Typos and small errors are sources of frustration, but you can reduce your aggravation by paying attention to detail, building code using preexisting sample blocks, and employing code-checking features that are built into browser-based code editing environments like *Google Colab*—often referred to as Integrated Development Environments (IDE).

Variables are a basic building block of code. A variable is a named container of data that stores some value; to stretch the cooking analogy, the variable could be the length of time to boil the sap or the size of the fire. Unlike many other programming languages, in Python you don't need to independently declare variables; they are created as you use them. Variables can be named nearly anything (except for words reserved for commands; see below) and Python can handle many variable types, including *string* (a series of characters), *integer* (a whole number), *float* (a number with a decimal point), and *boolean* (a condition of either true or false). For example, imagine trying to search through a vast quantity of social media posts for references to Giller Prize winners. The following code declares two string variables and an integer variable:

```
Giller_winner_2017 = "Michael Redhill"
Giller_winner_title_2017 = "Bellevue Square"
Giller_nominees_2017 = 5
```

This simple set of instructions stores references to 2017 Giller winner Michael Redhill, to his winning novel *Bellevue Square*, and to the number of shortlisted nominees in 2017, each in their own variable. Since variables cannot have spaces in their names, we have called our author variable `Giller_winner_2017` rather than `Giller winner 2017`. Note that Python's case sensitivity applies to variables too, so `giller_winner_2017` is not the same variable as `Giller_winner_2017`.

Python has a number of reserved words, many of which are built-in commands, such as `print`, `type`, `for`, `and`, and `False`; these cannot be used for variable names because they already have other assigned functions. As seen in the `Bonjour le monde` example at the start of the chapter, the `print` command prints (types out) the specified output to the screen. The `type` command, meanwhile, outputs the type of a variable or data type:

```
type(Giller_winner_2017)
>> str
```

The program's output (indicated by the >>) tells us that the variable named `Giller_winner_2017` is of type *string*. Note that Python is only able to tell us that the output (`Michael Redhill`) is a series of characters (a string); it cannot tell us what the string of characters means, since it is not able to interpret strings of text—that is our job. To the computer, Michael Redhill and *Bellevue Square* are each just a series of characters.[3]

The `len` command tells us the length of any data type. For example, imagine looking for trends among the titles of books that were Giller nominees. Titles range in length from one character (Marjorie Celona's *Y*, longlisted in 2012) to nearly fifty (Megan Gail Coles's *Small Game Hunting at the Local Coward Gun Club*, shortlisted in 2019). The `len` command can be used to count the number of characters in each:

```
print(len(Giller_winner_title_2017))
>> 15
```

You may be curious about the brackets in the above examples. Brackets tend to indicate the use of a function (sometimes referred to as a command). In general terms, a function is code that accepts an input (the content enclosed in brackets), performs an operation on the input, and then outputs the result. For example, the `print` function requires the user to include the string they want to print in the brackets (`"Bonjour le monde"`), whereas the `type` function requires the variable (or data type) the user wants to know the type of. In the above example, we are using nested brackets: the input for our `len` command is our variable `Giller_winner_title_2017` and the output for the `len` command becomes the input for our `print` command. In this case, the `len` command counts the total number of characters (individual letters, spaces, and punctuation) in the string variable and outputs `15` because there are 15 characters in *Bellevue Square* including spaces.

Like most programming languages, Python also allows you to add comments to your code using the # symbol. Comments are not part of the executable code, but rather are notes left by the programmer who is writing the code; you can use them to leave notes about things to return to later, or you can use them to provide future users with additional context. Anything that appears in a line after the # symbol is not part of the active code; Python ignores comments and the code to be performed only resumes on the next new line. For example, our Giller code could include the following reminder:

```
# Check the type of the variable to ensure it is correct:
type(Giller_winner_2017)
```

The first line is a note left by us to check that the type of variable is correct; the second line is the command itself. Comments can be used to document a code's rationale and logic. In DH, they provide an opportunity for the programmer to incorporate plain-language descriptions and explanations that can be referenced by future users who want to understand, and perhaps even reuse, the code.

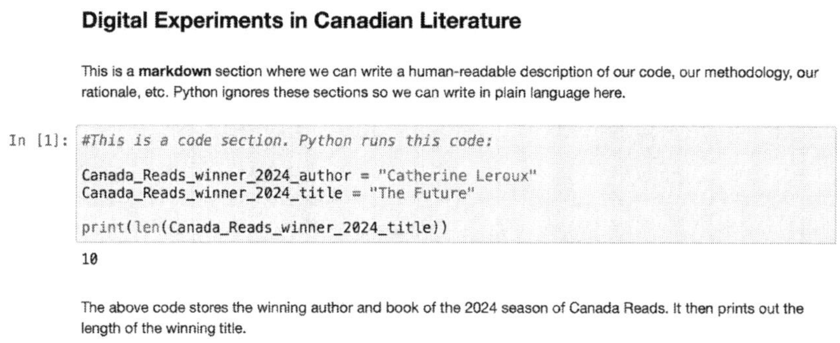

Digital Experiments in Canadian Literature

This is a **markdown** section where we can write a human-readable description of our code, our methodology, our rationale, etc. Python ignores these sections so we can write in plain language here.

```
In [1]: #This is a code section. Python runs this code:

        Canada_Reads_winner_2024_author = "Catherine Leroux"
        Canada_Reads_winner_2024_title = "The Future"

        print(len(Canada_Reads_winner_2024_title))
        10
```

The above code stores the winning author and book of the 2024 season of Canada Reads. It then prints out the length of the winning title.

FIGURE 14.1 *Jupyter* notebook combining Markdown and code sections.

DH projects often use *Jupyter*, which provides a method of writing Python that combines code with plaintext. *Jupyter* notebooks combine code sections with Markdown (plain text) sections, which we can use to intersperse lengthy explanations with our code. *Jupyter* notebooks (see Figure 14.1) are good for teaching because they are so similar to classroom textbooks in that they provide a convenient way of explaining code's logic.

Data types

Python stores information in a program using data types. Some information (say, the entirety of text that comprises Marian Engel's novel, *Bear*) is particularly suited to being stored in a string, whereas other information (say, the number of pages in an edition of *Bear*) is suited to being stored as an integer. There are also more complex data types: for example, if we wanted to store a list of all of Marian Engel's books along with their corresponding page numbers, we would use lists and dictionaries. Lists are, as one would expect, collections of individual objects. Lists are enclosed in square brackets with commas used to separate the items:

```
# Don't forget to finish this list
Engel_books = ["Bear", "The Honeyman Festival", "Monodromos", "Lunatic Villas", "No Clouds of Glory"]
```

Here we have created a list called `Engel_books`. The quotation marks around each entry tell Python that each of these objects is a string. Note also that we have added a comment to remind ourselves that the list is incomplete.

Dictionaries are also groupings of related objects where each object has a key and a value, akin to a word and its definition in a traditional dictionary. The key for any dictionary item must be unique. Dictionaries are created using curly brackets (sometimes called curly braces):

```
Engel_pages = {"Bear": 122, "The Honeyman Festival": 131,
"Monodromos": 250, "Lunatic Villas": 251, "No Clouds of
Glory": 181}
```

Here, we have created a dictionary, where the key (the first element, or the dictionary term to be defined) is the book's title and the value (the second element, or the definition) is the number of pages in our edition of that book.

Data types may seem a bit abstract, but their utility becomes apparent when we use them as part of datasets that are large, complex, or both. Methods allow users to perform additional operations on the data. For instance, the methods `append` and `remove` can be used (unsurprisingly) to add items to and remove items from a list. For example,

```
# Add an incorrect book to Engel_books
Engel_books.append("Fifth Business")
```

```
# Remove the incorrect book from the list
Engel_books.remove("Fifth Business")
```

In the above examples, we put `"Fifth Business"` in quotation marks to indicate that it is the string that is to be added to our list. We then removed the same string (the same incorrect book title) from the list. This function is especially useful for more complicated or in-progress datasets, which could well need ongoing adjustments: our dataset related to the Giller Prize would need updating annually with the names of that year's nominated books, their authors, and the prize's jury members; in the case of the 2024 prize and the controversy surrounding the sponsor, information would need adjusting as authors removed their books from contention.

Although we can add an incorrect title to our list, it is worth noting that Python does not allow code-based errors. If we tried to run the following code:

```
# Add Fifth Business without quotation marks
Engel_books.append(Fifth_Business)
```

Python would produce an error message. The quotation marks indicate that the user wants to add the string `"Fifth Business"` to the list, whereas `Fifth_Business` without quotation marks tells Python to look for a variable named `Fifth_Business` and append the contents of that variable to the list. Unless we've created the variable `Fifth_Business` in advance, this command won't execute. While no programming language is failsafe, in-built protections like these reduce the likelihood of entering mistakes. Lists and dictionaries are just two of the many data types available in Python. As you become more familiar with coding and Python, you will discover tools that allow them to perform a broad range of functions and therefore ask all kinds of interesting research questions.

Control structures

Computer programs run in a linear fashion until they reach the end or until the programmer tells the program that it should do otherwise. It can be useful to redirect the program if certain conditions are met or specific information is provided. When we want to do this, we use control structures such as *if statements*, *for loops*, and *while loops*.

An *if statement* is a conditional command that does something if a criterion is met:

```
Book_length = 314
if Book_length > 150:
    print("This is a novel.")
else:
    print("This is a novella.")
```

This code creates a variable called `Book_length` with a value of `314`. It then checks to see if `Book_length` is greater than 150 pages and, if so, prints that the book is a novel. If the length is not greater than 150 (`else`) it prints that the book is a novella (remember, this is just an example; there is no agreed-upon book length that differentiates novels from novellas). The indentation underneath the `if` and `else` statements are not just for style and ease of reading; Python requires indents and will automatically insert them as you are writing your code. If you remove these indents, the code will not function.

A *while loop* is another control structure that executes code while something is true:

```
giller_countdown = 10
while giller_countdown > 0:
    print(giller_countdown)
    giller_countdown = giller_countdown - 1
print("It's Giller Time!")
```

This code creates a variable called `giller_countdown` with a value of `10`. It then creates a while loop that says, "while `giller_countdown` is greater than 0 execute everything indented under the while statement." First, it prints the value of `giller_countdown` (10), then reduces `giller_countdown` by 1. Then it checks the *while loop*'s condition again, sees that `giller_countdown` is still greater than 0, and so executes the code under the *while loop* again: it prints the value of `giller_countdown` (9) and reduces it by 1. This repeats, printing and reducing the value of `giller_countdown` until its value is 0. When that condition is met, Python exits the *while loop* and prints `"It's Giller Time!"` The resulting output is

```
10, 9, 8, 7, 6, 5, 4, 3, 2, 1, It's Giller Time!
```
[4]

While loops are powerful tools so care needs to be taken when using them. If, for example, we were to accidentally change our code to `giller_countdown = giller_countdown + 1`, the loop would never stop running because our condition (`giller_countdown > 0`) would always be true. This would result in an infinite loop, and we would never get to the final line of code.

Another important control structure is a *for loop*. A *for loop* iterates over a series of items ("for every item in this list...") and performs an operation on the items:

```
Canadian_Michaels = ["Michael Redhill", "Michael Ondaatje", "Michael Winter"]
for item in Canadian_Michaels:
    print(item, "is a great Canadian Michael.")
```

In this code, (1) we create a list called `Canadian_Michaels`, and (2) for every item in the list, we have Python print a string that combines the item with `"is a great Canadian Michael."` The code in the *for loop* will execute once for each item in the list, and `item` will refer to whichever entry in the list the code is currently looking at (first `item = "Michael Redhill"`, then `item = "Michael Ondaatje"`, and so on). Note that the `item` reference in the loop is a placeholder for the object that Python is currently viewing; we could use any word instead of `item`.

If we want to be more complex in our use of control structures, we can combine them:

```
Canadian_Authors = ["Michael Redhill", "Dionne Brand", "Michael Ondaatje", "Michael Winter", "Michael Crummey", "Mordecai Richler", "Marie-Claire Blais"]
for item in Canadian_Authors:
    if "Michael" in item:
        print(item, "is a great Canadian Michael.")
```

```
elif "Mordecai" in item:
    print(item, "is a great Canadian Mordecai.")
else:
    print(item, "is still great.")
```

This code combines two of our control structures, a *for loop* and an *if statement*, and introduces the new term `elif`, which stands for *else if*. The *else if* code only runs if the first *if statement* is false and the *else if* condition (in this case, `Mordecai` appears in item) is true. If neither the *if* nor the *else if* conditions are true, the program executes the code under the *else* condition.

This code begins by creating a list of Canadian authors. For each author, it checks to see if the word *Michael* is in the writer's name. If so, it prints out that the author *is a great Canadian Michael*. If not, it then checks to see if the word *Mordecai* is in the writer's name. If so, it prints out that the author *is a great Canadian Mordecai*. If neither of those conditions are true, it prints out that the author *is still great*. Control structures are a key dimension of programming languages because they allow the program to make decisions depending on the input.

Application Programming Interfaces

An Application Programming Interface (API) is a link between your own Python code and an external service such as a website, social media platform, or database. APIs enable you to connect your code to those external services and to use Python to work with the data from those services. Each API is unique in its requirements, so the best way to start working with an API is to follow the instructions that are provided alongside it or to seek out generic instructions online. Some APIs require registering with an external service and acquiring a unique connection code (called a *key*); others require no registration.

Libraries

One of Python's most useful features is its libraries, which allow you to load commands and code directly into your Python environment. Libraries' preexisting code packages make some tasks easier; they are the recipe equivalent of making poutine starting with frozen fries instead of peeling and cutting fresh potatoes. Libraries are at the heart of the Python programming ethos, which is based on the idea that if someone else has written code you can use, you should use it—so long as you acknowledge your source. In this regard, Python has a lot in common with digital humanities, which is collaborative and community-oriented. There are thousands of libraries in Python ranging from Pokémon card databases to code for interacting with Spotify or Statistics Canada.

Gutenberg is a very convenient library for adding public domain texts directly into Python (see Chapter 11 for more about *Project Gutenberg* and its resources). Using the *Gutenberg* library and some blocks of Python code, we could explore the stylistic similarities of Susanna Moodie's *Roughing It in the Bush* (1852) and Mary Prince's *The History of Mary Prince* (1831) as we do in the case study discussed in the next chapter. Prince was an enslaved woman who, after being nominally dismissed from slavery in London (although never emancipated), published her life story; Moodie served as Prince's amanuensis for her slavery narrative and it remains unclear how much of Prince's narrative was shaped by Moodie's authorial intervention. Andrea Medovarski asks the provocative question,

> What happens if, instead of seeing Moodie's *Roughing It in the Bush* (1852) as one of the significant starting points for Canadian literature, we instead trace the literary tradition back to *The History of Mary Prince*? What does it mean for Moodie, and for subsequent Canadian writers, to write in the wake of a slave narrative?
>
> *(2014, 14)*

Tracing Canadian literature's origins back beyond Moodie's settler text to Prince's slavery narrative would transform the field's foundations. Digital humanities methodologies—such as using Python to compare full-text versions of the books downloaded for free from Project *Gutenberg*—can provide the basis for establishing the similarities of and differences between the two texts.

The first steps of this project would be to install the *Gutenberg* library and import the relevant texts. There can be slight variations in these steps depending on the computer operating system; instead of detailing these steps, we encourage you to search online, as there are plenty of system-specific reusable code blocks, step-by-step guides, and tutorials. Once the initial installation is complete, we use the import command to load a library into Python; from there it only takes a few short lines of code to download the entirety of Moodie's and Prince's books:

```
#Import the relevant library
from gutenberg.acquire import load_etext

#Load the two texts from Gutenberg into string variables
Prince_text = load_etext(17851)
Moodie_text = load_etext(4389)
```

The first code block uses the import command to load the relevant function (`load_etext`) from the *Gutenberg* library, which connects our code with *Gutenberg*. The second code block uses the `load_etext` function to load two books: Prince's *The History of Mary Prince* and Moodie's *Roughing It in the Bush*. Typing two lines of code is much faster than retyping two whole books.

In the second code block, note that the first part of each line (before the equals sign) uses the variables we have created to refer to the works: `Prince_text` and `Moodie_text` respectively. The second half of each line (after the equals sign) uses the numerical input in the `load_etext` functions (17851, 4389); these are the unique eBook identifiers for each book on the *Gutenberg* website. Searching for a book on *Gutenberg* will produce the relevant eBook identifier. The above code loads the two books and stores them in the appropriate variables (`Prince_text` and `Moodie_text`).

Once we have copies of the texts stored, we can do all kinds of programmatic analysis, such as looking for patterns of words that appear in both texts. This is only one example; preexisting code blocks are available online to borrow, reuse, and build upon.[5] Searching for patterns across the two texts uses code blocks for tokenizing words and removing stop words. *Tokenizing* breaks up large amount of text into machine-processable tokens that can be easily interpreted by a computer. In Python terms, tokenizing typically transforms a large string into a list of word tokens. For example, the opening line of Margaret Laurence's *The Diviners* (1974), "The river flowed both ways," becomes a list of words: ["The", "river", "flowed", "both", "ways"]. *Stop words* are generic, frequently occurring words (such as *it*, *and*, *the*) that we remove in order to focus the analysis on words that we deem to be more significant. Of course, discerning which words have significance for any particular corpus can be difficult, so removing stop words requires care.

To begin to analyze our text, we first need to tokenize it so that the code will treat each word as an individual item. One way to do this is to use the *Natural Language Toolkit* (NLTK) library, which includes useful commands for textual analysis and natural language[6] processing. The following code tokenizes our textual data:

```
import nltk
from nltk.tokenize import word_tokenize
nltk.download("punkt_tab")

Prince_words = word_tokenize(Prince_text)
Moodie_words = word_tokenize(Moodie_text)
```

Now `Prince_words` and `Moodie_words` are lists containing the tokenized versions of the text; we could use `type(Prince_words)` to confirm the type of these two lists.

Once the text is tokenized, we can then remove stop words with the following code:

```
nltk.download("stop words")
from nltk.corpus import stopwords

#Create a list of stop words from NLTK's list
stop_words = set(stopwords.words('english'))

#Create two empty lists where we will store our lists of
#words after removing the stop words
Moodie_words_cleaned = []
Prince_words_cleaned = []

#Loop once for every word in Moodie_words:
for word in Moodie_words:
    #If that word is not a stop word:
    if word not in stop_words:
        #Add that word to the 'cleaned' list
        Moodie_words_cleaned.append(word)

#Loop once for every word in Moodie_words:
for word in Prince_words:
    #If that word is not a stop word:
    if word not in stop_words:
        #Add that word to the 'cleaned' list
        Prince_words_cleaned.append(word)[7]
```

This code block will remove the stop words in Moodie's and Prince's texts using the NLTK stop words list,[8] and it will create two "clean" texts, which we can use in our analysis. We might, for instance, try to find all of the matching bi-grams and tri-grams (two- and three-word phrases, respectively) from both texts. We could use this list in all kinds of ways: for example, we could look for turns of phrase or sentence structures that overlap between Moodie and Prince's writing, or we could look for words that appear with high frequency across both texts. Stylistics is a complex and controversial method of textual analysis, and we are only scratching the surface here.

Using the following code, we could identify words greater than three characters in length (and that are also not the already removed stop words) that appear in both texts:

```
#For every word in our list of Prince words:
for word in Prince_words_cleaned:
    #If the length of the current word is > 3
    if len(word) > 3:
        if word in Moodie_words_cleaned:
            print(word)
```

In the case study discussed in the next chapter, we develop this comparison of Moodie's and Prince's texts to demonstrate some of the larger questions we can explore with digital textual analysis. Depending on the volume and content of the output, we could continue to explore using code, or we could take the results and input them into a tool such as *Voyant* (see Chapter 13) to create a visualization, or we could upload the full text to *LEAF-Writer* to tag and annotate it; we could also take the list offline and interrogate it using traditional literary analysis methods. As we develop our analysis further, we might count the most common words across both texts, or we could expand our Moodie corpus to include her other writings to further the possible connections we might make between Moodie and Prince (see Chapter 15).

Data cleaning

Removing stop words is an example of data cleaning, which is the process of removing anything incorrect or unnecessary from the data for the purpose of our analysis. As discussed in the previous chapter, data cleaning is essential for data scraped from the web, which is likely to include a substantial amount of HTML formatting and other irrelevant text. We also need to clean data when we are working with digitized publications where headers, footers, and page numbers are mixed into the body of the work. Cleaning is also an efficient way to correct errors inserted because of optical character recognition or to align variations across a dataset: for example, multiple ways of spelling an author's name or entering dates.

Data can be cleaned both programmatically and with tools that have user-friendly interfaces. To do so, DH practitioners who are comfortable with code often use a method of pattern matching called *regular expressions* (RegEx). Regular expressions have many functions, such as finding and removing or replacing text strings. For example, importing a list of Giller nominees could easily lead to errors in names with accents: André Alexis, André Forget, and André Narbonne might, because of the way computers treat accents, all appear as `AndrU+00E9` instead of *André*.[9] Using regular expressions, it would be easy to find and correct this and similar errors. Regular expressions use complex, rules-based codes, which can be confusing and difficult to remember, especially for those who do not use them often. Thankfully, there are online resources to help. We recommend the *Regular Expression Cheat Sheet*, available free online, for building regular expressions to match a particular case. In most cases, the expression that is required can be found in the cheat sheet or using a quick Internet search.

Regular expressions can be incorporated into Python code using the *re* library, or they can be used via interface-based tools. *OpenRefine* (2024) is a free tool for cleaning and curating data. Using drop-down menus and easy-to-navigate sidebars, users can clean and restructure data, for example, by correcting errors, splitting or joining text together, and removing blanks and duplicates; *OpenRefine* also allows you to do more complex cleaning using regular expressions. *OpenRefine* can also be used for some analysis: it has functions for clustering and filtering data, finding trends in data (referred to as faceting), and it can be used to enhance data by linking out to external databases by using a process called reconciliation—a method of linking an individual dataset to other datasets to confirm and augment information. *OpenRefine* is best for data that is structured (e.g., spreadsheets and tables). For example, it would be better suited to our dataset listing Giller nominees than our full text comparison of *Roughing It in the Bush* and *The History of Mary Prince*.

Although there are many powerful ways of transforming data, either using programming notebooks or GUI-based tools, it should be noted that you can do excellent work without them. As we have seen in the example of Jordan Abel's poetry, familiar functions such as *find and replace* in a word processor or the filters available in spreadsheet software can be used with great success. Regular expressions, stop words, variables, and functions are all great assets, but it is entirely possible for you to become a brilliant DH programmer without any of them. If you have been inspired to learn more, we encourage you to consult any of the free online resources mentioned in this chapter (and the further reading section at the end) that offer quick and easy examples of how to engage in textual analysis. Using a combination of code and literary analysis will allow you to pose new questions about collections of texts. The best way to get started with computational-aided textual analysis in Python is to work through an introduction, search for answers online, and experiment.

Bringing it all together

To close this chapter, we provide a final example in the form of a piece of code that brings together all the skills that have been discussed. If executed, this code loads *Gutenberg*'s version of *Anne of Green Gables* (1908) into Python, removes the *Gutenberg* headers, cleans the text using regular expressions, and removes a selection of stop words preloaded in the NLTK library.

```
#Import the regular expression library
import re
#Import the relevant Gutenberg library
from gutenberg.acquire import load_etext
from gutenberg.cleanup import strip_headers

#Import the relevant nltk libraries
import nltk
from nltk.tokenize import word_tokenize
from nltk.corpus import stopwords

#Store the entirety of the novel in the anne variable
anne = load_etext(64365)

#Remove the header & metadata from the novel
anne = strip_headers(anne).strip()

#Use RegEx to remove non-alphanumeric characters
anne = re.sub('[^A-Za-z ]+', '', anne)

#Convert the string of the novel into a list of word tokens
anne_words = word_tokenize(anne)

#Load the NLTK stop words
stop_words = set(stop_words.words('english'))

#Create an empty list that will store anne_words—stop words
anne_words_cleaned = []

#Append all words not in the stop word list to cleaned list
for word in anne_words:
    if word not in stop_words:
        anne_words_cleaned.append(word)
```

Once this code executes, the variable `anne` will contain the entirety of the novel, and `anne_words_cleaned` will contain a list of all the word tokens with stop words removed. From this we can begin to form our analysis, identifying frequent words, the words that tend to collocate across the novel, the verbs and nouns associated with individual characters, and more.

Notes

1 Many of these tools have engaging Graphical User Interfaces (GUI), which enable users to use complex DH tools with minimal computing knowledge. *Voyant* is perhaps the best introductory DH tool and offers an intuitive GUI atop powerful code.
2 At the time of writing, *Programming Historian*, a popular resource for self-guided DH lessons, has topic tags for only two programming languages, Python (thirty-four lessons) and R (eight lessons).
3 The code cannot distinguish between a person's name and a book name regardless of whether the book's name is obviously not a person's name, as in Redhill's 2017 winner, *Bellevue Square*, or his 2001 shortlisted title, *Martin Sloane* (which also happens to be a person's name). Some more complex programming could generate a count of Giller-nominated titles that are made up solely of a person's first and last name. In addition to *Martin Sloane*, this list would include Richard B. Wright's *Clara Callan* (2001), Anakana Schofield's *Martin John* (2015), Esi Edugyan's *Washington Black* (2018), and Joshua Whitehead's *Jonny Appleseed* (2018).
4 The output of this code will actually print each number (and the final message) on separate lines. We have put all of the output on one line in the interest of concision.
5 Increasingly, it is possible to generate functional custom code using AI. The ethics of using AI are complex, given that it is built on vast quantities of work for which no credit is provided, and its black-box design makes it impossible to determine whether AI-generated code is embedding bias in the research. Notwithstanding these problems, programmers at all levels have found AI a useful resource—albeit one that needs to be used thoughtfully.
6 *Natural language processing* is the computational term for linguistic analysis of any text or corpora. It typically begins by transforming a text into a collection of textual tokens (units of analysis) suited to a particular form of textual analysis (common words, concordance, words in context, topic modeling, sentiment analysis, etc.). See Chapter 13 for more information about natural language processing.
7 This is by far the longest code block we have used so far, but nearly three quarters (by word count) is comments. Remember too that code blocks such as this one can be found online and modified as needed; code editors will check your work in progress and Python will generate an error message for anything that cannot be run, which means you will have lots of feedback as you work.
8 NLTK's 127 English-language stop words are ["i", "me", "my", "myself", "we", "our", "ours", "ourselves", "you", "your", "yours", "yourself", "yourselves", "he", "him", "his", "himself", "she", "her", "hers", "herself", "it", "its", "itself", "they", "them", "their", "theirs", "themselves", "what", "which", "who", "whom", "this", "that", "these", "those", "am", "is", "are", "was", "were", "be", "been", "being", "have", "has", "had", "having", "do", "does", "did", "doing", "a", "an", "the", "and", "but", "if", "or", "because", "as", "until", "while", "of", "at", "by", "for", "with", "about", "against", "between", "into", "through", "during", "before", "after", "above", "below", "to", "from", "up", "down", "in", "out", "on", "off", "over", "under", "again", "further", "then", "once", "here", "there", "when", "where", "why", "how", "all", "any", "both", "each", "few", "more", "most", "other", "some", "such", "no", "nor", "not", "only", "own", "same", "so", "than", "too", "very", "s", "t", "can", "will", "just", "don", "should", "now"] (NLTK Project 2023).
9 When cutting and pasting from a word processor into Python or sending plain text files from one operating system to another, the computer typically converts the format of the text into ASCII (American Standard Code for Information

Interchange), a standardized format for representing characters across computing systems. This can result in messy data where accents are represented as numerical codes.

Further reading

Montfort, Nick. 2021. *Exploratory Programming for the Arts and Humanities*. Cambridge: The MIT Press.
Programming Historian. July 12, 2024. https://programminghistorian.org/.
Rockwell, Geoffrey, and Stéfan Sinclair. 2016. *Hermeneutica: Computer-Assisted Interpretation in the Humanities*. Cambridge: The MIT Press. https://doi.org/10.7551/mitpress/9780262034357.001.0001.
Walsh, Melaine. 2021. *Introduction to Cultural Analytics & Python*. Version 1. https://doi.org/10.5281/zenodo.4411250.

Works cited

cc:DH/HN. n.d. *The Canadian Certificate in Digital Humanities / Certificat canadien en Humanités Numériques*. Accessed July 12, 2024. https://ccdhhn.ca/.
Child, Dave. n.d. "Regular Expression Cheat Sheet." *Cheatography*. Accessed July 28, 2024. https://cheatography.com/davechild/cheat-sheets/regular-expressions/.
Google. n.d. *Google Colab*. Accessed September 8, 2024. https://colab.research.google.com/.
Hockey, Susan. 1980. *A Guide to Computer Applications in the Humanities*. Baltimore: Johns Hopkins University Press.
Jupyter. 2024. *Jupyter Notebook*. https://jupyter.org/.
Linked Editing Academic Framework. n.d. *LEAF-Writer*. Accessed September 8, 2024. https://leaf-writer.leaf-vre.org.
Medovarski, Andrea. 2014. "Roughing It in Bermuda: Mary Prince, Susanna Strickland Moodie, Dionne Brand, and the Black Diaspora." Special issue, Tracking CanLit, *Canadian Literature* 220: 94–114. https://doi.org/10.14288/cl.v0i220.192606.
Montfort, Nick. 2021. *Exploratory Programming for the Arts and Humanities*. Cambridge: The MIT Press.
NLTK Project. 2023. *Natural Language Toolkit*. Version 3.8.1, January 2, 2023. https://www.nltk.org/.
Nowviskie, Bethanie. 2014. "On the Origin of 'Hack' and 'Yack'." *Bethanie Nowviskie* (blog), January 8, 2014. https://nowviskie.org/2014/on-the-origin-of-hack-and-yack/.
OpenRefine. 2024. https://openrefine.org/.
Programming Historian. July 12, 2024. https://programminghistorian.org/.
Rockwell, Geoffrey, and Stéfan Sinclair. 2016. *Hermeneutica: Computer-Assisted Interpretation in the Humanities*. Cambridge: The MIT Press. https://doi.org/10.7551/mitpress/9780262034357.001.0001.
Spyral. 2024. *Spyral Notebook*. https://voyant-tools.org/spyral.
Voyant. 2024. *Voyant Tools*. Version 2.6.14. https://voyant-tools.org/.
Walsh, Melaine. 2021. *Introduction to Cultural Analytics & Python*. Version 1. https://doi.org/10.5281/zenodo.4411250.

15
MARY PRINCE AND SUSANNA MOODIE, A CASE STUDY

* * *

In what follows, we bring together ideas from previous sections to describe a (theoretical) Canadian literature digital humanities research project. Our description is not the only way to go about the project, but rather we present it as an example of how you might begin. There are lots of excellent how-to guides for those finding their footing in the field, many of which contain sample projects; we have suggested some in the further reading at the end of this section.

Starting points

At the start of a DH project, two early challenges are (1) creating your research questions, and (2) selecting your digital tools and approaches. In broad terms, these steps constitute the beginning of articulating your methodology. How do we combine our interest in literature with the available DH tools? Some researchers use digital tools to generate a hypothesis: they use a tool like *Voyant* to explore a corpus—to look for patterns or significant features that, in turn, prompt new questions and further explorations. Other researchers start with a research question, and they seek out suitable digital tools and methods to help them find the answer. In many respects, these approaches are not that different from traditional forms of humanities research, where researchers read a collection of texts, note patterns, generate questions and, eventually, devise some kind of thesis about the texts.

DOI: 10.4324/9781003318323-21

A difference between digital and traditional humanities emerges, however, in the challenges and opportunities of using digital tools to interpret cultural objects. As we have discussed, acquiring, digitizing, and curating cultural objects are non-trivial tasks. Because we see the relationship between corpus and research questions as dialogical, we draw on Tanya Clement's (2013) notion of differential reading to guide the project we imagine here. In other words, instead of pitting close and distant reading against one another (either reading strictly in a traditional sense or reading exclusively with digital tools), and instead of putting questions before tools or tools before questions, we move between the two: reading the texts closely *and* using digital tools to identify meaningful textual patterns. Combined, we generate a more complex understanding of the texts. Our chosen approach involves (1) looking through the corpus with our exploratory research questions in mind, (2) using digital tools to hone our research questions, and then (3) returning to the texts armed with our newly refined questions. This is an iterative process as we move between close and distant reading methods to refine our understanding of the texts.

In addition to devising research questions and selecting tools, from the start it is also worth considering the final form the published results will take. Is ours an article intended for a humanities audience? Will it be a presentation at a DH conference, part of a book, a website, or something else? Will our published results include code and other technical material and, if so, how will these materials be contextualized so a non-specialist audience can access, read, and reuse them? To what degree will our project include technical explanation and demonstrate reproducible results? Is there data that needs to be managed, stored, and shared? These are important questions to consider at the outset, but ones we will not answer here; our sample project is purely imaginary. For more on how to manage the data generated by a project, see Chapter 13.

Mary Prince and Susanna Moodie

The project we imagine here is motivated by Canadian literary and critical race studies scholar Andrea Medovarski's (2014) provocation that scholarship has yet to properly grasp the significance of Mary Prince's *The History of Mary Prince* (1831). As described in our preliminary discussion of this project in the previous chapter, Mary Prince was born into slavery in Bermuda in 1788; in 1828, after nearly forty years of slavery, Prince accompanied John Adams Wood, her fourth owner, to England. Prince knew that upon arriving in England she would be declared temporarily free, but that her status as a slave would be reinstated were she to return to the Caribbean. After some time, Prince left Wood and sought shelter with the

Moravian church and, eventually, the Anti-Slavery Society. While in England, Prince met John Pringle, a well-known abolitionist, and his protégé, Susanna Strickland (soon to be Susanna Moodie). Pringle was eager to publish Prince's life story as part of his abolitionist efforts, and Strickland agreed to serve as Prince's amanuensis. The recorded story was eventually published as *The History of Mary Prince* and its account of plantation slavery was integral to the abolitionist cause in Britain.

The relationship between Moodie and Prince is complex and merits a lengthy study in its own right—a project that is beyond the scope of what we can achieve here. Moodie was instrumental in shaping Prince's narrative to serve the pedagogical and propagandistic goals of the Anti-Slavery Society. This shaping required speaking for Prince, silencing parts of her story and reframing others such that her character aligned with Victorian ideals of womanhood and ensuring that her life served as a clear example for her readers. Thus, *The History of Mary Prince* is an ambivalent and complex text: it is an account of Prince's life and her struggle for freedom, yet it has also been shaped by a team of white editors to exclude any dimensions of Prince's experiences, desires, and hopes that are beyond the requirements of the abolitionist cause. The text critiques the institution of slavery without also critiquing British imperialism as a key reason for slavery's existence and, in doing so, ensures that it does not demand too much of white readers.

The complexity of *The History of Mary Prince* leads Gillian Whitlock to argue that there are at least "two oppositional agendas at work" in Prince's story:

> The first is the most obvious: the editor, Pringle, who wishes to put before the public a slave narrative which will have the marks of authenticity, but not the signs of what would be construed as depravity. The second is the concern of the narrator, Mary Prince, who desires that the good people of England might hear from a slave what a slave had felt and suffered.
>
> *(2000, 19)*

Yet, as Jenny Sharpe argues, "Slave tactics" for self-expression, agency, and power outside of Victorian feminine ideals, "are difficult to detect in the slave narrative, not only because they lack a language of their own, but also because they are overwritten by the moral discourse of the antislavery movement" (1996, 46).

The History of Mary Prince is also an important text for Canadian literature because of Susanna Moodie's role as Prince's amanuensis—and therefore her central role in shaping a Black woman's life story to suit white, European readership. The *History* was one of Moodie's earliest literary efforts, predating *Roughing It in the Bush* (1852) by just over twenty years. Yet, the relationship between Moodie's work on Prince's narrative and her later writing has yet to be properly explored. Notwithstanding a lack of study in this area, it seems plausible that Moodie's interest in ideas of freedom, female agency, empire, and race—all of which are threaded throughout her writing—may have been informed by her experience with Prince. *Roughing It in the Bush* begins, for example, with the verse,

> Canada, the blest—the free!
> With prophetic glance, I see
> Visions of thy future glory,
> Giving to the world's great story [...]
>
> Like one awaken'd from the dead,
> The peasant lifts his drooping head,
> No more oppress'd, no more a slave,
> Here freedom dwells beyond the wave.
> (1852)

Our research question, then, could be, to what extent are Moodie's immediate concern with freedom, the "opress'd," and being "no more a slave" shaped by her experience with Prince's account of slavery? Are her opening lines an example of Moodie finding common ground between the British poor and enslaved Black people, or is she appropriating Prince's experience to describe her own experience of migration? Medovarski asks,

> What happens if, instead of seeing Moodie's *Roughing It in the Bush* (1852) as one of the significant starting points for Canadian literature, we instead trace the literary tradition back to *The History of Mary Prince*? What does it mean for Moodie, and for subsequent Canadian writers, to write in the wake of a slave narrative?
> *(2014, 95)*

Medovarski's questions are important not just to the study of Moodie's writing but also for a deeper understanding of how Canadian literature—even in its earliest manifestations—is already informed by race, slavery, and empire. Questions about Canadian literature's colonial origins and ongoing legacy are central to the study of CanLit today.

For our project, we hone Medovarski's questions to focus on how digital methods of textual analysis can identify linguistic features shared by Prince's narrative and Moodie's subsequent works. For example, are there particular words or phrases that appear in both texts that might indicate Moodie's hand in shaping Prince's narrative? Can we use digital tools to argue for the import of Prince's narrative to Moodie's subsequent works and, in doing so, locate Prince's narrative as an important text to early Canadian literature? Such an analysis would "unsettle" (Medovarski 2014, 104) our understanding of early Canadian literature by stressing the import of Blackness, transnational movement, concerns with liberal individual notions of freedom, and early notions of what Daniel Coleman calls "white civility" (2008).

Data acquisition

Now that we have a collection of research questions informed by historical context and theoretical framings, we can begin to collect the relevant data. Both *The History of Mary Prince* and Moodie's works are available from gutenberg.org in a variety of formats (e.g., PDF, EPUB, and ZIP). Plain Text UTF-8 is the best choice for our textual analysis, as it provides us with just the text—no unnecessary formatting. Prince's text appears in Figure 15.1.

Saving the *Gutenberg* page in our web browser will save a local copy of the text file to our computer, which we can then edit. Each text includes header information describing the *Gutenberg* site, which we need to remove from our files so that we do not include it in our analysis; we also need to remove the metadata that appears at the end of all *Gutenberg* documents. To remove the unwanted data, we can use any of the data curation methods described in Chapter 11. The easiest method is to open the file in a text editor (the default editors are *Notepad* on Windows and *TextEdit* on a Mac), highlight the parts we want to remove, delete them, and resave the file. At this stage, we might choose to save the file with a new file name, so that we can keep separate the version that we have edited from the original version from *Gutenberg*.

Before proceeding with any analysis, we should check the file to confirm that it has the correct text and no additional, unwanted materials. A quick scan of the Prince text file reveals a great deal of supplementary information, including commentary from Pringle, letters from Prince's supporters, twenty-eight footnotes that provide context and frame Prince's narrative, and an additional, supplementary text—"The Narrative of Asa-Asa: A Captured African." We would have to decide whether to keep this material. Since we are looking for overlap between Prince's writing and Moodie's, we would probably remove some of this material. Finding a similar phrase in Moodie's writing and the letters from Prince's supporters would likely be happenstance (although an alternative, which is discovering that

Mary Prince and Susanna Moodie, a case study   **277**

```
The Project Gutenberg eBook of The History of Mary Prince, a West Indian Slave

This ebook is for the use of anyone anywhere in the United States and
most other parts of the world at no cost and with almost no restrictions
whatsoever. You may copy it, give it away or re-use it under the terms
of the Project Gutenberg License included with this ebook or online
at www.gutenberg.org. If you are not located in the United States,
you will have to check the laws of the country where you are located
before using this eBook.

Title: The History of Mary Prince, a West Indian Slave

Author: Mary Prince

Release date: February 24, 2006 [eBook #17851]

Language: English

Credits: Produced by Suzanne Shell, Sankar Viswanathan, and the
         Online Distributed Proofreading Team at http://www.pgdp.net


*** START OF THE PROJECT GUTENBERG EBOOK THE HISTORY OF MARY PRINCE, A WEST INDIAN SLAVE ***



Produced by Suzanne Shell, Sankar Viswanathan, and the
Online Distributed Proofreading Team at http://www.pgdp.net




                            THE
                    HISTORY OF MARY PRINCE,
                     A WEST INDIAN SLAVE.

                      RELATED BY HERSELF.

                WITH A SUPPLEMENT BY THE EDITOR.


                      To which is added,

                   THE NARRATIVE OF ASA-ASA,

                     A CAPTURED AFRICAN.
```

FIGURE 15.1   Plain text of *The History of Mary Prince*.

Moodie was influenced by or even might have written those too, would be revelatory).

Not all of these decisions are straightforward. In particular, the footnotes pose a challenge, as they are directly related to Prince's narrative and help readers understand the text and its constitution, while remaining apart from the narrative proper. Footnote three, for example, states that Mary's "strong expressions, and all of a similar character in this little narrative, are given verbatim as uttered by Mary Prince," and footnote sixteen explains "The whole of this paragraph especially, is given as nearly as was possible in Mary's precise words" (Prince 1831). The presence of these footnotes—and the curious phrase "as nearly as was possible"—implies that the rest of the text is *not* given verbatim, and that Prince's words have been altered during transcription and editing. Without delving into a lengthy discussion of paratextuality (although we hope this chapter inspires such discussions), it seems clear to us that the footnotes are significant components of the text (if not Prince's narrative), in that they help readers understand the text more completely. For the purposes of our analysis, however, we remove them as part of the supplementary materials, but we could justifiably also include them. This reshaping of the data of Prince's narrative is a good reminder of Johanna Drucker's distinction between data and capta (see Chapter 7), particularly as humanities research transforms data through the questions researchers ask.

Once we have downloaded and curated *The History of Mary Prince*, we need to repeat the process with Susanna Moodie's writing. For the purposes of this analysis, we have decided to save all Moodie's fifteen available works. Note that this does not include all her publications, just the ones on gutenberg.org; a more developed project would need to find and digitize the missing material.

We now have Prince's text and all fifteen files from Moodie's archive. Because we are working with multiple files, we would create a directory (or folder) on our computer just for these files; we would use this directory to store all the input files, our code, and our outputs. Having one place to save everything—plus a set of conventions for naming and versioning our files—will make our project far more manageable. It will ensure that our project files are not mixed up with each other or with other files, and it will also make it easier to back up, archive, and share our work.

Analyzing the texts using Voyant

Our next step is a preliminary analysis. For our project, we have chosen to start by identifying key terms in Prince's writing, which we can then use for our analysis of Moodie's text. This sort of task is well suited to *Voyant Tools*, which can easily identify textual features and even be used to create a list of stop words. Following the instructions from *Voyant*'s user documentation, we have loaded Prince's text to generate an analysis with *Voyant*'s pre-set five analysis panes (see Figure 15.2).

The most frequent words in the text according to *Voyant* are:

master (62); work (51); mr (51); mistress (51); slaves (49); said (48); went (47); mrs (45); time (43); house (42); poor (39); came (38); slave (37); great (33); wood (31); mother (31); come (30); till (28); got (28); day (27); people (26); little (26); good (26); away (26); woman (25); told (25); free (25); ill (24); home (24); heart (24); thought (23); night (23); england

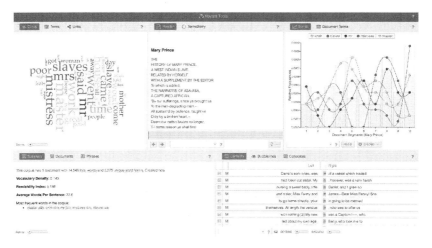

FIGURE 15.2 *Voyant* analysis of *The History of Mary Prince*.

(23); water (22); salt (21); took (20); think (20); long (20); like (20); heard (20); wash (19); used (19); say (19); quite (19); oh (19); hard (19); called (19); saw (18); old (18); miss (18).

From this list, terms such as *master*, *work*, and *slaves* jump out at us as relevant to Prince's narrative. Others appear to tell us something about Prince's daily life (*wash*, *water*, *wood*). Others still are from the pleas to consider the experiences of enslaved people (*heart*, *hard*). The prevalence of *time*, which appears forty-three times, is suggestive of the temporality of the text, of a longing for the time when slavery will be abolished, and of the routinized daily life of enslaved people. In contrast to the terms that seem particularly meaningful, terms such as *mr*, *mrs*, *mistress*, and *came* strike us as less particularly relevant to Prince's work (due to their general frequency of use across all texts, especially during the period in which it was written). If we were creating a list of stop words, we would consider removing these from our analysis.

In addition to using *Voyant* to generate a list of frequent words, we can also use its *trends* pane to isolate individual words and track their use across the text. Consider, for example, the word *free* (see Figure 15.3).

The increasing frequency of *free* is in line with the typical structure of slavery narratives, which move from slavery to freedom, not just because this is a logical structure for a linear narrative, but also because it serves the texts' pedagogical and propagandistic goals. As Sharpe explains, "*The History of Mary Prince* moves from ignorance to enlightenment and from slavery to freedom" (1996, 32); the steep increase in the use of the term

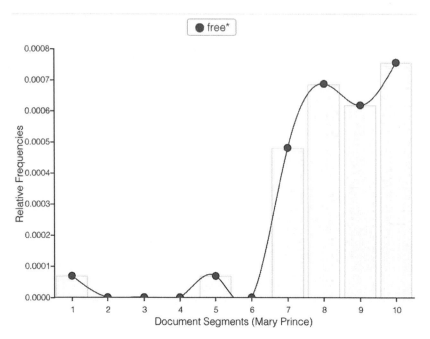

FIGURE 15.3 *Voyant* trends analysis of the word *free* in *The History of Mary Prince*.

free in the latter third of the text indicates Mary Prince's narrative conforms to these generic standards.

Alongside an analysis of Prince's text, we could do the same with Moodie's writing (see Figure 15.4), although we would have to be mindful of the fact that we were looking at an assemblage of her works, rather than a single, focused narrative. If we were so inclined, we could also look at each text individually, or we could choose a single text—say, *Roughing It in the Bush*—for a side-by-side comparison.

Some of the most frequent words in the Moodie corpus are:

said (2495); old (2022); man (1781); like (1525); good (1457); little (1322); heart (1305); mrs (1282); great (1190); long (1139); young (1131); mr (1108); poor (1033); Dorothy (983); house (962); love (956); life (956); mother (951); eyes (931); father (912); night (888); face (862); dear (838); thought (836); make (805); home (804); hand (794); woman (754); know (740); child (746); god (740); shall (736); mind (727).

Even though this list of words is less useful because it comes from many different texts, it still hints at some themes. Patterns such as the use of *heart* and *love* and the mention of family (*mother, father, child*) could be

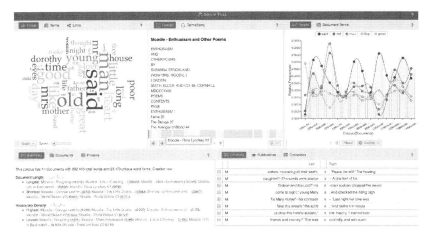

FIGURE 15.4   *Voyant* analysis of Susanna Moodie texts available on gutenberg.org.

the basis for a thematic analysis. More immediately, we can also put this list to use in combination with the list generated for Prince by assembling a list of stop words, which we can use to further refine and analyze our data using code.

Analyzing the texts using Python

Assessing our corpus at a high level using *Voyant* provides us with a general sense of what appears in the texts. From here, we are ready to analyze them in more detail. Using Python, we can create new corpuses for Prince's and Moodie's works from *Gutenberg*, remove headers and other irrelevant materials, and remove stop words based on both the *Natural Language Toolkit* standard list of stop words and the custom list of stop words that we prepared based on the most-frequent words we generated using *Voyant*. Iterating between the text, a high-level analysis via *Voyant*, and a closer analysis in Python enables us to engage in differential reading of the texts. We can then tokenize the corpuses to make the text machine-readable, and then we can lemmatize them, so that variations on the same word are treated as the same (e.g., *work*, *working*, *worked*, and *worker* will all be grouped as *work*). We can then create a list of the most common words in each of the two texts, compare these lists to find the most commonly used shared words, and also produce a list of shared tri-grams (three-word phrases).

```
# Import the relevant libraries
# re: regular expressions; nltk: natural language toolkit;
# Gutenberg
```

```
import re
import nltk
from gutenberg.acquire import load_etext
from gutenberg.cleanup import strip_headers
from nltk.corpus import stopwords
from nltk.tokenize import word_tokenize
from nltk.util import ngrams
from nltk import PorterStemmer
from nltk.stem import WordNetLemmatizer

# Load Mary Prince's text from Gutenberg. The strip_
# headers function removes the headers.
prince_text = strip_headers(load_etext(17851)).strip()

# Load Moodie texts from Gutenberg
moodie_roughing = strip_headers(load_etext(4389)).strip()
moodie_flora = strip_headers(load_etext(27373)).strip()
moodie_clearings = strip_headers(load_etext(8132)).strip()
moodie_backwoods = strip_headers(load_etext(8393)).strip()
moodie_brothers = strip_headers(load_etext(16836)).strip()
moodie_leatrim = strip_headers(load_etext(6454)).strip()

# Combine all of the Moodie texts into one large string
moodie_texts = moodie_roughing + moodie_flora + moodie_
clearings + moodie_backwoods + moodie_brothers +
moodie_leatrim

# Convert the text to lowercase
moodie_texts = moodie_texts.lower()

#Substitute non-alphanumeric characters
moodie_texts = re.sub(r'\W+',' ', moodie_texts)

#Remove numbers from the string
moodie_texts = re.sub(r'\d+',' ', moodie_texts)

# Remove remaining non-alphanumeric characters
moodie_texts = re.sub(r'[^a-zA-Z0-9]+', ' ', moodie_texts)

# Repeat the same pre-processing for the Prince text
prince_text = prince_text.lower()
prince_text = re.sub(r'\W+',' ', prince_text)
prince_text = re.sub(r'\d+',' ', prince_text)
prince_text = re.sub(r'[^a-zA-Z0-9]+', ' ', prince_text)

# Store the generic list of nltk's stop words in stop_words
stop_words = stopwords.words('english')
```

```python
# Add our own list of stop words
stop_words.extend(["the", "of", "and", "a", "to", "in",
"dr", "add", "cause", "james", "george", "mary", "i",
"that", "his", "wa", "it", "he", "said", "mr", "u"])

# Tokenize both the Prince and Moodie texts
prince_words = word_tokenize(prince_text)
moodie_words = word_tokenize(moodie_texts)

# Create two empty lists where we will store the list of
# tokens after the texts have been cleaned
prince_cleaned = []
moodie_cleaned = []

# Initialize the nltk lemmatizing function
lemmatizer = WordNetLemmatizer()

# You may need to uncomment the next line to run the code
# nltk.download('wordnet')

# Loop through every word in prince_words
for word in prince_words:
    # If that word is not in stop_words
    if word not in stop_words:
        # Append the lemmatized word
        prince_cleaned.append(lemmatizer.lemmatize(word))

# Repeat the process for moodie_words
for word in moodie_words:
    if word not in stop_words:
        moodie_cleaned.append(lemmatizer.lemmatize(word))

# Use the ngrams function to create a list of all of the
# tri-grams in Moodie's and Prince's texts
moodie_ngram = list(ngrams(moodie_cleaned, 3))
prince_ngram = list(ngrams(prince_cleaned, 3))

# Create an empty list to store the shared trigrams
shared_trigrams = []

# This is a Python concept called a list comprehension.
# It effectively says "for every tri-gram in prince_ngram if that
# tri-gram is also in Moodie_ngram, add it to the shared_
# trigram list"
shared_trigrams = [ngram for ngram in prince_ngram if ngram in moodie_ngram]
```

```python
# Print the number of shared tri-grams and the tri-grams
print(f"Number of shared trigrams: {len(shared_trigrams)}")
print(shared_trigrams)

# Use the frequency distribution to create a list of the
# most common words in both Moodie and Prince
moodie_most_common_words = nltk.FreqDist(moodie_cleaned)
prince_most_common_words = nltk.FreqDist(prince_cleaned)

# Get the most common 2500 words in Moodie and most common
# 500 words in Prince
# We have included a larger selection of Moodie's most
# common words because her corpus is much larger
moodie_top2500 = moodie_most_common_words.most_common(2500)
prince_top500 = prince_most_common_words.most_common(500)

# Note that moodie_top2500 & prince_top500 are "tuples"
# Each element contains the word itself and the number of
# times it appears in the corpus
# We are only interested in the words so we will use the
# following few lines to make lists of just the words

# Create two empty lists that store just the most-
# frequently occurring words
moodie_top2500_justwords = []
prince_top500_justwords = []

# Get the words from the tuples
for M_word in moodie_top2500:
    moodie_top2500_justwords.append(M_word[0])

for P_word in prince_top500:
    prince_top500_justwords.append(P_word[0])

# Create an empty list that will store the shared top words
shared_top_words = []
# For every word in the list of Moodie's top 2500 words
for moodie_word in moodie_top2500_justwords:
    # If that word is also in Prince's top 500 words
    if moodie_word in prince_top500_justwords:
        # Append it to the shared_top_words list
        shared_top_words.append(moodie_word)

# Print the list of the shared_top_words
print(shared_top_words)
```

This code provides us with a list of the most frequent words across the corpus, which includes:

['upon', 'would', 'one', 'could', 'old', 'man', 'never', 'u', 'day', 'like', 'child', 'good', 'little', 'great', 'time', 'heart', 'long', 'hand', 'house', 'eye', 'well', 'young', 'father', 'poor', 'thought', 'much', 'life', 'mr', 'woman', 'year', 'made', 'night', 'make', 'many', 'without', 'friend', 'home', 'must', 'first', 'see', 'country', 'may', 'girl', 'ever', 'place', 'every', 'water', 'dear', 'way', 'face', 'large', 'd', 'mind', 'take', 'last', 'husband', 'know', 'two', 'head', 'god', 'still', 'come', 'give', 'found', 'oh', 'son', 'came', 'left', 'wood', 'shall', 'think', 'look', 'boy', 'mother', 'back', 'thing', 'go', 'wife', 'brother', 'men', 'people', 'might', 'o', 'better', 'lady', 'away', 'person', 'say', 'word', 'door', 'small', 'hope', 'want', 'felt', 'tell', 'family', 'work', 'bed', 'part', 'gave', 'mean', 'took', 'fire', 'manner', 'light', 'captain', 'though', 'get', 'death', 'new', 'often', 'went', 'money', 'yet', 'another', 'always', 'soon', 'told', 'let', 'best', 'brought', 'spirit', 'put', 'saw', 'foot', 'among', 'far', 'indian', 'black', 'returned', 'called', 'morning', 'heard', 'miss', 'feel', 'whole', 'whose', 'cried', 'even', 'rest', 'name', 'shore', 'enough', 'leave', 'feeling', 'town', 'state', 'care', 'bad', 'several', 'find', 'creature', 'fellow', 'round', 'right', 'nothing', 'white', 'got', 'm', 'present', 'hard', 'bear', 'seen', 'wish', 'ill', 'knew', 'three', 'arm', 'return', 'kind', 'keep', 'least', 'done', 'near', 'next', 'almost', 'quite', 'full', 'happy', 'order', 'john', 'servant', 'master', 'age', 'circumstance', 'true', 'common', 'scarcely', 'help', 'le', 'going', 'week', 'received', 'sir', 'object', 'character', 'however', 'power', 'truth', 'subject', 'stood', 'believe', 'became', 'hear', 'since', 'asked', 'horse', 'together', 'sent', 'loved', 'hill', 'sea', 'followed', 'longer', 'towards', 'used', 'daughter', 'month', 'lay', 'human', 'open', 'given', 'strong', 'within', 'call', 'c', 'fell', 'letter', 'sleep', 'speak', 'grief', 'sorrow', 'situation', 'end', 'sister', 'length', 'four', 'free', 'broken', 'ran', 'society', 'live', 'taken', 'case', 'kept', 'account', 'bring', 'dreadful', 'short', 'sad', 'perhaps', 'living', 'led', 'cry', 'service', 'answer', 'english', 'indeed', 'vessel', 'run', 'effect', 'read', 'natural', 'till', 'heavy', 'business', 'church', 'known', 'late', 'conduct', 'died', 'colony', 'turn', 'public', 'food', 'fact', 'really', 'gone', 'doubt', 'thus', 'sweet', 'island', 'twenty', 'worse', 'board', 'cow', 'sick', 'hot', 'england', 'point', 'period', 'body', 'school', 'wished', 'six', 'view', 'nearly', 'clothes', 'reason', 'regard', 'stand', 'deal', 'lived', 'stay', 'fast', 'mistress', 'wanted', 'severe', 'passion', 'obliged', 'kindness', 'sum', 'term', 'five', 'reader', 'carried', 'law', 'clock', 'passage', 'suffering', 'following', 'street', 'comfortable', 'degree', 'paper', 'cattle', 'moral', 'story', 'ship', 'suffered', 'consider', 'pain', 'besides', 'prayer', 'send', 'nurse', 'former', 'offered', 'seems', 'please', 'different', 'whilst', 'forgive', 'cruel', 'usual', 'charge', 'note', 'domestic', 'sorry', 'whether', 'forward', 'task', 'notice', 'history', 'worst', 'carry', 'trunk', 'written', 'london', 'presented', 'opinion', 'blow', 'killed', 'female', 'easily', 'owner', 'stop', 'occasion', 'yard', 'constantly', 'remark', 'forced', 'taught', 'shame', 'consequence', 'hired', 'appear', 'ought', 'bought', 'sometimes', 'angry', 'fault', 'directly', 'value', 'fully', 'flesh', 'sold', 'page', 'treated', 'condition', 'buy', 'acquainted', 'sufficient', 'sell', 'suppose', 'allowed', 'skin', 'respectable', 'afterwards', 'treat', 'understand', 'wash', 'beat', 'also', 'slave', 'punishment', 'marriage', 'benevolent', 'refused', 'sale', 'appears', 'west', 'freedom', 'household', 'else', 'washed', 'statement', 'queen', 'serve', 'report', 'evidence', 'salt', 'limb', 'satisfaction', 'consent', 'sore', 'driven', 'worked', 'treatment', 'distressed', 'proof', 'ordered', 'induced'].

While some of these words are not immediately interesting, others offer potential inroads for analysis. For example, we could look further into depictions of race via the frequency and context of words like *slave*, *black*, and *white*. We could also explore depictions of family via words such as *father*, *mother*, *husband*, and *child*. Or, we could look at the texts shared language of domesticity and slavery via the frequency of words such as *skin*, *wash*, *beat*, *marriage*, *benevolent*, and more. Of course, identifying frequent words does not constitute an analysis on its own; rather, it serves as a starting point. With these words in hand, we are ready to move from our distant, computer-enabled reading to a closer reading of the texts themselves. To make this close reading easier, we could write some simple code to place each of the keywords in context. This, however, is beyond the scope of what we have shown in this book. If you would like to learn more about this approach, search online for Python implementations of keywords-in-context (kwic). Without writing any further code, we could also scan the material ourselves for each of our words of interest, or we could perform a CTRL+F search on our text files, or we could even use *Voyant* to find the contexts surrounding the relevant words (as shown in Figure 15.5).

A sample from *Voyant*'s keywords-in-context list for the word *slave* in Moodie's writing provides context of the use of the term:

> But, even if *slaves* had been allowed in the colony, the horror of colour is as great among the native-born Canadians as it is in the United States.
> *(Flora Lyndsay 1854)*

> to bid him stand up a free inheritor of a free soil, who so long laboured for a scanty pittance of bread, as an ignorant and degraded *slave*, in the

FIGURE 15.5 A selection of *Voyant*'s keywords-in-context for the word *slave* in the Moodie corpus.

country to which you now cling with such passionate fondness, and leave with such heart-breaking regret.

(Flora Lyndsay)

I was an irritable, volatile, spoilt child, and expected that everybody would yield to me, as readily as my *slave* attendants had done in Jamaica.

(Flora Lyndsay)

Now don't go and tell your husband that it was all my fault; if you had had a little patience, I would have come when you asked me, but I don't choose to be dictated to, and I won't be made a *slave* by you or any one else.

(Life in the Backwoods 1852)

I felt deeply my degradation—felt that I had become the *slave* to low vice; and in order to emancipate myself from the hateful tyranny of evil passions, I did a very rash and foolish thing.

(Roughing It in the Bush)

From these excerpts, we can begin to build an argument about how Prince's life and writing not only informed Moodie's view of slavery as an institution but also framed how Moodie viewed women's lives in the colonies. Indeed, further examination of these keywords in context demonstrates an uneasy truce between what Moodie identifies as the humanizing and civilizing project of empire and the abolishment of slavery. For Moodie, the institution of empire was a bulwark against what she perceives as the American institution of slavery. Contemporary readers would likely understand this to be a complete contradiction given that empire was built on the backs of enslaved people—contradictions Moodie uses literature to resolve.

Undertaking a similar analysis but for shared bi-grams (two consecutive words) in Moodie's and Prince's writing reveals that the phrase *salt water* appears in both. In her text, Mary Prince describes her memories of slavery as so harrowing that "they make the *salt water* come into my eyes;" Moodie uses the same expression throughout her oeuvre. For example, in *Matrimonial Speculations*, a captain exclaims, "A sight like that allers brings the *salt water* to my eyes," (256, emphasis added), while an enslaved Black woman named Minerva cries, "*salt water* in my heart—in my eyes" (218, emphasis added). Moodie's adaptation of the phrase "salt water to my eyes" is distinctive; a *Google Ngram* search for the same phrase in other writings produces no results. Therefore, it is likely that the phrase is either Moodie's own and one that she inserted into Prince's narrative, or it is one that she borrowed from Prince as part of her efforts to represent plantation slavery in her own work.

In this case study, we have just skimmed the surface of what is possible when we combine distant textual analysis with close reading. A list of shared tri-grams and frequent words is only the start of what is possible with tools like *Voyant* and a Python-based humanities analysis. We have shown how we might use these digital experiments to hone research questions and generate new avenues of exploration. We look forward to seeing how you take these tools and techniques in exciting new directions by applying them to texts of your own choosing and research questions of your own.

Further reading

Medovarski, Andrea. 2014. "Roughing It in Bermuda: Mary Prince, Susanna Strickland Moodie, Dionne Brand, and the Black Diaspora." Special issue, Tracking CanLit, *Canadian Literature* 220: 94–114. https://doi.org/10.14288/cl.v0i220.192606.

Walsh, Melaine. 2021. *Introduction to Cultural Analytics & Python*. Version 1. https://doi.org/10.5281/zenodo.4411250.

Works cited

Clement, Tanya. 2013. "Text Analysis, Data Mining, and Visualizations in Literary Scholarship." *Literary Studies in the Digital Age: An Evolving Anthology*. Modern Language Association. Knowledge Commons. https://doi.org/10.1632/lsda.2013.0.

Coleman, Daniel. 2008. *White Civility: The Literary Project of English Canada*. Toronto: University of Toronto Press.

Medovarski, Andrea. 2014. "Roughing It in Bermuda: Mary Prince, Susanna Strickland Moodie, Dionne Brand, and the Black Diaspora." Special issue, Tracking CanLit, *Canadian Literature* 220: 94–114. https://doi.org/10.14288/cl.v0i220.192606.

Moodie, Susanna. 1852 (2004). *Roughing It in the Bush*. Project Gutenberg. https://www.gutenberg.org/ebooks/4389.

Moodie, Susanna. 1852 (2005). *Life in the Backwoods*. Project Gutenberg. https://www.gutenberg.org/ebooks/8393.

Moodie, Susanna. 1854 (2008). *Flora Lyndsay; or, Passages in an Eventful Life*. https://www.gutenberg.org/ebooks/27373.

Moodie, Susanna. 1854. *Matrimonial Speculations*. London: Richard Bentley.

Prince, Mary. 1831 (2023). *The History of Mary Prince, a West Indian Slave, Related by Herself*. Project Gutenberg. https://www.gutenberg.org/ebooks/17851.

Sharpe, Jenny. 1996. "'Something Akin to Freedom': The Case of Mary Prince." *differences: A Journal of Feminist Cultural Studies* 8, no. 1: 31–56. https://doi.org/10.1215/10407391-8-1-31.

Whitlock, Gillian. 2000. *The Intimate Empire: Reading Women's Autobiography*. London: Bloomsbury.

PART VI

16
FUTURE THINKING

Developments and predictions for the twenty-first century

* * *

Throughout the 1970s Canadian writer Hugh MacLennan found himself overwhelmed by the radical social change that was taking place in his home of Montréal, across Canada, and across the globe. What others experienced as a necessary upheaval and transformation of a repressive social order—a call for change expressed in the demands of the civil rights movement, the women's movement, and the anti-war movement—MacLennan perceived as an erosion of social virtues and valuable traditions. He responded to this feeling of crisis by issuing a warning about the desire for unbridled social change in his final novel, *Voices in Time* (1980). The book depicts the fascists of World War II and the radicals of the Québécois separatist movement effectively as one and the same, insofar as both aimed to destroy a peaceable, liberal establishment. The narrative shifts between 1930s Europe, 1960s North America, and the 2030s, during which John Wellfleet, living in a post-apocalyptic Québec governed by an authoritarian bureaucracy and overseen by vast networks of computers, warns his contemporaries about the mistakes of the past. MacLennan intended his novel as a parable to teach young Canadians about the threats of radical change and the virtues of liberalism. However, it serves more effectively as a parable for the dangers of predicting the future, of misreading the changes of the present as crises, and of projecting contemporary worries in their worst forms onto some vision of the future. While (at our time of writing) it isn't quite 2030 yet, MacLennan's vision of a dystopian digital world has yet to materialize.

DOI: 10.4324/9781003318323-23

Predicting the future of DH research and teaching is, similarly, something of a fool's errand. This is particularly true given the shifting technologies and changing critical preoccupations that have transformed and will continue to transform DH in unpredictable ways. As Willard McCarty says, "predicting the future by projecting it from current technical know-how misleads: it ignores the multiple contingencies of history and human nature and so cannot prepare us to become knowing actors in making the future" (2013, 41). Instead, McCarty suggests that the best way to be ready for what comes next is to think critically about the past: "the history of the digital humanities … is essential to that preparation" (41). McCarty is certainly right that attempting to predict the future in a technologically deterministic way will miss the mark by a great deal, as we've shown throughout with asides from scholars and DH practitioners who have tried to anticipate the impact of then-new technologies. However, predictions have not been wholly wrong. For example, Frye's suggestion that "the most mind-numbing of humanist activities, the marking of undergraduate essays, would disappear as the essays were fed into a machine" equipped with "a complete file of the essays written in the fraud factories, and when it received one would start bellowing the name of the student who had bought it over a public address system" has proven partly true in the form of surveillance systems such as *Turnitin* and the use of AI to generate feedback on student work (Frye 1989, 458). As of January 2023, the University of Toronto has, chillingly, "several licensed software tools available for facilitating grading, such as SpeedGrader and Crowdmark … [for] supporting the grading process" (Office of the Vice-Provost 2024). One wonders about the forms of so-called support on offer and the paucity of a vision of education present in such pronouncements. Although McCarty's own prediction—that email "carefully managed, may be just what is needed to foster widespread humanistic discussion and collaboration in a world largely indifferent to its goals" (McCarty 1991, 206)—has not come to fruition, we cannot help but wonder whether the failure is due to the lack of *careful management* rather than the technology itself, as exemplified by the collapse of Twitter.

Where McCarty is indisputably right is in his suggestion that reflecting on new technological developments in relation to preceding history enables us to identify some of the concerns that will likely animate future DH teaching and research. The connection between what has come before and what has yet to come seems likely, given the patterns we've identified throughout this volume. Lynn Coady's monster at the end of the book could equally be reading, the Internet, AI, or something yet to be imagined. The earliest DH projects we discuss are the concordances created by Sandra Djwa, Robert Jay Glickman and Gerrit Joseph Staalman, and Father

Busa (see Chapter 3); the most recent technical applications we describe are topic modeling and the uses of linked open data—both of which provide computationally facilitated methods of identifying themes. *Plus ça change.*

Returning to DH's history may yet be a dimension of future DH work, particularly in Canada. While this book has only touched on the complexity of the history of the digital humanities in Canada, we are struck by the need for a more complete study of the history of DH scholarship and teaching here and elsewhere (although, as Frye might prompt us to ask, "Where is here?"). We have noted how many of the projects that comprise this history—projects to which researchers have dedicated significant portions of their scholarly lives—survive only as brief mentions in published materials. The history of DH in Canada exists only in fragments and, unsurprisingly, what has lasted are primarily large projects and traditional forms of publication: monographs, articles, and conference proceedings. Books such as Baron Brainerd's *Weighing Evidence in Language and Literature* (1974) and Susan Hockey's *A Guide to Computer Applications in the Humanities* (1980) are available both at libraries and online, whereas early digital projects such as *SwiftCurrent*, *The Hypertext Pratt*, and the *Canadian Poetry Collection* are no longer available in any form. When the University of Toronto's Centre for Computing in the Humanities was abruptly shuttered in the early 1990s, many of its files, a rich repository of humanities computing in Canada, were simply placed in the hallway to be disposed of.

Alongside this outright loss, there are many projects that are on the cusp of obsolescence: for example, the once vibrant but now languishing *L'infocentre littéraire des écrivains québécois*. The digital records of a great deal of DH history, code, concordances, servers, websites, archives, electronic messages, and more, have also been lost. Research projects such as our own *Canadians Read*, which is built on publicly available social media data, are increasingly rare as private interests make data access more difficult. This is a more recent phenomenon than one might imagine: even some of the DH work from the early 2000s now survives only in memory. How might historically minded Canadianists begin to reassemble some of this lost history?

Canadian DH scholars have identified this growing lacuna in our history and have developed new formats for designing projects for longevity and archiving digital projects. *Archives Unleashed* worked to make "petabytes of historical internet content accessible to scholars and others interested in researching the recent past" and has supported efforts to preserve and study recent online publications (2023). *The Endings Project* has been designed with this form of historicizing in mind: it promotes methods for DH projects looking to ensure their longevity. It poses the questions of "How ... should DH projects conclude?" "How should we preserve projects to retain their dynamic features?" "Where should projects be archived?" and it provides frameworks for researchers to address those questions in their own work (2024). *SpokenWeb*'s *Archive of the Digital Present* captures the network's ongoing work as a way of recognizing that

> Technology and mediation are instantiating factors of literary historical records and they impact how we understand ... an ever-expanding entity. That entity is a living archive that we are shaping through our archival practices ... and acting (and recording) in the present.
> *(SpokenWeb 2022)*

These projects are part of a wider effort to theorize and support the long-term preservation of digital cultural and historical artifacts, among them the work of the Digital Preservation Coalition, Open Preservation Foundation, and the European Archival Records and Knowledge Preservation Project. There are also individual projects that have sprung up in response to immediate needs. For example, *Saving Ukrainian Cultural Heritage Online* engages in "data-sitting" Ukrainian cultural heritage data until the country can rebuild. Meanwhile, open access and data management have taken on increasing importance with funders such as the Social Sciences and Humanities Research Council of Canada (SSHRC) (see Chapter 12).

Yet historicizing tends to further empower researchers who are already connected with the larger DH community, and futureproofing is easiest accomplished by those who have the time, funding, and support to do so. Indeed, it is primarily researchers who regularly attend conferences and symposia, who are invited to participate in multi-institutional research projects, and who find themselves at the centre of the Canadian DH community whose work has, up to now, been preserved. Those who are less established—and those in other fields who are doing DH work in everything but name (such as the Black and minority race scholars discussed in Chapter 9)—are more likely to miss out on the methodological discussions, training, and resources required to preserve their work. Going forward, we must ensure that the broadest possible range of DH researchers and projects are included in the historical archive.

This is not merely a matter of cultural capital or positioning but also one of precarity and labour. Tenured faculty members have the resources that their limited-term, tenuously employed, and alt-ac colleagues do not. As Jim McGrath notes, "The conditions of labor in higher education make it challenging for many digital humanists to take up project work if they reside outside of tenure-track and tenured hiring lines" (2021). McGrath, Christina Boyles, Anne Cong-Huyen, Carrie Johnston, and Amanda Phillips write that the value of adjuncts' digital humanities "labor has been challenged, taken for granted, dismissed outright, or explained away as at best a fad or at worst the manifestation of neoliberalism in its most craven form within the humanities" (2018, 693). As they note, while DH has opened additional full-time employment opportunities to some humanities scholars, the field continues to rely on a large body of precariously employed staff to support tenured faculty's research. This is a significant—and often-noted—equity concern in contemporary DH work, and it will only become more pronounced if we do not make changes now. To address these problems, we need to do more than just developing frameworks that call for support. UCLA Humanities Technology's "A Student Collaborators' Bill of Rights" (Di Pressi et al. 2015), the Postdoctoral Laborers Group's "Postdoctoral Laborers Bill of Rights" (Alpert-Abrams et al. 2019), and Media Commons Press's "Collaborators' Bill of Rights" (2011) are good places to start, but words must be backed up by action—and by resources.

These equity concerns are not new. Rather, as we have shown, they have been at the heart of DH since the earliest days, even if they have come into sharp relief in recent years. DH scholars have long worried about recognition of their work, about the field's position in relation to the broader humanities, about the stability of labs and programs, and of course about the meaning of the digital humanities. However, these questions are now inflected by broader concerns about labour, power, alterity, and equity in both research and public life. The digital humanities have always been *disruptive* (to draw on an overused and abused adjective) to traditional notions of the humanities, but we argue that the challenge of the digital humanities is now articulated less in terms of explicit methods (for instance, distant reading versus close reading) and more in terms of the questions of power and agency (whose labour, whose corpora).

Where digital humanities scholars might have been once happily cloistered from politics, today's DH community is deeply concerned with understanding how scholarly practice can intervene in questions of racism, colonialism, classism, religious and cultural discrimination, misogyny, heteronormativity, cissexism, ableism, and other forms of oppression. This is unsurprising given the ways that networked technologies have become so intimately entwined with systems of power and control. Discussions of the use of biometric scanning at the Canadian border (Akhmetova and Harris 2021) or the use of facial recognition by Canadian police (Jones and McKelvey 2024) are now well within the domain of digital humanities research. New generations of DH scholars are interrogating the digital humanities from the perspective of queer, Indigenous, and racialized epistemologies and are challenging DH's traditional lack of engagement with race, sexuality, and other forms of difference. It is significant that one of the most stringent critiques of racist systems of technology in this book comes from Katherine McKittrick, a Black studies scholar who sidesteps the language of digital humanities. It is also telling that among the most widely talked about digital humanities books of recent years are Safiya Noble's *Algorithms of Oppression* (2018) and Catherine D'Ignazio and Lauren F. Klein's *Data Feminism* (2023). Meanwhile, digital humanities scholars have turned the tools of DH on themselves, expanding the field to include such political topics as the gender and racial compositions of research teams, the invisible labour of DH work, the exploitation of sessional academic workers, the environmental and colonial effects of large computing projects—as well as the ways in which DH research challenges or reaffirms systems of power more generally.

As the DH tent has expanded, scholars trained in critical race theory, postcolonial studies, feminist studies, and other fields have become less concerned with the relationship between the digital and the humanities and more concerned with investigating what vision of the humanities is at stake in DH research. These scholars draw on the work of Donna Haraway, Sylvia Wynter, Edward Said, and others to take seriously Diana Brydon's call that "the humanities need a new humanism" (2011, 233). Amy Earhart, for example, encourages scholars

> to embrace digital humanities as the politically charged field it might become, rather than retreating to DH as merely a "neutral" academic study. By acceding that DH is just another research area, by denying that we might take on crucial issues of power, we will create just another area that, quite frankly, has little to say.
>
> *(2015)*

As it has been throughout the history of DH, Canadian scholars working in the field will have a great deal to contribute to the pragmatic and theoretical dimensions of these questions. DH research in Canada is in dialogue with, and being reframed by, Indigenous epistemologies in transformative ways (see Chapter 10). The creative and critical work of Jordan Abel and Joshua Whitehead, Indigenous approaches to digital forms of mapping that call into question Western approaches to land and space, and Indigenous archival projects all challenge the tenets of digital humanities in Canada.

As the number of digital Canadian literature projects has increased in the past decade, Canadian literature has, albeit slowly, engaged more substantially with digital humanities. A book such as *Refuse: CanLit in Ruins*

(2018) archives the online discourse of the first part of the twenty-first century, but it does not reflect on the implications of capturing an online discussion in the form of a book. New digital media such as tweets, YouTube videos, and online essays all affect how people discuss literature. We explore some of these concerns in our *Canadians Read* project where we trace the networks of online communication around the CBC program *Canada Reads*, asking how communication networks comprised of authors, critics, celebrities, industry insiders, and the public are structured, what their broader implications are for thinking about public discourse online, and how the actors in those networks discuss Canadian literature. What happens, for instance, to discourses of national literature when they move from the pages of a newspaper to discussions on a radio program such as *Canada Reads* to taking place on TikTok? As Canadian literary scholars explore these questions, they must grapple with the affordances of existing and emerging platforms, the interrelationships of networks, and the complexities of algorithms. Canadian literary study has a great number of contributions to make to these and other digital humanities concerns in terms of the attention to place; to discussions of bilingualism, multiculturalism, and antiracism; to the lengthy history of Canadian digital engagements with literature; to the histories of Canadian theories of media; and more.

In a surprising way, the shift into (seemingly immaterial) digital spaces reminds us of the importance of place, medium, and materiality. Canadian literature has undergone a turn towards place, informed, in part, by Indigenous thinkers, Indigenous epistemologies of place, and other challenges to the space of the nation. Canadian literary scholars are well poised to bring their thinking around place and environment to bear on the digital humanities. The same is true of materiality: *SpokenWeb*, for instance, makes the affordances of analog and digital poetry recordings a central component of their analysis. In a very practical sense, this ethos is evident in Canadian literary scholars' burgeoning interest in podcasting—an area that has emerged as one of the most significant forms of knowledge dissemination beyond the academy. A major component of *SpokenWeb*'s research is its podcast series, where researchers describe their archival finds and tell the stories behind their research. Scholars such as Linda Morra and Jessica McDonald host podcasts relevant to Canadian literature; Wilfrid Laurier Press has recently developed a framework for open peer review of podcasts and develops podcasts to accompany some of their scholarly titles.

It is undeniable that DH research and teaching is thriving in Canada. The Canadian Society for Digital Humanities / Société canadienne des humanités numériques (CSDH/SCHN) boasts a large conference each year; many of the papers presented there push at disciplinary boundaries. In 2024, the conference included papers from many of the established scholars cited throughout this book but also papers such as Tina Tang Sang's "A Dominating East: Techno-Orientalism in Narrative Building at the 2023 League of Legend's World Championship," Maya Karanouh's "Wicked Problems of Generative AI: Ethical Concerns and Early Adoption Challenges," and Kiera Obbard's "The Politics of Instagram: Analyzing the Facebook Papers with Voyant." As we write this, Toronto Metropolitan University is in the process of hiring for a Canada Research Chair in Digital Humanities with specialization in one or more of

> Asian, Black, or Indigenous studies, including critical race studies, decolonial studies, or transnational and diaspora studies; feminist and queer studies; game studies; computational humanities; critical code studies; electronic literature and digital arts; and machine learning/artificial intelligence.
>
> *(TMU 2024)*

Likewise, the Digital Humanities Summer Institute (DHSI) has grown from a small group of enthusiasts to an annual, two-week event featuring more than forty courses attended by hundreds of participants. Whereas DHSI of the early 2000s taught on topics such as "New Media Literacy" and "Humanities Computing in Text Oriented Studies," the curriculum has expanded. Sessions in 2024 included "Modeling Texts and Maps with Semantic Annotation," "Queer(ing) DH," "Deep Learning for Humanists," and "Pedagogy of the Digitally Oppressed: Anti-Colonial some DH projects Critiques & Praxis." DHSI also hosts a series of aligned conferences; in 2024, these included "Project Management in the Humanities" and "Open Digital Collaborative Project Preservation in the Humanities"—thus underscoring the above-mentioned recognition that, without concerted effort, some DH projects will rapidly become obsolete. The 2024 aligned conference on "Hypertext & Art: A Retrospective of Forms" suggests that, if we have reached a stage where hypertext is worthy of a retrospective, digital affordances are truly entrenched in our world. In addition to DHSI, training institutes are held at the University of Ottawa, the University of Guelph, St. Francis Xavier University, the annual Congress of the Humanities and Social Sciences, and beyond. The recent development of the Canadian Certificate in Digital Humanities (cc:DH/HN), a formal accreditation of the various skills on offer at these conferences and training institutes, demonstrates the ongoing appeal of and people's desire for affiliation with DH.

Yet even amid all this growth, the institutional future of digital humanities programs remains uncertain, as it is subject to the capriciousness of administrators, funders, and student engagement. At the University of Guelph, the Culture and Technology Studies program is a DH undergraduate program in all but name (undergraduate students largely did not understand what a digital humanities program would involve, just as they equally could not explain what constitutes the humanities). The program's course offerings include "DH and cultural difference," "Python Programming for the Humanities," "Ethics in AI," "Critical Making," and more. The University of Western Ontario has a DH undergraduate program, OCAD U offers MA, MDes, and MFA programs in Digital Futures, and the University of Alberta boasts a cross-disciplinary MA in Digital Humanities. McGill's English department lists an ad hoc MA Programs in Digital Humanities; indeed, the ad hoc nature of DH pedagogy in Canada has been one of its constant features. Yet history reminds us that growth is uneven and uncertain: not only did the graduate degree in DH that Ian Lancashire envisioned at the University of Toronto never come to fruition, but also a great deal of his work was undone with the shuttering of the Centre for Computing in the Humanities in the mid-1990s. Likewise, the Multimedia program at McMaster University closed soon after the program's founding personnel moved to new institutions. Geoffrey Rockwell's words reflecting on the history of DH remain true today: "Computing, in the humanities, has been plagued by resistance" (Meunier 2009). DH programs in Canada continue to depend on cross-disciplinary teaching provided by instructors from other departments, on centralized resources (such as those based in university libraries), and on institutional support.

It seems clear that, in the future, DH research will need to grapple not only with these historical (and continuing) challenges but also with emerging ones—particularly the ethics, methods, and broader social implications of AI. Large language models and AI are now sophisticated enough to mimic human prose, present compelling arguments, write functioning software, transform plain language into images and video at a level of quality on par with what humans can create, and much more. By the time you read this, AI will have likely developed in a range of unexpected ways. DH scholars are particularly suited to thinking about the social implications of these technologies and what they mean for the humanities. After all, humanities students are now beginning to question whether they *really* need to learn to craft arguments and write essays when AI can do it for them in a fraction of the time and with far fewer grammatical errors. Likewise, Computer Science students are questioning the need to learn programming fundamentals when AI can produce efficient code with ease. Digital humanities scholars can intervene in these discussions by offering new ways to think about the function of AI as a tool or replacement for human activity, especially with respect to the existing and emerging scholarship that emphasizes the ways in which technology perpetuates biases (see Chapters 8–10).

History also serves as a sobering force in this regard and is particularly necessary in the face of the techno-triumphalism that characterizes so much AI discussion. As we write this conclusion in September 2024, Open AI has just released *OpenAI o1*, the latest version of its large language model AI software, which it promises will "spend more time *thinking*" before returning more complex results (OpenAI 2024, emphasis added). This month, *ChatGPT* also briefly gave the impression of having reached artificial general intelligence (the point at which a machine will be deemed to have the same cognitive abilities as a human) as it began initiating conversations with people who had not even asked it a question; this was chalked up to a glitch (Eliot 2024). AI technologies are imagined by supporters as incredible new tools that will solve a range of social problems and by critics as solutions to problems that do not exist. As we discuss in the introduction to this book, it is incumbent on the digital humanities to make these technologies visible in all their complexity. What are the environmental implications of such technologies? What will the effects of AI be on notions of literacy and writing? What will their impact be on the labour market? What does OpenAI mean when it describes a large language model as spending more time *thinking*?

Fortunately, there is still time for us to interrogate these questions, as our jobs have yet to be usurped by machines—a point made by Sean Michaels in his 2023 novel, *Do You Remember Being Born?* The novel tells the story of Marian Ffarmer (modelled on the American poet Marianne Moore), who is invited by a Google-esque tech company to write a poem with its chatbot, Charlotte. The book documents Ffarmer's exchanges with Charlotte, whose words, as Michaels tells us at the end, were "generated with help from OpenAI's GPT-3 language model as well as Moorebot, a package of custom poetry-generation software designed by Sean Michaels and Katie O'Nell. Moorebot was trained on a corpus that includes the collected work of Marianne Moore" (Michaels 2023). About Charlotte's literary efforts, reviewer Steven W. Beattie notes,

> in many cases, the computer-generated lines are, to be polite, not of superior quality. They frequently appear simply extraneous: "I would propose a line, a portion of a line, and what the system spat back upended my expectations," Michaels writes in the voice of Marian. "I had been seduced by this surprise." To which the AI redundantly adds, "I had mistaken a fit of algorithmic exuberance for the truth."
> *(2023)*

With admirable restraint in not lamenting that his job as a reviewer now requires him to assess the poetic output of a machine, Beattie reassures his readers that computer code (even if trained on the works of a Pulitzer-prize-winning poet) has not bested Michaels (a Giller-prize-winning novelist). Perhaps not coincidentally, Beattie's comments appear in *Quill & Quire*, a magazine catering to the Canadian publishing industry. If there were any group other than the members of a university literature department who needed reassurance that robots have not yet come for their jobs, authors, editors, and publishers would be it. Ffarmer calls Charlotte's poetry "handsome nonsense"; her random strings of words are, in many regards, no different from the text fragments her arachnid namesake weaves into her web. If there is meaning in the poetry that Charlotte generates, it is because of the material on which she was trained, or because the reader imparts it through their reading—not because she has created it. As Beattie notes,

> The poetry in the book is largely doggerel, save a few inspired moments, such as the reference to "the days of prismatic color … when there was no smoke and color was / fine." It should come as little surprise that this and other similar instances are the verbatim work of Moore herself.

Michaels's novel not only captures a great deal of what we have surveyed in this book but is also a likely harbinger of things to come: Canadian authors experimenting in ways that point to both the creative promise and significant limitations of new technologies. His image, of snippets of text—be it stolen from a poet and inputted by a programmer or torn from the back of a box of soap flakes and ferried by a rat—provided to a chatbot named after a spider, suggests the strange menagerie of emerging digital forms of creation that have comprised this history and proliferate today. Yet it also suggests the increased importance of language and reading to parsing this new digital world. Indeed, despite the supposed promises of AI to shape the future, it is still writers, critics, and artists who will critically assess this digital world and offer us possibilities for how we might understand it. If AI and machine learning algorithms recycle the texts and knowledge of the past to offer a Potemkin form of knowledge and creation, it falls to writers and critics to seek something more original and substantial behind the façade. If MacLennan envisions the future digital world as dystopia and Michaels imagines it as a cybernetic menagerie, it is up to us to decide which vision resonates most.

In our previous book, *Future Horizons: Canadian Digital Humanities* (2023), we argued that the scholars working at the margins of digital humanities would have an outsized influence in determining its future.

In this book, we move away from the visionary mode and instead reflect on the lessons of the past to understand the relationship between Canadian literature and digital humanities. We thus conclude with the provocation that the future will reflect the past, particularly as researchers' future capability to navigate an increasingly novel and strange digital technologies will require "old fashioned" skills in hermeneutics, critical discourse analysis, historiography, archival studies, and analyses of power—but that these skills will, inevitably, need to be combined with a (theoretical, if not practical) grasp of code, algorithms, and digital forms of representation.

Working at the intersection of digital humanities and Canadian literature will require a bespoke set of critical reading *and* making practices and will increasingly mean contributing to feedback loops that are shaped by, and shape, institutional priorities, research methods, archives, and networks of power. When we participate in those networks and feedback loops, we both subject our work to those same forces while also transforming those networks in our critical interventions. If Willard McCarty is right, and we think he is, that digital humanities are a "space where machines interact asynchronously to deepen the fundamental problems, rather than solve them" (2013), then it will be up to humanities scholars, students, readers, and critics to plumb the depths of the problems of the digital, the literary, and the national. It is up to us to decide who or what is the monster at the end of the book, and who or what is its puppet (or muppet) master.

Works cited

Akhmetova, Roxana, and Erin Harris. 2021. "Politics of Technology: The Use of Artificial Intelligence by US and Canadian Immigration Agencies and Their Impacts on Human Rights." In *Digital Identity, Virtual Borders and Social Media: A Panacea for Migration Governance?*, edited by Emre E. Korkmaz, 52–72. Cheltenham: Elgar. https://doi.org/10.4337/9781789909159.00008.

Alpert-Abrams, Hannah, Heather Froehlich, Amanda Henrichs, Jim McGrath, and Kim Martin. 2019. "Postdoctoral Laborers Bill of Rights." *Knowledge Commons*. https://doi.org/10.17613/7fz6-ra81.

Archives Unleashed. 2023. "Welcome to the Archives Unleashed Project." Accessed September 5, 2024. https://archivesunleashed.org.

Barrett, Paul, and Sarah Roger. n.d. *Canadians Read*. Accessed October 10, 2024. https://canadiansread.ca/.

Barrett, Paul, and Sarah Roger, eds. 2023. *Future Horizons: Canadian Digital Humanities*. Ottawa: University of Ottawa Press. https://doi.org/10.2307/jj.17681834.

Beattie, Steven W. 2023. "*Do You Remember Being Born?* by Sean Michaels." *Quill & Quire*, September 2023. https://quillandquire.com/review/do-you-remember-being-born/.

Boyles, Christina, Anne Cong-Huyen, Carrie Johnston, Jim McGrath, and Amanda Philips. 2018. "Precarious Labor and Digital Humanities." *American Quarterly* 70, no. 3: 693–700. https://doi.org/10.1353/aq.2018.0054.

Brainerd, Barron. 1974. *Weighing Evidence in Language and Literature: A Statistical Approach.* Toronto: University of Toronto Press.

Brydon, Diana. 2011. "Do the Humanities Need a New Humanism?" *Retooling the Humanities: The Culture of Research in Canada*, edited by Daniel Coleman and Smaro Kamboureli, 233–62. Edmonton: University of Alberta Press. https://doi.org/10.1515/9780888646781-014.

cc:DH/HN. n.d. *The Canadian Certificate in Digital Humanities / Certificat canadien en Humanités Numériques.* Accessed July 12, 2024. https://ccdhhn.ca/.

DHSI. n.d. *Digital Humanities Summer Institute.* Accessed October 15, 2024. https://dhsi.org/.

D'Ignazio, Catherine, and Lauren F. Klein. 2023. *Data Feminism.* Cambridge: The MIT Press. https://doi.org/10.7551/mitpress/11805.001.0001.

Di Pressi, Haley, Stephanie Gorman, Miriam Posner, Raphael Sasayama, and Tori Schmitt. 2015. "A Student Collaborators' Bill of Rights." *UCLA Humanities Technology* (blog), June 8, 2015. https://humtech.ucla.edu/news/a-student-collaborators-bill-of-rights/.

Earhart, Amy E. 2015. "Digital Humanities Futures: Conflict, Power, and Public Knowledge." *Digital Studies / Le champ numérique* 6, no. 1. https://doi.org/10.16995/dscn.1.

Eliot, Lance. 2024. "ChatGPT Speak-First Incident Stirs Worries of Artificial General Intelligence." *Forbes*, September 18, 2024. https://www.forbes.com/sites/lanceeliot/2024/09/17/chatgpt-speak-first-incident-stirs-worries-that-generative-ai-is-getting-too-big-for-its-britches/.

Frye, Northrop. 1989. "Literary and Mechanical Models." In *The Secular Scripture and Other Writings on Critical Theory: 1976–1991*, edited by Joseph Adamson and Jean Wilson, 451–62. Toronto: University of Toronto Press. https://doi.org/10.3138/9781442627550.

Hockey, Susan. 1980. *A Guide to Computer Applications in the Humanities.* Baltimore: Johns Hopkins University Press.

Jones, Maurice, and Fenwick McKelvey. 2024. "Deconstructing Public Participation in the Governance of Facial Recognition Technologies in Canada." *AI & Society*, 2024: 14 pp. https://doi.org/10.1007/s00146-024-01952-w.

MacLennan, Hugh. 1980. *Voices in Time.* Montréal and Kingston: McGill-Queen's University Press.

McCarty, Willard. 1991. "HUMANIST: Lessons from a Global Electronic Seminar." *Computers and the Humanities* 26: 205–22. https://doi.org/10.1007/BF00058618.

McCarty, Willard. 2013. "The Future of Digital Humanities Is a Matter of Words." In *A Companion to New Media Dynamics*, edited by John Hartley, Jean Burgess, and Axel Bruns, 33–52. Hoboken: Blackwell. https://doi.org/10.1002/9781118321607.ch2.

McGrath, Jim. 2021. "Project Endings and Precarious Labor." *Jim McGrath* (blog). Updated July 19, 2023. https://jimmcgrath.us/teaching/project-endings-and-precarious-labor/.

McGregor, Hannah, Julie Rak, and Erin Wunker, eds. 2018. *Refuse: CanLit in Ruins*. Toronto: BookThug.
Media Commons Press. 2011. "Collaborators' Bill of Rights." *Media Commons Press*. https://mcpress.media-commons.org/offthetracks/part-one-models-for-collaboration-career-paths-acquiring-institutional-support-and-transformation-in-the-field/a-collaboration/collaborators%E2%80%99-bill-of-rights/.
Meunier, J. G. 2009. "CARAT—Computer-Assisted Reading and Analysis of Texts: The Appropriation of a Technology." *Digital Studies / Le champ numérique* 1, no. 3. https://doi.org/10.16995/dscn.263.
Michaels, Sean. 2023. *Do You Remember Being Born?* Toronto: Penguin Random House.
Noble, Safiya. 2018. *Algorithms of Oppression*. New York: NYU Press. https://doi.org/10.18574/nyu/9781479833641.001.0001.
Office of the Vice-Provost. 2024. "Generative Artificial Intelligence in the Classroom: FAQs." Office of the Vice-Provost, Innovations in Undergraduate Education, University of Toronto, August 29, 2024. https://www.viceprovostundergrad.utoronto.ca/16072-2/teaching-initiatives/generative-artificial-intelligence/.
Open AI. 2024. "Introducing OpenAI o1." September 20, 2024. https://openai.com/o1/.
SpokenWeb. 2022. *Archive of the Digital Present*. https://adp.spokenweb.ca.
SpokenWeb. 2024. *SpokenWeb*. https://spokenweb.ca/.
TMU. 2024. "Hiring Tier 2 Canada Research Chair in Digital Humanities." Toronto Metropolitan University, May 28, 2024. https://www.torontomu.ca/english/news-events/2024/05/dhc-hire/.

APPENDIX I

Digital humanities laboratories and centres at Canadian universities

* * *

The information below has been assembled in consultation with members of the laboratories and centres, where possible. We have limited ourselves to facilities with a digital humanities focus. Many Canadian universities also have makerspaces, (multi)media laboratories, VR and AR facilities, gaming spaces, and more, which we do not have space to include. Additional DH facilities will undoubtedly open in coming years—Brock University has a laboratory opening in fall 2024—and some of the spaces listed here may, unfortunately, close. The names and URLs are accurate as of summer 2024; for the most up-to-date details, we encourage you to consult the webpages provided below or search online.

Carleton University—Hyperlab
https://carleton.ca/hyperlab/

The Hyperlab is Carleton University's Digital Humanities research centre, co-directed by Brian Greenspan and Stuart Murray. Founded in 2008 with support from the Canada Foundation for Innovation (CFI) and the Social Sciences and Humanities Research Council (SSHRC), the lab's focus is on critical and creative approaches to digital text and narrative, game studies, locative media, XR storytelling, digital theatre, visual culture, and new media cultures. It comprises four spaces: a main lab with high-performance workstations for computation, gaming, and data visualization; a dedicated game lab; a reading room with specialist technologies for writing and reading; and a digital rhetorics and ethics lab for studying the user interfaces.

Carleton University—Cultural Heritage Informatics Collaboratory
https://carleton.ca/xlab/

Carleton University's Cultural Heritage Informatics Collaboratory (XLab) is a collective for exploring the intersection of cultural heritage, digital media, and computation. XLab is a "transdisciplinary 'skunkworks'"—a space for non-traditional, imaginative work undertaken by a loosely structured group of engaged individuals. Founded in 2019, it has been supported with funding from Carleton University (2021) and CFI (2024). XLab is located in Paterson Hall, where it provides space and equipment for students in the MA program with DH specialization as part of the StudioDH initiative. Led by Shawn Graham and Laura Banducci, the XLab supports research projects, organizes events, and provides student support via the George Garth Graham Undergraduate Digital History Research Fellowship.

McGill University—Digital Scholarship Hub
https://www.mcgill.ca/library/services/digital-scholarship-hub

Located in the McGill University library, the Digital Scholarship Hub (DSH) provides space for and access to equipment used for digital research, including high-powered workstations, specialized software, VR and AR equipment, 3D printers, and more. Rather than being a dedicated DH centre, it draws together expertise from across the university to support research using digital technologies and methods. First planned in 2017 and soft-launched in 2019, the DSH was founded by Jenn Riley (assistant director, digital archives) and Jeffrey Archer (assistant director, user services); it is currently led by Marcela Isuster, who works with the Digital Scholarship Hub's team of experts to organize nearly seventy workshops annually, serving over 1,500 members of the community.

McMaster University—Lewis & Ruth Sherman Centre for Digital Scholarship
https://scds.ca/

Located in Mills Memorial Library, the Sherman Centre provides consulting, instruction, and technical support to McMaster and its community for all aspects of digital scholarship—from teaching to research and knowledge mobilization. Co-directed by Andrea Zeffiro (academic director) and Jay Brodeur (administrative director)—and funded by a gift from the Lewis and Ruth Sherman Foundation and support from the Office of the Provost—its programming includes a graduate residency, speaker and workshop series, and undergraduate courses. The Sherman Centre provides access to tools such as advanced computing workstations and 3D printers.

Simon Fraser University—Digital Humanities Innovation Lab
https://www.lib.sfu.ca/help/publish/dh/dhil

Located in the W. A. C. Bennett Library at Simon Fraser University's Burnaby campus (and in shared meeting spaces on both the Vancouver and Surrey campuses), the Digital Humanities Innovation Lab provides support for the SFU community. Founded by Colette Colligan and Michelle Levy in 2016 and currently led by Rebecca Dowson (digital scholarship librarian and library collaborator), the Digital Humanities Innovation Lab's team of developers and fellows offers consultation, training, mentoring, research software development, and technical support.

Toronto Metropolitan University—Centre for Digital Humanities
https://www.torontomu.ca/centre-digital-humanities/

Based out of the Toronto Metropolitan University Library Building, the Centre for Digital Humanities (CDH) provides a home for collaborative, transdisciplinary research, with a focus on projects that join the material with the digital. The CDH supports faculty and students through training, mentorship, and access to digital resources. Co-founded in 2010 by Lorraine Janzen Kooistra (director emerita) and Dennis Denisoff (senior research associate), the CDH was established with support from TMU Libraries and the Faculty of Arts. The CDH is currently led by Jason Boyd (director) and with the support of centre manager Reg Beatty.

Université de Montréal—Centre de recherche interuniversitaire sur les humanités numériques
https://www.crihn.org/

Located at the Université de Montréal's Département des littératures et langues du monde, the Centre de recherche interuniversitaire sur les humanités numériques (CRIHN) is a hub for DH research at a dozen institutions across Québec. Since its founding in 2013, the centre has provided training and support for students and researchers, and it fosters collaboration through monthly meetings, workshops on digital tools, roundtables and guest speaker series, and annual conferences. CRIHN is led by Michael Sinatra (director) and Katrina Kaustinen (administrative coordinator), and it is supported by the Fonds de recherche du Québec—Société et culture.

University of Alberta—Digital Scholarship Centre
https://dsc.library.ualberta.ca/

Housed in the Cameron Science & Technology Library, the Digital Scholarship Centre (DSC) is a research and teaching facility for members of the University of Alberta. Since 2019, it has provided collaborative workspaces with access to resources such as a large-scale visualization wall, high-powered workstations with gaming and research software, a virtual reality space, a sound booth for quiet recording, a media room for video creation, and a makerspace featuring 3D printers, laser cutters, and textile tools. Led by Lydia Zvyagintseva (head, digital scholarship services) and Harvey Quamen (academic director), its team of librarians and digital scholarship specialists teaches workshops on digital scholarship practices and provides research support. The Centre's Digital Scholarship Fellowship Program provides students with resources, assistance from DSC staff, and a stipend to support their digital projects.

University of British Columbia Okanagan—AMP Lab
https://amplab.ok.ubc.ca/

The Audio Media Poetry Lab (AMP Lab), located in the Fipke Building on the UBC Okanagan (UBCO) campus, supports students and researchers through training and knowledge mobilization, and it provides access to specialized tools including equipment for working with legacy media. As the home of the UBCO branch of *SpokenWeb*, the AMP Lab provides a home for projects that investigate the relationship between digital and non-digital media to cultural heritage, with an emphasis on audio media and poetry. Originally founded as the Spark Lab (led by Constance Crompton in collaboration with Karis Shearer and Hussein Keshani) in 2013, the lab grew into the CFI-funded Humanities Data Lab, which is now based at the University of Ottawa (see below). In 2017, the UBC lab transformed into the AMP Lab, led by Karis Shearer (principal investigator). Emily Murphy joined the lab in 2019 and in 2022 launched the CFI-funded

(Re)Media Infrastructure for Multimedia Research and Creation, which partners the AMP Lab with resources in UBCO's Innovation Annex. AMP Lab is supported by UBCO, the BC Knowledge Development Fund, and CFI; its research projects are supported by SSHRC, funding from UBCO, the Digital Research Alliance of Canada (DRAC), and private donations.

University of Guelph—The Humanities Interdisciplinary Collaboration Lab
https://www.uoguelph.ca/arts/dhguelph/thinc

Located in the McLaughlin Library at the University of Guelph, The Humanities Interdisciplinary Collaboration Lab (THINC Lab) supports collaborative, interdisciplinary, and inclusive digital humanities research. Home to a number of digital humanities projects, THINC Lab provides collaborative and individual workspaces with access to data visualization touchscreens and other specialized equipment in a flexibly configured space suited for presentations, workshops, and meetings. THINC Lab supports students and faculty in DH research and pedagogy, and it offers graduate residencies, training, and mentoring, including through the Michael Ridley Postdoctoral Fellowship in Digital Humanities; it also supports students in Guelph's Culture and Technology Studies program in their capstone research projects. THINC Lab programming includes DH@Guelph talks, demonstrations, and summer workshops, the IF: Interdisciplinary/Intersectional Feminisms research series, wellbeing programming in collaboration with the library, and other events. It hosts visiting scholars, including through the Fulbright Canada Research Chair Awards Program. Led by Susan Brown (director) and Kim Martin (associate director), THINC Lab was built with funding from CFI and is supported by the College of Arts and the University of Guelph Library.

University of Ottawa—Labo de données en sciences humaines / The Humanities Data Lab
https://humanitiesdata.ca/

Located in the Faculty of Arts at the University of Ottawa, the Humanities Data Lab provides support for digital humanities research. Its programming includes knowledge mobilization events and training opportunities offered in collaboration with the University of Ottawa's DHSITE/SNTech summer school. Directed by Constance Crompton, the lab brings together projects with the shared goal of sustaining online access to libratory histories. The lab provides access to resources such as high-performance computers and large touchscreen monitors for data visualizations. Founded in 2017 and launched in its current location in 2020, the Humanities Data Lab is supported by the University of Ottawa's Faculty of Arts, DH@uOttawa, CFI, SSHRC, and DRAC.

University of Toronto—Critical Digital Humanities Initiative
https://dhn.utoronto.ca/

The Critical Digital Humanities Initiative (CDHI) supports digital humanities at the University of Toronto with a focus on digital research creation and digital knowledge mobilization, including a UX design for DH accelerator program, a digital research storytelling workshop, and praxis workshops for digital design and knowledge mobilization skills. Its team includes DH developers, UX designers, digital research creation specialists, research associates, and communications officer roles, alongside academic and staff leadership. It supports faculty and researchers through information sessions, workshops, project planning, coaching, and consultations, as well as by co-designing and developing digital projects. An initiative that supports all three of the University of Toronto campuses, it has a working space in the Jackman Humanities Building on the St. George (downtown Toronto) campus. The CDHI was founded in 2020 with support from the Jackman Humanities Institute; it is a project of the university's Digital Humanities Network, which itself began in 2014. CDHI was founded by Elspeth Brown (director) and co-developed by Danielle Taschereau Mamers (managing director).

University of Victoria—Electronic Textual Cultures Lab / Digital Scholarship Commons
https://etcl.uvic.ca/

Based in the Digital Scholarship Commons at the McPherson Library, the Electronic Textual Cultures Lab (ETCL) works at the intersection of textual communication, digital humanities research, project development, and open social scholarship. It is part of the Canadian Social Knowledge Institute, which also houses the Digital Humanities Summer Institute and the Implementing New Knowledge Environments Partnership. The Electronic Textual Cultures Lab provides support for students and researchers through training and knowledge mobilization events, access to resources, its Open Scholarship Awards program, and other open knowledge initiatives such as its Open Knowledge Practicum and Honorary Resident Wikipedian. The ETCL is led by Ray Siemens (director) and Graham Jensen (assistant director) supported with funding from SSHRC. Founded in 2004 with support from CFI, the Canada Research Chairs program, and the University of Victoria, it has also benefitted from the guidance of directorial group members Alyssa Arbuckle, Randa El Katib, Caroline Winter, and Jannaya Friggstad Jensen.

York University—Digital Scholarship Centre
https://www.library.yorku.ca/ds/

The Digital Scholarship Centre brings together York University library expertise in the areas of scholarly publishing, digitization, media creation and critical making, metadata and digital collections, digital humanities, research data management and research impact metrics, and data services including data curation and data visualization. It also serves as a hub for researchers looking to partner with the libraries on grant-funded projects. The Digital Scholarship Centre hosts workshops, panel discussions, and lectures related to the issues and practices surrounding digital scholarship, scholarly communications, and digital tools. It includes Making and Media Creation Lab spaces at Scott, Markham, and Glendon campus locations, where York community members can access AV recording and VR studios, a gaming and data visualization lab, a large makerspace, editing workstations, and a broad selection of equipment available to borrow. The Centre was launched in 2020 under the guidance of a digital scholarship steering committee, co-chaired by Andrea Kosavic and Kris Joseph; it was established with seed funding provided by the university's Vice-Provost for Teaching and Learning.

APPENDIX II

Digital humanities projects, tools and platforms, resources, and organizations

* * *

This appendix provides a list of the digital humanities projects, tools and platforms, resources, and organizations mentioned in the book. Where an entry could be listed in more than one category (e.g., digital humanities projects that also serve as a source for content that can be used to create a corpus for other projects), we have listed the project according to how we have principally discussed it in the text.

Projects

AMM Bibliography | https://www.ammbibliography.com/
The Anne of Green Gables Manuscript: L. M. Montgomery and the Creation of Anne | https://annemanuscript.ca/
Archive of the Digital Present (SpokenWeb) | https://adp.spokenweb.ca
Black Book Interactive Project | https://iopn.library.illinois.edu/omeka/s/BBIP/page/welcome
Black Loyalists: Our History, Our People | https://blackloyalist.com/cdc/documents/official/book_of_negroes.htm
The Black Past in Guelph: Remembered and Reclaimed | https://blackpastinguelph.com
Canada's Early Women Writers | https://cwrc.ca/project/canadas-early-women-writers
Canadian Jewish Women Writers | https://cwrc.ca/project/canadian-jewish-women-writers
Canadian Modernist Magazines Project | https://modernistmags.ca
Canadian Women Playwrights Online | https://cwrc.ca/cwpo
Canadians Read | https://canadiansread.ca/

Chugachmiut Heritage Library & Archive | https://archive.chugachmiut.org/
Digital Archaeological Archive of Comparative Slavery | https://www.daacs.org
The Digital Page: The Collected Works of P. K. Page | https://cwrc.ca/project/digitalpage
Distant Reading Mennonite Writing | https://ctms.uwinnipeg.ca/projects/drmw/
Editing Modernism in Canada (EMiC) | https://editingmodernism.ca/
The Family Camera Network | https://familycameranetwork.org
Feminist Caucus Living Archives | https://cwrc.ca/project/feminist-caucus-living-archives
FourDirectionsTeachings.com | https://www.fourdirectionsteachings.com/
Fred Wah Digital Archive | https://fredwah.ca
Genoa Indian School Digital Reconciliation Project | https://genoaindianschool.org/home
Great Lakes Research Alliance for the Study of Aboriginal Arts & Cultures (GRASAC) | https://grasac.artsci.utoronto.ca/
HistSex | https://histsex.org/
Huna Heritage Digital Archives | https://archives.hunaheritage.org/
Kiinawin Kawindomowin / Story Nations | https://storynations.utoronto.ca/
The Knowledge G.A.P. | https://knowledgegap.org
L. M. Montgomery Collection | https://cwrc.ca/lmmontgomery
Legends of Vancouver | https://www.legendsofvancouver.net/
Lesbian and Gay Liberation in Canada (LGLC) | https://lglc.ca/
LGBTQ Oral History Digital Collaboratory | https://lgbtqdigitalcollaboratory.org
Mapping Ontario's Black Archives | https://mobaprojects.ca/
Native American Women Playwrights Archive | https://spec.lib.miamioh.edu/home/nawpa
Native Land Digital | https://native-land.ca/
North Side Hip Hop Archive | https://www.nshharchive.ca
Ohneganos Ohnegahdę:gyo Water Research Program | https://explore.terrastories.app/community/ohneganos
The Orlando Project | https://orlando.cambridge.org/
Passamaquoddy Peoples' Knowledge Portal | https://passamaquoddypeople.com/
The People and the Text: Indigenous Writing in Lands Claimed by Canada (TPatT) | https://thepeopleandthetext.ca/
Plateau People's Web Portal Project | https://plateauportal.libraries.wsu.edu/
Race, Migration, and the Canadian Nation | https://racemigrationcanada.com
Respectful Terminology Platform Project | https://www.nikla-ancla.com/respectful-terminology
SlaveVoyages | https://www.slavevoyages.org
SpokenWeb | https://spokenweb.ca/
Stolen Relations: Recovering Stories of Indigenous Enslavement in the Americas | https://indigenousslavery.org/
Sustaining Digital Scholarship for Sustainable Culture | https://sustainableknowledgeproject.blogspot.com/
The "Use Our Words" Toolkit | https://indigenouslis.ca/the-use-our-words-toolkit/
Voices of the Land | https://voicesoftheland.org/
What Is Digital Humanities? | https://whatisdigitalhumanities.com/

Whose Land | https://www.whose.land/en/
Wikipetcia Atikamekw Nehiromowin | https://atj.wikipedia.org/wiki/Otitikowin
The Winnifred Eaton Archive | https://winnifredeatonarchive.org
Women's Writing and Reading in Canada from 1950 | https://cwrc.ca/canwwrfrom1950
Yellow Nineties 2.0 | https://1890s.ca/

Tools and platforms

Archives Unleashed | https://archivesunleashed.org/
Borealis: The Canadian Dataverse Repository | https://borealisdata.ca/
Canadian HSS Commons | https://hsscommons.ca/
Collaboratory for Writing and Research on Culture (CWRC) | https://cwrc.ca/
Constellate | https://constellate.org/
Collective Access | https://www.collectiveaccess.org/
Data Management Plan Assistant (DMP Assistant) | https://dmp-pgd.ca/
The Digital Documentation Process | https://digitalhumanitiesddp.com/
Digital Research Tools Wiki | https://digitalresearchtools.pbworks.com/
Dynamic Table of Contexts | https://dtoc.leaf-vre.org/
Federated Research Data Repository (FRDR) | https://www.frdr-dfdr.ca/repo/
Google Colab | https://colab.research.google.com/
Google Ngram Viewer | https://books.google.com/ngrams/
Great Lakes Research Alliance for the Study of Aboriginal Arts & Cultures (GRASAC) *Knowledge Sharing Platform* | https://gks.artsci.utoronto.ca/
HathiTrust Bookworm | https://bookworm.htrc.illinois.edu/develop/
Jupyter Notebook | https://jupyter.org/
Kaggle | https://www.kaggle.com/
Linked Editing Academic Framework-Virtual Research Environment (LEAF-VRE) | https://www.leaf-vre.org/
Linked Editing Academic Framework-Writer (LEAF-Writer) | https://leaf-writer.leaf-vre.org
Linked Infrastructure for Networked Cultural Scholarship (LINCS) | https://lincsproject.ca/
Murkutu CMS | https://mukurtu.org/
Natural Language Toolkit (NLTK) | https://www.nltk.org/
Omeka | https://omeka.org/
OpenRefine | https://openrefine.org/
Python | https://www.python.org/
SpaCy | https://spacy.io/
Spyral Notebook | https://voyant-tools.org/spyral
Text Analysis Portal for Research 3 (TAPoR) | https://tapor.ca/home
Terrastories | https://terrastories.app/
Voyant Tools | https://voyant-tools.org/spyral
Wget | https://www.gnu.org/software/wget/
Wikidata | https://www.wikidata.org/

Resources

The ArQuives: Canada's LGBTQ+ Archives | https://arquives.ca/
Black Digital Humanities Projects & Resources | https://bit.ly/Black-DH-List
Canadian Heritage Information Network (CHIN) *Data Dictionaries* | https://app.pch.gc.ca/application/ddrcip-chindd/description-about.app?lang=en
Canadian National Digital Heritage Index (CNDHI) | https://www.cndhi-ipnpc.ca/en
Canadiana | https://www.canadiana.ca/
CARE Principles for Indigenous Data Governance | https://www.gida-global.org/care
Creative Commons | https://creativecommons.org/
Dublin Core Metadata Initiative | https://www.dublincore.org/
The Endings Project | https://endings.uvic.ca/
Érudit | https://www.erudit.org/en/
FAIR Principles | https://www.go-fair.org/fair-principles/
Feminist Principles of the Internet | https://feministinternet.org/en
FemTechNet | https://www.femtechnet.org/
The First Nations Principles of OCAP® | https://fnigc.ca/ocap-training
Getty Vocabularies | https://www.getty.edu/research/tools/vocabularies/
GitHub | https://github.com/
GitLab | https://gitlab.com/
HathiTrust Digital Library | https://www.hathitrust.org/
Homosaurus: An International LGBTQ+ Linked Data Vocabulary | https://homosaurus.org/
Humanities Data | https://humanitiesdata.com/
MARC 21 Format for Bibliographic Data | https://www.loc.gov/marc/bibliographic/
Nomenclature for Museum Cataloguing (CHIN) | https://page.nomenclature.info/apropos-about.app?lang=en
Open Government | https://open.canada.ca/en
Open Source Initiative | https://opensource.org/
Open Researcher and Contributor ID (ORCID) | https://orcid.org/
Programming Historian | https://programminghistorian.org/
Project Gutenberg | https://www.gutenberg.org/
Regular Expression Cheat Sheet | https://cheatography.com/davechild/cheat-sheets/regular-expressions/
Representative Poetry Online | https://rpo.library.utoronto.ca/bibliography/canadian-poetry
TEI by Example | https://teibyexample.org/exist/
Text Encoding Initiative (TEI) | https://tei-c.org
Transgender Archives | https://www.uvic.ca/transgenderarchives/index.php
Traditional Knowledge Labels | https://localcontexts.org/labels/traditional-knowledge-labels/
UBC Library Open Collection | https://open.library.ubc.ca/
Virtual International Authority File (VIAF) | https://viaf.org/
Women Writers Online | https://www.wwp.northeastern.edu/wwo/
Zenodo | https://zenodo.org/

Organizations

Alliance of Digital Humanities Organizations (ADHO) | https://adho.org/
Canada Foundation for Innovation (CFI) | https://www.innovation.ca/
Canadian Certificate in Digital Humanities / Certificat canadien en humanités numériques (cc:DH/HN) | https://ccdhhn.ca/
Canadian Heritage Information Network (CHIN) | https://www.canada.ca/en/heritage-information-network.html
Canadian Research Knowledge Network (CRKN) | https://www.crkn-rcdr.ca/en
Canadian Society for Digital Humanities / Société canadienne des humanités numériques (CSDH/SCHN) | https://csdh-schn.org/
centerNet | https://dhcenternet.org/
Digital Humanities Summer Institute (DHSI) | https://dhsi.org/
Digital Research Alliance of Canada (DRAC) | https://alliancecan.ca/en
Humanities, Arts, Science and Technology Alliance (HASTAC) | https://hastac.hcommons.org/
Implementing New Knowledge Environments (INKE) | https://inke.ca/
National Indigenous Knowledge & Language Alliance / Alliance nationale des connaissances et des langues autochtones (NIKLA-ANCLA) | https://www.nikla-ancla.com/respectful-terminology
Social Sciences and Humanities Research Council of Canada (SSHRC) | https://www.sshrc-crsh.gc.ca/home-accueil-eng.aspx

INDEX

Note: *Italic* page numbers refer to figures and page numbers followed by "n" denote endnotes.

Abel, Jordan 7, 194–97, 199–200, 212, 215, 268, 298; *Injun* 7, 195; *Un/Inhabited* 195–96
algorithm 131, 148, 161, 164–66, 210, 242, 245–50, 254–69, 299, 302–4
Algorithms of Oppression (Noble) 161, 298
Alliance of Digital Humanities Organizations (ADHO) 30–32, 141–42, 151
Allison-Cassin, Stacy: *Respectful Terminology Platform Project* 187
AMM Bibliography 114–15, 213
Anarchists in the Academy (Spinosa) 119
Anatomy of Criticism (Frye) 108
Andromeda (Fisher) 111
Anne of Green Gables (Montgomery) 212, 218n3, 268; *Anne of Green Gables Manuscript, The* 212
Antoniak, Maria 170
Application Programming Interface (API) 263; Gutenberg API 213; Open Government API 214; UBC Libraries API 215
Aquin, Hubert: *Prochain episode* 16
Archive of the Digital Present (SpokenWeb) 95, 126, 247, 296

archives: digital 55, 58, 77, 88–95, 112, 126, 212–14; digital humanities and 8, 30, 33, 58, 87–99; Indigenous 183, 187–89, 192–96, 199–200, 201n5; LGBTQ+ and feminist 150–51; management of 221, 224–29; physical 47, 88; as sites of power or oppression 6–7, 33, 147–48, 153, 154, 164, 233n5; of slavery, colonialism, and Black life 134, 160–61, 166–69, 171–72, 174n4
artificial intelligence (AI) 1–2, 32, 111, 119, 161–62, 294; in literature 301–3
Artmob 6, 58–59, 63, 115
Atwood, Margaret 1, 2, 15, 20, 54, 73, 88, 150, 196; *Survival: A Thematic Guide to Canadian Literature* 22, 107, 110
augmented reality (AR) 111
Augustine, Saint: *The City of God* 71
Augustine, Stephen 190
Avison, Margaret 20, 23
Awad, Mona 1–2
Ayers, Edward L. 106

Bailey, Moya Z. 167, 169; *#HashtagActivism* 170
Bailey, Richard W. 64

Ballantyne, Emily: *The Digital Page* 113
Bantz, David A. 57
Bardy Google (Davey) 118–19
Barrett, Paul 10, 95, 227, 249; *Canadians Read* 133, 295, 299; *Future Horizons* 303
BASIC (programming language) 215
Battacharyya, Sayan 170
Baudot, Jean: *La Machine à écrire* 46
Bauman, Syd 239
Beattie, Steven W. 302–3
Bellevue Square (Redhill) 257–58, 270
Bentley, D. M. R. 17
Betts, Gregory 117
Bianco, Jamie Skye 128, 146–47
Birney, Earle 20, 88, 95, 117; "Space Conquest" 7
Black Book Interactive Project 169
Black digital humanities 99n1, 119–20, 133–34, 143–45, 147–48, 164–75
Black Past in Guelph, The 171
Blas, Zach 154–55
Blei, David 247–48
Blodgett, E. D. 72
Bode, Katherine 64, 239
Bonner, Claudine 171
Book of Canadian Poetry (Smith) 17
Book of Negroes (historical document) 133–34, 160; *Black Loyalists* 211
Book of Negroes, The (Hill) 133–34, 211
Bordalejo, Barbara 142–43
Borealis 115, 213–14, 222, 224, 231
Boyd, Jason 37, 144, 146, 309
Boyles, Christina 164, 297
bpNichol 7, 21, 95, 117–18, 215; *bpnichol.ca* 58; *First Screening* 7, 21, 117
Brainerd, Barron: *Weighing Evidence in Language and Literature* 47, 63, 295
Brand, Dionne 23; *What We All Long For* 231, 246
Brathwaite, Kamau 172
Bratley, Paul 50
Brossard, Nicole: *Le désert mauve* 21, 117
Brown, Elspeth 150, 312
Brown, Susan 4, 22, 37, 76, 80, 91, 106–8, 115–16, 120, 131, 154, 215, 311; *Collaboratory for Writing and Research on Culture* 93, 153; *Linked Infrastructure for Networked Cultural Scholarship* 231; *The Orlando Project* 59–61, 150, 153
Brydon, Diana 74, 298
Busa, Roberto 43, 45, 65n1, 65n3, 96, 294–95
Bush Garden, The (Frye) 22

C++ (programming language) 255
Callison, Camille: *Respectful Terminology Platform Project* 187
Cameron, Angus: *Computers and Old English Concordances* 46
Canada and the Spanish Civil War (Sharpe and Vautour) 95
Canada Council for the Arts 71, 72, 213
Canada Foundation for Innovation (CFI) 58, 61, 76–77, 79, 81–82, 91, 307–8, 310–12
Canada Reads 16, 25, 72, 133, 299
Canada Research Chair 76, 79, 300
Canada's Early Women Writers 90, 93
Canadiana 77, 90, 214
Canadian Broadcasting Corporation (CBC) 16, 25, 110, 299
Canadian Certificate in Digital Humanities (cc:DH/HN) 98, 256, 300
Canadian Heritage Information Network (CHIN) 229
Canadian Literary Prose (Cluett) 21, 48
Canadian Literature Archive (CLA) 225
Canadian Literature Centre (CLC) 105, 225
Canadian Literature in English (Moss and Sugars) 15
Canadian Modernist Magazines Project (CMMP) 63, 73, 114, 132, 151, 213
Canadian National Digital Heritage Index (CNDHI) 213
Canadian National Site Licensing Project (CNSLP) 77
Canadian Poetry Collection, The 6, 295
Canadian Research Knowledge Network (CRKN) 76–77, 213
Canadian Society for Digital Humanities / Société canadienne

des humanités numériques (CSDH/SCHN) 32, 56–57, 142, 299
Canadians Read 133, 295, 299
capta 129–31, 133, 217, 242, 278
CARE Principles for Indigenous Data Governance 185
Caribbean 172, 273–74
Carleton University: Cultural Heritage Informatics Collaboratory 308; Hyperlab 307–8; Transgender Media Lab 148
Carman, Bliss 20, 211
Caswell, Michelle 89
Cattapan, Alana 153
Centre d'application des médias technologiques à l'enseignement et à la recherche (CAMTER) 46
Centre for Computing in the Humanities (CCH) (University of Toronto) 52, 54–59, 65n6, 75, 295
ChatGPT 1–3, 302
Child, Lydia Maria 249
Chinese Head Tax policy 161, 171; *Register of Chinese Immigrants to Canada* 211
Cho, Alan 171
Cho, Lily: *Mass Capture* 161, 171
Christen, Kimberly 229; *Murkutu CMS* 188, 201n2
Chun, Wendy Hui Kyong: *Discriminating Data* 161, 164
Civil Elegies (Lee) 110
Clarke, Austin 73, 95, 244
Clement, Tanya 9, 240, 249, 273
Clements, Patricia 54, 61, 154; *The Orlando Project* 59–61
Cluett, Robert: *Canadian Literary Prose* 21, 48
Coach House Press 7, 22, 56, 58–59
Coady, Lynn: *Who Needs Book?* 2, 105, 125, 294
Coleman, Daniel 78, 276
collaboratories 87–99
Collaboratory for Writing and Research on Culture (CWRC) 90, 93–94, 130, 150–51, 193
Collins, Patricia Hill 145, 164
colonialism 2, 11n4, 25, 173, 174n2, 174n5, 180, 183, 186, 192, 194–99
Companion to Digital Humanities, A (Schreibman, Siemens, and Unsworth) 34–35

Complicated Kindness, A (Toews) 16
Compton, Wayde 119–20, 172
computational literary studies (CLS) 126
Computer Applications in Literary Studies (CCH) 54
Computer Applications to Medieval Studies (Gilmour-Bryson) 48
Computers and Old English Concordances (Angus, Frank, and Leyerle) 46
concordance, computational 46–47, 50, 52, 126, 237, 270n6; Busa 43, 65n1, 294–95; Djwa 5, 19–22, 27n4, 44–45, 113, 249, 294–95; Glickman and Staalman 27n4, 44–45, 294–95
Congress of the Humanities and Social Sciences 27, 300
Connell, Sarah 239
Consortium for Computers in the Humanities / Consortium pour ordinateurs en sciences humaines (COCH/COSH) 48, 56
Coombe, Rosemary J. 58; *Dynamic Fair Dealing* 107
Coupland, Douglas 1, 21; *JPod* 7; *Microserfs* 7
Craig, Hugh 239
Creative Commons 189, 228, 231
Crenshaw, Kimberlé 144–45
Crompton, Constance 36, 76, 311; *Lesbian and Gay Liberation in Canada* 151–52
Crow Eagle, Geoff 190
Crowshoe, Reg 190
Cummings, James 94
Cunningham, Richard 61
cyberspace 7, 111, 183
Cybertypes (Nakamura) 179

Da, Nan Z. 32, 108, 125–27
Danard, Deborah 183
data acquisition 209–18, 276–78
Data Feminism (D'Ignazio and Klein) 164, 298
data management 2, 98, 132–33, 273, 296, 313; ethics of 160–61, 164, 182–88, 201n2, 230, 233–34; guidelines for 77–78, 130, 184–86, 224–33; practice of 209–11, 214, 218, 221–33; projects and

platforms for 58–59, 62, 93–94, 115, 187, 223–24
data management plan (DMP) 222–24, 232
Data Management Plan Assistant (DMP Assistant) 222–23
Datapac network 20, 118
Davey, Frank 22–23, 109; *Bardy Google* 118–19; *SwiftCurrent* 5–6, 20, 56, 108, 121n5, 215
Dear Science and Other Stories (McKittrick) 164
Désert mauve, Le (Brossard) 21, 117
Devereux, Cecily 4, 215
Devor, Aaron 150
diaspora 119, 245, 247
Dietrich, Craig 188
differential reading 9, 240, 249, 273, 281
Digital Documentation Process, The 224
Digital Humanities Manifesto 2.0 33, 88
Digital Humanities Summer Institute (DHSI) 51, 58, 63, 83, 94, 98, 116, 300
Digital Object Identifier (DOI) 227
Digital Page, The (Pollock and Djwa) 5, 63, 113–14
Digital Research Alliance of Canada (DRAC) 91, 93, 98, 130, 182, 222, 233n2, 311, 312
digital scholarship 5, 19, 110–14, 310; ephemerality of 6; materiality of 146; sustainability of 80
Digital Studies / Le champ numérique 32–33, 61, 241
digitization 34, 108, 130, 132–33, 210–11
D'Ignazio, Catherine: *Data Feminism* 164, 298
disidentification 154–55
distant reading 49, 73, 115, 135n2, 170, 173, 240, 248–49, 273, 297
Distant Reading Mennonite Writing (DRMW) 115
Djwa, Sandra 5, 19–22, 25, 32, 44–45, 63, 96, 113, 249, 294; *The Digital Page* 5, 63, 113–14
Dobson, Teresa 61
Do You Remember Being Born? (Michaels) 7, 301–3

Drucker, Johanna 128–29, 217, 278
Dublin Core Metadata Initiative 226, 229
Dynamic Table of Contexts 94, 244

Earhart, Amy 298
Early Canadiana Online 90
Early Canadian Cultural Journals Index 90, 93
Eaton, Winnifred 151, 227; *The Winnifred Eaton Archive* 244
Editing Modernism in Canada (EMiC) 63, 73, 94–95, 99n3
Eichhorn, Kate 117, 120
Eichmann-Kalwara, Nickoal 141, 151
Ellegård, Alvar: *The Junius Letters* 48
email 7, 55, 65n7, 294
Endings Project, The 47, 126–27, 224, 295
Engel, Marian 218n2; *Bear* 259–60
Ermine, Willie 180
Érudit 214
Estill, Laura 76
Exploratory Programming for the Arts and Humanities (Montfort) 256

Facebook 215, 241, 300
FAIR Principles 130, 185, 224–32
Family Camera Network, The 172
Fan, Lai-Tze 76, 120
Fawcett Toolkit 63
Federated Research Data Repository (FRDR) 224
Fee, Margery 18, 188; *The People and the Text* 63, 73, 116
"Feminist Data Manifest-No" 186
FemTechNet 147–48, 153
Ferguson, Jade: *The Black Past in Guelph* 171
Fields, Erin 194
Findlay, Len 128
First Nations Information Governance Centre (FNIGC) 184
First Nations Principles of OCAP, The 184
First Screening (bpNichol) 7, 21, 117
Fisher, Caitlin: *Andromeda* 111; *These Waves of Girls* 7, 111; *200 Castles* 111
Fish, Stanley 31, 108, 125–26
Fitzpatrick, Kathleen 32

Fitzpatrick, Ryan 6, 63, 79, 115
Flanders, Julia 31, 129–30, 239
Flemmer, Kyle 116–17
Flennoy, Davonte 164–65
Fong, Deanna: *Fred Wah Digital Archive* 6, 63, 79, 115
Fortier, Paul A.: THEME (software) 46
FourDirectionsTeachings.com 6, 179, 189–90
Frank, Roberta: *Computers and Old English Concordances* 46
Fred Wah Digital Archive 6, 58, 63, 115, 226
Frye, Northrop 16, 19–22, 108–9, 121n2–4, 294; *Anatomy of Criticism* 108; *The Bush Garden* 22
full-metal indigiqueer (Whitehead) 197–99

Gaertner, David 181–83, 194, 197, 201n4
Gaffield, Chad 77
Galey, Alan 61, 112
Gallant, Mavis 15, 23, 73
Gallon, Kim 164, 166–67, 169, 173
Gao, Jin 142
gender 60, 142, 144–51, 154, 161
Gerson, Carole: *Canada's Early Women Writers Project* 90
Getty Vocabularies 229
Ghosh, Arjun 171
Gibson, William: *Neuromancer* 7, 111
Giller Prize 257–61, 267
Gilmour-Bryson, Ann 48–49
Glickman, Robert Jay 44–45, 294; *Manual for the Printing of Literary Texts and Concordances by Computer* 27n4, 44–45
Global Indigenous Data Alliance (GIDA) 185–86
Glover, Susan: *The People and the Text* 63, 73, 116
Goddard, Lisa 209, 229
Golumbia, David 125, 175n1
Good, Alex: *Revolutions* 121n1
Google 118–19, 215; *Bard* 119; *Books* 125, 242; *Colab* 255, 256; *Gemini* 162; *Ngram Viewer* 242, 243, 245, 288; *Translate* 198–99
Gordon, Neta: *AMM Bibliography* 114–15

Gouglas, Sean 46, 57
Graham, Shawn 62–63, 210, 308; *Failing Gloriously and Other Essays* 63
Grant, George 109–10, 196
Graphical User Interfaces (GUI) 240–43
Great Lakes Research Alliance for the Study of Aboriginal Arts & Cultures (GRASAC) 193; *Knowledge Sharing Platform* 193
Grundy, Isobel: *The Orlando Project* 59, 154
Guide to Computer Applications in the Humanities, A (Hockey) 47, 253, 295

Hammond, Adam 126
Haraway, Donna 298
Hartman, Saidiya 134, 166, 169, 171
HathiTrust: Bookworm 242, 243; *Digital Library* 212–13
Hayles, N. Katherine: *Writing Machines* 3
Head, Harold: *Canada in Us Now* 23
Healey, Antonette diPaolo 49
Henko (Murakami) 108
Hermeneutica (Rockwell and Sinclair) 63, 256
Higgins, Stefan 209, 229
Highway, Tomson 23
Hill, Heather V. 5, 32
Hill, Lawrence 15; *The Book of Negroes* 134, 211
Hill, Susan 180
History of Mary Prince, The (Prince) 264–65, 273–74, 277
HistSex 153
Hjartarson, Paul 111
Hockey, Susan 51, 238; *A Guide to Computer Applications in the Humanities* 47–48, 253–54, 295; *The Orlando Project* 59
Homosaurus 153
#HonouringIndigenousWriters 194
Howard, Liz 21, 111
Howe, James 144, 146
humanism 10, 70–73, 91, 173, 298; Christian 109; definition of 10n2; implied forms of 35; retro-humanism 128

Humanist (listserv) 38n2, 54–55, 65n1, 65n7, 82–83, 241
Humanities and the Computer (Miall) 57
Humanities and Social Sciences Commons (HSS Commons) 62
humanities computing 8, 19, 32, 34–35, 43–64, 83, 96, 244, 254, 295; infographic of 53
Hunter, C. Stuart 49
Hutcheon, Linda 23; *Other Solitudes* 23–24
hypertext 7, 9, 59, 111–12, 116, 146, 300
Hypertexte Potentiele (HyperPo) 63
Hypertext Pratt, The 108, 111–14, 130, 132, 295

IBM 19–20, 48, 51–52, 75, 160
Ide, Nancy M. 44, 244; *Pascal for the Humanities* 44
Ilovan, Mihaela 93, 150
Image, Text, Sound, and Technology program (SSHRC) 75
Imagining Canada's Future initiative (SSHRC) 78
Implementing New Knowledge Environments Partnership (INKE) 61, 62
Indigenous digital humanities projects and platforms 167, 169, 179–200
Indigenous Innovation Initiative 185
Indigenous knowledge and epistemologies 6, 179, 186–92, 200n1, 298–99; data sovereignty 182–88; survivance and resistance 200
Indigenous literature 194–200
Indigenous peoples: Haudenosaunee 180, 192; Rainy River First Nations 191; Warumungu 188
inequities, structural 24–25
infrastructure 63–64, 70–83, 93–94, 98–99, 99n2, 163, 223
Injun (Abel) 7, 195
Innes, Christopher 58
Instapoetry 21, 131
integrated development environment (IDE) 256

International Standard Book Number (ISBN) 226
intersectionality 34, 141–55, 163
Intimacies of Four Continents, The (Lowe) 160
Introduction to Cultural Analytics & Python (Walsh) 255
Irvine, Dean 80; *The Digital Page* 113–14; *Editing Modernism in Canada* 73, 94–95, 114
Iseke-Barnes, Judy 183

Jackson, Sarah J.: *#HashtagActivism* 170
Jakacki, Diane: LEAF 94
Java (programming language) 255
JavaScript (programming language) 117, 254
Jenik, Adriene 21, 117
Jensen, Graham H. 79, 133, 312; *Canadian Modernist Magazines Project* 63, 73, 114, 132–33, 151
Johnson, E. Pauline: *Legends of Vancouver* 116, 151, 211–12
Johnson, Jessica Marie 134, 168
Johnston, Carrie 297
Jonny Appleseed (Whitehead) 131, 197, 270n3
Jorgensen, Jeana 141, 151
Josephs, Kelly Baker 172–73; *The Digital Black Atlantic* 99n1, 175n6
Jupyter Notebook 255, 259
Justice, Daniel Heath 188, 198–200; *Why Indigenous Literatures Matter* 194; *A Year of #HonouringIndigenousWriters* 194

Kamboureli, Smaro 23, 24, 78
Kaur, Rupi 21, 131
Keeling, Kara 145, 147
Kellough, Kaie 119–20, 172
Kennedy, Bill: *Artmob* 115
keywords in context 48, 287; Python (kwic) 245; *Voyant* 241, 286–87, 287
Khair, Shahira 209, 229
Kiinawin Kawindomowin / Story Nations 191
Kirschenbaum, Matthew 31–34
Klein, Julie Thompson 20, 131
Klein, Lauren F. 164, 249, 298; *Data Feminism* 164, 298

Klinck, Carl F.: *Literary History of Canada* 16, 19, 72
knowledge mobilization 77, 79, 95, 309, 311, 312
Kooistra, Lorraine Janzen 309; *Yellow Nineties 2.0* 151

laboratories, digital humanities 87–99, 307–13
labour 45, 64, 79–81, 115, 146, 170, 201n2, 228, 232–33, 238, 296–98
Lai, Larissa 24
Lament for a Nation (Grant) 110
Lampman, Archibald 20, 212
Lancashire, Ian 48, 50–57, 53, 63n6, 75, 301
Land, Kaylin 148, 154
large language models (LLM) 1–3, 301
Latent Dirichlet Allocation (LDA) 248
Laurence, Margaret: *The Diviners* 265
Lave, Jean 92
Layton, Irving 20, 213
Lecker, Robert 17
Lee, Dennis 73, 83n2, 110; *Civil Elegies* 110
Lee, Mary 190
Legends of Vancouver (Johnson) 116, 212
Le-Khac, Long 170
Lesbian and Gay Liberation in Canada (LGLC) 151–52, 170
Letters in a Bruised Cosmos (Howard) 111
Lévesque, George Henri 71
Leyerle, John: *Computers and Old English Concordances* 46
LGBTQ Oral History Digital Collaboratory 150
libraries 263–67
Library and Archives Canada (LAC) 214
Library of Congress Subject Headings (LCSH) 186
linear regression 162
Linked Editing Academic Framework (LEAF) 94, 244; *LEAF-Writer* 244–45, 267; *Virtual Research Environment* (VRE) 94
Linked Infrastructure for Networked Cultural Scholarship (LINCS) 126, 132, 152, 182, 229, 231, 232
linked open data (LOD) 231–32, 295

"LISP Program for Use in Stylistic Analysis, A" 44
Literary History of Canada (Klinck et al.) 16–17, 19, 21, 110
Litt, Paul 71
Liu, Alan 64; diversity stack 163; meaning problem 9, 131, 238
Lives of Girls and Women (Munro) 113
Logan, Grace 48
Logan, Harry M. 50–51
LongPen 1, 10n1
Lowe, Lisa: *The Intimacies of Four Continents* 160

MacDonald, Ann-Marie: *AMM Bibliography* 114–15, 213; *Fall On Your Knees* 246
MacLennan, Hugh 15, 21, 23; *Voices in Time* 7, 111, 293, 303
Mair, Charles 20
Major Collaborative Research Initiative (MCRI) (SSHRC) 61
Making Love with the Land (Whitehead) 199
Manual for the Printing of Literary Texts and Concordances by Computer (Glickman and Staalman) 27n4, 44–45
Map of White Supremacy's Mob Violence 169
Mapping Ontario's Black Archives 172
MARC 21 Format for Bibliographic Data 226
Marche, Stephen 108, 125, 127
Martin-Hill, Dawn: *Ohneganos Ohnegahdę:gyo Water Research Program* 192
Massey Commission 71–72, 74, 80, 83n2, 108
McCarthy, Dermot 17
McCarty, Willard 5, 52, 54–55, 57, 70, 98, 294, 304
McConnel, J. Colin: THEME (software) 46
McDonald, Jessica 299
McDougall, Aislinn Clare 195
McGill University: Digital Scholarship Hub 308
McGrath, Jim 296–97
McGregor, Hannah 295; *Refuse* 25–26, 298–99

McKinnon, Alistair 48
McKittrick, Katherine 164–67, 298; *Dear Science and Other Stories* 164–65
McLeod, Don: *Lesbian and Gay Liberation in Canada* 152
McLeod, Katherine 91
McLuhan, Marshall 4, 5, 21, 109, 111, 119
McMaster University 48, 50, 57, 240; Lewis & Ruth Sherman Centre for Digital Humanities 308–9
McNeillie, Andrew 34
McPherson, Tara 145, 162–63
Medovarski, Andrea 264, 273, 275–76
metadata 114, 126, 132, 135n1; creation and management 80, 93, 130, 218, 222–28, 231–33; meaning in 133–34, 143, 186, 210–11, 230–31, 233n1; working with 95, 215–16, 269, 276, 313
methodology 36–38, 98
Meunier, Jean-Guy 46
Miall, David S.: *Humanities and the Computer* 57
Michaels, Sean: *Do You Remember Being Born?* 7, 301–3
Miki, Roy 95
Mohabir, Nalini 172
Monster at the End of This Book, The 105, 108–9, 121n1, 125, 294, 304
Montfort, Nick: *Exploratory Programming for the Arts and Humanities* 256
Montgomery, Lucy Maud 15, 151; *Anne of Green Gables* 212, 268, 218n3; *The Blue Castle* 218n3
Moodie, Susanna 212, 264–67, 272–88; *Roughing It in the Bush* 264–65, 275, 280
Morra, Linda 91, 299
Moss, Laura: *Canadian Literature in English* 15
Mount, Nick 17, 26n2, 72–73
Mouré, Erin: *Pillage Laud* 21, 117–18
multiculturalism 23, 163, 174n2, 242–43, 247, 299
Muñoz, Trevor 129–30
Munro, Alice 218n1; *Lives of Girls and Women* 113

Murakami, Sachiko 215; *Figure* 108; *Henko* 108
Murchison, Carole 50
Murkutu CMS 188, 201n2

n-gram 242–43
Nakamura, Lisa: *Cybertypes* 179
named entity recognition 244–45
Nardocchio, Elaine 48, 55; *Theatre* (software) 51, 55
National Indigenous Knowledge & Language Alliance / Alliance nationale desconnaissances et des langues autochtones (NIKLA-ANCLA) 187, 229, 233n5
national literatures 17, 27n3, 70–83
Native Land Digital 191–92
natural language processing 265, 270n6
Natural Language Toolkit (NLTK) 217, 245, 265, 281
network analysis 246–47
Neuromancer (Gibson) 7, 111
New Companion to Digital Humanities, A (2016) 35
New Oxford English Dictionary 51
Nindokiikayencikewin Indigenous Knowledges & Data Governance Protocol 185
Noble, Safiya 164; *Algorithms of Oppression* 161, 298
Nomenclature for Museum Cataloguing (CHIN) 229
Northside Hip Hop Archive 172

Obbard, Kiera 241, 300
Ohneganos Ohnegahdę:gyo Water Research Program 192
Oldenburg, Ray 96, 99n4
Omeka 153, 223
Ondaatje, Michael 15, 23, 245, 262
O'Neil, Cathy: *Weapons of Math Destruction* 161
O'Neill, Heather: *The Girl Who Was Saturday Night* 244; *Lullabies for Little Criminals* 16
O'Nell, Katie 302
Ontario Consortium for Computers and the Humanities (OCCH) 55–56
Ontario Humanities Computing Newsletter 55

OpenAI 1–3, 302
Open Government 214
OpenRefine 268
Open Researcher and Contributor ID (ORCID) 227, 231
Open Source Initiative 228, 231
OpenText 51
oppression 10, 24–25, 163, 199, 297–98; data 6–7, 161–63; power and 145, 153–54, 164–66
Orlando Project, The 59–61, 75, 76, 149–50
Other Solitudes (Richmond and Hutcheon) 23, 24
Outer Harbour, The (Compton) 119

Page, P. K. 20, 27n5, 151; *The Digital Page* 5, 63, 113–14
Pannapacker, William 35
Pascal for the Humanities (Ide) 44
People and the Text, The (TPatT) 63, 73, 116, 192–93
persistent identifier (PID) 225–27
personography 151, 155n1
Philip, M. NourbeSe 25
Phillips, Amanda 297
Pillage Laud (Mouré) 21, 117–18
Pitawanakwat, Lillian 190
poetry 5–6, 20–21, 24, 54, 95, 109; digital 6–7, 115–20, 131, 195–97, 302–3
Pollock, Zailig 5, 63, 115; *The Digital Page* 5, 63, 113–14; *The Hypertext Pratt* 111–13
Polster, Claire 78
Popham, Elizabeth: *The Hypertext Pratt* 111–13
Porter, Tom 190
Posner, Miriam 144, 230
Potter, Rosanne G. 64, 126–27, 131
power 2, 9, 19, 33, 89, 110–11, 134, 144, 160–73; abuses of 24; archives 153; digital tools 149; institutional 25; oppression and 145
Pratt, E. J. 15, 20–21, 72, 109; *The Hypertext Pratt* 108, 111–14, 130, 132, 295
Prince, Mary 264–67, 272–88; *The History of Mary Prince* 264–65, 268, 273–81, 277, 279, 280
Pringle, John 274, 276

Prochain episode (Aquin) 16
Program for Research on Romance Authors (PRORA) (software) 45
programming: historical examples of 27n4, 44–46, 51, 54, 59, 117–18; introduction to 216–18, 243, 245–50, 253–71; problems with 65n3, 161–63, 237–38, 242; text analysis with 281–88; value of 81, 108
Programming Historian 255–56, 270n2
Project Gutenberg 195, 211–13, 216, 218n3, 264–65, 268–69, 276, 278, 281–82
prosopography 155n1
Punzalan, Ricardo 89
Purdy, Al 23, 72
Python (programming language): benefits of 243, 254–56; demonstration of 281–88; introduction to 256–271; sentiment analysis 246; text analysis 245–46

Quamen, Harvey 36, 111, 310
Queer OS (Keeling) 145

R (programming language) 243, 254
race and racism 25, 133, 144, 154, 160–73; digital humanities and 162–66; literature and culture 169–72
Radzikowska, Milena 37, 240
Rak, Julie 25; *Refuse* 25–26, 298–99
Ramadan, Danny 1–2
Reddon, Madeleine: *The People and the Text* 63, 73, 116
Reder, Deanna 188; *The People and the Text* 63, 73, 116
Redhill, Michael 257, 262, 270n3
Redlining Culture (So) 169
Refuse (McGregor, Rak, and Wunker) 25–26, 298–99
Register of Chinese Immigrants to Canada 211; *see also* Chinese Head Tax policy
regular expressions 267–99
replatforming 89, 95, 99n1, 195
Representative Poetry Online 54
research capitalism 78–82
research data management (RDM) *see* data management
Research Organization Registry (ROR) 227

Resource Description Framework (RDF) 231
Respectful Terminology Platform Project 187
retro-humanism 128
Revolutions (Good) 121n1
Richmond, Marion: *Other Solitudes* 23–24
Risam, Roopika 147, 163, 174n5; *The Digital Black Atlantic* 99n1, 175n6
Ritter, Kathleen 196
Robertson, Bruce G.: *Fawcett Toolkit* 63
Rockwell, Geoffrey 36, 37, 54, 57–58, 256, 301; *Hermeneutica* 38n2, 63, 249n1, 256; TAPoR 58, 63, 240; *Voyant Tools* 63, 238, 240–41, 249n1
Roger, Sarah 10; *Canadians Read* 133, 295, 299; *Future Horizons* 303
romantic nationalism 18
Rommel, Thomas 239
Rosenthal, Caitlin 160
Roughing It in the Bush (Moodie) 264–65, 275, 280
Royal Commission on National Development in the Arts, Letters, and Sciences; *see* Massey Commission
Ruberg, Bonnie 144–45
Rubinski, Yuri 59
Rudy, Susan 80, 115
Ruecker, Stan 36, 61, 112

Said, Edward 10, 298
Sample, Mark 33
Sangwand, T-Kay 89
Saving Ukrainian Cultural Heritage Online 296
Schmaltz, Eric 196
Schreibman, Susan 61, 88; *A Companion to Digital Humanities* 34–35
Schwartz, Michelle: *Lesbian and Gay Liberation in Canada* 151–52
Scott, Duncan Campbell 20
secretarial assistance 45
Sedelow, Sally 43–44
sentiment analysis 240, 246
Shadd, Mary Ann 249
Sharpe, Emily Robbins 95
Sharpe, Jenny 274, 279

Shield, Alix: *The People and the Text* 63, 73, 116
Siemens, Lynne 75, 80, 81
Siemens, Ray 54, 61, 76, 80–83, 88, 312; *A Companion to Digital Humanities* 34–35; Digital Humanities Summer Institute 83, 98; Implementing New Knowledge Environments Partnership 83
Simon Fraser University 50, 91; Digital Humanities Innovation Lab 309
Sinclair, Stéfan 37–38, 57, 63, 98, 238, 241, 256; Digital Humanities Summer Institute 98; *Hermeneutica* 38n2, 63, 249n1, 256; *HyperPo* 63; TAPoR 58; *Voyant Tools* 63, 238, 240–41, 249n1
slavery 134, 160–61, 274
Slemon, Stephen 82–83
Slocombe, David 59
Smith, A. J. M. 17, 20; *Book of Canadian Poetry* 17
Smith, John B. 44, 126
SNOBOL (programming language) 253–54
So, Richard Jean: *Redlining Culture* 169–70
social change and movements 2, 82, 83n1, 109, 145, 148, 163, 293, 301
social media 25, 131, 133, 211, 215
Social Sciences and Humanities Research Council of Canada (SSHRC) 72, 233n1, 307; funding 48, 61–62, 73, 75–78, 81, 90–91, 93, 98, 106, 112, 224; policies and initiatives 74–76, 214, 221–22, 228, 296, 311, 312, 318; research capitalism 79
Society for Digital Humanities / Société pour l'étude des medias interactifs (SDH/SEMI) 56
SoftQuad 59
Sperberg-McQueen, Michael 44, 50, 244
Spinosa, Dani 79, 119–20; *Anarchists in the Academy* 119
Spivak, Gayatri 170
SpokenWeb 38n1, 93, 95, 126; *Archive of the Digital Present* 95, 126, 247, 296, 299
Spyral Notebooks 249n1, 254
Srinivasan, D. 47

Staalman, Gerrit Joseph 44–45, 294; *Manual for the Printing of Literary Texts and Concordances by Computer* 27n4, 44–45
Starosielski, Nicole 146
statistics 44, 47–48, 168, 238, 240, 247–49
stop words 216–17, 265–69, 270n8, 281, 283
stylometrics 31
Sugars, Cynthia: *Canadian Literature in English* 15
Sula, Chris Alen 5, 32, 38n1
Survival (Atwood) 22, 107, 110
Svensson, Patrik 33–34
SwiftCurrent (Davey and Wah) 6, 20, 56, 108, 117–19, 216, 295
Systeme d'analyse des textes par ordinateur (SATO) 46
Szumigalski, Anne 213

"Teaching Computers and the Humanities Courses" 51
Technology & Empire (Grant) 110
terra nullius 183, 195
Terras, Melissa 6, 31, 65n3
Terrastories 192
Text Analysis Computing Tools (TACT) 54, 108
Text Analysis Portal for Research (TAPoR) 58, 240
text encoding 94, 239–40, 243–44
Text Encoding Initiative (TEI) 44, 112, 152, 229, 240, 243–44; Guidelines for Electronic Text Encoding and Interchange 244
textual analysis: concept of 125–27, 237–40, 272–73; example of 272–88; history in digital humanities 30, 32–33, 46–51, 54–56, 59–61, 64, 64–65n1–2; materials for 211–18; programmatic 245–249, 281–88; projects 93–95, 114–17, 169–70, 194–97; tool-based 237, 240–44, 241, 243, 278–81
Theatre: Software for the Analysis of Dramatic Dialogue (software) 51, 55
thematicism 22–23
THEME: *A System for Computer-Aided Theme Searches of French Texts* (software) 46

These Waves of Girls (Fisher) 7, 111
third place communities 96, 99n4
Thompson, Cheryl: *Mapping Ontario's Black Archives* 172
TikTok 26, 299
Toews, Miriam: *A Complicated Kindness* 16
topic modeling 247–49
Toronto Metropolitan University 151, 172, 213, 300; Centre for Digital Humanities 309
Traditional Knowledge Labels (TK Labels) 187–88, 226
Trans-Atlantic Slave Trade Database 168
transgender 143, 148–52, 194
Transgender Archives 150
Transgender Media Portal 148
Tremblay, Michel 50
Tri-Agency Research Data Management Policy 77, 222
Twitter 25–26, 133, 172, 215, 294, 299; *Canadians Read* 133; #HashtagActivism 170; *A Year of #HonouringIndigenousWriters* 194
200 Castles (Fisher) 111
Two Solitudes (MacLennan) 23

Ulysses (Joyce) 217
Uniform Resource Identifier (URI) 231
Un/inhabited (Abel) 7, 195–96
United Nations Declaration on the Rights of Indigenous Peoples (UNDRIP) 185
Université de Montréal 46, 50, 98; Centre de recherche interuniversitaire sur les humanités numériques 309–10
University of Alberta 36, 49, 55, 57–59, 61, 78, 105, 189, 301; Canadian Literature Centre 105; Collaboratory for Writing and Research on Culture 93; Digital Scholarship Centre 310
University of British Columbia: Computing Centre 19–20, 45; *Open Collections* 211
University of British Columbia Okanagan: AMP Lab 310–11
University of Guelph 49, 55, 94, 98, 148, 300–1; The Humanities Interdisciplinary Collaboration Lab 311

University of Ottawa 94, 98, 300, 310; Labo de données en sciences humaines / The Humanities Data Lab 311–12
University of Toronto 22, 44–48, 50–59, 88, 108, 171, 207, 294, 301; Centre for Computing in the Humanities 52, 54–59, 65n6, 75, 295; Computing Services 48–49; Critical Digital Humanities Initiative 150, 312; *LGBTQ Oral History Digital Collaboratory* 150; Press 44–45; Thomas Fisher Rare Book Library 88
University of Victoria 58, 63, 98, 224; Electronic Textual Cultures Lab / Digital Scholarship Commons 312–13; *Transgender Archives* 150
(Un)Silencing Slavery 166, 167
Unsworth, John 88, 112; *A Companion to Digital Humanities* 34–35
"Use Our Words" Toolkit, The 187

Vandendorpe, Christian 62
variables 161, 165, 257–58, 260–61, 264–65, 268, 269
Vassanji, M. G. 23
Vermette, Katherena 23
Vernon, Karina 25
Vincent, Tom 90
Vipond, Mary 5, 128
Virtual International Authority File (VIAF) 227
Voices in Time (MacLennan) 7, 111, 293
Voices of the Land 189
Voyant Tools 5, 37, 54, 63, 237–38, 241–42, 241, 249n1, 254, 267, 270n1, 272, 300; *The History of Mary Prince* 278–81, 279, 280, 286; keywords-in-context 286–87, 287

Wah, Fred 95; *Fred Wah Digital Archive* 6, 63, 115, 226; *SwiftCurrent* 5–6, 20, 56, 108, 118, 121n5, 215
Walsh, Melanie: *Introduction to Cultural Analytics & Python* 255
Warwick, Claire 61
Watanna, Onoto 227; as Winnifred Eaton 151, 244
Watson, B. M. 153
Watson, Sheila 20–21, 111; *The Double Hook* 111

Watson, Wilfrid 20–21, 111
Wattpad 1
Weapons of Math Destruction (O'Neil) 161
Weighing Evidence in Language and Literature (Brainerd) 47, 63, 295
Weingart, Scott B. 141–42, 151
Welles, Brooke Foucault 170
Wemigwans, Jennifer 189; *FourDirectionsTeachings.com* 6, 179, 189–90
Wenger, Etienne 92
Wernimont, Jacqueline 147–48, 154
Wershler, Darren 58, 80, 91, 99n2, 107, 115; *Artmob* 115; *Dynamic Fair Dealing* 107
Wget 216, 218n4
What We All Long For (Brand) 231, 246
white civility 276
Whitehead, Joshua 21, 25, 131, 194–95, 197–200, 201n6, 298; full-metal indigiqueer 197–99; *Jonny Appleseed* 131, 197, 270n3; *Making Love with the Land* 199
Whitlock, Gillian 274
Who Needs Books? (Coady) 2, 105
Whose Land 191–92
Why Indigenous Literatures Matter (Justice) 194
Wikidata 230, 232, 233n5
Wikipedia 193–94, 221, 312
Wikipetcia Atikamekw Nehiromowin 193–94
Wisbey, R. A. 48
Women Writers Online 150
Wood, John Adams 273–74
World Wide Web Consortium (W3C) 44
Writing Machines (Hayles) 3
Wunker, Erin 25; *Refuse* 25–26, 298–99
Wynter, Sylvia 10, 173, 298

Yellow Nineties 2.0 151
York University 6, 20, 48, 58, 118; Digital Scholarship Centre 313

Zacharias, Robert: *Distant Reading Mennonite Writing* 115
Zeilinger, Martin: *Dynamic Fair Dealing* 107
Zenodo 214, 222, 224
Zhang, Sarah 171

Printed in the United States
by Baker & Taylor Publisher Services